Beta Edition

Revolutions

AND

Constitutions

The United States
The USSR
The Islamic Republic of Iran

Paul W. Werth

LINUS Learning

Published by Linus Learning.

Ronkonkoma, NY 11779

ISBN 10: 1-60797-570-X

ISBN 13: 978-1-60797-570-0

Printed in the United States of America.

This book is printed on acid-free paper.

Print Number   5   4   3   2   1

TABLE OF CONTENTS

UNIT ONE: UNITED STATES

CHAPTER 1
English Antecedents 3

CHAPTER 2
From Confederation to Federation 15

CHAPTER 3
The US Constitution and the Bill of Rights 23

CHAPTER 4
Later Evolutions and the Case of Nevada 31

UNIT TWO: RUSSIA AND THE SOVIET UNION

CHAPTER 5
Tsarist Russia and its Regime 53

CHAPTER 6
The Regime's Opponents and the Revolution of 1905 67

CHAPTER 7
The Revolutions of 1917 & the New Communist State 83

CHAPTER 8
The Civil War and the Creation of the USSR 103

CHAPTER 9
The Stalin Revolution and the Constitution of 1936 121

UNIT THREE: IRAN

CHAPTER 10
Early Iran and Islam 145

CHAPTER 11
Revolutionary Upheaval & Autocratic Modernization to the 1970s 153

CHAPTER 12
Opposition to the Shah 161

CHAPTER 13
From Revolution to Constitution in Iran 177

INDEX 195

CITATION INFORMATION

INTRODUCTION

REVOLUTIONS AND CONSTITUTIONS: THE UNITED STATES, THE USSR, AND THE ISLAMIC REPUBLIC OF IRAN

Revolutions and constitutions have played a fundamental role in creating the modern society in which we live. Although definitions of "revolution" vary, most societies in the world have experienced some kind of political and or social upheaval that has been labeled "revolutionary." For some countries this happened a relatively long time ago. Thus Great Britain experienced a revolution in the 1640s, the American colonies in the 1770s, and France for a decade or so beginning in 1789. Other countries have experienced revolutions relatively recently—for example, Iran in 1979 and a number of Arab countries in 2011 (the so-called "Arab Spring"). Looking across the globe, one would find it hard to identify many societies that have not experienced some kind of revolutionary upheaval.

This observation is even truer with respect to constitutions. Although a few countries continue to have only "unwritten constitutions" (something that we will address below), the vast majority of societies have a specific document that they regard as a constitution.[1] In short, it is impossible to understand the modern world today without some grasp of both revolutions and constitutions. This proposition is the starting point for this book and for this course, which examine three revolutions and sets of constitutions that had tremendous worldwide significance at different stages of human history: the United States, Russia, and Iran.

But we can go further still. In fundamental ways revolutions and constitutions are connected. Even in cases where constitutions emerged gradually, revolutionary change proved critical to their appearance. Great Britain's constitution is perhaps the one that appeared most gradually, and there were of course many factors that went into its composition. But dramatic events that can be seen as revolutionary—the English Civil War in the mid-17th century and the so-called Glorious Revolution of 1688-89—were central to the constitution's appearance. The connection between revolution and constitution is even clearer in those countries where the drafting of a new fundamental legal document followed quickly on the heels of the rejection or destruction of the previous political order. Thus Americans moved quickly to produce state constitutions after declaring independence from Britain in 1776, and drafted the Articles of the Confederation in 1777 (although that document was not formally ratified until 1781). Likewise, in Russia the seizure of power by radical socialists called "Bolsheviks" in October of 1917 was followed by the creation of the first Soviet constitution by the next summer. In Iran the process was almost equally rapid: a constitution for the newly proclaimed Islamic Republic went into force ten months after the previous ruler, the Shah, had been overthrown in February of 1979. In short, in most cases in modern history, constitutions emerged more or less directly from a revolutionary experience. They represent the products of dramatic political and social change. They are efforts to codify the values of the given revolution and to construct new institutions by which the transformed society will live.

This book begins from the premise that one of the most productive and insightful ways to study the United States Constitution (1787) and the constitution of the State of Nevada (1864) is, first, to analyze those documents in relation to the preceding revolution against Great Britain; and, second, to consider the American experience in comparative perspective. By "comparative," we mean that we examine several different cases and ask the same or similar questions of each of them. This exercise reveals both similarities and differences from case to case, which in turn allows us to understand each individual case better. This comparative approach has the added benefit of allowing us to learn about

---

1   See for example the list at https://www.cia.gov/library/publications/the-world-factbook/fields/2063.html.

different parts of the world, thus enhancing our awareness of the increasingly globalized context in which we live.

In this course we focus on three revolutions that occurred at different times and produced very different outcomes. The first is the American Revolution and Constitution, with which most students are already at least somewhat familiar. The American Revolution, which occurred towards the end of the eighteenth century, may be seen as a liberal-democratic revolution in light of the social and political order that it helped to create. The second case is the Russian Revolution, which occurred in the early twentieth century. In fact, there were two revolutions in Russia in 1917—one that overthrew the regime of the Tsar, or Emperor, in favor of a Provisional Government that sought to create the conditions for a new democratic society; and a second revolution that saw a group of radical socialists, known as the "Bolsheviks," take power and embark on a remarkable but also destructive experiment lasting a good portion of the twentieth century. The third revolution that we will examine took place in Iran towards the end of the twentieth century. Here, a movement inspired by a combination of socialism, Islam, and opposition to foreign interference overthrew the Shah, or king, and replaced his regime with a new entity known as the Islamic Republic. Thus a fundamentally new political order appeared in Iran at the beginning of 1979.

In the case of each revolution, we see the creation of a new state that was defined, in part at least, by a new constitution. In each case a form of monarchy (a political system ruled by a king, tsar, or shah) was replaced by a republic, although each republic was quite distinct in character. The American Revolution saw a wave of new constitutions, first for the individual states such as Pennsylvania and Virginia, and then for the new country as a whole, in the form of the Articles of Confederation. Yet for the first decade or so after the American Declaration of Independence, it was unclear whether there was really one new country or thirteen. The Articles themselves reflect that confusion and ambivalence, as we shall see. The Constitution of 1787 clarified the question somewhat, although there were still many issues that remained unresolved, not least of all the question of slavery. Some of those could be resolved only by a bloody

civil war in the 1860s, and still others, for example the relationship between the states and federal government, continue to shape our modern politics today. In Russia, the new Bolshevik regime fairly quickly declared the existence of a new country—the Russian Soviet Federated Socialist Republic, or RSFSR—and by the summer of 1918 the Bolsheviks had produced a new constitution for the republic. That constitution was supplemented several years later by a treaty that created the Union of Soviet Socialist Republics—the USSR, or "Soviet Union." Finally, in Iran the new regime of the Ayatollah Ruhollah Khomeini produced a new constitution in the fall of 1979. It, too, sought to express the values of the revolution and also the political aspirations of the new republic's leadership.

To say that each new state produced a constitution (or several of them) is not to say that constitutions had the same significance in each country. Much depended on the conception of law that existed in each society. Thus a constitution could serve as a form of law that genuinely restrained governmental power, at least most of the time; or it could represent primarily an article of propaganda or an instrument that the new regime sought to use in consolidating its power and achieving its goals. As we go forward with our analysis, we should think about the different functions that constitutions can perform, and which of those functions has been most important at any given time.

Each of these three revolutions represents an event of world significance. The American Revolution articulated a set of values that were understood to apply to all of humanity, and at least some of those values have indeed been broadly embraced across much of the world. The Bolshevik Revolution established communism as an alternative to liberal capitalist development; it made German Nazism possible and also represents the foundation for the Cold War that followed World War II and shaped the second half of the twentieth century. The Iranian Revolution, finally, occurred in the midst of crucial shifts in the world order and revealed the possibility that religiously inspired ideologies, which were assumed to be irrelevant in an increasingly secular age, could actually obtain substantial support. This course accordingly rests on the proposition that these three revolutions offer major insights for understanding the world in which we live.

As we begin our investigation of these three revolutions, it is worthwhile to keep in mind a set of questions that we may pose of each of them. This will allow us to engage in effective and meaningful comparative analysis. The first question involves the pressures and antagonisms that produced revolutionary change in each case. What kinds of social and political problems appeared in each case to create a crisis sufficient to allow a revolution to occur? And why in each case was the old regime unable to deal with these challenges? Here we should avoid the temptation to conclude simply that revolutions occur when people are oppressed and their dissatisfaction reaches a critical point. The fact of the matter is that oppression is quite common in human history, while revolutions are quite rare.

A second question concerns the experiences with constitutions or constitutional ideas that each society had *prior* to those revolutions. We shall see that in each case there were some efforts at constitution-making prior to the revolution. In the case of the American Revolution, we will look back to seventeenth-century England to investigate important political developments that created part of the ideological foundations for the American revolt in 1776. In the case of Russia, we will see that in 1905—some twelve years *before* the Bolshevik Revolution—the old monarchy was compelled by political crisis to create a new parliament, grant basic civil rights to the population, and revise its fundamental law in such a way as to give it constitutional significance. And in the case of Iran, we will see that even before the revolution of 1979, the country had a constitution that had originally been created in 1906, when the country experienced an earlier political revolution. These earlier constitutional experiences all have distinct importance for the constitutional development of these societies *after* their respective revolutions.

A third set of questions involves the relationship between revolution and war. We shall see that each case of revolution was accompanied by some form of major warfare. In the case of the American colonies, war with Great Britain actually began in 1775, even before the Declaration of Independence. That war continued for several years, ending only in 1783, when the colonies finally secured their independence. Moreover, the American Civil War in 1861-65 also had tremendous constitutional implications, with regard both to the reasons for the war's outbreak and to the fundamentally important amendments

to the Constitution that followed shortly after the war's end, in 1865-70. War was even more central for the revolutionary experience in Russia. The Russian Empire had entered the First World War in 1914, and the strains after three years of devastating military conflict were undoubtedly a crucial factor in producing the revolutionary situation that appeared in 1917. No less important, within a few months of having taken power, the Bolsheviks faced an array of political opponents who were prepared to take up arms against them. Thus Russia experienced a brutal and taxing civil war between 1918 and 1921, leaving the country exhausted and famine-stricken. Nor, finally, did Iran escape warfare as part of its revolutionary experience. Conflict within Iran to determine the future of the revolution arguably took the form of a civil war between socialists and those with a more religious orientation—although it was rare that people referred to it explicitly as a civil war. More dramatically, the Iraqi dictator Saddam Hussein, both fearing the spread of revolutionary upheaval from Iran and also sensing an opportunity to take advantage of that country's chaos to acquire more territory for himself, launched an invasion of his neighbor in 1981. This conflict came to an end only in 1988. Thus the new Iranian regime had to fight a major war for its very survival, much like its American and Bolshevik counterparts. The importance of warfare for all three revolutions is therefore an issue that warrants our attention.

Fourth, we should inquire into the nature of constitutional change. In none of the cases that we will analyze were constitutions left unchanged, even after they had been ratified and implemented. In some cases, one constitution was simply discarded in favor of another. Thus the Philadelphia Convention, even as it was convened in 1787 merely to revise the Articles of Confederation, chose instead to jettison that earlier constitution and to produce an entirely new one in its place. Likewise, early Soviet constitutions were simply replaced by the new Stalin constitution of 1936 (which was itself replaced by the Brezhnev constitution of 1977, though this is beyond our purview in this course). In other cases, existing constitutions have been modified by amendments or other modifications. The US Constitution has been modified 27 times since its ratification, and several of those changes had fundamental significance for how we understand it. Likewise, the constitution of Iran was significantly modified in 1989, with important implications for political life in that country.

A fifth question pertains to federalism. The relationship between a central government and the states has remained a central issue in American history from the moment of the thirteen colonies' declaration of independence. The Articles of Confederation proposed one solution to this conundrum, but one found wanting. The Constitution of 1787 offered a different solution, but even then modifications were required—beginning with the Bill of Rights—to resolve one set of lingering issues, while a civil war proved necessary to resolve others. Even today the balance between federal and state power remains a matter of dispute. Federalism has also proved an important issue in Soviet history, but in a very different way. From the beginning, the young Soviet republic declared itself to be a federation (the "F" in RSFSR stood for "Federated"), but without actually investing that concept with very much actual content. The USSR, likewise, was explicitly a federal state—a "Union of Soviet Socialist Republics"—but with a highly centralized Communist Party, the country's federal character proved to be something of a fiction. In any event, comparison between these two cases offers interesting material for thinking about what federalism actually means.

A final question concerns revolutionary ends. At what point can we say that a revolution is "over"? This question proved especially complicated for the USSR and Iran. At some point it proved desirable for the leaders of the new regime to stabilize their rule and to declare revolutionary goals "accomplished." We shall see that this was a main purpose of the Stalin constitution of 1936, as the dictator sought to solidify his rule after tumultuous changes over the previous two decades. Contemporary Iran faces the dilemma of deciding whether the revolution of 1979 is complete. The revolution gives the current leadership legitimacy, yet most of the country's current population was born after the revolution occurred, or at least has no memory of it. At what point can a regime safely say that it is no longer "revolutionary" by nature but only by origin?

DEFINITIONS

Before turning to our first case—the British colonies of North America—we need to define a few terms. We do this partly because some of the terms that we need to use may simply be unfamiliar to students,

but also because any good scholar is careful to define clearly the concepts that form the basis for his or her analysis. With this in mind, here are a few key concepts that we will use in this course, along with their derivations and definitions.[2]

Autocracy – independent, self-derived power; uncontrolled authority; monarchy rooted in claim of absolute right (from *autos* = self; *kratos* = strength). This concept includes two key ideas: first, the idea of unlimited power and authority; and second, authority derived from ruler himself, not from any other source (except perhaps for God). This is a term that we will use with regard to both the Russian Emperor and the Iranian Shah.

Monarchy – a government in which a single person is sovereign (from *monos* = one; and *archien* = to rule). Thus any country ruled by a king/queen or an emperor/empress is a monarchy, since there is only that single ruler. However, we need to acknowledge the possibility that a monarchy can be limited. Thus a "constitutional monarchy" is one in which the power of the monarch is limited by law, and this would describe modern monarchies in Europe like the ones in the United Kingdom and Denmark (in both countries the monarch has become largely ceremonial). In contrast a "constitutional autocracy" is an oxymoron, because autocracy is by definition unlimited, while a constitution suggests limits.

Republic – a state in which sovereign power resides in a certain body of the people (the electorate) and is exercised by representatives elected by them (from *res* = thing, affair; *publicus* = public). Notably, each of the three revolutions in this course involved the termination of monarchy (at least within the given territory) in favor of a republic. At the same time, they were very different republics: one (the US) became a liberal-democratic republic, Russia (the USSR) became a socialist republic, and Iran became an Islamic republic. We will learn more about these differences later.

Sovereignty – supreme political power or authority (from *super* = above). This concept is a bit more abstract than the others, but we will find it to be critical to our analysis in all three cases. The basic issue at stake here involves the question: from where does political power/authority derive? Who

---

2   These definitions come primarily from the Oxford English Dictionary.

or what is ultimately sovereign in a given society? We will find different answers to this question as we go forward in this course.

Federation & Confederation – I put these two concepts together because they are obviously related. For our purposes they refer to different ways of organizing and distributing political power in a country. Here it is best to imagine a spectrum, where at one end one has a country in which all political power is concentrated in one place (a centralized state), and at the other end one has a country where political power is fragmented throughout the entire realm (a decentralized state). A federation and confederation are both somewhere in between and feature the centralization of some powers, but the decentralization of others. A federation is closer to a centralized state, but reserves some powers to political units at a lower level (for example, states); a confederation features more decentralization, but still grants some powers to a central government.

Constitution – the system or body of fundamental principles according to which a nation, state, or body politic is constituted or established) and governed. Note that the focus in this definition is on the *system* or the *principles* involved in governing a country. In light of this definition, a constitution can take two different forms: On the one hand, this system and its principles can be established gradually by precedent, without being written down in one particular place or document. This is true for the British Constitution, because it does not take the form of a single document. Alternatively, a constitution may be formally set forth in a document framed and adopted on a particular occasion by members of a commonwealth or their representatives. This what as was done in the American case. Similarly most constitutions are indeed written. But even today a few countries—the UK, Israel, and New Zealand—still have "unwritten constitutions." In short, "constitution" refers both to the system or principles of governance and—in the case of written document—to that document itself. But whether written or unwritten, the basic idea is that a constitution is more fundamental than any other law, and that it therefore contains the principles with which all other legislation must be in harmony.

Our final term—**Revolution**—is even more complicated. Scholars who study revolutions often cannot agree on a single definition, because they are inclined to emphasize different dimensions of the political and social change in question. This makes it hard even to say with certainty which historical or contemporary events "count" as revolutions (although few would deny that our three cases would all qualify). It might be interesting to compare definitions in different languages. The *Oxford English Dictionary* offers the following: "A complete overthrow of the established government or state by those who were previously subject to it; a forcible substitution of a new ruler or from of government." This definition focuses on the *political* dimension of the question; the emphasis is on the government or the state, and the issue is the substitution of one ruler or set of rulers by another. This nicely captures the essence of revolutions such as the American one or the so-called Glorious Revolution in England in 1688-89. What is absent from the definition is any focus on *social* change. Things look different if we look at a Russian (Soviet) definition of "revolution": "A fundamental overturning in the life of a society that leads to the liquidation of an obsolete social and political order and transfers power into the hands of the foremost class." Note here that the focus is on both the political *and* the social order. The Soviet conception includes the idea of the transfer of power to a *new social class* of people. It implies an extensive and thorough structural transformation and massive class upheaval. This definition better describes revolutions like those in France (1789), Russia (1917), and China (1949). A Persian definition of "revolution" looks like this: "To overturn, to capsize; upheaval; an insurgency to topple the existing regime and establish some new governance." Here the political dimension is again prominent, as in English definition. (Curiously, this same term in Persian can mean "restlessness" and "anxiety" in a medical context.)

These, then, are the key concepts that we will be using in this course. It might make sense to come back to these definitions from time to time, but at present we are now prepared to investigate our first case of revolution and constitution: the American one.

ACKNOWLEDGEMENTS

"For their help in assembling materials, providing essays, and reviewing the text, I thank Stephen Bohigian, John Curry, Michael Green, Heather Nepa, Lindsay Oden, Jaycie Weeks, and Daniel Werth."

UNIT ONE

The United States

CHAPTER 1

ENGLISH ANTECEDENTS

Most of Great Britain's North American colonies broke away from their mother country in 1776 and in due course created a new country with distinct traditions and mentalities. At the same time, the early history of the United States is in no small measure an extension of the history of Great Britain (and, in the West, of Spain and Mexico). As a result, in order to understand the political culture of the American colonists who broke away from Britain, we need also to understand elements of British history as well. Of course, there is a lot to understand, and we can manage to focus only on a few specific elements here. But by doing so, we may better understand how Americans both drew on English political traditions and departed from them.

In order to clarify these connections, let us focus on two texts that played an important role in shaping English—and thus American—thinking about what made government legitimate, and the conditions under which it was possible to reject a government and create something new in its place. These are the English Declaration of Right (1689) and John Locke's *Second Treatise on Government* (1690). In order to analyze these two texts, we need to understand the historical context in which they appeared. Both were closely connected with a political crisis in Britain known as the Glorious Revolution of 1688 (note the dates of the texts in relation to this set of events). And to understand that historical context, we need to delve a bit deeper into the history of Great Britain in the seventeenth century (that is, in the 1600s).

That history is enormously complex (and very interesting), but for our purposes we can identify two major axes of conflict that shaped political life in Britain in the seventeenth century. One axis concerned religion. Christianity had appeared in England as early as the third century, when Britain was still part of the Roman Empire. Before the Protestant Reformation, the vast majority of Western Europe, including England, was Catholic, which meant that clergy and parishioners accepted Rome's teaching of Christianity and recognized the authority of the Pope. With the appearance of the Reformation in Germany in the early 1500s, however, significant portions of Europe, especially in the north, rejected Rome and established Protestant churches. True, most of southern Europe—Italy, Portugal, Spain, and France—remained staunchly Roman Catholic. But significant portions Germany and all of Scandinavia created Lutheran churches, while much of the Netherlands and Scotland, as well as parts of Switzerland, became Presbyterian, or Calvinist. Smaller communities of Protestants appeared in countries like Poland and Hungary, although they remained distinct minorities. In many countries with mixed populations there was significant conflict, and in certain cases frightful violence, between Catholics and Protestants. The period roughly from 1500 to 1650 is sometimes therefore called "the Age of Religious Wars."

In England, first King Henry VIII (reigned 1509-1547) and then Queen Elizabeth I (1558-1603) effectuated the break from Rome and the creation of the Anglican Church, an official Protestant church for the country. Yet even as it broke from Rome and rejected the Pope's authority, the Anglican Church retained certain elements of Catholicism in its liturgy and its organizational structure. For example, the prominent place of bishops in the Anglican Church represented a significant element of continuity with Catholicism. There were other Protestants in Britain who wanted to go further with reform. Called "dissenters" because they rejected the official Anglican Church, they wanted a fuller and cleaner break from Catholic practices and the elimination of anything and everything that looked, smelled, or felt Catholic. Thus, for example, they wanted to do away entirely with bishops in favor of alternative forms of church organization. Finally, even as the country as a whole broke from Rome, some people in England continued to embrace Catholicism. True, they were a small minority, but some of them were quite powerful and influential. They held out the hope that the Protestant Reformation was just a passing crisis, and that it would be possible, eventually, to return Britain to Rome's embrace and to render it a Catholic country again. Not surprisingly, many English Protestants harbored strong suspicions about English Catholics, presuming that they were treasonous because they maintained ties with Rome and Catholic countries like France. The result was that Catholics faced tremendous hatred and discrimination and were at points the objects of persecution. This is another way of saying that religion and politics in England, as in most of Europe, were thoroughly intertwined at this point, so that things that we today might regard as purely spiritual always had political significance as well, just as politics sometimes occurred in a religious key.

If religion was one axis for political conflict in Britain, then the second concerned the relationship between the King and the Parliament. Monarchy had long been the main political institution of England, as a long line of kings and queens over the century attests. By 1603 the Stuart dynasty, a royal house originally founded in Scotland, had become the ruling family in England as well. The king enjoyed extensive executive powers but was dependent on Parliament financially—that is, he was limited in his ability to raise revenues without Parliament's consent. The problem in the seventeenth century was that the precise relationship between king and Parliament remained unclear. Both recognized that the other had certain powers and prerogatives, but the balance between the two was nowhere clearly defined, thus creating the basis for disagreement and conflict. Nor did England have a written constitution that could regulate the relationship between the two. Here it is worth noting that elsewhere in Europe, especially in nearby France, monarchs were making extensive efforts to concentrate their power and to erode the resistance of rival institutions—the church, local assemblies, powerful nobles, etc. King Louis XIV of France (1643-1715) was proving especially successful in this regard, and he therefore is often invoked as a premier example of "absolutism," the tendency to create an absolute monarchy, unrestricted by other institutions. The British kings of the seventeenth century shared some of these aspirations, although they proved far less effective than their French counterparts in realizing them. Indeed, Parliament proved exceptionally stubborn in defending its prerogatives, and the result, by the end of the century, was that Britain had become a constitutional monarchy rather than an example of absolutism.

Two political crises in the seventeenth century demonstrate the entanglement of these two sources of political conflict. The first crisis was the English Civil War, which is far too complicated to recount here. Suffice it to say that both religion and the conflict between King and Parliament were major sources of the conflict, and that the country reached a level of crisis that culminated in the execution of King Charles I in 1649. For the next decade, England accordingly became a republic, although it might be better to regard it as a kind of military dictatorship under the rule of Oliver Cromwell (1599-1658). When Cromwell died in 1658, there was really no one of his stature to replace him, and in any event the country was exhausted by some two decades of conflict. The obvious solution was to invite the son of the executed king, then in exile, to return to England and become king. Parliament did precisely this in 1660, and in this way the monarchy was restored and Charles II (reigned 1660-85) became the new king of England.

What is striking about this restoration of the monarchy was that it was essentially unconditional. In a constitutional sense, England simply returned to the situation that had existed before the civil war. This meant that fundamental religious issues remained unresolved, as did critical questions about the relationship between King and Parliament. For several decades, political life remained reasonably stable, since no one wished to precipitate a new crisis. Yet the underlying tensions persisted. The battle for sovereignty between Crown and Parliament continued, while the religious tensions among Anglicans, dissidents, and Catholics persisted as well. Potentially destabilizing was the fact that Charles II exhibited a distinct preference for Roman Catholicism over English Protestantism, and he also admired the absolutism that Louis XIV was constructing in France. He was careful not to be too obvious about these preferences, but he secretly promised Louis XIV that he would return England to Catholicism as soon as conditions might permit. And even as his Parliament, consisting mostly of ardent Anglicans, sought to impose persecuting laws on religious nonconformists, Charles tried to limit restrictions on Catholics. In 1668 there appeared a dangerous rumor that the Catholic pope and his supporters were planning to assassinate Charles, massacre English Protestants, and place the King's brother James II, a zealous convert to Catholicism, on the throne. This created a wave of anti-Catholic hysteria that continued into the 1680s. Meanwhile, Charles, like his predecessor, tried to rule without Parliament after 1681. In short, religious and political conflict continued in England along roughly the same lines that it had earlier in the century.

Tensions were already high when Charles II died in 1685 and his brother became **King James II** (reigned 1685-88). As an ardent Catholic, James proved far less restrained than his brother in his promotion of Catholicism. "We cannot but heartily wish," he told his subjects at one point, "that all the people of our dominions were members of the Catholic Church."[1] He accordingly sought to undermine the Anglican establishment by suspending repressive laws against Catholics and dissidents in a new decree on religious toleration. His call for Anglican clergy to read his toleration decree from their pulpits produced a serious backlash from the bishops of the established church. But the critical event producing a full-blown crisis proved to be the birth of a son to James II in 1688. Up until that point, the laws of succession dictated that the crown pass after James's death to his daughter, Mary, who was married to William of Orange in the Netherlands.[2]

Both **William and Mary** were Protestants, which meant that after James the succession would return to Protestant rulers. The birth of a son changed the picture dramatically. By Britain's law of succession, male claimants to the throne had precedence over females, which meant that James's son—surely to be baptized a Catholic—would gain the crown over his sister. Thus Britain, a predominantly Protestant country, was faced with the prospect of a permanent Catholic monarchy. This was something that most Englishmen could not accept, and James's strong-armed tactics against Parliament provided an extra incentive to be rid of him. A number of English aristocrats accordingly invited William and Mary to bring a foreign army to England to restore their religion and liberty. William responded to the call, landing with his army in November in 1688. As the chief men of the country went over to William's side, James found himself without any basis to resist the invasion and decided instead to flee to France. In February of 1689 a parliamentary assembly declared that James had abdicated the throne and offered the crown to William and Mary. This remarkable coup d'état was labeled the "Glorious Revolution."

This, then, was the context for the two documents that follow. The first is the **English Declaration of Rights**, sometimes also called Parliament's Bill of Rights. This document outlined the rights of England's population and its Parliament, and, as one historian has written, it "epitomized England's evolution into a constitutional monarchy, in which the king governed by parliamentary consent and was subject to law."[3] It is one of several documents and traditions that are at the foundation of Great Britain's constitution, which is sometimes referred to as "unwritten" because it is not codified as a single document. The Declaration also served as a basis in many ways for the Bill of Rights in the United States. As you read the Declaration, try to identify the principal rights that the authors of the English Bill of Rights of 1689 assert against the King. Why did they feel the need to make such an assertion? Also, consider how the propositions outlined here relate to John Locke's assertions in doc. 1.2.

---

1   Cited in Richard S. Dunn, *The Age of Religious Wars, 1559-1715* (New York: W. W. Norton, 1979), 194.

2   In this case "of Orange" refers to a ruling dynasty in

the Netherlands called "the House of Orange." Fans of World Cup soccer (football) will note the color of the Dutch team's uniform.

3   Dunn, *Age of Religious Wars*, 195.

DOCUMENT 1.1

THE ENGLISH DECLARATION OF RIGHTS (1689)

An Act Declaring the Rights and Liberties of the Subject and Settling the Succession of the Crown

Whereas the Lords Spiritual and Temporal and Commons assembled at Westminster,[4] lawfully, fully and freely representing all the estates of the people of this realm, did upon the thirteenth day of February in the year of our Lord one thousand six hundred eighty-eight [old style date] present unto their Majesties, then called and known by the names and style of William and Mary, prince and princess of Orange, being present in their proper persons, a certain declaration in writing made by the said Lords and Commons in the words following, viz.:

Whereas the late King James the Second, by the assistance of diverse evil counsellors, judges and ministers employed by him, did endeavor to subvert and extirpate the Protestant religion and the laws and liberties of this kingdom;

By assuming and exercising a power of dispensing with and suspending of laws and the execution of laws without consent of Parliament; By committing and prosecuting divers worthy prelates for humbly petitioning to be excused from concurring to the said assumed power;

By issuing and causing to be executed a commission under the great seal for erecting a court called the Court of Commissioners for Ecclesiastical Causes;

By levying money for and to the use of the Crown by pretence of prerogative for other time and in other manner than the same was granted by Parliament;

By raising and keeping a standing army within this kingdom in time of peace without consent of Parliament, and quartering soldiers contrary to law;

By causing several good subjects being Protestants to be disarmed at the same time when papists were both armed and employed contrary to law;

By violating the freedom of election of members to serve in Parliament;

By prosecutions in the Court of King's Bench for matters and causes cognizable only in Parliament, and by divers other arbitrary and illegal courses;

And whereas of late years partial corrupt and unqualified persons have been returned and served on juries in trials, and particularly divers jurors in trials for high treason which were not freeholders;

And excessive bail hath been required of persons committed in criminal cases to elude the benefit of the laws made for the liberty of the subjects;

And excessive fines have been imposed;

And illegal and cruel punishments inflicted;

And several grants and promises made of fines and forfeitures before any conviction or judgment against the persons upon whom the same were to be levied;

All which are utterly and directly contrary to the known laws and statutes and freedom of this realm;

And whereas the said late King James the Second having abdicated the government and the throne being thereby vacant, his Highness the prince of Orange (whom it hath pleased Almighty God to make the glorious instrument of delivering this kingdom from popery and arbitrary power)[5] did (by the advice of the Lords Spiritual and Temporal and divers principal persons of the Commons) cause letters to be written to the Lords Spiritual and Temporal being Protestants, and other letters to the several counties, cities, universities, boroughs and cinque ports, for the choosing of such persons to represent them as were of right to be sent to Parliament, to meet and sit at Westminster upon the two and twentieth day of January in this year one thousand six hundred eighty and eight [old style date], in order to such an establishment as that their religion, laws and liberties might not again be in danger of being subverted, upon which letters elections having been accordingly made;

---

4   This long phrase is simply another (and formal) way of saying "Parliament."

5   "Popery" is a derogatory, or insulting, term for Catholicism, based on the idea that Catholics are all followers of the pope and his arbitrary rule.

And thereupon the said Lords Spiritual and Temporal and Commons, pursuant to their respective letters and elections, being now assembled in a full and free representative of this nation, taking into their most serious consideration the best means for attaining the ends aforesaid, do in the first place (as their ancestors in like case have usually done) for the vindicating and asserting their ancient rights and liberties declare:

That the pretended power of suspending the laws or the execution of laws by regal authority without consent of Parliament is illegal;

That the pretended power of dispensing with laws or the execution of laws by regal authority, as it hath been assumed and exercised of late, is illegal;

That the commission for erecting the late Court of Commissioners for Ecclesiastical Causes, and all other commissions and courts of like nature, are illegal and pernicious;

That levying money for or to the use of the Crown by pretense of prerogative, without grant of Parliament, for longer time, or in other manner than the same is or shall be granted, is illegal;

That it is the right of the subjects to petition the king, and all commitments and prosecutions for such petitioning are illegal;

That the raising or keeping a standing army within the kingdom in time of peace, unless it be with consent of Parliament, is against law;

That the subjects which are Protestants may have arms for their defense suitable to their conditions and as allowed by law;

That election of members of Parliament ought to be free;

That the freedom of speech and debates or proceedings in Parliament ought not to be impeached or questioned in any court or place out of Parliament;

That excessive bail ought not to be required, nor excessive fines imposed, nor cruel and unusual punishments inflicted;

That jurors ought to be duly impanelled and returned, and jurors which pass upon men in trials for high treason ought to be freeholders;

That all grants and promises of fines and forfeitures of particular persons before conviction are illegal and void;

And that for redress of all grievances, and for the amending, strengthening and preserving of the laws, Parliaments ought to be held frequently.

And they do claim, demand and insist upon all and singular the premises as their undoubted rights and liberties....

And whereas it hath been found by experience that it is inconsistent with the safety and welfare of this Protestant kingdom to be governed by a popish prince, or by any king or queen marrying a papist, the said Lords Spiritual and Temporal and Commons do further pray that it may be enacted, that all and every person and persons that is, are or shall be reconciled to or shall hold communion with the see or Church of Rome, or shall profess the popish religion, or shall marry a papist, shall be excluded and be for ever incapable to inherit, possess or enjoy the crown and government of this realm and Ireland and the dominions thereunto belonging or any part of the same, or to have, use or exercise any regal power, authority or jurisdiction within the same....

End of document 1.1

If the Declaration of Rights was one critical document to emerge from the Glorious Revolution, another was the *Second Treatise on Government* by John Locke (1632-1704). Though published in 1690, the bulk of the *Second Treatise* was probably written in the early 1680s, even before Locke was compelled to flee to the Netherlands under suspicion of being involved in a plot to assassinate the King, then Charles II (Locke seems actually not to have been directly involved in this plot). After the Glorious Revolution in 1688-89, Locke was able to return to England, where the ideas he had articulated in the *Second Treatise* proved useful in justifying the overthrow of James II in favor of William and Mary.

Many historians regard Locke as standing at the origins of a remarkable intellectual movement known as the Enlightenment, which began in the late seventeenth century and continued throughout most of the eighteenth. Central to the Enlightenment were an optimistic view of humans and their potential; a critical attitude towards existing institutions and practices; a practical orientation directed towards reform and human improvement; and an emphasis on liberty as a dominant value over order. Even as an early author of the Enlightenment, Locke reflects several of these values. *His Essay Concerning Human Understanding* (1690) was designed to show that people are born without innate ideas or principles; the human mind at birth was instead a blank slate, or *tabula rasa*, which meant that he effectively rejected the conventional Christian emphasis on original sin. Locke's *Letter Concerning Toleration* (1689) rejected the idea that Christianity could be promoted or defended by force and proposed that there was no harm in a wide variety of religious practices (although Locke notably refused to extend toleration to Catholics).

The *Second Treatise* proved highly influential also in other contexts, most notably for American political thinking. Indeed, as you read the materials later in this course on the American colonies and the United States, you might consider how Locke's ideas are reflected in them. At present, try to keep in mind the following questions as you analyze the text below: According to John Locke, for what purpose do people form government? What do they hope to gain or protect by doing so? According to Locke, in what ways and for what reasons is the power of the legislature (that is, of the government) limited? What are the sources of these limitations? On what basis do they exist? How does Locke define "tyranny," and what are people entitled to do when faced with such tyranny?

The selection here begins after Locke has made the point that in the state of "nature"—that is, before the establishment of government—people existed in a state of "freedom." Why then, Locke asks, would people want to give up such freedom? Why would they leave the state of "nature" and become a "society" under government? One of his goals in the text is to provide an answer.

DOCUMENT 1.2

JOHN LOCKE, THE SECOND TREATISE OF GOVERNMENT (1690)[6]

CHAP. IX.
Of the Ends of Political Society and Government

§ 123. IF man in the state of nature be so free, as has been said; if he be absolute lord of his own person and possessions, equal to the greatest, and subject to no body, why will he part with his freedom? why will he give up this empire, and subject himself to the dominion and control of any other power? To which it is obvious to answer, that though in the state of nature he hath such a right, yet the enjoyment of it is very uncertain, and constantly exposed to the invasion of others: for all being kings as much as he, every man his equal, and the greater part no strict observers of equity and justice, the enjoyment of the property he has in this state is very unsafe, very unsecure. This makes him willing to quit a condition, which, however free, is full of fears and continual dangers: and it is not without reason, that he seeks out, and is willing to join in society with others, who are already united, or have a mind to unite, for the mutual *preservation* of their lives, liberties and estates, which I call by the general name, *property*.

§ 124. The great and *chief end*, therefore, of men's uniting into commonwealths, and putting themselves under government, *is the preservation of their property*. To which in the state of nature there are many things wanting.

CHAP. XI.
Of the Extent of the Legislative Power

Locke goes on to make the case that legislative power, which can take a number of different forms, is "supreme power" in the commonwealth, in the sense that there is no power or authority that stands above

---

6   Abridged from the text posted at: http://oregonstate.edu/instruct/phl302/texts/locke/locke2/locke2nd-d.html#CHAP.%20 XVIII. Several long footnotes have been eliminated from this portion of the original text.

it. The legislative has this authority, Locke proposes, because "the public" has chosen and appointed it to secure "the preservation of their property," as just noted above. Thus only an edict produced by this legislative power can have the force of law, and it is to this legislative power that people owe their obedience. But this does not mean that this legislative power is arbitrary. On the contrary, it exists within certain limits. Locke discusses those at some length.

§ 135. Though the *legislative,* whether placed in one or more, whether it be always in being, or only by intervals, though it be the *supreme* power in every common-wealth; yet,

First, It is *not,* nor can possibly be absolutely *arbitrary* over the lives and fortunes of the people: for it being but the joint power of every member of the society given up to that person, or assembly, which is legislator; it can be no more than those persons had in a state of nature before they entered into society, and gave up to the community: for no body can transfer to another more power than he has in himself; and no body has an absolute arbitrary power over himself, or over any other, to destroy his own life, or take away the life or property of another…. [Legislative] power, in the utmost bounds of it, is *limited to the public good* of the society. It is a power, that hath no other end but preservation, and therefore can never have a right to destroy, enslave, or designedly to impoverish the subjects. The obligations of the law of nature cease not in society, but only in many cases are drawn closer, and have by human laws known penalties annexed to them, to enforce their observation. Thus the law of nature stands as an eternal rule to all men, *legislators* as well as others. The rules that they make for other men's actions, must, as well as their own and other men's actions, be conformable to the law of nature, i.e. to the will of God, of which that is a declaration, and the fundamental law of nature being the preservation of mankind, no human sanction can be good, or valid against it.

§ 136. *Secondly,* The *legislative,* or supreme authority, cannot assume to its self a power to rule by extemporary arbitrary decrees, but *is bound to dispense justice,* and decide the rights of the subject *by promulgated standing laws, and known authorized judges:* for the law of nature being unwritten, and so no where to be found but in the minds of men, they who through passion or interest shall miscite, or misapply it, cannot so easily be convinced of their mistake where there is no established judge… To avoid these inconveniences, which disorder men's properties in the state of nature, men unite into societies, that they may have the united strength of the whole society to secure and defend their properties, and may have *standing rules* to bound it, by which every one may know what is his. To this end it is that men give up all their natural power to the society which they enter into, and the community put the legislative power into such hands as they think fit, with this trust, that they shall be governed by *declared laws,* or else their peace, quiet, and property will still be at the same uncertainty, as it was in the state of nature.

§ 138. *Thirdly,* The *supreme power cannot take* from any man any part of his *property* without his own consent: for the preservation of property being the end of government, and that for which men enter into society, it necessarily supposes and requires, that the people should *have property,* without which they must be supposed to lose that, by entering into society, which was the end for which they entered into it; too gross an absurdity for any man to own…. Hence it is a mistake to think, that the *supreme* or *legislative power* of any common-wealth, can do what it will, and dispose of the estates of the subject *arbitrarily,* or take any part of them at pleasure. This is not much to be feared in governments where the *legislative* consists, wholly or in part, in assemblies which are variable, whose members, upon the dissolution of the assembly, are subjects under the common laws of their country, equally with the rest. But in governments, where the *legislative* is in one lasting assembly always in being, or in one man, as in absolute monarchies, there is danger still, that they will think themselves to have a distinct interest from the rest of the community; and so will be apt to increase their own riches and power, by taking what they think fit from the people…

§ 141. *Fourthly,* The *legislative cannot transfer the power of making laws* to any other hands: for it being but a delegated power from the people, they who have it cannot pass it over to others. The people alone can appoint the form of the commonwealth, which is by constituting the legislative, and appointing in whose hands that shall be. And when the people have said, We will submit to rules, and be governed by *laws* made by such men, and in such forms, no body else can say other men shall make *laws* for them….

§ 142. These are the *bounds* which the trust, that is put in them by the society, and the law of God and nature, have *set to the legislative power* of every common-wealth, in all forms of government.

First, They are to govern by *promulgated established laws,* not to be varied in particular cases, but to have one rule for rich and poor, for the favourite at court, and the country man at plough.

Secondly, These laws also ought to be designed *for* no other end ultimately, but *the good of the people.*

Thirdly, They must *not raise taxes* on the *property of the people, without the consent of the people,* given by themselves, or their deputies....

Fourthly, The *legislative* neither must *nor can transfer the power of making laws* to any body else, or place it anywhere, but where the people have.

CHAP. XVIII
Of TYRANNY

> *In the previous sections, Locke establishes a set of principles that describe the limits, or "bounds," of legislative power. His main point was that there were certain things that legislative power could not legitimately do. Yet there was also the question about what should be done if the legislative power did, in fact, violate these limits. Locke's discussion of "tyranny" is designed to address this question.*

§ 199. AS usurpation is the exercise of power, which another hath a right to; so *tyranny is the exercise of power beyond right,* which no body can have a right to. And this is making use of the power any one has in his hands, not for the good of those who are under it, but for his own private separate advantage. When the governor, however entitled, makes not the law, but his will, the rule; and his commands and actions are not directed to the preservation of the properties of his people, but the satisfaction of his own ambition, revenge, covetousness, or any other irregular passion.

§ 222. The reason why men enter into society, is the preservation of their property; and the end why they choose and authorize a legislative, is, that there may be laws made, and rules set, as guards and fences to the properties of all the members of the society, to limit the power, and moderate the dominion, of every part and member of the society: for since it can never be supposed to be the will of the society, that the legislative should have a power to destroy that which every one designs to secure, by entering into society, and for which the people submitted themselves to legislators of their own making; whenever the *legislators endeavor to take away, and destroy the property of the people,* or to reduce them to slavery under arbitrary power, they put themselves into a state of war with the people, who are thereupon absolved from any farther obedience, and are left to the common refuge, which God hath provided for all men, against force and violence. Whensoever therefore the *legislative* shall transgress this fundamental rule of society; and either by ambition, fear, folly or corruption, *endeavor to grasp* themselves, *or put into the hands of any other, an absolute power* over the lives, liberties, and estates of the people; by this breach of trust they *forfeit the power* the people had put into their hands for quite contrary ends, and it devolves to the people, who. have a right to resume their original liberty, and, by the establishment of a new legislative, (such as they shall think fit) provide for their own safety and security, which is the end for which they are in society....

§ 223. To this perhaps it will be said, that the people being ignorant, and always discontented, to lay the foundation of government in the unsteady opinion and uncertain humor of the people, is to expose it to certain ruin; and *no government will be able long to subsist,* if the people may set up a new legislative, whenever they take offence at the old one. To this I answer, Quite the contrary. People are not so easily got out of their old forms, as some are apt to suggest. They are hardly to be prevailed with to amend the acknowledged faults in the frame they have been accustomed to. And if there be any original defects, or adventitious ones introduced by time, or corruption; it is not an easy thing to get them changed, even when all the world sees there is an opportunity for it. This slowness and aversion in the people to quit their old constitutions, has, in the many revolutions which have been seen in this kingdom, in this and former ages, still kept us to, or, after some interval of fruitless attempts, still brought us back again to our old legislative of king, lords and commons: and whatever provocations have made the crown be taken from some of our princes heads, they never carried the people so far as to place it in another line.

§ 224. But it will be said, this *hypothesis* lays a *ferment for* frequent *rebellion.* To which I answer,

First, No more than any other *hypothesis:* for when the people are made miserable, and find themselves *exposed to the ill usage of arbitrary power,* cry up their governors, as much as you will, for sons of *Jupiter;* let them be sacred and divine, descended, or authorized from heaven; give them out for whom or what you please, the same will happen. *The people generally ill treated,* and contrary to right, will be ready upon any occasion to ease themselves of a burden that sits heavy upon them. They will wish, and seek for the opportunity, which in the change, weakness and accidents of human affairs, seldom delays long to offer itself....

§ 225. *Secondly,* I answer, such *revolutions happen* not upon every little mismanagement in public affairs. *Great mistakes* in the ruling part, many wrong and inconvenient laws, and all the *slips* of human frailty, will be *born by the people* without mutiny or murmur. But if a long train of abuses, prevarications and artifices, all tending the same way, make the design visible to the people, and they cannot but feel what they lie under, and see whither they are going; it is not to be wondered, that they should then rouse themselves, and endeavor to put the rule into such hands which may secure to them the ends for which government was at first erected; and without which, ancient names, and specious forms, are so far from being better, that they are much worse, than the state of nature, or pure anarchy; the inconveniencies being all as great and as near, but the remedy farther off and more difficult.

§ 226. *Thirdly,* I answer, that *this doctrine* of a power in the people of providing for their safety a-new, by a new legislative, when their legislators have acted contrary to their trust, by invading their property, is *the best fence against rebellion,* and the probablest means to hinder it: for *rebellion* being an opposition, not to persons, but authority, which is founded only in the constitutions and laws of the government; those, whoever they be, who by force break through, and by force justify their violation of them, are truly and properly *rebels:* for when men, by entering into society and civil-government, have excluded force, and introduced laws for the preservation of property, peace, and unity amongst themselves, those who set up force again in opposition to the laws, do *rebellare,* that is, bring back again the state of war, and are properly rebels: which they who are in power, (by the pretense they have to authority, the temptation of force they have in their hands, and the flattery of those about them) being likeliest to do; the properest way to prevent the evil, is to shew them the danger and injustice of it, who are under the greatest temptation to run into it.

End of document 1.2

THE AMERICAN DECLARATION OF INDEPENDENCE

The broad circumstances leading to the American **Declaration of Independence** are covered by Gordon Wood in *The American Revolution,* so here we will note merely that the Declaration was written primarily by Thomas Jefferson (1743-1826) to justify the American colonists' break with Great Britain, once war had broken out with the mother country in 1775. In reading through the Declaration, is worth considering the extent to which the English experience in the foregoing documents is reflected here. Which ideas in the first two documents find expression here as well? Are there particular passages or phrases that connect the either of the two English documents with the American one? Is there a way in which the Declaration of Independence is similar to one of the other documents in terms of its structure?

DOCUMENT 1.3

DECLARATION OF INDEPENDENCE (1776)

IN CONGRESS, JULY 4, 1776
The unanimous Declaration of the thirteen United States of America

When in the Course of human events it becomes necessary for one people to dissolve the political bands which have connected them with another and to assume among the powers of the earth, the separate and equal station to which the Laws of Nature and of Nature's God entitle them, a decent respect to the opinions of mankind requires that they should declare the causes which impel them to the separation.

We hold these truths to be self-evident, that all men are created equal, that they are endowed by their Creator with certain unalienable Rights, that among these are Life, Liberty and the pursuit of Happiness. — That to secure these rights, Governments are instituted among Men, deriving their just powers from the consent of the governed, — That whenever any Form of Government becomes destructive of these ends, it is the Right of the People to alter or to abolish it, and to institute new Government, laying its foundation on such principles and organizing its powers in such form, as to them shall seem most likely to effect their Safety and Happiness. Prudence, indeed, will dictate that Governments long established should not be changed for light and transient causes; and accordingly all experience hath shewn that mankind are more disposed to suffer, while evils are sufferable than to right themselves by abolishing the forms to which they are accustomed. But when a long train of abuses and usurpations, pursuing invariably the same Object evinces a design to reduce them under absolute Despotism, it is their right, it is their duty, to throw off such Government, and to provide new Guards for their future security. — Such has been the patient sufferance of these Colonies; and such is now the necessity which constrains them to alter their former Systems of Government. The history of the present King of Great Britain is a history of repeated injuries and usurpations, all having in direct object the establishment of an absolute Tyranny over these States. To prove this, let Facts be submitted to a candid world.

He has refused his Assent to Laws, the most wholesome and necessary for the public good.

He has forbidden his Governors to pass Laws of immediate and pressing importance, unless suspended in their operation till his Assent should be obtained; and when so suspended, he has utterly neglected to attend to them.

He has refused to pass other Laws for the accommodation of large districts of people, unless those people would relinquish the right of Representation in the Legislature, a right inestimable to them and formidable to tyrants only.

He has called together legislative bodies at places unusual, uncomfortable, and distant from the depository of their Public Records, for the sole purpose of fatiguing them into compliance with his measures.

He has dissolved Representative Houses repeatedly, for opposing with manly firmness his invasions on the rights of the people.

He has refused for a long time, after such dissolutions, to cause others to be elected, whereby the Legislative Powers, incapable of Annihilation, have returned to the People at large for their exercise; the State remaining in the mean time exposed to all the dangers of invasion from without, and convulsions within.

He has endeavored to prevent the population of these States; for that purpose obstructing the Laws for Naturalization of Foreigners; refusing to pass others to encourage their migrations hither, and raising the conditions of new Appropriations of Lands.

He has obstructed the Administration of Justice by refusing his Assent to Laws for establishing Judiciary Powers.

He has made Judges dependent on his Will alone for the tenure of their offices, and the amount and payment of their salaries.

He has erected a multitude of New Offices, and sent hither swarms of Officers to harass our people and eat out their substance.

He has kept among us, in times of peace, Standing Armies without the Consent of our legislatures.

He has affected to render the Military independent of and superior to the Civil Power.

He has combined with others to subject us to a jurisdiction foreign to our constitution, and unacknowledged by our laws; giving his Assent to their Acts of pretended Legislation:

For quartering large bodies of armed troops among us:

For protecting them, by a mock Trial from punishment for any Murders which they should commit on the Inhabitants of these States:

For cutting off our Trade with all parts of the world:

For imposing Taxes on us without our Consent:

For depriving us in many cases, of the benefit of Trial by Jury:

For transporting us beyond Seas to be tried for pretended offences:

For abolishing the free System of English Laws in a neighbouring Province, establishing therein an Arbitrary government, and enlarging its Boundaries so as to render it at once an example and fit instrument for introducing the same absolute rule into these Colonies.

For taking away our Charters, abolishing our most valuable Laws and altering fundamentally the Forms of our Governments:

For suspending our own Legislatures, and declaring themselves invested with power to legislate for us in all cases whatsoever.

He has abdicated Government here, by declaring us out of his Protection and waging War against us.

He has plundered our seas, ravaged our coasts, burnt our towns, and destroyed the lives of our people.

He is at this time transporting large Armies of foreign Mercenaries to complete the works of death, desolation, and tyranny, already begun with circumstances of Cruelty & Perfidy scarcely paralleled in the most barbarous ages, and totally unworthy the Head of a civilized nation.

He has constrained our fellow Citizens taken Captive on the high Seas to bear Arms against their Country, to become the executioners of their friends and Brethren, or to fall themselves by their Hands.

He has excited domestic insurrections amongst us, and has endeavored to bring on the inhabitants of our frontiers, the merciless Indian Savages whose known rule of warfare, is an undistinguished destruction of all ages, sexes and conditions.

In every stage of these Oppressions We have Petitioned for Redress in the most humble terms: Our repeated Petitions have been answered only by repeated injury. A Prince, whose character is thus marked by every act which may define a Tyrant, is unfit to be the ruler of a free people.

Nor have We been wanting in attentions to our British brethren. We have warned them from time to time of attempts by their legislature to extend an unwarrantable jurisdiction over us. We have reminded them of the circumstances of our emigration and settlement here. We have appealed to their native justice and magnanimity, and we have conjured them by the ties of our common kindred to disavow these usurpations, which would inevitably interrupt our connections and correspondence. They too have been deaf to the voice of justice and of consanguinity. We must, therefore, acquiesce in the necessity, which denounces our Separation, and hold them, as we hold the rest of mankind, Enemies in War, in Peace Friends.

We, therefore, the Representatives of the united States of America, in General Congress, Assembled, appealing to the Supreme Judge of the world for the rectitude of our intentions, do, in the Name, and by Authority of the good People of these Colonies, solemnly publish and declare, That these united Colonies are, and of Right ought to be Free and Independent States, that they are Absolved from all Allegiance to the British Crown, and that all political connection between them and the State of Great Britain, is and ought to be totally dissolved; and that as Free and Independent States, they have full Power to levy War, conclude Peace, contract Alliances, establish Commerce, and to do all other Acts and Things which Independent States may of right do. — And for the support of this Declaration, with a firm reliance on the protection of Divine Providence, we mutually pledge to each other our Lives, our Fortunes, and our sacred Honor.

[Signatures follow]

End of document 1.3

Further Reading:

Richard S. Dunn, *The Age of Religious Wars, 1559-1715*. New York: W. W. Norton, 1979.

Thomas Munck, *Seventeenth Century Europe, 1598-1700*. New York, St. Martin's Press, 1989.

CHAPTER 2

FROM CONFEDERATION TO FEDERATION

FIRST SOLUTION: CONFEDERATION

The Declaration of Independence of 1776 was undertaken by thirteen separate colonies, which thereafter became states. It may be tempting to suppose that already in 1776 a single new country had emerged on the North American continent, but it is far from clear that this was actually the case. Arguably, there were now thirteen distinct political entities, and the very use of the word "states" to describe them would confirm this proposition.[1] Aside from their connection to the mother country in Britain, there was little that formally united the colonies of North America. It is true that some people had begun to think about greater unity among the American colonies even before the political crisis of the 1770s. For example, in 1754 Benjamin Franklin proposed a "Grand Council" consisting of eleven colonies.[2] This council would have consisted of delegates elected by assemblies of each colony, and would have been presided over by a president-general appointed by the British Crown, with the right of veto. But colonial legislators rejected this proposal, because it would have entailed shifting

power away from themselves towards the new Council. The implication is clear: Most colonists were still focused principally upon their own colony and were apparently satisfied being connected to the other colonies through the British Crown. The situation of course changed fundamentally with the colonies' declaration of independence from Britain, but this by itself did not mean that the colonies suddenly became a single, unified country. In fact, the states focused first and foremost on producing their own individual constitutions, the first of these being the constitution of Pennsylvania (28 September 1776). Thus, in a basic sense people at the time were faced with the question of whether there was one new country or thirteen. We ourselves must grapple with the same question.

One solution to the conundrum was to create a **confederation**, which the *Oxford English Dictionary* defines as "a more or less permanent union of countries with some or most political power vested in a central authority." This was the solution that the new American states adopted when they produced the **Articles of Confederation** (Document 1.4 below). This solution allowed the states to unite for certain limited purposes while retaining their sovereignty (see for example article II of the Articles). It is noteworthy that even as the individual states produced their own constitutions fairly rapidly after the Declaration of Independence, the Articles of Confederation were completed by Congress only on 15 November 1777 and ratified only more than three years later, on 1 March 1781.

---

1   The word "state" has eventually come to signify "an organized political community or area forming part of a federal republic," but in a more fundamental sense it is defined as "a nation or territory considered as an organized political community under one government" (both definitions are from the *Oxford English Dictionary*).

2   The plan subsumed Delaware within Pennsylvania and excluded Georgia, which was the newest and least organized colony.

As you read the Articles below (an abridged version), keep in mind the following questions: to what extent are the "United States" in this document construed as a single entity, and to what extent were they thirteen distinct ones? And looking ahead: in what fundamental ways do the Articles differ from the Constitution ratified a decade later?

DOCUMENT 1.4

ARTICLES OF THE CONFEDERATION (1777/1781)

Nov. 15, 1777

To all to whom these Presents shall come, we the undersigned Delegates of the States affixed to our Names send greeting.

Articles of Confederation and perpetual Union between the states of New Hampshire, Massachusetts-bay Rhode Island and Providence Plantations, Connecticut, New York, New Jersey, Pennsylvania, Delaware, Maryland, Virginia, North Carolina, South Carolina and Georgia.

I.   The Stile of this Confederacy shall be "The United States of America."

II. Each state retains its sovereignty, freedom, and independence, and every power, jurisdiction, and right, which is not by this Confederation expressly delegated to the United States, in Congress assembled.

III. The said States hereby severally enter into a firm league of friendship with each other, for their common defense, the security of their liberties, and their mutual and general welfare, binding themselves to assist each other, against all force offered to, or attacks made upon them, or any of them, on account of religion, sovereignty, trade, or any other pretense whatever.

IV. The better to secure and perpetuate mutual friendship and intercourse among the people of the different States in this Union, the free inhabitants of each of these States, paupers, vagabonds, and fugitives from justice excepted, shall be entitled to all privileges and immunities of free citizens in the several States; and the people of each State shall free ingress and regress to and from any other State, and shall enjoy therein all the privileges of trade and commerce…. If any person guilty of, or charged with, treason, felony, or other high misdemeanor in any State, shall flee from justice, and be found in any of the United States, he shall, upon demand of the Governor or executive power of the State from which he fled, be delivered up and removed to the State having jurisdiction of his offense….

V.   For the most convenient management of the general interests of the United States, delegates shall be annually appointed in such manner as the legislatures of each State shall direct, to meet in Congress on the first Monday in November, in every year, with a power reserved to each State to recall its delegates, or any of them, at any time within the year, and to send others in their stead for the remainder of the year…. In determining questions in the United States in Congress assembled, each State shall have one vote…

VI. No State, without the consent of the United States in Congress assembled, shall send any embassy to, or receive any embassy from, or enter into any conference, agreement, alliance or treaty with any King, Prince or State; nor shall any person holding any office of profit or trust under the United States, or any of them, accept any present, emolument, office or title of any kind whatever from any King, Prince or foreign State; nor shall the United States in Congress assembled, or any of them, grant any title of nobility…. No State shall engage in any war without the consent of the United States in Congress assembled, unless such State be actually invaded by enemies, or shall have received certain advice of a resolution being formed by some nation of Indians to invade such State, and the danger is so imminent as not to admit of a delay till the United States in Congress assembled can be consulted…

IX. The United States in Congress assembled, shall have the sole and exclusive right and power of determining on peace and war, except in the cases mentioned in the sixth article.

   ❖   of sending and receiving ambassadors

   ❖   entering into treaties and alliances…

- ❖ of establishing rules for deciding in all cases, what captures on land or water shall be legal…
- ❖ of granting letters of marque[3] and reprisal in times of peace
- ❖ appointing courts for the trial of piracies and felonies committed on the high seas and establishing courts for receiving and determining finally appeals in all cases of captures…

The United States in Congress assembled shall also be the last resort on appeal in all disputes and differences now subsisting or that hereafter may arise between two or more States concerning boundary, jurisdiction or any other causes whatever…

The United States in Congress assembled shall also have the sole and exclusive right and power of regulating the alloy and value of coin struck by their own authority, or by that of the respective States.

- ❖ fixing the standards of weights and measures throughout the United States
- ❖ regulating the trade and managing all affairs with the Indians…
- ❖ establishing or regulating post offices from one State to another…
- ❖ appointing all officers of the land forces, in the service of the United States, excepting regimental officers.
- ❖ appointing all the officers of the naval forces, and commissioning all officers whatever in the service of the United States.
- ❖ making rules for the government and regulation of the said land and naval forces, and directing their operations.

The United States in Congress assembled shall have authority to appoint a committee, to sit in the recess of Congress, to be denominated 'A Committee of the States,' and to consist of one delegate from each State…

The United States in Congress assembled shall never engage in a war, nor grant letters of marque or reprisal in time of peace, nor enter into any treaties or alliances, nor coin money, nor regulate the value thereof, nor ascertain the sums and expenses necessary for the defense and welfare of the United States, or any of them, nor emit bills, nor borrow money on the credit of the United States, nor appropriate money, nor agree upon the number of vessels of war, to be built or purchased, or the number of land or sea forces to be raised, nor appoint a commander in chief of the army or navy, unless nine States assent to the same: nor shall a question on any other point, except for adjourning from day to day be determined, unless by the votes of the majority of the United States in Congress assembled.

XI. Canada acceding to this confederation, and adjoining in the measures of the United States, shall be admitted into, and entitled to all the advantages of this Union; but no other colony shall be admitted into the same, unless such admission be agreed to by nine States.

XII. All bills of credit emitted, monies borrowed, and debts contracted by, or under the authority of Congress, before the assembling of the United States, in pursuance of the present confederation, shall be deemed and considered as a charge against the United States, for payment and satisfaction whereof the said United States, and the public faith are hereby solemnly pledged.

XIII. Every State shall abide by the determination of the United States in Congress assembled, on all questions which by this confederation are submitted to them. And the Articles of this Confederation shall be inviolably observed by every State, and the Union shall be perpetual; nor shall any alteration at any time hereafter be made in any of them; unless such alteration be agreed to in a Congress of the United States, and be afterwards confirmed by the legislatures of every State.

End of document 1.4

---

3   A "letter of marque" was authorization by a government to attack and capture enemy sailing vessels.

DEBATING THE SECOND SOLUTION: FEDERATION

The Articles of Confederation proved unable to meet the needs of the thirteen states, and the Confederation Congress accordingly authorized a convention, to be held in Philadelphia in 1787, to revise the Articles. Instead, the participants of the convention produced an entirely new constitution, which proposed the creation of a **federation**. It is worth emphasizing that the convention had not actually been empowered to propose a whole new constitution, and for that reason alone there was likely to be opposition to the new document.

Indeed, there proved to be both opponents and proponents of approving the proposed Constitution, and therefore considerable debate ignited among Americans about its merits. Notably, while modifications to the Articles of Confederation would have required the *unanimous* assent of all the states, then Article VII of the proposed Constitution specified that *nine states* were sufficient for the document in order for it to go into effect. And yet even with this lower threshold, ratification of the constitution was by no means guaranteed. All of this suggests that good students of the constitution should pay at least some attention to the ratification process, which is actually a critical part of the history of the Constitution. James Madison himself—one of the Constitution's authors, no less—emphasized in 1796 that as the proposed constitution emerged from Philadelphia, "it was nothing more than the draught [draft] of a plan, nothing but a dead letter, until life and validity were breathed into it by the voice of the people, speaking through the several state conventions. If we were to look therefore, for the meaning of the instrument [the constitution] beyond the face of the instrument, we must look for it not in the general convention [in Philadelphia], which proposed, but in the state conventions, which accepted and ratified the constitution."[4] In short, even the main author of the Constitution believed that the document's ratification was as important as its composition.

Among the more articulate opponents of ratification was an author who wrote under the penname of "**Brutus.**" There is consensus among historians that this was probably **Robert Yates** (1783-1801), who had served on the New York Supreme Court during the Revolutionary War and was well known for his opposition to the Constitution. In his Second Essay, reproduced below, Brutus was concerned above all with the danger of "the destruction of [our] liberties." In reading the Essay, consider the ways in which the thought of John Locke is present in Brutus's thinking. Think also about the relationship that Brutus posits between states and the central (federal) government. Moreover, what connection would you draw between the Essay here and the approval of the Bill of Rights (the first 10 amendments of the US Constitution), discussed later in this book?

DOCUMENT 1.5

BRUTUS [ROBERT YATES?], SECOND ESSAY OPPOSING THE CONSTITUTION (1787)

To the Citizens of the State of New-York.

I flatter myself that my last address established this position, that to reduce the Thirteen States into one government, would prove the destruction of your liberties.

But lest this truth should be doubted by some, I will now proceed to consider its merits.

Though it should be admitted, that the argument[s] against reducing all the states into one consolidated government, are not sufficient fully to establish this point; yet they will, at least, justify this conclusion, that in forming a constitution for such a country, great care should be taken to limit and definite its powers, adjust its parts, and guard against an abuse of authority....

If we may collect the sentiments of the people of America, from their own most solemn declarations, they hold this truth as self evident, that all men are by nature free. No one man, therefore, or any class of men, have a right, by the law of nature, or of God, to assume or exercise authority over their fellows. The

---

4   Pauline Maier, *Ratification: The People Debate the Constitution, 1787-1788* (New York: Simon & Schuster, 2010), xvii.

origin of society then is to be sought, not in any natural right which one man has to exercise authority over another, but in the united consent of those who associate…. The common good, therefore, is the end of civil government, and common consent, the foundation on which it is established. To effect this end, it was necessary that a certain portion of natural liberty should be surrendered, in order, that what remained should be preserved…. But it is not necessary, for this purpose, that individuals should relinquish all their natural rights. Some are of such a nature that they cannot be surrendered. Of this kind are the rights of conscience, the right of enjoying and defending life, etc….

Those who have governed, have been found in all ages ever active to enlarge their powers and abridge the public liberty. This has induced the people in all countries, where any sense of freedom remained, to fix barriers against the encroachments of their rulers. The country from which we have derived our origin, is an eminent example of this. Their magna charta and bill of rights have long been the boast, as well as the security, of that nation. I need say no more, I presume, to an American, than, that this principle is a fundamental one, in all the constitutions of our own states; there is not one of them but what is either founded on a declaration or bill of rights, or has certain express reservation of rights interwoven in the body of them….

It has been said, in answer to this objection, that such declaration[s] of rights, however requisite they might be in the constitutions of the states, are not necessary in the general constitution, because, "in the former case, every thing which is not reserved is given, but in the latter the reverse of the proposition prevails, and every thing which is not given is reserved." It requires but little attention to discover, that this mode of reasoning is rather specious than solid. The powers, rights, and authority, granted to the general government by this constitution, are as complete, with respect to every object to which they extend, as that of any state government — It reaches to every thing which concerns human happiness — Life, liberty, and property, are under its control. There is the same reason, therefore, that the exercise of power, in this case, should be restrained within proper limits, as in that of the state governments….

The same security [that one finds in the bills of rights of the constitutions of the individual states] is as necessary in this constitution, and much more so; for the general government will have the sole power to raise and to pay armies, and are under no control in the exercise of it; yet nothing of this is to be found in this new system….

This system, if it is possible for the people of America to accede to it, will be an original compact: and being the last, will, in the nature of things, vacate every former agreement inconsistent with it. For it being a plan of government received and ratified by the whole people, all other forms, which are in existence at the time of its adoption, must yield to it. This is expressed in positive and unequivocal terms, in the 6th article, "That this constitution and the laws of the United States, which shall be made in pursuance thereof, and all treaties made, or which shall be made, under the authority of the United States, shall be the supreme law of the land; and the judges in every state shall be bound thereby, any thing in the constitution, or laws of any state, to the contrary notwithstanding." […]

It is therefore not only necessarily implied thereby, but positively expressed, that the different state constitutions are repealed and entirely done away, so far as they are inconsistent with this, with the laws which shall be made in pursuance thereof, or with treaties made, or which shall be made, under the authority of the United States; of what avail will the constitutions of the respective states be to preserve the rights of its citizens? …

This will appear the more necessary, when it is considered, that not only the constitution and laws made in pursuance thereof, but all treaties made, or which shall be made, under the authority of the United States, are the supreme law of the land, and supersede the constitutions of all the states. The power to make treaties, is vested in the president, by and with the advice and consent of two thirds of the senate. I do not find any limitation, or restriction, to the exercise of this power. The most important article in any constitution may therefore be repealed, even without a legislative act. Ought not a government, vested with such extensive and indefinite authority, to have been restricted by a declaration of rights? It certainly ought.

So clear a point is this, that I cannot help suspecting, that persons who attempt to persuade people, that such reservations were less necessary under this constitution than under those of the states, are wilfully endeavouring to deceive, and to lead you into an absolute state of vassalage.

End of document 1.5

If Brutus was a prominent voice in opposition to the US Constitution, then *The Federalist Papers* offered a series of arguments in favor of its ratification. In all, *The Federalist Papers* consist of 85 articles composed in 1787-88 and designed to promote ratification of the Constitution. Written under the pseudonym "Publius," the articles were actually authored by **Alexander Hamilton** (51 articles), **James Madison** (29 articles), and **John Jay** (5 articles). They were directed above all to the people of New York, who were among the most skeptical about the proposed Constitution.

Federalist no. 41, reproduced below, was written by Madison, who more than anyone else merits being considered the author of the Constitution itself. The most famous and the most philosophically important of the *Federalist Papers* was no. 10, in which Madison addressed the means of preventing factions and advocated an extended republic. But the importance of no. 10 for people at the time of ratification has often been exaggerated, and the geopolitical implications of the Constitution were also prominent in the minds of the document's supporters. Some of these are addressed in no. 41. As you read, consider the dangers that Madison saw in the disunion of the states. How does Madison respond to worries that the Constitution would increase the likelihood of there being a large standing army in the country? Why does he propose that disunion would be likely to reproduce the problems that had appeared in continental Europe? How in his view would disunion foster the existence of "standing armies and perpetual taxes"? In what specific ways does Madison regard the US as being similar to Great Britain, and what does he see as being the principal benefit of this similarity?

DOCUMENT 1.6

PUBLIUS [JAMES MADISON], *THE FEDERALIST*, **NO. 41 (1788)**

To the People of the State of New York:

THE Constitution proposed by the convention may be considered under two general points of view. The FIRST relates to the sum or quantity of power which it vests in the government, including the restraints imposed on the States. The SECOND, to the particular structure of the government, and the distribution of this power among its several branches.

Under the first view of the subject, two important questions arise: 1. Whether any part of the powers transferred to the general government be unnecessary or improper? 2. Whether the entire mass of them be dangerous to the portion of jurisdiction left in the several States?

Is the aggregate power of the general government greater than ought to have been vested in it? This is the first question.

It cannot have escaped those who have attended with candor to the arguments employed against the extensive powers of the government, that the authors of them have very little considered how far these powers were necessary means of attaining a necessary end. They have chosen rather to dwell on the inconveniences which must be unavoidably blended with all political advantages; and on the possible abuses which must be incident to every power or trust, of which a beneficial use can be made… [B]ut cool and candid people will at once reflect, that the purest of human blessings must have a portion of alloy in them; that the choice must always be made, if not of the lesser evil, at least of the GREATER, not the PERFECT, good; and that in every political institution, a power to advance the public happiness involves a discretion which may be misapplied and abused. They will see, therefore, that in all cases where power is to be conferred, the point first to be decided is, whether such a power be necessary to the public good; as the next will be, in case of an affirmative decision, to guard as effectually as possible against a perversion of the power to the public detriment.

That we may form a correct judgment on this subject, it will be proper to review the several powers conferred on the government of the Union; and that this may be the more conveniently done they may be reduced into different classes as they relate to the following different objects: 1. Security against foreign danger; 2. Regulation of the intercourse with foreign nations; 3. Maintenance of harmony and proper intercourse among the States; 4. Certain miscellaneous objects of general utility; 5. Restraint of the States from certain injurious acts; 6. Provisions for giving due efficacy to all these powers.

The powers falling within the first class are those of declaring war and granting letters of marque; of providing armies and fleets; of regulating and calling forth the militia; of levying and borrowing money.

Security against foreign danger is one of the primitive objects of civil society. It is an avowed and essential object of the American Union. The powers requisite for attaining it must be effectually confided to the federal councils.

Is the power of declaring war necessary? No man will answer this question in the negative. It would be superfluous, therefore, to enter into a proof of the affirmative. The existing Confederation establishes this power in the most ample form.

Is the power of raising armies and equipping fleets necessary? This is involved in the foregoing power. It is involved in the power of self-defense.

But was it necessary to give an INDEFINITE POWER of raising TROOPS, as well as providing fleets; and of maintaining both in PEACE, as well as in WAR?

[…] The answer indeed seems to be so obvious and conclusive as scarcely to justify such a discussion in any place. With what color of propriety could the force necessary for defense be limited by those who cannot limit the force of offense? If a federal Constitution could chain the ambition or set bounds to the exertions of all other nations, then indeed might it prudently chain the discretion of its own government, and set bounds to the exertions for its own safety…. A standing force, therefore, is a dangerous, at the same time that it may be a necessary, provision. On the smallest scale it has its inconveniences. On an extensive scale its consequences may be fatal. On any scale it is an object of laudable circumspection and precaution. A wise nation will combine all these considerations; and, whilst it does not rashly preclude itself from any resource which may become essential to its safety, will exert all its prudence in diminishing both the necessity and the danger of resorting to one which may be inauspicious to its liberties.

The clearest marks of this prudence are stamped on the proposed Constitution. The Union itself, which it cements and secures, destroys every pretext for a military establishment which could be dangerous. America united, with a handful of troops, or without a single soldier, exhibits a more forbidding posture to foreign ambition than America disunited, with a hundred thousand veterans ready for combat. It was remarked, on a former occasion, that the want of this pretext had saved the liberties of one nation in Europe. Being rendered by her insular situation and her maritime resources impregnable to the armies of her neighbors, the rulers of Great Britain have never been able, by real or artificial dangers, to cheat the public into an extensive peace establishment. The distance of the United States from the powerful nations of the world gives them the same happy security. A dangerous establishment can never be necessary or plausible, so long as they continue a united people. But let it never, for a moment, be forgotten that they are indebted for this advantage to the Union alone. The moment of its dissolution will be the date of a new order of things….

This picture of the consequences of disunion cannot be too highly colored, or too often exhibited. Every man who loves peace, every man who loves his country, every man who loves liberty, ought to have it ever before his eyes, that he may cherish in his heart a due attachment to the Union of America, and be able to set a due value on the means of preserving it.

Next to the effectual establishment of the Union, the best possible precaution against danger from standing armies is a limitation of the term for which revenue may be appropriated to their support. This precaution the Constitution has prudently added…. Now, if in Great Britain, where the House of Commons is elected for seven years; where so great a proportion of the members are elected by so small a proportion of the people; where the electors are so corrupted by the representatives, and the representatives so corrupted by the Crown, the representative body can possess a power to make appropriations to the army for an indefinite term, without desiring, or without daring, to extend the term beyond a single year, ought not suspicion herself to blush, in pretending that the representatives of the United States, elected FREELY by the WHOLE BODY of the people, every SECOND YEAR, cannot be safely entrusted with the discretion over such appropriations, expressly limited to the short period of TWO YEARS?

[N]ot only has the constitution provided the most effectual guards against danger from that quarter, but nothing short of a Constitution fully adequate to the national defense and the preservation of the Union, can save America from as many standing armies as it may be split into States or Confederacies, and from such a progressive augmentation, of these establishments in each, as will render them as burdensome to the properties and ominous to the liberties of the people, as any establishment that can become necessary, under a united and efficient government, must be tolerable to the former and safe to the latter….

Some, who have not denied the necessity of the power of taxation, have grounded a very fierce attack against the Constitution, on the language in which it is defined. It has been urged and echoed, that the power "to lay and collect taxes, duties, imposts, and excises, to pay the debts, and provide for the common defense and general welfare of the United States," amounts to an unlimited commission to exercise every power which may be alleged to be necessary for the common defense or general welfare. No stronger proof could be given of the distress under which these writers labor for objections, than their stooping to such a misconstruction.

Had no other enumeration or definition of the powers of the Congress been found in the Constitution, than the general expressions just cited, the authors of the objection might have had some color for it... But what color can the objection have, when a specification of the objects alluded to by these general terms immediately follows, and is not even separated by a longer pause than a semicolon? If the different parts of the same instrument ought to be so expounded, as to give meaning to every part which will bear it, shall one part of the same sentence be excluded altogether from a share in the meaning; and shall the more doubtful and indefinite terms be retained in their full extent, and the clear and precise expressions be denied any signification whatsoever? [...]

The objection here is the more extraordinary, as it appears that the language used by the convention is a copy from the articles of Confederation. The objects of the Union among the States, as described in article third, are "their common defense, security of their liberties, and mutual and general welfare." The terms of article eighth are still more identical: "All charges of war and all other expenses that shall be incurred for the common defense or general welfare, and allowed by the United States in Congress, shall be defrayed out of a common treasury," etc. A similar language again occurs in article ninth. Construe either of these articles by the rules which would justify the construction put on the new Constitution, and they vest in the existing Congress a power to legislate in all cases whatsoever. But what would have been thought of that assembly, if, attaching themselves to these general expressions, and disregarding the specifications which ascertain and limit their import, they had exercised an unlimited power of providing for the common defense and general welfare? I appeal to the objectors themselves, whether they would in that case have employed the same reasoning in justification of Congress as they now make use of against the convention. How difficult it is for error to escape its own condemnation!

PUBLIUS

End of document 1.6

Further Reading:

Akhil Reed Amar, *America's Constitution: A Biography*. New York: Random House, 2005.

Pauline Maier, *Ratification: The People Debate the Constitution, 1787-1788*. New York: Simon & Schuster, 2010.

Gordon S. Wood, *The Creation of the American Republic, 1776-1787*. New York: W. W. Norton, 1969.

Gordon S. Wood, *The Radicalism of the American Revolution*. New York: Vintage, 1991.

THE US CONSTITUTION AND THE BILL OF RIGHTS

THE US CONSTITUTION

The US Constitution was adopted by the Constitutional Convention in Philadelphia in September of 1787 and was then submitted to the states for ratification, as we saw in the previous chapter. Article VII provided that when nine states had ratified, the Constitution would go into effect. When New Hampshire became the ninth state to ratify in June of 1788, the Congress of the Confederation set a timetable for the federal government to begin functioning. This occurred in March of 1789. It is worth noting that ratification was favored only by a very slim majority in New York (30 votes vs. 27) and Rhode Island (34 vs. 32), but eventually all thirteen colonies—as well as Vermont, which was not a colony—had ratified by 1791.

For this course, we will read the Constitution in parts, so that we can give proper attention to each of them within in its historical context. Immediately below is the original Constitution, in the sense that this was what was produced at the convention in Philadelphia in 1787. The amendments follow further below and in a later section of this book.

As you read the Constitution, consider how the document in its various parts does and does not address the important issues raised by the English Declaration of Rights, the thirteen colonies' Declaration of Independence, Locke, Brutus, and Publius. What important issues seem to remain unresolved in the Constitution?

DOCUMENT 1.7 [PART A]

US CONSTITUTION (1787)

[Preamble]

We the People of the United States, in Order to form a more perfect Union, establish Justice, insure domestic Tranquility, provide for the common defence, promote the general Welfare, and secure the Blessings of Liberty to ourselves and our Posterity, do ordain and establish this Constitution for the United States of America.

ARTICLE I

Section 1. All legislative Powers herein granted shall be vested in a Congress of the United States, which shall consist of a Senate and House of Representatives.

Section 2. The House of Representatives shall be composed of Members chosen every second Year by the People of the several States, and the Electors in each State shall have the Qualifications requisite for Electors of the most numerous Branch of the State Legislature.

No Person shall be a Representative who shall not have attained to the Age of twenty five Years, and been seven Years a Citizen of the United States, and who shall not, when elected, be an Inhabitant of that State in which he shall be chosen.

Representatives and direct Taxes shall be apportioned among the several States which may be included within this Union, according to their respective Numbers, which shall be determined by adding to the whole Number of free Persons, including those bound to Service for a Term of Years, and excluding Indians not taxed, three fifths of all other Persons. The actual Enumeration shall be made within three Years after the first Meeting of the Congress of the United States, and within every subsequent Term of ten Years, in such Manner as they shall by Law direct. The Number of Representatives shall not exceed one for every thirty Thousand, but each State shall have at Least one Representative; and until such enumeration shall be made, the State of New Hampshire shall be entitled to chuse three, Massachusetts eight, Rhode-Island and Providence Plantations one, Connecticut five, New-York six, New Jersey four, Pennsylvania eight, Delaware one, Maryland six, Virginia ten, North Carolina five, South Carolina five, and Georgia three.

When vacancies happen in the Representation from any State, the Executive Authority thereof shall issue Writs of Election to fill such Vacancies.

The House of Representatives shall chuse their Speaker and other Officers; and shall have the sole Power of Impeachment.

Section 3. The Senate of the United States shall be composed of two Senators from each State, chosen by the Legislature thereof, for six Years; and each Senator shall have one Vote.

Immediately after they shall be assembled in Consequence of the first Election, they shall be divided as equally as may be into three Classes. The Seats of the Senators of the first Class shall be vacated at the Expiration of the second Year, of the second Class at the Expiration of the fourth Year, and of the third Class at the Expiration of the sixth Year, so that one third may be chosen every second Year; and if Vacancies happen by Resignation, or otherwise, during the Recess of the Legislature of any State, the Executive thereof may make temporary Appointments until the next Meeting of the Legislature, which shall then fill such Vacancies.

No Person shall be a Senator who shall not have attained to the Age of thirty Years, and been nine Years a Citizen of the United States, and who shall not, when elected, be an Inhabitant of that State for which he shall be chosen.

The Vice President of the United States shall be President of the Senate, but shall have no Vote, unless they be equally divided.

The Senate shall chuse their other Officers, and also a President pro tempore, in the Absence of the Vice President, or when he shall exercise the Office of President of the United States.

The Senate shall have the sole Power to try all Impeachments. When sitting for that Purpose, they shall be on Oath or Affirmation. When the President of the United States is tried, the Chief Justice shall preside: And no Person shall be convicted without the Concurrence of two thirds of the Members present.

Judgment in Cases of Impeachment shall not extend further than to removal from Office, and disqualification to hold and enjoy any Office of honor, Trust or Profit under the United States: but the Party convicted shall nevertheless be liable and subject to Indictment, Trial, Judgment and Punishment, according to Law.

Section 4. The Times, Places and Manner of holding Elections for Senators and Representatives, shall be prescribed in each State by the Legislature thereof; but the Congress may at any time by Law make or alter such Regulations, except as to the Places of chusing Senators.

The Congress shall assemble at least once in every Year, and such Meeting shall be on the first Monday in December, unless they shall by Law appoint a different Day.

Section 5. Each House shall be the Judge of the Elections, Returns and Qualifications of its own Members, and a Majority of each shall constitute a Quorum to do Business; but a smaller Number may adjourn from day to day, and may be authorized to compel the Attendance of absent Members, in such Manner, and under such Penalties as each House may provide.

Each House may determine the Rules of its Proceedings, punish its Members for disorderly Behaviour, and, with the Concurrence of two thirds, expel a Member.

Each House shall keep a Journal of its Proceedings, and from time to time publish the same, excepting such Parts as may in their Judgment require Secrecy; and the Yeas and Nays of the Members of either House on any question shall, at the Desire of one fifth of those Present, be entered on the Journal.

Neither House, during the Session of Congress, shall, without the Consent of the other, adjourn for more than three days, nor to any other Place than that in which the two Houses shall be sitting.

Section 6. The Senators and Representatives shall receive a Compensation for their Services, to be ascertained by Law, and paid out of the Treasury of the United States. They shall in all Cases, except Treason, Felony and Breach of the Peace, be privileged from Arrest during their Attendance at the Session of their respective Houses, and in going to and returning from the same; and for any Speech or Debate in either House, they shall not be questioned in any other Place.

No Senator or Representative shall, during the Time for which he was elected, be appointed to any civil Office under the Authority of the United States, which shall have been created, or the Emoluments whereof shall have been encreased during such time; and no Person holding any Office under the United States, shall be a Member of either House during his Continuance in Office.

Section 7. All Bills for raising Revenue shall originate in the House of Representatives; but the Senate may propose or concur with Amendments as on other Bills.

Every Bill which shall have passed the House of Representatives and the Senate, shall, before it become a Law, be presented to the President of the United States; If he approve he shall sign it, but if not he shall return it, with his Objections to that House in which it shall have originated, who shall enter the Objections at large on their Journal, and proceed to reconsider it. If after such Reconsideration two thirds of that House shall agree to pass the Bill, it shall be sent, together with the Objections, to the other House, by which it shall likewise be reconsidered, and if approved by two thirds of that House, it shall become a Law. But in all such Cases the Votes of both Houses shall be determined by yeas and Nays, and the Names of the Persons voting for and against the Bill shall be entered on the Journal of each House respectively. If any Bill shall not be returned by the President within ten Days (Sundays excepted) after it shall have been presented to him, the Same shall be a Law, in like Manner as if he had signed it, unless the Congress by their Adjournment prevent its Return, in which Case it shall not be a Law.

Every Order, Resolution, or Vote to which the Concurrence of the Senate and House of Representatives may be necessary (except on a question of Adjournment) shall be presented to the President of the United States; and before the Same shall take Effect, shall be approved by him, or being disapproved by him, shall be repassed by two thirds of the Senate and House of Representatives, according to the Rules and Limitations prescribed in the Case of a Bill.

Section 8. The Congress shall have Power to lay and collect Taxes, Duties, Imposts and Excises, to pay the Debts and provide for the common Defence and general Welfare of the United States; but all Duties, Imposts and Excises shall be uniform throughout the United States;

To borrow Money on the credit of the United States;

To regulate Commerce with foreign Nations, and among the several States, and with the Indian Tribes;

To establish an uniform Rule of Naturalization, and uniform Laws on the subject of Bankruptcies throughout the United States;

To coin Money, regulate the Value thereof, and of foreign Coin, and fix the Standard of Weights and Measures;

To provide for the Punishment of counterfeiting the Securities and current Coin of the United States;

To establish Post Offices and post Roads;

To promote the Progress of Science and useful Arts, by securing for limited Times to Authors and Inventors the exclusive Right to their respective Writings and Discoveries;

To constitute Tribunals inferior to the supreme Court;

To define and punish Piracies and Felonies committed on the high Seas, and Offences against the Law of Nations;

To declare War, grant Letters of Marque and Reprisal, and make Rules concerning Captures on Land and Water;

To raise and support Armies, but no Appropriation of Money to that Use shall be for a longer Term than two Years;

To provide and maintain a Navy;

To make Rules for the Government and Regulation of the land and naval Forces;

To provide for calling forth the Militia to execute the Laws of the Union, suppress Insurrections and repel Invasions;

To provide for organizing, arming, and disciplining, the Militia, and for governing such Part of them as may be employed in the Service of the United States, reserving to the States respectively, the Appointment of the Officers, and the Authority of training the Militia according to the discipline prescribed by Congress;

To exercise exclusive Legislation in all Cases whatsoever, over such District (not exceeding ten Miles square) as may, by Cession of particular States, and the Acceptance of Congress, become the Seat of the Government of the United States, and to exercise like Authority over all Places purchased by the Consent of the Legislature of the State in which the Same shall be, for the Erection of Forts, Magazines, Arsenals, dock-Yards, and other needful Buildings; — And

To make all Laws which shall be necessary and proper for carrying into Execution the foregoing Powers, and all other Powers vested by this Constitution in the Government of the United States, or in any Department or Officer thereof.

Section 9. The Migration or Importation of such Persons as any of the States now existing shall think proper to admit, shall not be prohibited by the Congress prior to the Year one thousand eight hundred and eight, but a Tax or duty may be imposed on such Importation, not exceeding ten dollars for each Person.

The Privilege of the Writ of Habeas Corpus shall not be suspended, unless when in Cases of Rebellion or Invasion the public Safety may require it.

No Bill of Attainder or ex post facto Law shall be passed.

No Capitation, or other direct, Tax shall be laid, unless in Proportion to the Census or Enumeration herein before directed to be taken.

No Tax or Duty shall be laid on Articles exported from any State.

No Preference shall be given by any Regulation of Commerce or Revenue to the Ports of one State over those of another; nor shall Vessels bound to, or from, one State, be obliged to enter, clear, or pay Duties in another.

No Money shall be drawn from the Treasury, but in Consequence of Appropriations made by Law; and a regular Statement and Account of the Receipts and Expenditures of all public Money shall be published from time to time.

No Title of Nobility shall be granted by the United States: And no Person holding any Office of Profit or Trust under them, shall, without the Consent of the Congress, accept of any present, Emolument, Office, or Title, of any kind whatever, from any King, Prince, or foreign State.

Section 10. No State shall enter into any Treaty, Alliance, or Confederation; grant Letters of Marque and Reprisal; coin Money; emit Bills of Credit; make any Thing but gold and silver Coin a Tender in Payment of Debts; pass any Bill of Attainder, ex post facto Law, or Law impairing the Obligation of Contracts, or grant any Title of Nobility.

No State shall, without the Consent of the Congress, lay any Imposts or Duties on Imports or Exports, except what may be absolutely necessary for executing it's inspection Laws; and the net Produce of all Duties and Imposts, laid by any State on Imports or Exports, shall be for the Use of the Treasury of the United States; and all such Laws shall be subject to the Revision and Controul of the Congress.

No State shall, without the Consent of Congress, lay any Duty of Tonnage, keep Troops, or Ships of War in time of Peace, enter into any Agreement or Compact with another State, or with a foreign Power, or engage in War, unless actually invaded, or in such imminent Danger as will not admit of delay.

ARTICLE II

Section 1. The executive Power shall be vested in a President of the United States of America. He shall hold his Office during the Term of four Years, and, together with the Vice President, chosen for the same Term, be elected, as follows:

Each State shall appoint, in such Manner as the Legislature thereof may direct, a Number of Electors, equal to the whole Number of Senators and Representatives to which the State may be entitled in the Congress: but no Senator or Representative, or Person holding an Office of Trust or Profit under the United States, shall be appointed an Elector.

The Electors shall meet in their respective States, and vote by Ballot for two Persons, of whom one at least shall not be an Inhabitant of the same State with themselves. And they shall make a List of all the Persons voted for, and of the Number of Votes for each; which List they shall sign and certify, and transmit sealed to the Seat of the Government of the United States, directed to the President of the Senate. The President of the Senate shall, in the Presence of the Senate and House of Representatives, open all the Certificates, and the Votes shall then be counted. The Person having the greatest Number of Votes shall be the President, if such Number be a Majority of the whole Number of Electors appointed; and if there be more than one who have such Majority, and have an equal Number of Votes, then the House of Representatives shall immediately chuse by Ballot one of them for President; and if no Person have a Majority, then from the five highest on the List the said House shall in like Manner chuse the President. But in chusing the President, the Votes shall be taken by States, the Representation from each State having one Vote; a quorum for this Purpose shall consist of a Member or Members from two thirds of the States, and a Majority of all the States shall be necessary to a Choice. In every Case, after the Choice of the President, the Person having the greatest Number of Votes of the Electors shall be the Vice President. But if there should remain two or more who have equal Votes, the Senate shall chuse from them by Ballot the Vice President.

The Congress may determine the Time of chusing the Electors, and the Day on which they shall give their Votes; which Day shall be the same throughout the United States.

No Person except a natural born Citizen, or a Citizen of the United States, at the time of the Adoption of this Constitution, shall be eligible to the Office of President; neither shall any Person be eligible to that Office who shall not have attained to the Age of thirty five Years, and been fourteen Years a Resident within the United States.

In Case of the Removal of the President from Office, or of his Death, Resignation, or Inability to discharge the Powers and Duties of the said Office, the Same shall devolve on the Vice President, and the Congress may by Law provide for the Case of Removal, Death, Resignation or Inability, both of the President and Vice President, declaring what Officer shall then act as President, and such Officer shall act accordingly, until the Disability be removed, or a President shall be elected.

The President shall, at stated Times, receive for his Services, a Compensation, which shall neither be increased nor diminished during the Period for which he shall have been elected, and he shall not receive within that Period any other Emolument from the United States, or any of them.

Before he enter on the Execution of his Office, he shall take the following Oath or Affirmation: — "I do solemnly swear (or affirm) that I will faithfully execute the Office of President of the United States, and will to the best of my Ability, preserve, protect and defend the Constitution of the United States."

Section 2. The President shall be Commander in Chief of the Army and Navy of the United States, and of the Militia of the several States, when called into the actual Service of the United States; he may require the Opinion, in writing, of the principal Officer in each of the executive Departments, upon any Subject relating to the Duties of their respective Offices, and he shall have Power to grant Reprieves and Pardons for Offences against the United States, except in Cases of Impeachment.

He shall have Power, by and with the Advice and Consent of the Senate, to make Treaties, provided two thirds of the Senators present concur; and he shall nominate, and by and with the Advice and Consent of the Senate, shall appoint Ambassadors, other public Ministers and Consuls, Judges of the supreme Court, and all other Officers of the United States, whose Appointments are not herein otherwise provided for, and which shall be established by Law: but the Congress may by Law vest the Appointment of such inferior Officers, as they think proper, in the President alone, in the Courts of Law, or in the Heads of Departments.

The President shall have Power to fill up all Vacancies that may happen during the Recess of the Senate, by granting Commissions which shall expire at the End of their next Session.

Section 3. He shall from time to time give to the Congress Information of the State of the Union, and recommend to their Consideration such Measures as he shall judge necessary and expedient; he may, on extraordinary Occasions, convene both Houses, or either of them, and in Case of Disagreement between them, with Respect to the Time of Adjournment, he may adjourn them to such Time as he shall think proper; he shall receive Ambassadors and other public Ministers; he shall take Care that the Laws be faithfully executed, and shall Commission all the Officers of the United States.

Section 4. The President, Vice President and all civil Officers of the United States, shall be removed from Office on Impeachment for, and Conviction of, Treason, Bribery, or other high Crimes and Misdemeanors.

ARTICLE III

Section 1. The judicial Power of the United States shall be vested in one supreme Court, and in such inferior Courts as the Congress may from time to time ordain and establish. The Judges, both of the supreme and inferior Courts, shall hold their Offices during good Behaviour, and shall, at stated Times, receive for their Services a Compensation, which shall not be diminished during their Continuance in Office.

Section 2. The judicial Power shall extend to all Cases, in Law and Equity, arising under this Constitution, the Laws of the United States, and Treaties made, or which shall be made, under their Authority; — to all Cases affecting Ambassadors, other public Ministers and Consuls; — to all Cases of admiralty and maritime Jurisdiction; — to Controversies to which the United States shall be a Party; — to Controversies between two or more States; — between a State and Citizens of another State; — between Citizens of different States; — between Citizens of the same State claiming Lands under Grants of different States, and between a State, or the Citizens thereof, and foreign States, Citizens or Subjects.

In all Cases affecting Ambassadors, other public Ministers and Consuls, and those in which a State shall be Party, the supreme Court shall have original Jurisdiction. In all the other Cases before mentioned, the supreme Court shall have appellate Jurisdiction, both as to Law and Fact, with such Exceptions, and under such Regulations as the Congress shall make.

The Trial of all Crimes, except in Cases of Impeachment, shall be by Jury; and such Trial shall be held in the State where the said Crimes shall have been committed; but when not committed within any State, the Trial shall be at such Place or Places as the Congress may by Law have directed.

Section 3. Treason against the United States shall consist only in levying War against them, or in adhering to their Enemies, giving them Aid and Comfort. No Person shall be convicted of Treason unless on the Testimony of two Witnesses to the same overt Act, or on Confession in open Court.

The Congress shall have Power to declare the Punishment of Treason, but no Attainder of Treason shall work Corruption of Blood, or Forfeiture except during the Life of the Person attainted.

ARTICLE IV

Section 1. Full Faith and Credit shall be given in each State to the public Acts, Records, and judicial Proceedings of every other State. And the Congress may by general Laws prescribe the Manner in which such Acts, Records and Proceedings shall be proved, and the Effect thereof.

Section 2. The Citizens of each State shall be entitled to all Privileges and Immunities of Citizens in the several States.

A Person charged in any State with Treason, Felony, or other Crime, who shall flee from Justice, and be found in another State, shall on Demand of the executive Authority of the State from which he fled, be delivered up, to be removed to the State having Jurisdiction of the Crime.

No Person held to Service or Labor in one State, under the Laws thereof, escaping into another, shall, in Consequence of any Law or Regulation therein, be discharged from such Service or Labor, but shall be delivered up on Claim of the Party to whom such Service or Labor may be due.

Section 3. New States may be admitted by the Congress into this Union; but no new State shall be formed or erected within the Jurisdiction of any other State; nor any State be formed by the Junction of two or more States, or Parts of States, without the Consent of the Legislatures of the States concerned as well as of the Congress.

The Congress shall have Power to dispose of and make all needful Rules and Regulations respecting the Territory or other Property belonging to the United States; and nothing in this Constitution shall be so construed as to Prejudice any Claims of the United States, or of any particular State.

Section 4. The United States shall guarantee to every State in this Union a Republican Form of Government, and shall protect each of them against Invasion; and on Application of the Legislature, or of the Executive (when the Legislature cannot be convened), against domestic Violence.

ARTICLE V

The Congress, whenever two thirds of both Houses shall deem it necessary, shall propose Amendments to this Constitution, or, on the Application of the Legislatures of two thirds of the several States, shall call a Convention for proposing Amendments, which, in either Case, shall be valid to all Intents and Purposes, as Part of this Constitution, when ratified by the Legislatures of three fourths of the several States, or by Conventions in three fourths thereof, as the one or the other Mode of Ratification may be proposed by the Congress; Provided that no Amendment which may be made prior to the Year One thousand eight hundred and eight shall in any Manner affect the first and fourth Clauses in the Ninth Section of the first Article; and that no State, without its Consent, shall be deprived of its equal Suffrage in the Senate.

ARTICLE VI

All Debts contracted and Engagements entered into, before the Adoption of this Constitution, shall be as valid against the United States under this Constitution, as under the Confederation.

This Constitution, and the Laws of the United States which shall be made in Pursuance thereof; and all Treaties made, or which shall be made, under the Authority of the United States, shall be the supreme Law of the Land; and the Judges in every State shall be bound thereby, any Thing in the Constitution or Laws of any State to the Contrary notwithstanding.

The Senators and Representatives before mentioned, and the Members of the several State Legislatures, and all executive and judicial Officers, both of the United States and of the several States, shall be bound by Oath or Affirmation, to support this Constitution; but no religious Test shall ever be required as a Qualification to any Office or public Trust under the United States.

ARTICLE VII

The Ratification of the Conventions of nine States, shall be sufficient for the Establishment of this Constitution between the States so ratifying the Same.

End of Document 1.7, part A

THE BILL OF RIGHTS

The essay above by Brutus (document 1.5) shows that the absence of a clear enumeration of rights in the original Constitution was an important reason for opposing ratification. Indeed, through several of the state ratifying conventions, the American people had demanded various amendments that would clarify implicit limits on federal power and add new limits. Some participants in those conventions even raised the idea of calling yet another constitutional convention in order to produce yet another constitution. Moreover, the states of North Carolina and Rhode Island had not yet ratified the Constitution, and many thought that appropriate amendments could secure their agreement. This gave the Congress good reason to move quickly to modify the existing Constitution.

In fairly short order, Madison submitted a series of amendments to the First US Congress, proposing among other things that they could serve as an olive branch to those who had opposed the Constitution. He thus wrote, "There is a great number of our constituents who are dissatisfied with [the Constitution]; among them are many respectable for their talents and patriotism [and who are] inclined to join their support to the cause … if they were satisfied on this one point. We ought not to disregard their inclination, but, on principles of amity and moderation, conform to their wishes, and expressly declare the great rights of mankind secured under this constitution."[1] By the end of 1791, three-quarters of the states had approved ten of the proposed amendments (there were twelve originally), and these subsequently became known as the Bill of Rights. This Bill—the first ten amendments to the Constitution—bears a close, organic relationship to the original document. The same, in fact, can be said for the other seventeen amendments, which are also reproduced in a subsequent section of this book. Indeed, in some interpretations, the fourteenth amendment altered the Constitution in important ways. Thus when we attempt to ascertain the "original meaning" or the

---

1 Cited in Akhil Reed Amar, *America's Constitution: A Biography* (New York, 2005), 318.

"original intent" of the authors of the Constitution, we must pay attention as much to the authors of subsequent amendments as we do to the "Founding Fathers."

DOCUMENT 1.7 [PART B]

BILL OF RIGHTS, OR AMENDMENTS 1-10 (1791)

The conventions of a number of the States having at the time of their adopting the Constitution, expressed a desire, in order to prevent misconstruction or abuse of its powers, that further declaratory and restrictive clauses should be added.

Amendment I. Congress shall make no law respecting an establishment of religion, or prohibiting the free exercise thereof; or abridging the freedom of speech, or of the press; or the right of the people peaceably to assemble, and to petition the Government for a redress of grievances.

Amendment II. A well regulated Militia, being necessary to the security of a free State, the right of the people to keep and bear Arms, shall not be infringed.

Amendment III. No Soldier shall, in time of peace be quartered in any house, without the consent of the Owner, nor in time of war, but in a manner to be prescribed by law.

Amendment IV. The right of the people to be secure in their persons, houses, papers, and effects, against unreasonable searches and seizures, shall not be violated, and no Warrants shall issue, but upon probable cause, supported by Oath or affirmation, and particularly describing the place to be searched, and the persons or things to be seized.

Amendment V. No person shall be held to answer for a capital, or otherwise infamous crime, unless on a presentment or indictment of a Grand Jury, except in cases arising in the land or naval forces, or in the Militia, when in actual service in time of War or public danger; nor shall any person be subject for the same offence to be twice put in jeopardy of life or limb; nor shall be compelled in any criminal case to be a witness against himself, nor be deprived of life, liberty, or property, without due process of law; nor shall private property be taken for public use, without just compensation.

Amendment VI. In all criminal prosecutions, the accused shall enjoy the right to a speedy and public trial, by an impartial jury of the State and district wherein the crime shall have been committed, which district shall have been previously ascertained by law, and to be informed of the nature and cause of the accusation; to be confronted with the witnesses against him; to have compulsory process for obtaining witnesses in his favor, and to have the Assistance of Counsel for his defence.

Amendment VII. In Suits at common law, where the value in controversy shall exceed twenty dollars, the right of trial by jury shall be preserved, and no fact tried by a jury, shall be otherwise re-examined in any Court of the United States, than according to the rules of the common law.

Amendment VIII. Excessive bail shall not be required, nor excessive fines imposed, nor cruel and unusual punishments inflicted.

Amendment IX. The enumeration in the Constitution, of certain rights, shall not be construed to deny or disparage others retained by the people.

Amendment X. The powers not delegated to the United States by the Constitution, nor prohibited by it to the States, are reserved to the States respectively, or to the people.

End of Document 1.7, Part B

Further Reading:

Akhil Reed Amar. *The Bill of Rights.* New Haven: Yale University Press, 1998.

Akhil Reed Amar, *America's Constitution: A Biography.* New York: Random House, 2005.

Gordon S. Wood, *The Creation of the American Republic, 1776-1787.* New York: W. W. Norton, 1969.

Gordon S. Wood, *The Radicalism of the American Revolution.* New York: Vintage, 1991.

LATER EVOLUTIONS AND THE CASE OF NEVADA

AMENDMENTS 11 AND 12

As we noted previously, the first ten amendments to the Constitution—now known as the Bill of Rights—were ratified in 1791, only shortly after the original Constitution itself. For a long time thereafter, we see only small changes to the Constitution. Before the **Civil War** (1861-1865) there were only two amendments, and these arguably involved primarily clarifications and some tweaking. The first of these, no. 11 in 1798, specifies a certain limitation on federal judicial power and thus merely clarified Article 3, Section 2 of the original Constitution. As one scholar of the Constitution has written, the amendment "aimed to rein in federal judges who seemed at risk of going too far—indeed had already gone too far."[1] It came as a response to an important Supreme Court decision in 1792, *Chisholm v. Georgia*, but the details need not detain us here. Amendment 12 in 1804—among the lengthiest—is too complicated for extensive commentary here, so it might be enough to remark simply that it clarified the process of electing the President, so that a party that commanded an electoral-vote majority would automatically win both presidency and vice-presidency. The effects of the amendment were these: First, by facilitating the efforts of political parties to run tickets with both president and vice-president, the amendment

paved the way for the increased involvement of ordinary citizens in the selection of the president. The amendment correspondingly reduced the role of Congress in selecting the President. Second, by the 12th amendment the vice-president became a rather diminished figure in comparison to what was envisioned in the original Constitution of 1787. Finally, the amendment created a new kind of President, who was more likely to be openly populist and partisan than his predecessors.[2] The two amendments are provided below.

These observations point to two larger points that are worth emphasizing. On the one hand, the amendments—as the very term "amendment": suggests—altered the Constitution. Thus both the president and vice-president became something different after 1804 than they had been before. On the other hand, the amendments are as much a part of the Constitution as was the original text produced in Philadelphia in 1787. This means that the intentions of those who produced and ratified the amendments are in many ways as important as the intentions of the "Founding Fathers." Thus for any question of constitutional significance, we cannot only go back to 1787 in order to determine what the original intent was, but must also consider the motivations of those who altered the Constitution subsequently.

1   Akhil Reed Amar, *America's Constitution: A Biography* (New York, 2005), 332.

2   Reed, *America's Constitution*, 342-44.

DOCUMENT 1.7 [PART C]

AMENDMENTS 11 AND 12 TO THE US CONSTITUTION

Article XI [Proposed 1794; Ratified 1798]. The Judicial power of the United States shall not be construed to extend to any suit in law or equity, commenced or prosecuted against one of the United States by Citizens of another State, or by Citizens or Subjects of any Foreign State.

Article XII. [Proposed 1803; Ratified 1804]. The Electors shall meet in their respective states, and vote by ballot for President and Vice-President, one of whom, at least, shall not be an inhabitant of the same state with themselves; they shall name in their ballots the person voted for as President, and in distinct ballots the person voted for as Vice-President, and they shall make distinct lists of all persons voted for as President, and of all persons voted for as Vice-President, and of the number of votes for each, which lists they shall sign and certify, and transmit sealed to the seat of the government of the United States, directed to the President of the Senate; — The President of the Senate shall, in the presence of the Senate and House of Representatives, open all the certificates and the votes shall then be counted; — The person having the greatest number of votes for President, shall be the President, if such number be a majority of the whole number of Electors appointed; and if no person have such majority, then from the persons having the highest numbers not exceeding three on the list of those voted for as President, the House of Representatives shall choose immediately, by ballot, the President. But in choosing the President, the votes shall be taken by states, the representation from each state having one vote; a quorum for this purpose shall consist of a member or members from two-thirds of the states, and a majority of all the states shall be necessary to a choice. And if the House of Representatives shall not choose a President whenever the right of choice shall devolve upon them, before the fourth day of March next following, then the Vice-President shall act as President, as in the case of the death or other constitutional disability of the President. — The person having the greatest number of votes as Vice-President, shall be the Vice-President, if such number be a majority of the whole number of Electors appointed, and if no person have a majority, then from the two highest numbers on the list, the Senate shall choose the Vice-President; a quorum for the purpose shall consist of two-thirds of the whole number of Senators, and a majority of the whole number shall be necessary to a choice. But no person constitutionally ineligible to the office of President shall be eligible to that of Vice-President of the United States.

End of Doc. 1.7 [Part C]

ENDING SLAVERY, EXTENDING RIGHTS—WITH DIFFICULTY

After the 12th Amendment, no new changes occurred to the Constitution until after the Civil War ended in 1865. This is the longest period—61 years—in US history without any constitutional amendments. It is not surprising that the country changed immensely over the course of that period, and a number of developments and questions that appeared are important to note in order to make sense of the next amendments, nos. 13-15, which appeared in the half-decade or so after the Civil War (1865-70).

One question concerned the basic identity of the United States. By 1860, there were 33 states rather than the original 13. This means that most states at the time had not been among the original 13 colonies and had had no existence prior to the creation of the Union and thus no history independent of the Union. On the contrary, those newer states had been brought into being by the Union. The result was that a feeling of *national* identity—that is, a sense of allegiance directed towards the country as a whole—now rivaled a feeling of identity focused primarily on the states. President Abraham Lincoln captured this sense in his famous **Gettysburg Address** of 1863. After noting that the country's predecessors ("our fathers") had "brought forth on this continent, a new nation, conceived in liberty, and dedicated to the proposition that all men are created equal," Lincoln remarked, "Now we are engaged in a great civil war, testing whether that nation, or any nation so conceived and so dedicated, can long endure."[3] In this speech, Lincoln identified "the people" with the nation as a whole, rather than with the states, and he in effect proposed that that nation was more than

---

3   The speech can be found at http://www.ourdocuments. gov/doc.php?doc=36&page=transcript.

just the sum of its parts. Instead, the nation was an enduring entity, one that could not be dismembered. But this is not to say that allegiance to states had disappeared. In fact, the Civil War represented, among other things, an assertion of individual states (in this case the southern ones) against the Union. So in effect a big question remained to be answered: did the Union proceed (or flow) from the states; or did the states proceed (flow) from the Union?

Another development in the years between the 12th and 13th Amendment needs to be noted as well. In 1833, an important Supreme Court case (**Barron v. Mayor & City Council of Baltimore**) raised the question as to whether the 5th amendment prevented states as well as the federal government from taking property without due compensation. The Court held that the 5th amendment applied only to the national government and not to the states. In that case, the Court wrote, "The counsel for the plaintiff in error insists that the constitution was intended to secure the people of the several states against the undue exercise of power by their respective state governments; as well as against that which might be attempted by their general government." In other words, the plaintiff was incorrect to suppose that the 5th Amendment was enforceable against the states. Rather, that amendment was designed to restrain the *federal* government. The Court went on to indicate that when the authors of the original Constitution sought to restrain the states from a particular action, they wrote "No state shall…" (for examples, look at section 10 of article 1 of the original constitution). The Court concluded, "We are of opinion that the provision in the fifth amendment to the constitution, declaring that private property shall not be taken for public use without just compensation, is intended solely as a limitation on the exercise of power by the government of the United States, and *is not applicable to the legislation of the States*" (emphasis added).[4] The implications were significant, because the same reasoning could be extended to many of the other provisions in the Bill of Rights. This indeed was the interpretation accepted before the Civil War: that the Bill of Rights was enforceable only against the federal government, not against the states.

A third issue concerned the character of government at the state level and the matter of citizenship for blacks. Recall that the Constitution declares, "The United States shall guarantee to every State in this Union a Republican Form of Government" (art. 4, sec. 4). Yet given the degree to which even black males (let alone females of any race) were excluded from participation in politics, there arose a question as to whether the southern states actually offered "a republican form of government." In states such as South Carolina and Mississippi, blacks constituted a very significant portion of the population, and at some level their disenfranchisement seemed to some inconsistent with republicanism. The issue of black citizenship was even more problematic and points to significant exclusions in the American political community. In 1823, the Supreme Court explicitly rejected the proposition that Native Americans were citizens, and federal law rectified that decision only in 1924. In a famous Supreme Court case of 1857 (Dred Scott v. Sanford) the question arose as to whether blacks were citizens—or as the Court itself posed the question, "Can a negro, whose ancestors were imported into this country and sold as slaves, become a member of the political community formed and brought into existence by the Constitution of the United States, and as such become entitled to all the rights, and privileges, and immunities, guaranteed by that instrument to the citizen?" The Court concluded that blacks "are not included, and were not intended to be included, under the word 'citizens' in the Constitution, and can therefore claim none of the rights and privileges which that instrument provides for and secures to citizens of the United States." On the contrary, the Court wrote, "they were at that time considered as a subordinate and inferior class of beings, who had been subjugated by the dominant race, and, whether emancipated or not, yet remained subject to their authority, and had no rights or privileges but such as those who held the power and the government might choose to grant them." The Court even recognized that the language of the Declaration of Independence—that "all men are created equal"—might seem to include "the whole human family," but rejected that idea, declaring, "But it is too clear for dispute, that the enslaved African race were not intended to be included, and formed no part of the people who framed and adopted this declaration." In short, blacks were not citizens.[5]

---

4   The full Barron decision, from which the citations here are taken, can be found at http://press-pubs.uchicago.edu/founders/documents/amendV_due_processs26.html

5   The key portions of the Dred Scott decision, from which the citations here are taken, can be found at http://www.blackpast.org/primary/dred-scott-decision

And then, of course, there was slavery. A striking feature of the original constitution was its refusal actually to use the word "slavery" even as it made numerous comprises with that institution. Indeed, slavery is inscribed on the original Constitution in a number of places. For example, the 3/5 compromise allowed southern states to count 3/5 of their slaves for the purposes of calculating their representation in the House of Representatives and by extension in the Electoral College. Yet the Constitution makes oblique reference only to "three fifths of all other Persons," thus preventing slavery from being named (art. 1, sec. 2). The original Constitution also included a provision that blocked any prohibition on the importation of slaves until the year 1808. Here, too, the authors of the Constitution avoided the term "slaves" by writing about "the Migration or Importation of such Persons as any State now existing shall think proper to admit" (art. 1, sec. 9). Probably the closest the original Constitution came to acknowledging slavery came where it declared, "No Person held to Service or Labor in one State, under the Laws thereof, escaping into another, shall, in Consequence of any Law or Regulation therein, be discharged from such Service or Labor, but shall be delivered up on Claim of the Party to whom such Service or Labor may be due." In other words, runaway slaves should be returned to their place and condition of servitude. The very fact that the authors of the Constitution tried to avoid referring to slavery even as they acknowledged it, suggests that already in 1787 some people were uncomfortable with that institution. But there were of course many who remained in favor of it, for a cluster of economic and ideological reasons—and this was not only people in the South.

The three Civil War Amendments (nos. 13-15) were designed to address the critical issues just described. Taken together, they arguably represent the greatest transformation of the Constitution at any point since the late 18th century, and it is therefore worth giving these amendments particular attention.

In order better to understand the 13th amendment, which eliminated slavery definitively, it is worth considering other ways in which Lincoln—the country's first openly anti-slavery president—sought to end the Civil War and to terminate slavery in a gradual fashion. He proposed such a plan in an **address to Congress on 1 December 1862** (doc. 1.8), but this plan needs to be read closely in conjunction with the following document, the **Emancipation Proclamation** (doc. 1.9). Note that the latter document, though it went into effect on 1 January 1863, was actually proposed on 22 September 1862—that is over two months *before* the address to Congress. One could thereby argue that in the fall of 1862 Lincoln was threatening the southern states with immediate emancipation, on the one hand, and offering them a gradual emancipation as a more attractive alternative, on the other. Thus in his address to Congress, Lincoln was in effect saying to the southern states: you can agree to my plan, as a result of which slavery will be ended gradually and slave owners will be compensated for their lost slaves; or you can reject my proposal and expect the Union Army to liberate slaves wherever it can.

The first part of Lincoln's address concerns foreign relations, the conditions of the country's finances, and the possibility of African-American emigration to Haiti, Liberia and other possible destinations, and several other issues. Perhaps the most interesting part of the speech, however, is the portion reproduced below, where Lincoln proposes what he calls "compensated emancipation" in order to resolve what he now regards as the central cause of the Civil War. As you read, think about how this proposal relates to the Emancipation Proclamation and to the 13th amendment. You might also how the geopolitical arguments in Lincoln's address relate to the points made by Madison in *Federalist* no. 41.

DOCUMENT 1.8

ABRAHAM LINCOLN, ANNUAL MESSAGE TO CONGRESS (1 DEC. 1862)[6]

On the 22nd day of September last a proclamation was issued by the Executive, a copy of which is herewith submitted.[7]

---

6   A full version of the speech: http://www.geocities.com/presidentialspeeches/1862.htm

7   The reference here is precisely to the Emancipation Proclamation.

In accordance with the purpose expressed in the second paragraph of that paper, I now respectfully recall your attention to what may be called "compensated emancipation"....

That portion of the earth's surface which is owned and inhabited by the people of the United States, is well adapted to be the home of one national family; and it is not well adapted for two, or more. Its vast extent, and its variety of climate and productions, are of advantage, in this age, for one people, whatever they might have been in former ages. Steam, telegraphs, and intelligence, have brought these, to be an advantageous combination, for one united people.

In the inaugural address I briefly pointed out the total inadequacy of disunion, as a remedy for the differences between the people of the two sections. I did so in language which I cannot improve, and which, therefore, I beg to repeat:

> One section of our country believes slavery is right, and ought to be extended, while the other believes it is wrong, and ought not to be extended. This is the only substantial dispute....

> Physically speaking, we cannot separate. We cannot remove our respective sections from each other, nor build an impassable wall between them. A husband and wife may be divorced, and go out of the presence, and beyond the reach of each other; but the different parts of our country cannot do this. They cannot but remain face to face; and intercourse, either amicable or hostile, must continue between them. Is it possible, then, to make that intercourse more advantageous, or more satisfactory, after separation than before? Can aliens make treaties, easier than friends can make laws? Can treaties be more faithfully enforced between aliens, than laws can among friends? Suppose you go to war, you cannot fight always; and when, after much loss on both sides, and no gain on either, you cease fighting, the identical old questions, as to terms of intercourse, are again upon you.

There is no line, straight or crooked, suitable for a national boundary, upon which to divide. Trace through, from east to west, upon the line between the free and slave country, and we shall find a little more than one-third of its length are rivers, easy to be crossed, and populated, or soon to be populated, thickly upon both sides; while nearly all its remaining length, are merely surveyor's lines, over which people may walk back and forth without any consciousness of their presence. No part of this line can be made any more difficult to pass, by writing it down on paper, or parchment, as a national boundary. The fact of separation, if it comes, gives up, on the part of the seceding section, the fugitive slave clause, along with all other constitutional obligations upon the section seceded from, while I should expect no treaty stipulation would ever be made to take its place.

But there is another difficulty. The great interior region, bounded east by the Alleghanies, north by the British dominions, west by the Rocky mountains, and south by the line along which the culture of corn and cotton meets, and which includes part of Virginia, part of Tennessee, all of Kentucky, Ohio, Indiana, Michigan, Wisconsin, Illinois, Missouri, Kansas, Iowa, Minnesota and the Territories of Dakota, Nebraska, and part of Colorado, already has above ten millions of people, and will have fifty millions within fifty years, if not prevented by any political folly or mistake. It contains more than one-third of the country owned by the United States—certainly more than one million of square miles. Once half as populous as Massachusetts already is, it would have more than seventy-five millions of people. A glance at the map shows that, territorially speaking, it is the great body of the republic... And yet this region has no sea-coast, touches no ocean anywhere. As part of one nation, its people now find, and may forever find, their way to Europe by New York, to South America and Africa by New Orleans, and to Asia by San Francisco. But separate our common country into two nations, as designed by the present rebellion, and every man of this great interior region is thereby cut off from some one or more of these outlets, not, perhaps, by a physical barrier, but by embarrassing and onerous trade regulations.

And this is true, wherever a dividing, or boundary line, may be fixed. Place it between the now free and slave country, or place it south of Kentucky, or north of Ohio, and still the truth remains, that none south of it, can trade to any port or place north of it, and none north of it, can trade to any port or place south of it, except upon terms dictated by a government foreign to them. These outlets, east, west, and south, are indispensable to the well-being of the people inhabiting, and to inhabit, this vast interior region. Which of the three may be the best, is no proper question. All, are better than either, and all, of right, belong to that people, and to their successors forever. True to themselves, they will not ask where a line of separation shall be, but will vow, rather, that there shall be no such line....

Our national strife springs not from our permanent part; not from the land we inhabit; not from our national homestead. There is no possible severing of this, but would multiply, and not mitigate, evils among us. In all its adaptations and aptitudes, it demands union, and abhors separation. In fact, it would, ere long, force re-union, however much of blood and treasure the separation might have cost....

In this view, I recommend the adoption of the following resolution and articles amendatory to the Constitution of the United States....

Article —.

Every State, wherein slavery now exists, which shall abolish the same therein, at any time, or times, before the first day of January, in the year of our Lord one thousand and nine hundred, shall receive compensation from the United States as follows, to wit:

The President of the United States shall deliver to every such State, bonds of the United States, bearing interest at the rate of __ per cent, per annum, to an amount equal to the aggregate sum of for each slave shown to have been therein, by the eighth census of the United States, said bonds to be delivered to such State by instalments, or in one parcel, at the completion of the abolishment, accordingly as the same shall have been gradual, or at one time, within such State; and interest shall begin to run upon any such bond, only from the proper time of its delivery as aforesaid. Any State having received bonds as aforesaid, and afterwards reintroducing or tolerating slavery therein, shall refund to the United States the bonds so received, or the value thereof, and all interest paid thereon.

Article —.

All slaves who shall have enjoyed actual freedom by the chances of the war, at any time before the end of the rebellion, shall be forever free; but all owners of such, who shall not have been disloyal, shall be compensated for them, at the same rates as is provided for States adopting abolishment of slavery, but in such way, that no slave shall be twice accounted for.

Article —.

Congress may appropriate money, and otherwise provide, for colonizing free colored persons, with their own consent, at any place or places without the United States.

I beg indulgence to discuss these proposed articles at some length. Without slavery the rebellion could never have existed; without slavery it could not continue.

Among the friends of the Union there is great diversity, of sentiment, and of policy, in regard to slavery, and the African race amongst us. Some would perpetuate slavery; some would abolish it suddenly, and without compensation; some would abolish it gradually, and with compensation; some would remove the freed people from us, and some would retain them with us; and there are yet other minor diversities. Because of these diversities, we waste much strength in struggles among ourselves. By mutual concession we should harmonize, and act together. This would be compromise; but it would be compromise among the friends, and not with the enemies of the Union. These articles are intended to embody a plan of such mutual concessions. If the plan shall be adopted, it is assumed that emancipation will follow, at least, in several of the States.

As to the first article, the main points are: first, the emancipation; secondly, the length of time for consummating it—thirty-seven years; and thirdly, the compensation.

The emancipation will be unsatisfactory to the advocates of perpetual slavery; but the length of time should greatly mitigate their dissatisfaction.... Another class will hail the prospect of emancipation, but will deprecate the length of time. They will feel that it gives too little to the now living slaves. But it really gives them much. It saves them from the vagrant destitution which must largely attend immediate emancipation in localities where their numbers are very great; and it gives the inspiring assurance that their posterity shall be free forever. The plan leaves to each State, choosing to act under it, to abolish slavery now, or at the end of the century, or at any intermediate time, or by degrees, extending over the whole or any part of the period; and it obliges no two states to proceed alike. It also provides for compensation, and generally the mode of making it. This, it would seem, must further mitigate the dissatisfaction of those who favor perpetual slavery, and especially of those who are to receive the compensation. Doubtless some of those who are to pay, and not to receive will object. Yet the measure is both just and economical. In a certain sense the liberation of slaves is the destruction of property–property acquired by descent, or by purchased, the same as any other property. It is no less true for having been often said, that the people of the south are not more responsible for the original introduction of this property, than are the people of the north; and when it is remembered how unhesitatingly we all use cotton and sugar, and share the profits of dealing in them, it may not be quite safe to say, that the south has been more responsible than the north for its continuance. If then, for a common object, this property is to be sacrificed is it not just that it be done at a common charge?

And if, with less money, or money more easily paid, we can preserve the benefits of the Union by this means, than we can by the war alone, is it not also economical to do it? [...] The war requires large sums, and requires them at once. The aggregate sum necessary for compensated emancipation, of course, would be large. But it would require no ready cash; nor the bonds even, any faster than the emancipation progresses. This might not, and probably would not, close before the end of the thirty-seven years. At that time we shall probably have a 100 millions of people to share the burden, instead of 31 millions, as now…

The proposed emancipation would shorten the war, perpetuate peace, insure this increase of population, and proportionately the wealth of the country. With these, we should pay all the emancipation would cost, together with our other debt, easier than we should pay our other debt, without it.…

But it is dreaded that the freed people will swarm forth, and cover the whole land? Are they not already in the land? Will liberation make them any more numerous? Equally distributed among the whites of the whole country, and there would be but one colored to seven whites. Could the one, in any way, greatly disturb the seven? There are many communities now, having more than one free colored person, to seven whites; and this, without any apparent consciousness of evil from it.… [W]hy should emancipation south, send the free people north? People, of any color, seldom run, unless there be something to run from. Heretofore colored people, to some extent, have fled north from bondage; and now, perhaps, from both bondage and destitution. But if gradual emancipation and deportation be adopted, they will have neither to flee from. Their old masters will give them wages at least until new laborers can be procured; and the freed men, in turn, will gladly give their labor for the wages, till new homes can be found for them, in congenial climes, and with people of their own blood and race. This proposition can be trusted on the mutual interests involved. And, in any event, cannot the north decide for itself, whether to receive them?

The plan consisting of these articles is recommended, not but that a restoration of the national authority would be accepted without its adoption.

Nor will the war, nor proceedings under the proclamation of September 22, 1862, be stayed because of the recommendation of this plan. Its timely adoption, I doubt not, would bring restoration and thereby stay both.…

Is it doubted, then, that the plan I propose, if adopted, would shorten the war, and thus lessen its expenditure of money and of blood? Is it doubted that it would restore the national authority and national prosperity, and perpetuate both indefinitely? Is it doubted that we here–Congress and Executive–can secure its adoption? Will not the good people respond to a united, and earnest appeal from us? Can we, can they, by any other means, so certainly, or so speedily, assure these vital objects? We can succeed only by concert. It is not "can any of us imagine better?" but "can we all do better?" Object whatsoever is possible, still the question recurs "can we do better?" [...]

End of Document 1.8

The southern states did not accept Lincoln's proposal of "emancipated compensation." Thus when 1863 began, the immediate emancipation that Lincoln had threatened in September of 1862 now went into effect. It is worth noting, however, that emancipation pertained only to those states and parts of states that were still in rebellion against the Union. This meant, among other things, that slavery continued to exist in those slave states that had not joined the Confederacy in the south.

DOCUMENT 1.9

THE EMANCIPATION PROCLAMATION (1863)[8]

Whereas, on the 22nd day of September, in the year of our Lord 1862, a proclamation was issued by the President of the United States, containing, among other things, the following, to wit:

---

8   Source: John G. Nicolay and John Hay, Complete Works of *Abraham Lincoln*, vol. 9 (1905), 161.

"That on the first day of January, in the year of our Lord 1863, all persons held as slaves within any State, or designated part of a State, the people whereof shall then be in rebellion against the United States, shall be then, thenceforward, and forever free; and the Executive Government of the United States, including the military and naval authority thereof, will recognize and maintain the freedom of such persons, and will do no act or acts to repress such persons, or any of them, in any efforts they may make for their actual freedom."

"That the Executive will, on the first day of January aforesaid, by proclamation, designate the States and parts of States, if any, in which the people thereof respectively shall then be in rebellion against the United States; and the fact that any State, or the people thereof, shall on that day be in good faith represented in the Congress of the United States by members chosen thereto at elections wherein a majority of the qualified voters of such State shall have participated, shall in the absence of strong countervailing testimony be deemed conclusive evidence that such State and the people thereof are not then in rebellion against the United States."

Now, therefore, I, Abraham Lincoln, President of the United States, by virtue of the power in me vested as commander-in-chief of the army and navy of the United States, in time of actual armed rebellion against the authority and government of the United States, and as a fit and necessary war measure for suppressing said rebellion, do, on this first day of January, in the year of our Lord 1863, and in accordance with my purpose so to do, publicly proclaimed for the full period of 100 days from the day first above mentioned, order and designate as the States and parts of States wherein the people thereof, respectively, are this day in rebellion against the United States, the following, to wit:

Arkansas, Texas, Louisiana (except the parishes of St. Bernard, Plaquemines, Jefferson, St. John, St. Charles, St. James, Ascension, Assumption, Terre Bonne, Lafourche, St. Mary, St. Martin, and Orleans, including the city of New Orleans), Mississippi, Alabama, Florida, Georgia, South Carolina, North Carolina, and Virginia (except the forty-eight counties designated as West Virginia, and also the counties of Berkeley, Accomac, Northampton, Elizabeth City, York, Princess Anne, and Norfolk, including the cities of Norfolk and Portsmouth), and which excepted parts are for the present left precisely as if this proclamation were not issued.

And by virtue of the power and for the purpose aforesaid, I do order and declare that all persons held as slaves within said designated States and parts of States are, and henceforward shall be, free; and that the Executive Government of the United States, including the military and naval authorities thereof, will recognize and maintain the freedom of said persons....

Done at the city of Washington, this first day of January, in the year of our Lord one thousand eight hundred and sixty-three, and of the independence of the United States of America the eighty-seventh.

Abraham Lincoln

End of Document 1.9

Lincoln's plan of "compensated emancipation" would not have ended slavery immediately—indeed, the proposition was that the gradual character of the emancipation on Lincoln's proposal would make it more palatable to the southern states (although this did not turn out to be the case). The Emancipation Proclamation, for its part, did not end slavery everywhere in the United States, since it pertained only to those states, or parts of them, that were in rebellion against the Union. So as the Civil War was ending, there was a need to end slavery completely, definitely, and permanently.

This was accomplished by the 13th amendment. Yet the significance of that amendment extends beyond the issue if slavery alone. Indeed, all the three of the amendments after the Civil War (nos. 13-15) represented a significant expansion of federal power at the expense of the states. It is partly for this reason that these amendments are so important.

As you read the three amendments, think also about the issues aside from slavery that these amendments addressed. What did they mean for citizenship or for the relationship of the Bill of Rights to the states?

DOCUMENT 1.7 [PART D]

AMENDMENTS 13-15 TO THE US CONSTITUTION

ARTICLE XIII [PROPOSED 1865; RATIFIED 1865].

Section. 1. Neither slavery nor involuntary servitude, except as a punishment for crime whereof the party shall have been duly convicted, shall exist within the United States, or any place subject to their jurisdiction.

Section. 2. Congress shall have power to enforce this article by appropriate legislation.

ARTICLE XIV [PROPOSED 1866; RATIFIED 1868]

Section. 1. All persons born or naturalized in the United States, and subject to the jurisdiction thereof, are citizens of the United States and of the State wherein they reside. No State shall make or enforce any law which shall abridge the privileges or immunities of citizens of the United States; nor shall any State deprive any person of life, liberty, or property, without due process of law; nor deny to any person within its jurisdiction the equal protection of the laws.

Section. 2. Representatives shall be apportioned among the several States according to their respective numbers, counting the whole number of persons in each State, excluding Indians not taxed. But when the right to vote at any election for the choice of electors for President and Vice President of the United States, Representatives in Congress, the Executive and Judicial officers of a State, or the members of the Legislature thereof, is denied to any of the male inhabitants of such State, being twenty-one years of age, and citizens of the United States, or in any way abridged, except for participation in rebellion, or other crime, the basis of representation therein shall be reduced in the proportion which the number of such male citizens shall bear to the whole number of male citizens twenty-one years of age in such State.

Section. 3. No person shall be a Senator or Representative in Congress, or elector of President and Vice President, or hold any office, civil or military, under the United States, or under any State, who, having previously taken an oath, as a member of Congress, or as an officer of the United States, or as a member of any State legislature, or as an executive or judicial officer of any State, to support the Constitution of the United States, shall have engaged in insurrection or rebellion against the same, or given aid or comfort to the enemies thereof. But Congress may by a vote of two-thirds of each House, remove such disability.

Section. 4. The validity of the public debt of the United States, authorized by law, including debts incurred for payment of pensions and bounties for services in suppressing insurrection or rebellion, shall not be questioned. But neither the United States nor any State shall assume or pay any debt or obligation incurred in aid of insurrection or rebellion against the United States, or any claim for the loss or emancipation of any slave; but all such debts, obligations and claims shall be held illegal and void.

Section. 5. The Congress shall have power to enforce, by appropriate legislation, the provisions of this article.

ARTICLE. XV [PROPOSED 1869; RATIFIED 1870].

Section. 1. The right of citizens of the United States to vote shall not be denied or abridged by the United States or by any State on account of race, color, or previous condition of servitude.

Section. 2. The Congress shall have power to enforce this article by appropriate legislation.

End of Document 1.7 (Part D)

Emancipation and the associated amendments offered great promise to African Americans, now free from servitude. And in the period known as **Reconstruction** (1865-77), blacks indeed gained considerable new opportunities, for example for participation in political life. But the end of Reconstruction undermined many of those achievements, and numerous limitations on the rights of African Americans appeared. One observer of these developments was **Frederick Douglass** (1818-1895).

Douglass is among the most important figures in African-African—and indeed US—history. Born as a slave in Maryland, Douglass learned to read and later escaped from slavery and became an abolitionist in the North. His best-known work was an autobiography, *Narrative of the Life of Frederick Douglass, an American Slave*, which was published in

1845. In the selection below, Douglass assesses the impact of the Civil War amendments on the lives of former slaves. He provides clear testimony that we cannot always assume that laws are actually put into practice. According to Douglass, to what extent were the 14th and 15th amendments actually being observed in the US South? To what extent had the relationship between master and slave changed by 1880?

DOCUMENT 1.11

FREDERICK DOUGLASS ASSESSES THE MEANING OF EMANCIPATION (1880)[9]

How stands the case with the recently emancipated millions of colored people in our own country? What is their condition to-day? What is their relation to the people who formerly held them as slaves? These are important questions, and they are such as trouble the minds of thoughtful men of all colors, at home and abroad. By law, by the constitution of the United States, slavery has no existence in our country. The legal form has been abolished. By the law and the constitution, the Negro is a man and a citizen, and has all the rights and liberties guaranteed to any other variety of the human family, residing in the United States....

In pursuance of this idea, the Negro was made free, made a citizen, made eligible to hold office, to be a juryman, a legislator, and a magistrate. To this end, several amendments to the constitution were proposed, recommended, and adopted.... This is our condition on paper and parchment. If only from the national statute book we were left to learn the true condition of the colored race, the result would be altogether creditable to the American people....

We have laid the heavy hand of the constitution upon the matchless meanness of caste, as well as upon the hell-black crime of slavery.... But today, in most of the Southern States, the fourteenth and fifteenth amendments are virtually nullified.

The rights which they were intended to guarantee are denied and held in contempt. The citizenship granted in the fourteenth amendment is practically a mockery, and the right to vote, provided for in the fifteenth amendment, is literally stamped out in face of government. The old master class is today triumphant, and the newly-enfranchised class in a condition but little above that in which they were found before the rebellion.

Do you ask me how, after all that has been done, this state of things has been made possible? I will tell you. Our reconstruction measures were radically defective. They left the former slave completely in the power of the old master, the loyal citizen in the hands of the disloyal rebel against the government. Wise, grand, and comprehensive in scope and desire as were the reconstruction measures, high and honorable as were the intentions of the statesmen by whom they were framed and adopted, time and experience, which try all things, have demonstrated that they did not successfully meet the case.

In the hurry and confusion of the hour, and the eager desire to have the Union restored, there was more care for the sublime superstructure of the republic than for the solid foundation upon which it could alone be upheld.... The old master class was not deprived of the power of life and death, which was the soul of the relation of master and slave. They could not, of course, sell their former slaves, but they retained the power to starve them to death, and wherever this power is held there is the power of slavery. He who can say to his fellow-man, "You shall serve me or starve," is a master and his subject is a slave.... Though no longer a slave, he is in a thralldom grievous and intolerable, compelled to work for whatever his employer is pleased to pay him, swindled out of his hard earnings by money orders redeemed in stores, compelled to pay the prince of an acre of ground for its use during a single year, to pay four times more than a fair price for a pound of bacon and to be kept upon the narrowest margin between life and starvation....

When the serfs of Russia were emancipated, they were given three acres of ground upon which they could live and make a living. But not so when our slaves were emancipated. They were sent away empty-handed, without money, without friends and without a foot of land upon which to stand....

Greatness does not come on flowery beds of ease to any people. We must fight to win the prize. No people to whom liberty is given, can hold it as firmly and wear it as grandly as those who wrench liberty

9   Source: *Life and Times of Frederick Douglass* (Boston, 1892).

from the iron hand of the tyrant. The hardships and dangers involved in the struggle give strength and toughness to the character, and enable it to stand firm in storm as well as in sunshine.

End of Document 1.11

SUBSEQUENT AMENDMENTS

There have arguably been two great periods of constitutional change since 1787. The Civil War amendments constitute the most important shift. The second came in the Progressive Period, in the early 20th century (usually dated 1900-1920).

As had been the case between the 12th and 13th amendments, a long period of time elapsed between the 15th and 16th—a full 43 years—and once again the country had changed quite dramatically in the meantime. Most notably, industrialization had taken off and was quickly making the United States the largest industrial power in the world—greater even than Great Britain and Germany. This period accordingly featured tremendous growth in US cities, rapid increases in the number of new immigrants to the US, the development of large-scale capitalism, and growing concentrations of wealth. This meant that there were many new problems requiring attention, and some people began to worry about corruption, the strength of monopolies, and the ill distribution of wealth. In this context a strong movement for political reform began to appear.

That reform, often called Progressivism, occurred in a number of ways, but one of them was constitutional amendment. Amendments 16-19 may all be regarded as Progressive amendments, because they reflected the spirit of that movement. By creating an income tax, democratizing elections of the Senate, and granting the vote to women—the single largest expansion of democracy in the history of the country—these amendments served to create better conditions for the equality of American citizens. The odd amendment in the group is no. 18, which outlawed the "manufacture, sale, or transportation" of alcohol, though it was consistent with the reformist spirit of the times. It is worth emphasizing that this, the only amendment that imposed a prohibition on American citizens, was repealed in 1933 by the 21st amendment.

It is difficult to summarize the rest of the amendments, though it is possible to make a generalization—namely that, on balance there is a general tendency towards expanding democracy and including broader segments of the population of the United States in politics and civil rights.

DOCUMENT 1.7 [PART E]

AMENDMENTS 16-27 TO THE US CONSTITUTION

ARTICLE XVI [PROPOSED 1909; RATIFIED 1913]. The Congress shall have power to lay and collect taxes on incomes, from whatever source derived, without apportionment among the several States, and without regard to any census or enumeration.

ARTICLE XVII. [PROPOSED 1912; RATIFIED 1913]. The Senate of the United States shall be composed of two Senators from each State, elected by the people thereof, for six years; and each Senator shall have one vote. The electors in each State shall have the qualifications requisite for electors of the most numerous branch of the State legislatures. When vacancies happen in the representation of any State in the Senate, the executive authority of such State shall issue writs of election to fill such vacancies: Provided, That the legislature of any State may empower the executive thereof to make temporary appointments until the people fill the vacancies by election as the legislature may direct. This amendment shall not be so construed as to affect the election or term of any Senator chosen before it becomes valid as part of the Constitution.

ARTICLE XVIII [PROPOSED 1917; RATIFIED 1919; REPEALED 1933].

Section. 1. After one year from the ratification of this article the manufacture, sale, or transportation of intoxicating liquors within, the importation thereof into, or the exportation thereof from the United States and all territory subject to the jurisdiction thereof for beverage purposes is hereby prohibited.

Section. 2. The Congress and the several States shall have concurrent power to enforce this article by appropriate legislation.

Section. 3. This article shall be inoperative unless it shall have been ratified as an amendment to the Constitution by the legislatures of the several States, as provided in the Constitution, within seven years from the date of the submission hereof to the States by the Congress.

ARTICLE XIX [PROPOSED 1919; RATIFIED 1920]. The right of citizens of the United States to vote shall not be denied or abridged by the United States or by any State on account of sex. Congress shall have power to enforce this article by appropriate legislation.

ARTICLE XX [PROPOSED 1932; RATIFIED 1933].

Section. 1. The terms of the President and Vice President shall end at noon on the 20th day of January, and the terms of Senators and Representatives at noon on the 3d day of January, of the years in which such terms would have ended if this article had not been ratified; and the terms of their successors shall then begin.

Section. 2. The Congress shall assemble at least once in every year, and such meeting shall begin at noon on the 3d day of January, unless they shall by law appoint a different day.

Section. 3. If, at the time fixed for the beginning of the term of the President, the President elect shall have died, the Vice President elect shall become President. If a President shall not have been chosen before the time fixed for the beginning of his term, or if the President elect shall have failed to qualify, then the Vice President elect shall act as President until a President shall have qualified; and the Congress may by law provide for the case wherein neither a President elect nor a Vice President elect shall have qualified, declaring who shall then act as President, or the manner in which one who is to act shall be selected, and such person shall act accordingly until a President or Vice President shall have qualified.

Section. 4. The Congress may by law provide for the case of the death of any of the persons from whom the House of Representatives may choose a President whenever the right of choice shall have devolved upon them, and for the case of the death of any of the persons from whom the Senate may choose a Vice President whenever the right of choice shall have devolved upon them.

Section. 5. Sections 1 and 2 shall take effect on the 15th day of October following the ratification of this article.

Section. 6. This article shall be inoperative unless it shall have been ratified as an amendment to the Constitution by the legislatures of three-fourths of the several States within seven years from the date of its submission.

ARTICLE XXI [PROPOSED 1933; RATIFIED 1933].

Section. 1. The eighteenth article of amendment to the Constitution of the United States is hereby repealed.

Section. 2. The transportation or importation into any State, Territory, or possession of the United States for delivery or use therein of intoxicating liquors, in violation of the laws thereof, is hereby prohibited.

Section. 3. This article shall be inoperative unless it shall have been ratified as an amendment to the Constitution by conventions in the several States, as provided in the Constitution, within seven years from the date of the submission hereof to the States by the Congress.

ARTICLE XXII [PROPOSED 1947; RATIFIED 1951].

Section. 1. No person shall be elected to the office of the President more than twice, and no person who has held the office of President, or acted as President, for more than two years of a term to which some other person was elected President shall be elected to the office of the President more than once. But this Article shall not apply to any person holding the office of President when this Article was proposed by the Congress, and shall not prevent any person who may be holding the office of President, or acting as President, during the term within which this Article becomes operative from holding the office of President or acting as President during the remainder of such term.

Section. 2. This article shall be inoperative unless it shall have been ratified as an amendment to the Constitution by the legislatures of three-fourths of the several States within seven years from the date of its submission to the States by the Congress.

ARTICLE XXIII [PROPOSED 1960; RATIFIED 1961].

Section. 1. The District constituting the seat of Government of the United States shall appoint in such manner as the Congress may direct: A number of electors of President and Vice President equal to the whole number of Senators and Representatives in Congress to which the District would be entitled if it were a State, but in no event more than the least populous State; they shall be in addition to those appointed by the States, but they shall be considered, for the purposes of the election of President and Vice President, to be electors appointed by a State; and they shall meet in the District and perform such duties as provided by the twelfth article of amendment.

Section. 2. The Congress shall have power to enforce this article by appropriate legislation.

ARTICLE XXIV [PROPOSED 1962; RATIFIED 1964].

Section. 1. The right of citizens of the United States to vote in any primary or other election for President or Vice President, for electors for President or Vice President, or for Senator or Representative in Congress, shall not be denied or abridged by the United States or any State by reason of failure to pay any poll tax or other tax.

Section. 2. The Congress shall have power to enforce this article by appropriate legislation.

ARTICLE XXV [PROPOSED 1965; RATIFIED 1967]

Section. 1. In case of the removal of the President from office or of his death or resignation, the Vice President shall become President.

Section. 2. Whenever there is a vacancy in the office of the Vice President, the President shall nominate a Vice President who shall take office upon confirmation by a majority vote of both Houses of Congress.

Section. 3. Whenever the President transmits to the President pro tempore of the Senate and the Speaker of the House of Representatives his written declaration that he is unable to discharge the powers and duties of his office, and until he transmits to them a written declaration to the contrary, such powers and duties shall be discharged by the Vice President as Acting President.

Section. 4. Whenever the Vice President and a majority of either the principal officers of the executive departments or of such other body as Congress may by law provide, transmit to the President pro tempore of the Senate and the Speaker of the House of Representatives their written declaration that the President is unable to discharge the powers and duties of his office, the Vice President shall immediately assume the powers and duties of the office as Acting President.

Thereafter, when the President transmits to the President pro tempore of the Senate and the Speaker of the House of Representatives his written declaration that no inability exists, he shall resume the powers and duties of his office unless the Vice President and a majority of either the principal officers of the executive department or of such other body as Congress may by law provide, transmit within four days to the President pro tempore of the Senate and the Speaker of the House of Representatives their written declaration that the President is unable to discharge the powers and duties of his office. Thereupon Congress shall decide the issue, assembling within forty-eight hours for that purpose if not in session. If the Congress, within twenty-one days after receipt of the latter written declaration, or, if Congress is not in session, within twenty-one days after Congress is required to assemble, determines by two-thirds vote of both Houses that the President is unable to discharge the powers and duties of his office, the Vice President shall continue to discharge the same as Acting President; otherwise, the President shall resume the powers and duties of his office.

ARTICLE XXVI [PROPOSED 1971; RATIFIED 1971].

Section. 1. The right of citizens of the United States, who are eighteen years of age or older, to vote shall not be denied or abridged by the United States or by any State on account of age.

Section. 2. The Congress shall have power to enforce this article by appropriate legislation.

ARTICLE XXVII [PROPOSED 1789; RATIFIED 1992]. No law, varying the compensation for the services of the Senators and Representatives, shall take effect, until an election of Representatives shall have intervened.

NEW STATES AND NEVADA

As noted above, by 1860 there were 33 states in the union, and two more were created during the Civil War—West Virginia and our own Nevada. The creation of Nevada and the appearance of its constitution (both in 1864) need to be understood in terms of two broader issues of large significance for US history. One is the expansion of the country—in effect, the creation of an American continental empire—and the other is the vexed relationship between states and the federal government.

The expansion of the United States westward had many dimensions: the movement of settlers westward, the dispossession and confinement of Native Americans, and war with Mexico in the 1840s (to acquire a large portion of the US West including Nevada and California) and later with Mexico (to acquire the Philippines and Puerto Rico). It is a noteworthy feature of the United States, however, that territories could become new states with the same status as the old ones. That is, there was no preference for the original 13 colonies over the newer states. The basic provisions for the creation of new states were outlined in the **Northwest Ordinance** of 1787 and the Constitution of the same year. The two were distinct but related. The ordinance provided that once a territory had 5000 male inhabitants, it could elect its own assembly (although a governor maintained an absolute veto). When the population reached 60,000, a territory could enter the Union on an equal basis with existing states. The Constitution provided that "New States may be admitted by the Congress into this Union" (art. 4, sec. 3), with a few basic conditions regulating that process. The Constitution did not actually promise that all federal territory would become states, but the structure and context imply such an outcome. Even so, there are still US territories that have not become states, such as Puerto Rico and Guam.

Nevada became a state at a particular moment in the country's history—in the midst of the Civil War—and this had significant implications for the state's constitution, especially for how that constitution defines the relationship between the state and the entire Union. To address that particular issue and others relating to Nevada's constitution, **Dr. Michael Green** of the University of Nevada, Las Vegas has produced the synopsis below, which provides an excellent overview. Dr. Green is the premier historian of Nevada, and his account can thus be regarded as a definitive one.[10]

READING 1.1

THE CONSTITUTION OF NEVADA: A BRIEF HISTORICAL SYNOPSIS

Michael Green

Nevada calls itself "Battle Born" because it achieved statehood during the Civil War (1861-65). Just as the Civil War created the conditions for statehood, it also shaped the constitution that governs Nevada. Disputes over the powers of federal and state governments helped prompt the South to secede from the Union, and the authors of the Nevada Constitution addressed those conflicts in hopes of preventing similar disagreements in the future. Like the rest of the country, Nevada still wrestles with matters of state and federal power in its constitution and in political processes, despite acknowledging the supremacy of the federal government. Southerners likewise felt alienated from the growing democratic society in the North, so Nevada's current constitution also reflects both the nineteenth century's democratic advances and later reform movements that would make our constitutional system far more participatory than at the federal level.

THE NEVADA CONSTITUTION: CONTEXT

Many forces that shaped Nevada's Constitution and led to statehood also influenced the creation of the Nevada territory. The United States acquired the land that includes Nevada in the Treaty of Guadalupe Hidalgo of 2 February 1848, ending the Mexican-American War. Only nine days before, prospectors had discovered gold at Sutter's Mill near Sacramento, California. The resulting gold rush prompted many gold-seekers to cross into what is now Nevada. The first settlers in present-day Nevada were Salt

---

10   He is the author of a definitive history of the state, *Nevada: A History of the Silver State* (Reno: University of Nevada Press, 2014).

Lake City Mormons who saw opportunity in opening a trading post for travelers en route to the Gold Rush, some of whom began prospecting the eastern foothills of the Sierra Nevada. Congress approved California's statehood and created two new territories, Utah and New Mexico, in the Compromise of 1850. Northern Nevada, then part of Utah territory, needed governing but was too far removed from other settlements and was locally divided between a small population of Mormons and non-Mormons. In 1859, the Comstock Lode's discovery in the Sierra Nevada foothills of modern Northern Nevada, led to a significant mining boom and the influx of enough people into the region to justify a separate government for the area.

Nevada's future soon became caught up in the swirl of national events, especially divisions between the North and South over the spread of slavery and the Civil War that followed. Debates over slavery dated to the 1787 Constitutional Convention and then to on-going discussions in Congress over the governing of the U.S. as a whole, the individual states, and U.S. territories. Although anti-slavery sentiment long had existed in the country, a series of reform movements and religious revivals during the first half of the nineteenth century encouraged, among other groups, abolitionists and opponents of the growth of slavery to advocate their cause.

Although abolitionism never became a mass movement, anti-slavery politicians came together during the 1850s in the newly created Republican Party, which sought to keep slavery from expanding into new territories, and succeeded in electing its presidential candidate, Abraham Lincoln, in 1860. Nevada became a territory on March 2, 1861, soon after seven southern states seceded from the Union and formed the Confederate States of America. Abraham Lincoln took the oath of office as president two days later. The Civil War itself began with the firing on Fort Sumter less than six weeks later. Thus, Nevada's birth and the Civil War became intertwined.

When Lincoln made appointments to government positions, he emphasized loyalty to the Union even more than loyalty to his political party. But in choosing territorial officials whom he could count on to support the Union, he selected loyal Republicans with connections to his administration. His choice for territorial governor, James W. Nye of New York, was a political ally of Lincoln's secretary of state, William Henry Seward. Nye stressed loyalty to the Union and urged territorial legislators to allow African Americans to serve in the militia and on juries, but those lawmakers refused. The territorial secretary, Orion Clemens, had worked in the St. Louis law office of Attorney General Edward Bates. Clemens handled administrative duties and inspired his brother Samuel to come west; Samuel started writing for newspapers and adopted the name Mark Twain. Nye often left Orion Clemens in charge of territorial affairs while he went to San Francisco and Washington, D.C. to lobby for statehood for Nevada Territory. He did this both to promote unionism and to satisfy his own ambition of becoming a U.S. senator.

Nevadans were eager enough for statehood to ignore federal law. In 1863 they held a constitutional convention even though Congress had yet to pass an enabling act that would authorize their efforts. The gathering included leaders of opposing factions who fought over how the mining industry, which dominated the state's economy, would be taxed. When advocates of taxing the mines like any other industry won the fight, the losing side nonetheless supported the constitution. But its leader, mining attorney William M. Stewart, claimed that under his interpretation of the document, mining would still receive a tax break. Nevadans resented his claims and his arrogance, and because the ballot on the constitution also included disliked candidates for office in the proposed new state, the proposed constitution was overwhelmingly defeated in January of 1864.

Less than two months later, Congress passed an enabling act for Nevada to seek statehood. Another constitutional convention accordingly met in the summer of 1864. This time, delegates did not include the most prominent advocates on both sides of the mining tax issue, and the state constitution gave the mining industry the tax break its leaders desired: a limit on the rate at which mining revenues could be taxed, and taxing net revenues rather than gross revenues, meaning that mining corporations could deduct expenses first. Also, the convention delegates scheduled the public vote two months before the general election, so that the constitution would be the only issue. On 7 September 1864, it passed by a 4-1 margin.

Even so, Lincoln had yet to issue a proclamation of statehood for Nevada. Although Nye sent the constitution back to Washington, Lincoln never received it and, despite the pleas of Nye's old friend Seward, refused to approve statehood without seeing the document first. With the 1864 presidential and state elections approaching, Nye had the **Nevada Constitution** telegraphed to Washington at a cost of more than $4,300 (today it would cost about $60,000, unless it was a .PDF file attached to an email). Having received the constitution in this fashion, Lincoln signed the proclamation of statehood on 31 October 1864, declaring Nevada would enjoy "equal footing with the original States." In other words, even as the thirty-sixth state, Nevada would enjoy all of the same privileges as the previously admitted states. On 8 November, Nevadans chose presidential electors, their congressional representative, state and local officials, and a state legislature that elected their first two U.S. senators: Stewart (the mining attorney) and Nye (the former territorial governor).

One of Nevada's greatest myths is that Lincoln supported statehood because he wanted gold and silver from the Comstock Lode. Since Nevada was a U.S. territory, the ore already was available to him. What was in fact more important was that Lincoln and his party hoped to win the electoral votes of the new state of Nevada for the president's reelection in 1864, and to gain extra support in Congress for the Thirteenth Amendment, which was designed to end slavery and to rebuild the country once the South surrendered. Lincoln indeed carried the state in the 1864 election, securing two electoral votes (the third elector was caught in a blizzard and unable to vote). Lincoln won an overwhelming Electoral College majority of 212-21. On 16 February 1865, just over two weeks after Congress sent it to the states for their approval, Nevada's legislators made theirs the sixteenth state to ratify the Thirteenth Amendment.

THE NEVADA CONSTITUTION: INFLUENCES

The Civil War. The constitution reflected the war's causes and effects. Article I, Section 2 declared unequivocally: "Paramount Allegiance of every citizen [of Nevada] is due to the Federal Government in the exercise of all its Constitutional powers as the same have been or may be defined by the Supreme Court of the United States; and no power exists in the people of this or any other State ... to dissolve their connection therewith." The Nevada constitution also stated that if an individual or group were to secede from the Union or were "forcibly [to] resist the Execution of its laws, the Federal Government may, by warrant of the Constitution, employ armed forces in compelling obedience to its Authority." Thus, in light of the South's rebellion against the Union, the Nevada Constitution left no doubt that every citizen owed allegiance to the Union before his or her state, and that there was no legal basis for secession from, or destruction of, the Union.

Just as slavery divided northerners and southerners, driving the country into the Civil War, it played a visible role in Nevada's constitution. Although it was written six months before Congress passed the Thirteenth Amendment to the U.S. Constitution, the Nevada Constitution outlawed slavery explicitly, as mandated in the act that Congress approved to permit Nevada to seek statehood. Also, Nevada denied the right to vote to any "person who, after arriving at the age of eighteen years, shall have voluntarily borne arms against the United States, or held civil or military office under the so-called Confederate States."

Still another section of the Nevada Constitution tied to the Civil War and the doctrine of federal supremacy remains relevant: the opening Ordinance declares that Nevadans "forever disclaim all right and title to the unappropriated lands lying within said territory, and that the same shall be and remain at the sole and entire disposition of the United States." This was true already, since the U.S. controlled what is now Nevada as part of the treaty ending the Mexican-American War. Today, the federal government controls about eighty-seven percent of Nevada's land. Many Nevadans, especially in rural areas outside of Las Vegas and Reno, have objected to this provision, leading in the late 1970s to the "Sagebrush Rebellion," whose leaders demanded state control of federal lands. Although the amount of regulation of federal land and the fees required for its use have varied by presidential administration, federal ownership and control of the vast majority of Nevada's land remains unchanged.

Federalism/The U.S. Constitution. Given that the Civil War resulted in part from differing interpretations of federal and state power, the Nevada Constitution's Declaration of Rights (Article I) was much more explicit and detailed than the federal Bill of Rights, requiring twice as many sections. Some of these now seem redundant, but they reflect concerns regarding protection of freedoms extending far back into American history. The Massachusetts Bay Colony had outlined a Body of Liberties as early as 1641, and the new states created from the colonies during the Revolutionary War had listed the rights of their citizens. The original U.S. Constitution lacked a Bill of Rights, but concerns about individual liberties, and the desire to win additional support for ratification, prompted the Founding Fathers to promise to amend the original document. The Bill of Rights kept that promise. However, those guarantees originally applied only at the federal level—that is, in relation to the central government in Washington—and not to the states. The "Civil War Amendments" (the Thirteenth, Fourteenth, and Fifteenth), passed between 1865 and 1870 in response to the issues leading to and created by the war, guaranteed these rights against the state governments, some specifically and some through the process of selective incorporation (by which judicial decisions applied the federal protections in the Bill of Rights to the state level). So, while it may seem redundant now, the Nevada Constitution's Declaration of Rights was an additional bulwark for the protection of individual freedoms and reflects the evolution of federalism and constitutional interpretation.

The U.S. Constitution is the central document in American federalism, and the original Nevada Constitution reflected its influence in a variety of ways. Like the federal document, Nevada's features a preamble acknowledging the separation of powers and checks and balances between the legislative, executive, and judicial branches; and it likewise devotes the most attention to legislative powers. Both documents outline the requirements for holding elective office and the lengths of terms, and how to impeach and remove an officeholder. Both constitutions give the executive the power to sign or veto legislation and the command of the armed forces. Neither originally set limits on how long the executive could serve, but both were amended to limit the president and the governor to two terms, plus no more than two years of his or her predecessor's term. Both empower the executive to make appointments, but while the U.S. Constitution gives the Senate the right to "advise and consent," the Nevada Constitution leaves it up to the governor to appoint judges and state board members and department heads without any confirmation process involving the legislature. Just as the Founding Fathers were concerned about presidential power in the wake of rebelling against the rule of King George III of England, the Nevada Constitution's framers preferred a weaker executive: the governor runs for office separately from the lieutenant governor and other state officials.

The federal Bill of Rights similarly influenced Nevada's Declaration of Rights. Nevada more specifically limits freedom of religion or conscience, so that it "shall not be so construed, as to excuse acts of licentiousness or justify practices inconsistent with the peace, or safety of this State." Many consider this an implied criticism of plural marriage, which the Mormon Church then permitted. Section 11 of Article I reflects and refines the Second Amendment of the U.S. Constitution by saying, "Every citizen has the right to keep and bear arms for security and defense, for lawful hunting and recreational use and for other lawful purposes." This formulation is more detailed than the federal amendment and its reference to a militia, and allows the state to define just what "security" and "defense" mean.

The Age of Reform and Jacksonian Democracy. In addition to the influence of the anti-slavery movement, the women's rights movement had prompted the Seneca Falls Convention of 1848, which declared, drawing on the language of the Declaration of Independence of 1776, that "all men and women are created equal." While Nevada declined to include such a declaration in its founding document, its constitution acknowledged these reformers by allowing women to own property separately from men.

In the 1820s and 1830s, just as Great Britain had expanded the right to vote, the proponents of Jacksonian Democracy in the U.S. had supported voting rights for white men whether or not they owned property. Democrats also promoted individual rights and limited government power. In turn, the Nevada Constitution included a large number of elective statewide offices, which limited the governor's power to make appointments and empowered the public to choose such officials as the state printer and the state superintendent of public instruction (although Nevadans eventually amended their constitution to make these appointive). Nevada's Constitution reflected the expansion of American democracy during this period by outlining voting rights in its second article; the U.S. Constitution, written before widespread popular voting, offered no such instructions.

The Western Frontier. Reflecting the desire for population growth and the realization that many Nevadans had moved to the area only recently, the constitution assured residents of the right to vote within six months of arriving and guaranteed the foreign-born "the same rights in respect to the possession, enjoyment and inheritance of property, as native-born citizens"—a provision repealed in 1924 amid nationwide efforts to restrict immigration. Westerners generally preferred more limited government and a greater diffusion of power than their eastern counterparts, and they acted on that preference in Nevada's Constitution by limiting the legislature to sessions biennially (every two years), with legislators paid only for the first sixty days of a session, which encouraged them to finish their business quickly.

THE NEVADA CONSTITUTION: A LIVING DOCUMENT

Like the U.S. Constitution's framers, delegates to the Nevada constitutional convention made it possible, but not easy, to amend their work. Befitting the greater emphasis that the Nevada Constitution places on democracy, it allowed voters to decide on amendments after—and only if—the legislature had approved amendments at consecutive sessions. Amendments were rare in the nineteenth century: in 1869, the legislature approved women's suffrage, and if the 1871 legislature had done the same and the voters had approved the measure, Nevada would have been the first state to enfranchise women. But the 1871 legislature defeated the amendment, and Nevada instead became one of the last states to approve votes for women, in 1914.

That decision reflected the era that led to the greatest changes in the Nevada Constitution: the Progressive Era. From about 1900 to 1920, several countries throughout the world engaged in liberal reform, with varying results: Great Britain reduced the power of the House of Lords and approved women's suffrage after lengthy battles; Russia created representative government after 1905 but a democratic government collapsed in 1917 and gave way to communist rule. In the U.S., Progressives pursued a variety of policies intended to manage government, the economy, and individual lives more efficiently, for good and ill. They also believed in more democracy.

Nevada was very much part of this movement. With the state dominated by mining and railroad interests, its reforms had limits—but national Progressives similarly varied in just how reform-minded they were, and reacted in part to more radical demands for change from Socialists and Communists. Not only did Nevada approve women's suffrage and ratify the Nineteenth Amendment to the U.S. Constitution, but it also added the **initiative** and **referendum**, which allows voters to legislate and amend the constitution on their own (bypassing legislators), and the **recall**, which enables them to remove elected officials. In 1912, Nevadans approved another progressive idea, the recall: If one-quarter of those who voted in the last election of a state or local politician (members of Congress cannot be recalled) sign a petition seeking his or her removal, an election must be held in thirty days, and the recalled candidate may appear on the ballot and stay in office if successful.

These changes continue to affect Nevadans' lives. Nevada's voters initiated a change to the constitution in 2002 to prohibit same sex marriage (the provision was held to be unconstitutional in federal court in 2014). During the 1990s, initiatives led to amendments requiring a two-thirds vote of the legislature to increase taxes and limiting lawmakers to no more than twelve years in the assembly or the state senate. This is a sign that Nevadans remain doubtful about how active and large their government should be, as both significantly affect what the legislature does and how it does it. While Nevadans have recalled few officeholders, they have removed city council members.

The general beliefs of the Progressives animated such liberal reforms as Franklin Roosevelt's New Deal of the 1930s and, in the 1950s and 1960s, the civil rights movement and the War on Poverty. National reform efforts, such as these, have helped shape the modern Nevada Constitution. Amendments to the U.S. Constitution have enfranchised African Americans, women, and people between the ages of 18 and 21; an amendment has also eliminated a poll tax that forced citizens to pay for the privilege of exercising their right to vote. Decades after the Progressive Era, the progressive idea of better management of government and industry helped inspire a Judicial Selection Commission that narrows the field from which the governor chooses to appoint judges.

One of the key changes in Nevada's political and governmental system resulted from the rulings of the U.S. Supreme Court under Chief Justice Earl Warren in the 1960s. The U.S. Constitution requires all states to have a "republican form of government." In *Reynolds v. Sims* (1964), the U.S. Supreme Court ruled that states were violating that provision of the Constitution by not having fair representation. At the time, Nevada based its representation on the "little federal plan." The assembly, loosely based on population, resembled the House of Representatives. Emulating the U.S. Senate's two members per state, Nevada's State Senate had one senator per county, but this meant that the larger counties, Clark (Las Vegas) and Washoe (Reno), had the same number of senators as the smallest counties. Due to *Reynolds* and a lower federal court decision in *Dungan v. Sawyer*, Nevada was compelled to reapportion its legislature to reflect its population. As a result, since Clark County has nearly three-fourths of Nevada's population, it has a corresponding number of legislators—15 of 21 in the state senate, 31 of 42 in the assembly (in 2015).

THE NEVADA CONSTITUTION: WHAT IT DOES AND MEANS

The most current text of the Nevada Constitution, including amendments and references to relevant laws, is at https://www.leg.state.nv.us/const/nvconst.html. Like the U.S. Constitution, it provides an extensive outline for our government system. Its nineteen sections address the three branches of government, the tax system, the educational system, finance, and state debt. The amount of guidance it gives varies: while the Nevada Constitution is more detailed than the U.S. Constitution, both leave room for interpretation and additional lawmaking. The Nevada Revised Statutes and various city and county ordinances are the laws that govern us, and they must be in accord with both the U.S. and Nevada Constitutions.

In many ways, the Nevada Constitution is like other state constitutions. But it also has allowed Nevadans to create the government that they want, and to change it when they see fit. Nevadans long have believed in a more limited, smaller state government. Thus, theirs is one of the few states where the legislature still meets every other year, instead of annually. They have joined other states in restricting the ability of legislators to raise taxes, and in enabling the public to legislate through the initiative and referendum, thus bypassing the legislature.

But the Nevada Constitution also raises questions for the state today—and some of these resemble questions about the U.S. Constitution. When the U.S. Constitution took effect in 1788, the U.S. consisted of thirteen states, the nation's western border was the Mississippi River, and the population was about four million—a far cry from the fifty states from the Atlantic to the Pacific and beyond, with a population approaching 310 million in the 2010 census. Similarly, Nevada's population in 1864 was less than 30,000, mostly a short distance from the state capital. With Nevada's twenty-first century population ninety times what it was in 1864, do the Nevada Constitution and the state government it designed properly serve Nevadans today? Does the state government's expansion meet the requirements of this greater population, especially when Nevada is becoming a majority-minority state in which more of its people are Hispanic than Caucasian? Since the original Nevada Constitution did not contemplate this growth, is it right that the governor can make appointments without legislative confirmation? Should Nevada's legislature meet more often? Is it possible for Clark County, with its percentage of the population, to have too much power, or should it exercise more power?

Early in the twenty-first century, Nevada ranked poorly in many categories that measure social progress, including the number of suicides, the percentage of high school graduates going to college, high school dropouts, pregnant teens, unimmunized children, killings related to domestic violence, health care, and smoking. The Tenth Amendment of the U.S. Constitution left powers to the states, and Nevada has taken advantage of that right, for good and for ill, to legalize gambling and to facilitate divorce, among other actions. The Nevada Constitution, in turn, means Nevadans have the freedom to make these decisions—and, once they make them, to change their minds.

End of Reading 1.1

Further Reading:

Akhil Reed Amar, *America's Constitution: A Biography*. New York: Random House, 2005.

Eric Foner. *Reconstruction: America's Unfinished Revolution, 1863-1877*. New York: Perennial Classics, 1988.

Michael Green, *Nevada: A History of the Silver State*. Reno: University of Nevada Press, 2014.

UNIT TWO

Russia and the Soviet Union

CHAPTER 5

TSARIST RUSSIA AND ITS REGIME

INTRODUCTION

The American Revolution was a remarkable event with worldwide significance. At the same time, the American colonies were far away from many parts of the world, and the revolution had not actually ended the monarchy, which continued to exist in Great Britain, as it does to this day. To be sure, there were important colonial revolutions elsewhere in the western hemisphere not long after the American. In the 1810-20s many countries in Latin America achieved their independence from Spain and Portugal. But to follow the history of revolution, we really need to return to Europe, where revolution became a major factor of political life over the course of the nineteenth century. The Russian revolution(s) of 1917 should be understood within this broader history of revolution.

Before we can turn to 1917, however, we need to consider a number of other issues, since only in this way can we understand how a group of radical socialists, the Bolsheviks, came to power in 1917. There are three clusters of issues that merit our attention. First, we will consider the spread of revolution to Europe, beginning with the great French Revolution in 1789. We will see that revolution became a fundamental part of European politics, especially in the first half of the nineteenth century. We will also note that whereas no successful revolution in Russia occurred in this period, there was an *attempted* revolution in 1825.

Second, we will briefly explore Russian history before and during the 19th century, focusing primarily on the creation of a massive multiethnic empire ruled by an autocracy under the emperor, or tsar. We will also see that the institution of serfdom played a key role in the making of Russia. While emphasizing the deep conservatism of the tsarist regime, we will note that tsarist leaders were willing to undertake some reform, for example under Peter the Great (1682-1725) and during the era of the Great Reforms (the 1860s). More reluctantly, the regime eventually promoted industrialization, and we will see why tsarist leaders were nervous about doing so.

Third, we briefly explore constitutional issues in Russian history before the 20th century, noting that the Russian emperors, as autocrats, strongly resisted either introducing or respecting constitutions except in a few distinct cases. At the same time we consider a few attempts at writing constitutions or plans for political change. The main lesson is that whereas the tsarist regime was prepared to promote certain kinds of social and economic reform, it was much more hostile to political change. Two documents will help us to understand the perspectives of Russian conservatives.

A REVOLUTIONARY ERA IN EUROPE

The most important event in this regard was the French Revolution, which began in 1789 and ended the monarchy in favor of a republic. The events of the French Revolution were nothing if not dramatic, featuring the execution of the king and queen, the elimination of various forms of privilege, the creation of modern notions of citizenship (at least for men), and a revolutionary terror featuring the liberal use of the guillotine and other forms of execution. The Revolution also had dramatic consequences for the rest of Europe and even the wider world, especially once Napoleon Bonaparte had come to power just before the turn of the century. Europe found itself constantly in warfare until Napoleon was finally defeated definitively in 1815, and the French brought their revolutionary enthusiasm to other parts of Europe and even the Middle East by force of arms. For anyone who subscribed to the values of the old regime—monarchy, religion and the church, hierarchy, authority, and rule by social elites—the French Revolution and its principles represented a serious threat.

Even once Napoleon was defeated and the monarchy had been restored in France in 1815, the revolutionary genie was out of the bottle. Indeed, every politically conscious person in Europe in the nineteenth was compelled to define himself or herself as either a proponent or opponent of the ideals of the French Revolution. This meant, first of all, that people could now contemplate revolution in a much more conscious fashion than they had in the past. Previously, revolutions had typically begun almost "by accident," often with people actually seeking to *restore* a previous golden age rather than trying to create something new. Note, for example, that the American colonists had initially cast their opposition to Parliament as a matter of protecting their "ancient liberties" as Englishmen rather than as an attempt to embark on revolutionary change. Now, with the experience of the French Revolution behind them, those people seeking change had a model to follow, as well as a set of slogans with which they could mobilize others. Secondly, the new political atmosphere meant that proponents of the "old order"—the political and social arrangements that had not yet been affected by revolutionary change—could no longer take that order for granted. Instead, they had to articulate the reasons why that old order was worth preserving. In this sense, the age of revolution unleashed by the events in France signaled also the birth of conservatism—that is, the deliberate and conscious effort to justify monarchy, the church, and a hierarchical (unequal) social order.

In the three decades after the restoration of the monarchy in France in 1815, revolution in fact became a frequent occurrence. There were a series of largely unsuccessful revolutions in the 1820s in places as diverse as Greece, Russia, Spain, and parts of Italy. In 1830 revolution overtook France once again, replacing one dynasty with a more liberal one. Neighboring Belgium also experienced revolution the same year, which was at least partly responsible for it becoming an independent country, while Poles revolted against their Russian overlords as well. The culmination of this tendency came in 1848, when revolution engulfed much of the European continent. The results were uneven, with disappointment for most of the revolutionaries. In France the revolution of 1848 produced the second republic with universal manhood suffrage (that is, all adult men could now vote), although a few years later Napoleon III subverted the new republic and converted France into an empire with himself at its head. In most other places where revolution had been temporarily successful in 1848, previous rulers were back in power by 1849, and elected assemblies had been dissolved. Where constitutions had been granted, they were later withdrawn or replaced with more conservative documents proclaiming different principles. But even if the revolutions seemed to have been in vain, the revolutionaries of 1848 "set precedents for subsequent generations of European liberals and democrats." Universal male suffrage survived in France, never to the lost again, and this principle "became the goal of democrats and radicals throughout Europe."[1] This was an important consequence of the **Revolutions of 1848**.

Constitutions occupied an important place in the aspirations of revolutionaries. For example, France produced a series of constitutions—in 1791, 1793, 1795, and 1804—each corresponding to a different stage in the country's revolutionary trajectory. For others, too, constitutions were central to revolutionary programs and even more moderate liberals. As two historians write about central, southern, and eastern Europe, where constitutions and representative institutions were almost non-existent before 1850, "the goal of liberals was a written constitution which would limit the authority of the ruler and provide for an elected parliament or assembly that would share in the formulation

---

1   Charles Breunig and Matthew Levinger, *The Revolutionary Era, 1789-1830*, 3rd ed. (New York, 2002), 294-95.

of laws. The word *constitution* took on an almost mystical significance for liberals in some of the German and Italian states, who assumed that by its mere existence such a document would solve all their problems."[2]

Two major European countries are notable for not having been touched by the Revolutions of 1848: Great Britain and Russia. As we know, Great Britain had experienced revolutionary upheaval in the seventeenth century, but in the nineteenth century it was much more stable than most other European countries. Arguably, after the English Civil War in the 1640s Britain had proved able to manage political and social change sufficiently well not to succumb to revolutionary upheaval. Russia escaped revolution for rather different reasons. In many ways, Russia's social and political order had not evolved enough yet in order to produce major revolutionary pressures. Russia retained the institution of serfdom—effectively a kind of slavery—all the way until 1861. Although some elements of industrialization had begun to appear already in the eighteenth century, in general Russia remained a more agrarian country far longer than lands like Britain, France, and Germany. Even at the start of the twentieth century probably some 85% of the population were peasants, and there was only a very small working class, or **proletariat**. Education remained the preserve of a relatively small elite until fairly late in the nineteenth century. To be sure, some peasants—boys sooner than girls—began to receive a basic education over the course of the century, but the school program featured a heavy dose of religion, which was designed to instill submission in the population. In short, basic preconditions for revolution were simply not yet in place in Russia.

Yet this is not to say that revolution was completely absent in Russia. In 1825, a group of enlightened army officers known as the **Decembrists** tried to incite a revolution and establish a new political order in Russia. These were young, educated men who had fought in the Russian army against Napoleon and had experienced Western Europe first hand. Many were fluent in several languages and thus had read important works of political philosophy written in French, German, and English. They could also look to the young United States and France as models for how to promote dramatic change—and what mistakes to avoid.

The Decembrists were planning an uprising for 1826, but when emperor Alexander I (1801-1825) died suddenly in 1825 and there was confusion about the succession,[3] some of these would-be revolutionaries decided to seize the opportunity and initiate a revolution. They were not terribly successful. They gathered their forces on a public square in St. Petersburg on 14 December 1825 (it was for this reason that they became known afterwards as "Decembrists"), but the new emperor Nicholas I (1825-1855), after encouraging them to acknowledge his authority, ordered his troops to fire into their midst. Many were killed, while others were arrested. After trials that followed, five Decembrists were executed, and their companions were sent into exile in Siberia. But however unsuccessful the Decembrists were, "This was the first time that an educated elite with its own considered program of social reform had taken up arms against the Russian autocracy."[4] In short, revolution had now reached Russia, at least as an ideal and an aspiration.

RUSSIAN HISTORY AND CHANGE

What kind of a country was Russia, and how did it become so prominent in European and world history? Russians typically trace their history back to the city of Kiev (now in Ukraine), where the first organized state appeared among the East Slavs in the ninth century.[5] But the government that existed in Russia in the 19th century was more directly descended from a medieval principality based in **Moscow**. At first, in around 1300, the principality of Moscow was quite small, and it faced significant competition from rival principalities based in cities located in what his now Russia, Ukraine, and Belarus. These principalities fought among themselves for power and influence, and it was only by a combination of skill and luck that Moscow emerged as the most prominent and powerful of these principalities. Moscow steadily amassed power and was gradually able to conquer

---

2   Breunig and Levinger, *Revolutionary* Era, 164.

3   Alexander had no children, and one brother, Constantine, had secretly renounced the throne in 1823 in favor of his younger brother Nicholas. This created confusion, since not everyone knew who the successor was.

4   Andzrej Walicki, *A History of Russian Thought from the Enlightenment to Marxism* (Stanford, 1979), 69.

5   By "East Slavs" we mean the people who are today Russians, Ukrainians, and Belarusians, although the distinction between the three appeared only a good deal later in history.

its rivals, incorporating those principalities into its own territory. By the mid-sixteenth century, Moscow had become the most important power in the northeastern part of Europe, where it faced competition primarily from Sweden and Poland in the west, the Ottoman Empire in the south, and the remnants of the Mongol Empire in the east. Eventually it challenged these major powers as well and in due course brought both Poland and several khanates (Turkic principalities to the east) under its rule.

Indeed, most historians would say that in 1552, when it conquered the Islamic khanate based in the city of Kazan (on the Volga River), Moscow became an empire, in the sense that it gained control over populations that were not Russian. This process of imperial expansion and the incorporation of non-Russian lands continued all the way into the early twentieth century. The result was one of the largest empires in the world, extending from the Baltic Sea in the west all the way to the Pacific Ocean in the east. The country consisted of Russians, who represented the core of the country's population, but also numerous non-Russian peoples, who spoke an extraordinary range of languages and were strikingly diverse in their ways of life. Russians themselves were mostly Orthodox Christians (an early Russian prince and his entourage had converted to Christianity in the year 988), while non-Russians confessed a wide range of religions including Islam, Judaism, Buddhism, and various denominations of Christianity, such as Lutheranism and Catholicism. The following table shows the distribution of Russia's population by faith according to an imperial census of 1897, and thus gives some indication as to the country's diversity:[6]

Moscow's rulers were initially princes, who subsequently styled themselves "grand princes" to signify their growing power and authority. They also used the title "tsar" (related to the word "caesar"), which is why one sometimes sees references to "tsarist Russia." In 1721 **Peter the Great** (1682-1725) formally adopted the title "Emperor," and his country now officially became "the Russian Empire," the designation it would have until 1917. Russia's grand princes, tsars, and emperors were all **autocrats**, which is to say that they ruled without

Faith	Population	Percent of Total
Orthodox Christians	87,123,604	69.3%
Muslims	13,906,972	11.1%
Roman Catholics	11,506,809	9.2%
Jews	5,215,805	4.2%
Protestants	3,762,756	3.0%
Old Believers	2,204,596	1.8%
Armenian "Gregorians"	1,179,266	0.9%
Buddhists	433,863	<0.5%
Karaites	12,894	<0.5%
Other non-Christians	285,321	<0.5%
Other Christians	8135	<0.5%

any formal legal limits to their power. Of course, the vast expanses of the country factually limited the rulers' power, in the sense that they could not actually rule such an enormous country directly but had to rely on governors. Moreover, there was also a ruling elite, whose interests could never be entirely ignored. But neither of these circumstances imposed any *formal* limits on the power of the ruler. There was certainly no constitution, nor were there any institutions with elected representatives, like a congress or a parliament. Russia's grand princes and emperors explicitly titled themselves "autocrats" in order to emphasize their unlimited power. Here we may observe a certain contrast between Russia and many other countries in Europe: in the west, most rulers proved unable to exercise unlimited power, because there were other organized political forces that prevented them from doing so. Recall, for example, that in England the Parliament prevented the king from accumulating too much power. In France, kings like Louis XIV proved adept at creating an absolutist regime, but this was eventually destroyed in the French Revolution. In Russia, rival political forces proved too weak or uninterested to contest the power of the ruler. For example, the tsars were able to secure the elite's acceptance of their rule by providing new land from their conquest of neighboring principalities and ensuring a guaranteed and cheap labor source for that land's exploitation by instituting serfdom, which bound peasants to the land and in many ways resembled

---

6   The table is taken from Paul W. Werth, *The Tsar's Foreign Faiths: Toleration and the Fate of Religious Freedom in Imperial Russia* (Oxford: Oxford University Press, 2014), 4.

slavery. The result was that Russia entered the 19th century with its autocratic system still unchallenged.

Indeed, the institution of autocracy proved enormously successful in Russia, which is one of the reasons why it lasted as long as it did. It had allowed the tsars to amass great power and to defeat their rival principalities. It had permitted them to mobilize resources for building one of greatest empires ever seen. It had allowed Russia to go from being a marginal and insignificant principality deep in the forests of northeastern Europe into one of the foremost players in European and indeed world politics. And when Russia was attacked by the army of Napoleon—which had managed to subdue almost the entire European continent before sending its armies towards Moscow in 1812—the autocracy managed to organize the defense of the country and to repel the invasion, thereby contributing mightily to Napoleon's final defeat. To be sure, not everyone benefitted from autocracy, but in terms of building an empire and securing the interests of its elite, the institution of autocracy had racked up successes with which it was hard to argue. This, surely, is one of the reasons why few in Russia were willing to challenge Russia's existing order.

If autocracy was one pillar of Russia's social and political order going into the 19th century, then serfdom was another. Serfdom was a system whereby peasants, rather than being free to move from one place to another in search of a better life, were legally bound to the land that they cultivated on behalf of their landlord. In effect, it was a form of slavery, and some scholars have indeed pointed to similarities between Russian serfdom and American slavery (although there were of course differences as well).[7] The basic arrangement was that nobles recognized the tsar's authority and provided military service to the ruler in campaigns undertaken against rival principalities and empires; in return, nobles received land (the most valuable resource in most pre-modern societies) and labor (without which the land was worthless). The system, which appeared gradually from around 1580 until around 1650, thus mobilized the society's resources for expansion, while also creating an alliance of sorts between the ruler and his elite. Like autocracy, then, serfdom played a critical role in Russia's geopolitical successes and in securing political stability. By

giving the country's noble elite land and labor, the tsars purchased the support of the one group that was most able to resist autocratic power. Serfdom, in other words, gave Russia's nobles an interest in the country's social and political order, making them less inclined to challenge the ruler's authority in favor of an alternative.

And yet Russia was also changing over time, as was the world around it. Russia's very successes created new challenges, because the country accordingly faced new rivals. Moreover, as military technology and forms of statecraft evolved, Russia felt pressure to make adjustments to its social and governmental order. Perhaps the most dramatic adjustments in this regard date to the reign of Peter the Great. We have already noted that Peter changed the title of the ruler to "emperor" and the name of the country to "the Russian Empire" in 1721. This was just one manifestation of the many changes that Peter brought to Russia, most of them involving the adoption of institutions, practices, and expertise from countries further west. Peter forced the Russian elite to adopt western forms of dress; he adopted western forms of statecraft; he built Russia's first navy; he reformed the Orthodox Church along western lines; he established scientific organizations akin to those in the west; and he moved the capital from the old city of Moscow to a new capital, **St. Petersburg**, that was founded in 1703. In fact, the list of reforms could go on, but the larger point is that Peter sought energetically to reform Russia along western lines, and his successors, though perhaps not to the same extent or with the same enthusiasm, continued to cast themselves as "reforming tsars" (or tsarinas) for the next century-and-a-half.[8] At the same time, neither Peter nor his immediate successors sought to eliminate either serfdom or autocracy. Indeed, over time Russian rulers became less enthusiastic about change and more inclined to conservatism. The last two emperors in particular—**Alexander III** (1881-1894) and **Nicholas II** (1894-1917)—were sooner backward looking than enthusiasts for a modern future. They tended to look back to an idealized past, when tsar and people had supposedly coexisted in harmony and mutual love.

Still, even those later Russian tsars recognized that times were dynamic, and that Russia could not

7   Peter Kolchin, *Unfree Labor: American Slavery and Russian Serfdom* (Cambridge, Mass., 1987).

8   Cynthia Hyla Whittaker, *Russian Monarchy: Eighteen-Century Rulers and Writers in Political Dialogue* (DeKalb, 2003), esp. 33-58.

avoid certain changes if the country was to remain competitive with its European rivals. True, they tended to be very cautious. But even conservative autocrats realized that Russia could not afford simply to put its head in the sand. Moreover, as the country grew and Russian society gradually became more complex, the autocracy realized that it needed new institutions and practices in order to rule the country. Finally, because Russia had expanded to include non-Russian parts of Europe, tsarist rulers recognized the benefits of accepting certain institutions in those parts of the country even if they were not acceptable elsewhere. As we shall see, this included constitutions in two parts of the empire.

Probably the biggest wave of reform in modern Russia came in the 1860s, in the aftermath of the Crimean War (1853-55). Recall that Russia had contributed fundamentally to the defeat of Napoleon's army in 1812-15, and partly for this reason the country became complacent, thinking that it did not need to make any major changes. In the meantime, the industrial revolution had begun to have dramatic effects in other parts of Europe, leading to the creation of new factories, the construction of new railways, and the development of new technologies. Many of these developments had military applications, and the result was that when Russia found itself at war with Britain, France, and the Ottoman Empire in 1853, it proved unable to match their military strength. The war, in short, proved to be a shock that convinced the new emperor, **Alexander II** (1855-81), that Russia had to embark on a project of reform, which eventually became known as the **Great Reforms**. The most important reform was the elimination of serfdom in 1861, as a result of which some 19 million peasants became at least formally free. The reforms also created an element of elective self-government at the local level, introduced trial by jury for at least some of the country's population, and established a more modern army based on universal military service and a system of reserves. These were very important changes, but it is noteworthy that none of them had a political component. That is, there was no talk of national elections, or a parliament, or a constitution, or any limitation on the power of the autocrat.

The Great Reforms also did not immediately involve promotion of **industrialization**. Russian rulers were frightened by the idea of industrialization, because they thought—rightly, it should be

noted—it had the potential to destabilize Russia's social order. For example, if peasants made their way into cities and factories, they would become disconnected from the structures of authority that existed in the countryside—their parents, the church, village elders, and so on. They might start to develop radical ideas, become atheists, or start drinking heavily—all of which were likely to have disruptive effects. Therefore, for a time the tsars were reluctant to promote industrialization. By the 1880s and 1890s, however, they realized that industrialization, too, would be necessary for Russia to remain competitive. Just next door, Germany had united into a single country in 1871 after defeating France impressively in the Franco-Prussian War. Industrialization unfolded rapidly in Germany, which soon overtook Great Britain as the largest industrial power in Europe (it was second only to the United States, which was also industrializing rapidly). Russian tsars realized that Germany represented a significant rival, and that to be in any position to resist German power Russia would have to embark on a more active program of industrialization as well. This began in the 1880s and picked up considerably in the 1890s. New factories began to appear with growing rapidity; Russia actively built railways, including one all the way across Siberia to the Pacific Ocean; and cities—especially St. Petersburg and Moscow, but also Warsaw, Kiev, and others—grew rapidly. To be sure, the vast majority of the population continued to be peasants all the way to 1917, and the Russian working class, or proletariat, was correspondingly small. But it was growing quickly and it was concentrated in a few major urban centers. The larger point is that even as Russian rulers had resisted industrialization for a time, they eventually realized that it was necessary for the country to remain competitive. More generally, one can say that Russian rulers were strikingly conservative, but they also realized that some change was necessary and proved willing to promote certain kinds of reform, albeit reluctantly and cautiously.

A SHORT CONSTITUTIONAL HISTORY OF RUSSIA

But despite the Great Reforms in the 1860s and the cautious promotion of industrialization by the 1880s-90s, Russian autocrats proved unwilling to engage in any substantial political reform. They regarded politics as their monopoly. By virtually any definition of the term, Russia as a whole had no constitution before 1906. The Russian emperor, or tsar, remained an autocrat throughout the 19th century. There were no formal limitations on his power, and there were no institutions of political representation at the national level, precisely because politics remained the monopoly of the autocrat and the bureaucracy that served him. In fact, for Russia's ruling elite, who were firm proponents of the old order, words like "constitution" and "democracy" had a clearly negative connotation, and any plan of political reform submitted to the emperor had to be careful to avoid them. It is easy to be cynical about the Russian emperors and to declare that they were simply jealous of their power. Undoubtedly, this is true on some level. But it is worth remembering that each emperor had received autocratic power from his predecessor and felt bound to maintain autocracy going forward. In general, rulers and indeed many subjects in Russia felt that autocracy had served the country well, by unifying diverse realms, making Russia into a great power on the European geopolitical stage, enabling the country to expand all the way to the Pacific Ocean and even into North America, and mobilizing the country against the Napoleonic invasion. Some were convinced that Russia, though broadly a part of Europe, was nonetheless distinct and needed to have its own social and political order, whatever Europeans further west chose to do. Russian rulers were generally convinced that autocracy was the only institution that could hold a country as large and diverse as Russia together. And they had a point. It is worth noting that shortly after the autocracy was toppled in 1917, the country began to disintegrate, and it took a new form of autocracy—Bolshevism—to reassemble the country again as the Soviet Union.

But to say that Russian autocrats successfully resisted the introduction of a constitution and popular representation until the early twentieth century is not to deny that some Russians—even ones closely associated with the regime—thought about constitutions and the law. For example, in the early 19th century the tsarist statesmen did a great deal of work compiling and codifying Russian laws. This meant gathering all the various laws and decrees that had been produced or promulgated for some two centuries and organizing that material first chronologically and then topically. The result

was a "law digest," published in 1832, the first volume of which was labeled the **Fundamental Law**. It might be tempting to see this already as an actual constitution. And, to be sure, the very label "Fundamental Law" was arguably a translation of the German word for "constitution" (*Grundgesetz*). Yet there are good reasons for concluding that this was not a constitution. Certainly most contemporaries did not treat it as one. But these efforts at codification, though they did not add up to a constitution, nonetheless were an important step in the development of law in Russia.

Moreover, there were particular parts of Russia that did have constitutions, at least for a time. As a result of the Napoleonic wars, Russia acquired two important territories with more developed constitutional traditions: **Finland** in 1809 and **Poland** in 1815. In both cases Alexander I accepted the idea of a constitution, and in the case of Poland even promoted it. In the case of Finland, when Russia acquired that territory from Sweden in 1809, Alexander made several statements in which he expressed his willingness to respect Finland's "constitutions" (he frequently used the plural). Thus in 1808, on the eve of the annexation, he told the Finns, "The old constitutions and privileges of your land shall be maintained sacredly." In 1809 he declared, "I have promised to maintain your constitutions, your fundamental laws." And in 1810, he remarked that he was "resolved to govern this country [Finland] as a free nation, enjoying the rights that its constitution guaranteed it." Here we see again clear confirmation of the idea that the word "constitution" in some cases referred not to a concrete written document—Finland did not have one—but rather the system or body of fundamental principles according to which a nation, state, or body politic is constituted or established and governed (see the introduction to this book). Alexander's point was that although Russia was annexing Finland, inhabitants there would not suffer any loss of their safety, rights, or privileges as a result.[9] Thus while the Finnish case reveals the tsar's respect for the local political arrangements, we may call the situation for Finns "constitutional" only in the unwritten sense of that term. Still, this was more than Russians received in the center of the country.

9   C. Leonard Lundin, "Finland," in Edward C. Thaden, ed., *Russification in the Baltic Provinces and Finland, 1855-1914* (Princeton, 1981), 360-62.

Even more complicated was the case of Poland, where an actual written constitution appeared in 1815. Poland itself had already experimented with a constitution in 1791, on the eve of the country's destruction.[10] After the Napoleonic wars, Alexander I became convinced that the portion of Poland that had been incorporated into Russia—it was called the **Kingdom of Poland**—needed its own constitutional identity in order to secure the country and the loyalty of its population. In November of 1815 he promulgated a new constitution for the Kingdom. Although the constitution reserved most authority for the tsar or his deputy, it created "a political system as progressive as any on the European mainland" and was "a liberal and enlightened document" by the standards of the day.[11] Parliaments were to meet at least every two years, and the inhabitants of the Kingdom acquired freedom of press, habeas corpus, freedom of religion, and other civil rights. The Kingdom was granted a broad and comprehensive autonomy. Thus a very strange situation had appeared in 1815: Alexander I was simultaneously an autocrat in Russia and a constitutional monarch in the Kingdom of Poland. But there was no fundamental contradiction. The fact was that in promoting constitutionalism in Poland, Alexander was not merely attempting to gain the Poles' loyalty, but also to use the Kingdom as a testing ground for new political institutions that might eventually be extended to the entire country—that is, to the rest of Russia. In other words, constitutional reform for all of Russia would begin with Poland. In the end, however, the constitutional experiment proved short-lived, even in Poland itself. Towards the end of his reign, Alexander became more concerned about the threat of revolution—there were several revolutions elsewhere in Europe in the early 1820s—and his enthusiasm for constitutionalism accordingly waned. Shortly before his death in 1825, he revised the constitution to make it more conservative. When Poland revolted against Russian rule in 1830-31, Alexander's brother and successor, Nicholas I, used the occasion to abrogate the Polish constitution. Thus Russia's experimentation with constitutionalism ended in its Polish borderlands.

There was one other occasion when the autocracy itself actually promoted constitutionalism—in this case beyond the borders of the country. In 1878, after liberating **Bulgaria** from Ottoman rule, tsarist occupation forces made it a priority to create a constitution for the newly autonomous country in order to stabilize its internal affairs and thus prevent other European states from undermining Russian influence there. Thus representatives of the tsar in Bulgaria drafted a new constitution for the country, allowing a constitutional assembly in Bulgaria itself to produce the final version, which proved to be "an extremely liberal document."[12] The larger picture that emerges, then, is that Russian rulers proved willing to respect or even promote constitutionalism at the very edges of the Russian Empire (in Finland and Poland) or even beyond its borders (in Bulgaria), but proved far more reluctant to engage in constitutional change for the core Russian territories of the empire at home.

Some of the regime's opponents were more enthusiastic constitutionalists. Several of the Decembrists who revolted unsuccessfully against the monarchy in 1825 produced draft constitutions as part of the preparations for their insurrection. Thus Nikita Murav'ev, a Decembrist, produced a text clearly based in part on the United States Constitution, although he was in favor of a constitutional monarchy rather than a republic. After the revolution that he envisioned, the emperor would remain but would become the "supreme official of the Russian government," subject to certain distinct limitations on his power and obligated to take an oath to the constitution. Murav'ev proposed a federation, again based on the US model, while also excluding nomadic tribes from citizenship—much like Native Americans in the United States. Women were also largely excluded. Thus Murav'ev's plan offered the ideal of popular sovereignty but a citizenry that probably would have excluded more people than it would have included. More radical than Murav'ev was Pavel Pestel', who produced a draft constitution known

---

10 Between 1772 and 1795, Poland was divided up, or partitioned, by three neighboring powers: Austria, Prussia, and Russia.

11 David Saunders, *Russia in the Age of Reaction and Reform, 1801-1881* (New York, 1992), 71; Michael T. Florinsky, *Russia: A History and an Interpretation*, vol. 2 (New York, 1953), 707.

12 Barbara and Charles Jelavich, *The Establishment of the Balkan National States, 1804-1920* (Seattle, 1986), 158-60 (citation at 160).

"the Russian Truth." Pestel' looked sooner to the radical tradition of revolution in France than to the more moderate United States. He rejected the idea of federalism and instead advocated a centralized republic, while also envisioning a quite radical plan for assimilating non-Russian peoples (except Poles). The projects of people like Murav'ev and Pestel' are interesting, and it can be curious (and a tad frightening) to contemplate what would have happened in Russia if they had come to power. In the event, however, they did not, but instead were either executed or exiled to Siberia. Their projects are interesting for us primarily because they show that constitutional thinking was developing in Russia in the 1820s.

For most of the 19th century, there was little more by way of actual constitutional reform. There were, however, two moments when statesmen proposed modest political changes that had, or could have had, constitutional significance if they had been adopted. The first case came in 1863, when the minister of the interior Peter Valuev proposed the creation of a representative body of prominent nobles, city-dwellers, and religious clerics—hardly radicals—to advise the emperor on important questions of the day. Valuev was careful to specify that these people would be appointed by the ruler, not elected by the people, and he was also careful to avoid the word "constitution," since he knew that the very use of that term would doom the project. Indeed, he made clear that the idea of allowing a few carefully chosen subjects to participate "to some extent in matters of legislation and general state administration does not imply an encroachment on the sovereign rights of the Autocratic power of Your Majesty." Rather, Valuev wrote, "The striving for this participation is an expression of the desire to draw nearer to Your Majesty's Throne, to take a place in those institutions through which Your Sovereign's will is made known."[13] But even this seemingly innocuous idea proved unacceptable to Alexander II, who continued to regard the person of the autocrat— that is, himself—as the very embodiment of the state. He therefore rejected Valuev's plan.

A second proposed change came in 1881. By the late 1870s, the Russian government faced a serious challenge from revolutionary terrorists (see below), who had become disappointed with pace of change and therefore sought to assassinate Emperor Alexander II as a way of precipitating a revolutionary crisis. In this context interior minister **Michael Loris-Melikov** proposed that modest political reform could perhaps help in combating these terrorists. The problem, as he saw it, was that the terrorists enjoyed support from segments of educated Russian society, who were frustrated by the absence of real political reform in Russia and by the arbitrary nature of the government's actions. These sympathies emerged dramatically in 1878, when a young woman, Vera Zasulich, attempted to murder the governor-general of St. Petersburg in his own office and was then acquitted by a jury. Zasulich had shot at the governor-general point-blank—there was no doubt that she had intended to kill him. Yet a jury sympathized with her rather than with the government and acquitted her. This outcome showed that the autocracy was dangerously isolated, and Loris-Melikov therefore regarded it as critical to restore confidence in the government among moderately liberal and potentially loyal segments of Russia's educated and economic elite, so as to deprive the terrorists of the sympathy that they otherwise enjoyed. His idea, then, was to defeat radical revolutionary ideologies by granting society a limited opportunity to participate in the formulation of laws and other measures for the benefit of the country. By making a small compromise with moderate elements in society, Loris-Melikov believed, they could be drawn away from the opposition camp and would become supporters of the regime *against* the radical threat. His goal, in short, was to split the opposition by granting limited political concessions, which would leave the radical opposition isolated and weakened. Even so, the limited nature of the concessions that Loris-Melikov proposed is striking. He emphasized that western models were not relevant to Russia and that his proposal "has nothing in common with Western constitutional forms." Indeed, he declared, the emperor would retain "fully and exclusively the right to introduce legislative matters at the time and within the limits which [he] deems desirable." In short, this was not a constitution or a limitation on autocrat's power, but instead merely a mechanism for allowing *some* participation of the country's responsible subjects in politics and legislation. One could say that Loris-Melikov was proposing a chance for their voice to

---

13   Valuev's project is in Marc Raeff, *Plans for Political Reform in Imperial Russia, 1730-1905* (Englewood Cliffs, 1966), 121-31 (citation at 125).

be heard while retaining for the autocrat the right to ignore it.[14] And yet even this proposal proved to be too much. True, Alexander II seems to have been prepared to accept this proposal in some form. But in the event, terrorists assassinated the emperor before he was able to approve the proposal formally, and his assassination pulled the rug out from under the plan. The terrorist act gave powerful ammunition to unrepentant conservatives to resist these projects.

To understand these conservative sentiments, we can do no better than to read the following speech, delivered a week after Alexander II's assassination. The author is **Konstantin Pobedonostsev** (1827-1907), the foremost representative of conservative political thought in late imperial Russia. An accomplished lawyer and tutor for the future Alexander III, in 1880 Pobedonostsev became chief procurator of the Holy Synod, the highest administrative position in the Russian Orthodox Church. He also served as a member of the State Council, a legislative body of the autocracy. The speech reproduced below was given on 8 March 1881, in the presence of the new autocrat, Alexander III, the son of the just-murdered tsar. The speech is produced here on the basis of the recollections of one of those present at the discussion, and therefore it remains difficult to state with certainty that these were the exact words of Pobedonostsev. Nonetheless, the sentiments expressed below seem broadly consistent with Pobedonostsev's views as we know them from other sources, and at the very least they tell us how his views were recalled by others who had contact with him.

DOCUMENT 2.1

SPEECH OF KONSTANTIN POBEDONOSTSEV[15]

Your Majesty! By oath and by conscience I am obliged to express all that is on my soul. I find myself not only in a state of confusion, but also one of despair…. In considering the plan submitted for Your consideration, one's heart sinks. In this plan one detects falsehood; I will say more: it reeks of falsehood. We are told that for the better elaboration of legislative bills, we must include those who know the life of the people, we must listen to experts. I would have nothing against this, if this were all that was to be done. Experts have in fact been consulted in previous times, but not in the way that is being proposed now. No! In Russia people want to introduce a constitution, if not immediately, then they at least they want to take the first step in that direction… But what is a constitution? Western Europe provides an answer to this question. Constitutions existing there are in essence instruments for every kind of untruth, the source of all kinds of intrigue…. But is it really the case that those people who will appear here to consider legislative bills will be genuine expressions of the people's opinion? I assure you that they will not. They will express only their own personal opinions….

And people want to introduce this falsehood in an alien form that is not suitable to us, to our detriment and to our ruin. Russia was strong thanks to autocracy, thanks to the unlimited mutual trust and close connection between the people and their Tsar. This connection between the Russian Tsar and his people is an incalculable good. Our people are the guardian of all our valor and our good moral qualities. One may learn a lot from them! The so-called representatives in the zemstvos[16] only disconnect the Tsar from the people. Meanwhile, the government must concern itself with the people, it must learn about its genuine needs, it must help the people to cope with their often perpetual needs. This is the goal to which one must aspire; these are the true tasks of the new reign. And instead of this we are being offered a talking-shop akin to the French Estates-General.[17] Even without this we already suffer from talking-shops, which, under the influence of worthless, good-for-nothing journalists, merely go about igniting popular passions. Thanks to empty chatterers, what became of the elevated plans of the deceased,

---

14   The project itself is in Raeff, *Plans for Political Reform*, 132-40.

15   Originally printed in *Russkii Arkhiv*, no. 5 (1907): 103-105. Translated by Paul W. Werth.

16   Created in 1864 as part of the Great Reforms, zemstvos were local councils of self-government at the provincial and district levels charged with overseeing certain local affairs.

17   The Estates-General was the French parliament.

unforgettable Sovereign, who at the end of his reign took upon himself the martyr's crown? To what has the great, holy idea of the peasants' emancipation led? They have been granted freedom, but the power needed over them—power that the dark masses cannot do without—has not been established. More than this, taverns have been opened everywhere. The poor people, left to their own devices and without any oversight, has begun to drink and to be lazy with regard to work, and has thus become the unhappy victim of tax collectors, kulaks [rich peasants], Yids [Jews], and all kinds of money-lenders. Then rural and urban institutions were opened—talking-shops, in which participants do not occupy themselves with real affairs, but pronounce lofty phrases all over the place about the most important affairs of state, which do not at all belong to their jurisdiction. And who pronounces these lofty phrases? Who bosses these talking-shops around? Immoral good-for-nothings, among whom a visible position is occupied by people who do not live with their families, who give themselves over to depravity, and who are thinking only about their personal gain, who are seeking popularity and who are introducing all kinds of sedition into everything. Then new judicial institutions were opened, new talking-shops, talking-shops of lawyers, thanks to whom the most frightful crimes, unquestioned murders and other grave evil deeds remain unpunished. Finally, freedom was granted to the press, the worst talking-shop of all, which conveys abuse and censure of the authorities to all ends of the unbounded Russian land, across thousands and tens of thousands of versts,[18] and sows the seeds of discord and dissatisfaction among peaceful and honest people, enflames passions, and incites the people to the most frightful forms of lawlessness. And, Sovereign, when is it that they propose establishing, on a foreign model, a new, supreme talking-shop? Precisely now, when only a few days have passed since the commission of the most frightful crime, one having never occurred before in Russia, when on the other side of the Neva, a stone's throw from here, the unburied ashes of the placid Russian Tsar lie in the Peter and Paul cathedral—the Tsar who was torn to pieces by Russian people in broad daylight....[19] We must all repent.

End of Document 2.1

Following Pobedonostev's advice, Alexander III rejected the plan, writing on it in his own hand, "Thank God that this criminal and hasty step toward [a] constitution was not taken." Interior Minister Loris-Melikov was accordingly dismissed in favor of a more conservative successor. No further efforts at political reform were attempted until the Revolution of 1905 (see below). Even so, because the country continued to change, conservatives like Pobedonostsev felt that they had to combat liberals and radicals who favored parliaments, elections, civil rights, and democracy.

A striking example of such conservative thought, again from the pen of Konstantin Pobedonostsev, was *The Falsehood of Democracy*, a collection of essays published in 1896. A selection from one of those essays is reproduced here. As you read the selection below, which was published in 1896, try to ascertain Pobedonostsev's reasons for opposing democracy. What dangers did he see in such a system? Who did he think was actually likely to rule in a democratic system? And in what ways did he find the idea of popular sovereignty objectionable?

DOCUMENT 2.2

KONSTANTIN POBEDONOSTEV, *THE FALSEHOOD OF DEMOCRACY* (1896)

What is this freedom by which so many minds are agitated, which inspires so many insensate actions, so many wild speeches, which leads the people so often to misfortune? In the democratic sense of the word, freedom is the right of political power, or, to express it otherwise, the right to participate in the government of the State. This universal aspiration for a share in government has no constant limitations, and seeks no definite issue, but incessantly extends.... Forever extending its base, the new Democracy now

---

18   A *verst* was an old unit of measurement roughly equivalent to a kilometer.

19   The Neva River flowed through the city of St. Petersburg. The Winter Palace, in which this speech was delivered, was located across the river from the Peter and Paul fortress, at the center of which stood the cathedral where most Russian sovereigns of the imperial period are buried.

aspires to universal suffrage – a fatal error, and one of the most remarkable in the history of mankind. By this means, the political power so passionately demanded by Democracy would be shattered into a number of infinitesimal bits, of which each citizen acquires a single one. What will he do with it, then? How will he employ it? In the result it has undoubtedly been shown that in the attainment of this aim Democracy violates its sacred formula of "Freedom indissolubly joined with Equality." It is shown that this apparently equal distribution of "freedom" among all involves the total destruction of equality. Each vote, representing an inconsiderable fragment of power, by itself signifies nothing; an aggregation of votes alone has a relative value. The result may be likened to the general meetings of shareholders in public companies. By themselves individuals are ineffective, but he who controls a number of these fragmentary forces is master of all power and directs all decisions and dispositions. We may well ask in what consists the superiority of Democracy. Everywhere the strongest man becomes master of the state; sometimes a fortunate and resolute general, sometimes a monarch or administrator with knowledge, dexterity, a clear plan of action, and a determined will. In a Democracy, the real rulers are the dexterous manipulators of votes, with their placemen, the mechanics who so skillfully operate the hidden springs which move the puppets in the area of democratic elections. Men of this kind are ever ready with loud speeches lauding equality; in reality, they rule the people as any despot or military dictator might rule it. The extension of the right to participate in elections is regarded as progress and as the conquest of freedom by democratic theorists, who hold that the more numerous the participants in political rights, the greater is the probability that all will employ this right in the interests of the public welfare, and for the increase of the freedom of the people. Experience proves a very different thing. The history of mankind bears witness that the most necessary and fruitful reforms—the most durable measures—emanated from the supreme will of statesmen, or from a minority enlightened by lofty ideas and deep knowledge, and that, on the contrary, the extension of the representative principle is accompanied by an abasement of political ideas and the vulgarization of opinions in the mass of the electors. It shows also that this extension—in great States—was inspired by secret aims to the centralization of power, or led directly to dictatorship....

The manipulation of votes in the game of Democracy is of the commonest occurrence in most European states, and its falsehood, it would seem, has been exposed to all; yet few dare openly to rebel against it.... But to an impartial mind, all this is nothing better than a struggle of parties, and a shuffling with numbers and names. The voters, by themselves inconsiderable unities, acquire a value in the hands of dexterous agents. This value is realized by many means—mainly, by bribery in innumerable forms, from gifts of money and trifling articles, to the distribution of places in the services, the financial departments, and the administration. Little by little a class of electors has been formed which lives by the sale of votes to one or another of the political organizations. So far has this gone in France, for instance, that serious, intelligent, and industrious citizens in immense numbers abstain from voting, through the difficulty of contending with the cliques of political agents. With bribery go violence and threats, and reigns of terror are organized at elections, by the help of which the respective cliques advance their candidates; hence the stormy scenes at electoral demonstrations, in which arms have been used, and the field of battle strewn with the bodies of the killed and wounded....

Among the falsest of political principles is the principle of the sovereignty of the people, the principle that all power issues from the people, and is based upon the national will—a principle which has unhappily become more firmly established since the time of the French Revolution. Thence proceeds the theory of Parliamentarism, which, up to the present day, has deluded much of the so-called "intelligentsia," and unhappily infatuated certain foolish Russians. It continues to maintain its hold on many minds with the obstinacy of a narrow fanaticism, although every day its falsehood is exposed more clearly to the world.

In what does the theory of Parliamentarism consist? It is supposed that the people in its assemblies makes its own law, and elects responsible officers to execute its will. Such is the ideal conception.... It may act successfully only when the delegates of the people abdicate their personalities; when on the benches of Parliament sit mechanical fulfillers of the people's behests; when the ministers of State remain impersonal, absolute executors of the will of the majority; when the elected representatives of the people are capable of understanding precisely, and executing conscientiously, the program of activity, mathematically expressed, which has been delivered to them....

Such is the theory. Let us look at the practice. Even in the classic countries of Parliamentarism it would satisfy not one of the conditions enumerated. The elections in no way express the will of the electors. The popular representatives are in no way restricted by the opinions of their constituents, but are guided by their own views and considerations, modified by the tactics of their opponents. In reality, ministers are autocratic, and they rule, rather than are ruled by, Parliament. They attain power, and lose power, not by virtue of the will of the people, but through immense personal influence, or the influence of a strong party which places them in power, or drives them from it. They dispose of the force and resources of the nation at will, they grant immunities and favors, they maintain a multitude of idlers at the expense of the people, and they fear no censure while they enjoy the support in Parliament of a majority which they maintain by the distribution of bounties from the rich tables which the State has put at their disposal. In reality, the ministers are as irresponsible as the representatives of the people. Mistakes, abuse of power, and arbitrary acts are of daily occurrence, yet how often do we hear of the grave responsibility of a minister? It may be once in fifty years a minister is tried for his crimes, with a result contemptible when compared with the celebrity gained by the solemn procedure.

Were we to attempt a true definition of Parliament, we should say that Parliament is an institution serving for the satisfaction of the personal ambition, vanity, and self-interest of its members. The institution of Parliament is indeed one of the greatest illustrations of human delusion. Enduring in the course of centuries the tyranny of autocratic and oligarchical governments, and ignoring that the evils of autocracy are the evils of society itself, men of intellect and knowledge have laid the responsibility for their misfortunes on their rulers and on their systems of government, and imagined that by substituting for these systems government by the will of the people, or representative government, society would be delivered from all the evils and violence which it endured. What is the result? The result is that, *mutato nomine*, all has remained essentially as before, and men, retaining the weaknesses and failings of their nature, have transfused in the new institutions their former impulses and tendencies. As before, they are ruled by personal will, and in the interests of privileged persons, but this personal will is no longer embodied in the person of the sovereign, but in the person of the leader of a party; and privilege no longer belongs to an aristocracy of birth, but to a majority ruling in Parliament and controlling the State...

Such is the Parliamentary institution, exalted as the summit and crown of the edifice of State. It is sad to think that even in Russia there are men who aspire to the establishment of this falsehood among us; that our professors glorify to their young pupils representative government as the ideal of political science; that our newspapers pursue it in their articles and feuilletons, under the name of justice and order, without troubling to examine without prejudice the working of the parliamentary machine. Yet even where centuries have sanctified its existence, faith already decays; the Liberal intelligentsia exalts it, but the people groans under its despotism and recognizes its falsehood. We may not see, but our children and grandchildren assuredly will see, the overthrow of this idol, which contemporary thought in its vanity continues still to worship.

End of Document 2.2

So let us summarize a few main points based on the foregoing discussion. First, Russia was a massive, multiethnic empire ruled by a tsar or emperor who enjoyed autocratic powers. Autocracy had proved remarkably successful in building the Russian Empire, in making Russia a world power and one of the major players of Europe, and in defeating Napoleonic France in 1812-15. Partly for this reason, the tsarist regime was profoundly conservative and proved reluctant to introduce even modest political reform, such as the plan of Loris-Melikov in 1881. Conservatives like Pobedonstsev expressed the regime's hostile attitude towards constitutions, parliaments, and democracy. At the same time, tsarist leaders recognized the need for modest and cautious change. Most strikingly, they oversaw the emancipation of Russia's serfs (notably *without* a civil war, as had been required in the US to secure the emancipation of slaves), introduced other changes in the Great Reforms, and, albeit reluctantly, began to promote industrialization by the 1880s and 1890s. We also noted that for a time the tsars had proved willing to recognize or create constitutions in Poland and Finland (whether written or unwritten), as well as one for Bulgaria in 1878.

Second, beginning with France in 1789, the idea of revolution became an important feature of European political thought and action. A number of revolutions occurred in Europe over the 19th century, while the appearance of Marxism from around 1848 (see the next chapter) signalled a new form of revolutionary ideology in European politics. There were no successful revolutions in Russia itself in the 19th century, but there were attempts, beginning with the Decembrists in 1825. Other attempts would follow, and it is to those that we turn in the next chapter.

Further Reading:

Charles Breunig and Matthew Levinger, *The Revolutionary Era, 1789-1830*, 3rd ed. New York: W. W. Norton, 2002.

Michael T. Florinsky, *Russia: A History and an Interpretation*, vol. 2. New York: Macmillan, 1953.

Peter Kolchin, *Unfree Labor: American Slavery and Russian Serfdom*. Cambridge, Mass.: Harvard University Press, 1987.

C. Leonard Lundin, "Finland," in Edward C. Thaden, ed., *Russification in the Baltic Provinces and Finland, 1855-191*. Princeton: Princeton University Press, 1981.

Marc Raeff, *Plans for Political Reform in Imperial Russia, 1730-1905*. Englewood Cliffs: Prentice Hall, 1966.

David Saunders, *Russia in the Age of Reaction and Reform, 1801-1881*. New York: Longman, 1992.

Andzrej Walicki, *A History of Russian Thought from the Enlightenment to Marxism*. Stanford: Stanford University Press, 1979.

Cynthia Hyla Whittaker, *Russian Monarchy: Eighteen-Century Rulers and Writers in Political Dialogue*. DeKalb: Northern Illinois University Press, 2003.

CHAPTER 6

THE REGIME'S OPPONENTS AND THE REVOLUTION OF 1905

In the previous chapter, we identified what could be regarded as the first revolutionary challenge to the tsarist order—the Decembrists. In this chapter we investigate other forms of opposition to the autocracy. After briefly noting Russian liberals, we focus on two main strands of radical thought in Russia: populism and Marxism. Though different from one another in important ways, both sought to destroy the tsarist regime through revolution and to create a new order based on the idea of socialism.

Thereafter, we turn to the Revolution of 1905, sometimes called the "dress rehearsal" for the Bolshevik Revolution of 1917. The Revolution, which actually extended from 1905 to 1907, failed to overthrown the tsarist order, but it did introduce important changes to the country's political system. Russia received its first parliament, the Duma, as well as a new version of its Fundamental Law, which now became something closer to a constitution, in that same year. A big question for us is whether Russia had become a constitutional state after 1905.

OPPONENTS OF THE TSARIST REGIME

If conservatives like Pobedonostsev tried to prevent social and political change, there were others in Russia who tried to promote it. Simplifying greatly, we can point to two main strands of opposition to the tsarist regime: a more moderate, liberal opposition (on the one hand) and a more radical, revolutionary opposition (on the other). Liberals were those who wished to convert Russia into a constitutional state with formal political representation (an assembly or parliament of some sort) and strong guarantees for basic civil rights and freedoms (for example of speech, assembly, print, religion, etc.). Some were prepared to accept a constitutional monarchy—that is, they wanted primarily to impose limitations on the tsar—while others preferred to see the creation of a republic in place of the monarchy. Either way, we can say that liberals sought to convert the country's subjects—or at least some of them—into citizens. They were less enthusiastic about rights for women, and they also had considerable doubts about the readiness of peasants, who had been liberated from serfdom only in 1861, to become active citizens. And then there was also all the non-Russian peoples, especially in the south and east of the country, who also did not seem ready for full participation in the political system, because they were considered to be especially "backward," "ignorant, "dark." Thus liberals envisioned a fairly limited group as being involved in politics, but it needs to be remembered that this was the way things had developed in other parts of Europe and the United States. For example, women in France gained the right to vote only in 1945, and in Switzerland—incredibly—only in 1971. Liberals were usually well-educated members of the society: professors, journalists, lawyers, etc. (although of course some of the people in those professions were conservative as well). It was in large measure people like these whom Loris-

Melikov, in his unsuccessful plan of 1881, sought cautiously to enlist in the governance of the country, precisely with the idea that they would cease to oppose the regime if they had the opportunity to participate in politics even a little bit.

Then there were radicals. These were people who wanted to destroy not only the monarchy, but the entire social order that existed in Russia at the time. It is worth emphasizing that even though serfdom had been eliminated, Russia was still a fundamentally unequal society. This was true not only in the sense that there were rich people and poor people—one can find this in virtually any society— but that distinctions between social groups were legally defined. Members of the nobility, for example, enjoyed certain distinct privileges and benefits, ones that peasants did not. This is another way of saying that Russian society did not even pretend to be equal, but was still based on the ideal of hierarchy and inequality. Although historians debate about how poor peasants really were, it is clear that poverty and occasionally famine were serious problems, especially given that the population was growing quite rapidly. In the cities, as industrialization began to take shape, workers—many of whom were really just peasants who had left the villages a short time before—faced long hours and grueling conditions in factories. Radicals were partly reacting to these conditions and came to the conclusion that only a revolution—a violent overthrow of the old order— could actually solve all these social problems.

Most radicals subscribed to ideas of socialism, a new ideology that appeared in response to the changes that Europe was experiencing over the course of the 19th century. The term "socialism" itself was apparently first used in France in 1832. Socialism reflected the combined influence of the French Revolution and the industrial revolution and proposed "that the uncontrolled concentration of wealth and unbridled competition were bound to lead to increasing misery and crises, and that the system must be replaced by one in which the organization of production and exchange would do away with poverty and oppression and bring about a redistribution of the world's goods on a basis of equality." The first socialists, dating to the 1830s and 40s, were labeled utopian socialists, and they envisioned an ideal society "founded on the premise that all human beings possess the same dignity by virtue of their humanity, and that, whatever the innate differences among individuals, they are identical as far as their rights and duties are concerned." Prominent in the writings of the utopian socialists was the idea that people were intended to live in a state of equality and mutual love, and that exploitation and conflict were contrary to nature's order. Less clear was how exactly to construct such a new society, especially as there were people with wealth and privilege who could be expected to oppose the establishment of socialism.[1]

With a bit of delay, these early socialist ideas began to make their way into Russia. In this regard, the Great Reforms occupied an important place. Many in Russia were of course pleased to see the serfs finally emancipated, but they felt that the emancipation had not gone far enough. Most importantly, peasants were not given land as property after their liberation, but rather had to pay for it: that is, they were granted access to a plot of land but had to pay for it over the course of the next 49 years. This meant that—somewhat like the United States after the emancipation of slaves—a modified form of serfdom continued to exist. Many radical Russians were thus dissatisfied with the emancipation and felt that a much more dramatic break with the past was required. These radicals identified precisely with Russia's peasants, seeing them as "the people." Because they sought to defend and promote the interests of peasants, these radicals were known as **populists** and their ideology as **populism**.

These populist radicals were not entirely sure how to promote the revolution that they envisioned. Many initially tried to conduct "agitation" and "propaganda"—that is, they went out into the countryside and tried to convince peasants that their situation would improve only if they destroyed the tsarist order. These efforts at propaganda were not terribly successful, as many peasants viewed these educated radicals as alien and had difficulty understanding their arguments. As these propaganda efforts foundered, some radicals concluded that it might require acts of **terrorism** to compel the tsarist regime to do more. Some even concluded that they should try to assassinate the tsar. The first attempt on the life of the tsar came in 1866 and in some sense signals "the birth of terrorism," as one historian has argued.[2]

---

1   Leszek Kolakowski, *Main Currents of Marxism* (New York, 2005), 150-180 (quotations at 150 and 179).

2   Claudia Verhoeven, *The Odd Man Karakozov: Imperial Russia, Modernity, and the Birth of Terrorism* (Ithaca, 2009).

Eventually terrorist groups formed in Russia. The most prominent, formed in 1879, was **People's Will**, whose members proposed that if they could assassinate the tsar, that would precipitate a mass revolt of the peasantry that would destroy the old order and usher in a new age of socialism. The selection from the party's program below gives some sense for their outlooks. As you read, think about the place that terrorism occupied in the program, and what the members of People's Will thought it would achieve. In what ways did the revolutionaries see their own movement as a product of specific historical circumstances? What relationship did the revolutionaries posit between "the Supreme Power" and the people? Where did they locate sovereignty?

DOCUMENT 2.3

PARTY PROGRAM OF PEOPLE'S WILL, 1879[3]

By fundamental conviction we are socialists and democrats. We are satisfied that only through socialistic principles can the human race acquire liberty, equality, and fraternity; secure the full and harmonious development of the individual as well as the material prosperity of all; and thus make progress. We are convinced that all social forms must rest upon the sanction of the people themselves, and that popular development is permanent only when it proceeds freely and independently, and when every idea that is to be embodied in the people's life has first passed through the people's consciousness and has been acted upon by the people's will. The welfare of the people and the will of the people are our two most sacred and most inseparable principles.

If we look at the environment in which the Russian people are forced to live and act, we see that they are, economically and politically, in a state of absolute slavery. As laborers, they are deprived of all rights. Not only does the actual state of things fail to answer their will; they cannot even think what is good and what is bad for them; the very thought that they can have a will is regarded as a crime against the State. Enmeshed on all sides, they are being reduced to a state of physical degeneration, intellectual stolidity, and general inferiority.

Around the enchained people we see a class of exploiters whom the state creates and protects. The state itself is the greatest capitalistic power in the land; it constitutes the sole political oppressor of the people, and only through its aid and support can the lesser robbers exist.... It is not sanctioned by the people; it rules by arbitrary violence, and it adopts and enforces governmental and economic forms and principles that have nothing whatever in common with the people's wishes and ideals.

In the nation we can see, crushed but still living, its old traditional principles, such as the right of the people to the land, communal and local self-government, freedom of speech and of conscience, and the rudiments of federal organization. These principles would develop broadly, and would give an entirely different and more popular direction to our whole history, if the nation could live and organize in accordance with its own wishes and its own tendencies.

We are of opinion, therefore, that it is our first duty, as socialists and democrats, to free the people from the oppression of the present government, and bring about a political revolution, in order to transfer the supreme power to the nation. By means of this revolution we shall afford the people an opportunity to develop, henceforth, independently, and shall cause to be recognized and supported, in Russian life, many purely socialistic principles that are common to us and to the Russian people.

In view of the stated aim of the party its operations may be classified as follows:

1. *Propaganda and agitation.* Our propaganda has for its object the popularization, in all social classes, of the idea of a political and democratic revolution as a means of social reform, as well as popularization of the party's own program. Its essential features are criticism of the existing order of things, and a statement and explanation of revolutionary methods.... The popular protest may take the form of meetings, demonstrations, petitions, leading addresses, refusals to pay taxes, and so forth.

2. *Destructive and terroristic activity.* Terroristic activity consists in the destruction of the most harmful persons in the Government, the protection of the party from spies, and the punishment

3   Source: George Kennan, *Siberia and the Exile System* (New York, 1891), 495-503.

of official lawlessness and violence in all the more prominent and important cases in which such lawlessness and violence are manifested. The aim of such activity is to break down the prestige of Governmental power, to furnish continuous proof of the possibility of carrying on a contest with the Government, to raise in that way the revolutionary spirit of the people and inspire belief in the practicability of revolution, and finally, to form a body suited and accustomed to warfare.

3. *The organization of secret societies and arrangement of them in connected groups around a single center.* The organization of small secret societies with all sorts of revolutionary aim is indispensable, both as a means of executing the numerous functions of the party and of finishing the political training of its members. In order, however, that the work may be carried on harmoniously, it is necessary that these small bodies should be grouped about one common center, upon the principle either of complete identification or of federal union....

End of Document 2.3

People's Will scored a stunning success on 1 March 1881 when its members managed to assassinate Emperor Alexander II. However, their expectation that this success would precipitate a popular revolt against the autocracy proved misguided. In fact, nothing happened. The peasants did not rise up. Alexander II was succeeded by his more conservative son, Alexander III, who as we saw above rejected even Loris-Melikov's modest plan for political reform. Meanwhile the tsarist police was able to infiltrate and arrest many of the key members of People's Will, with the result that by the mid-1880s the party was only a shadow of itself. For the time being, then, terrorism seemed like a dead-end, and all the hopes that populist radicals had placed in the peasantry came to nothing. For frustrated revolutionaries, it was not at all clear what they should do next.

But as chance would have it, a different variant of socialism was available: **scientific socialism**. The main theorist of this brand of socialism was the German **Karl Marx** (1818-1883), who unquestionably was one the most important thinkers of modern history. Marx had begun writing as early as the 1840s, and he found himself disagreeing with the utopian socialists. Many of these disagreements were deeply philosophical and are too complicated to be addressed here. For us the main difference is that Marx claimed to have discerned fundamental laws of historical development that effectively applied to any and all human societies (although he was thinking primarily about Europe). In this sense, he proposed, his idea of socialism was "scientific" because it was based on laws of human history, just as the laws of physics regulated the physical world. For him, the appearance of socialism was not only desirable, but inevitable: socialism was the endpoint of human history.

How did Marx reach this conclusion? He first of all proposed that **class struggle**—conflict between different social groups—was the driving force of human history. In almost every socio-economic order, one class dominated and exploited another. Thus under the feudal order from which Europe was only then emerging, a landlord class exploited peasants—that is, peasants performed the labor, but landlords received most of the product of their labor. Under capitalism, which was then developing in countries like Britain, France, and Germany, it was the capitalists (or the bourgeoisie) that exploited the working class (or the proletariat). Here again, workers performed much of the labor, but capitalists received most of the benefits. Every society, Marx proposed, essentially had to go through these different stages of historical development: first feudalism (peasants in conflict with landlords), then **capitalism** (proletariat in conflict with bourgeoisie), and then eventually socialism. The transition from one socio-economic order to the next was made possible by revolution. Thus, when class conflict between peasants and landlords became sufficiently great, a revolution would occur to destroy that old order and create a new one in its place. Thus the French Revolution, Marx thought, destroyed the feudal order and created the foundations of the new order of capitalism. Marx and his contemporaries were observing the development of this capitalist stage, and Marx sensed growing conflict between the proletariat and the bourgeoisie. It was in this context that Marx, together with his colleague Friedrich Engels (1821-1895), produced the famous *Communist Manifesto*, which advocated the overthrow of capitalism and the establishment of a socialist society. A few excerpts from that propaganda text should provide some sense for Marx's argument.

DOCUMENT 2.4

KARL MARX AND FRIEDRICH ENGELS, *THE COMMUNIST MANIFESTO* (1848)[4]

The history of all hitherto existing society is the history of class struggles. Freeman and slave, patrician and plebeian, lord and serf, guild-master and journeyman, in a word, oppressor and oppressed, stood in constant opposition to one another, carried on an uninterrupted, now hidden, now open fight, a fight that each time ended, either in a revolutionary reconstitution of society at large, or in the common ruin of the contending classes. The modern bourgeois society that has sprouted from the ruins of feudal society has not done away with class antagonisms. It has but established new classes, new conditions of oppression, new forms of struggle in place of the old ones.

Our epoch, the epoch of the bourgeoisie, possesses, however, this distinct feature: it has simplified class antagonisms. Society as a whole is more and more splitting up into two great hostile camps, into two great classes directly facing each other — Bourgeoisie and Proletariat....

But with the development of industry, the proletariat not only increases in number; it becomes concentrated in greater masses, its strength grows, and it feels that strength more. The various interests and conditions of life within the ranks of the proletariat are more and more equalized, in proportion as machinery obliterates all distinctions of labor, and nearly everywhere reduces wages to the same low level. The growing competition among the bourgeois, and the resulting commercial crises, make the wages of the workers ever more fluctuating. The increasing improvement of machinery, ever more rapidly developing, makes their livelihood more and more precarious; the collisions between individual workmen and individual bourgeois take more and more the character of collisions between two classes. Thereupon, the workers begin to form combinations (Trades' Unions) against the bourgeois; they club together in order to keep up the rate of wages; they found permanent associations in order to make provision beforehand for these occasional revolts. Here and there, the contest breaks out into riots.

Now and then the workers are victorious, but only for a time. The real fruit of their battles lies, not in the immediate result, but in the ever expanding union of the workers....

The essential conditions for the existence and for the sway of the bourgeois class is the formation and augmentation of capital; the condition for capital is wage-labour. Wage-labour rests exclusively on competition between the labourers. The advance of industry, whose involuntary promoter is the bourgeoisie, replaces the isolation of the labourers, due to competition, by the revolutionary combination, due to association. The development of Modern Industry, therefore, cuts from under its feet the very foundation on which the bourgeoisie produces and appropriates products. What the bourgeoisie therefore produces, above all, are its own grave-diggers. Its fall and the victory of the proletariat are equally inevitable....

The immediate aim of the Communists is the same as that of all other proletarian parties: formation of the proletariat into a class, overthrow of the bourgeois supremacy, conquest of political power by the proletariat....

The Communist revolution is the most radical rupture with traditional property relations; no wonder that its development involved the most radical rupture with traditional ideas....

We have seen above, that the first step in the revolution by the working class is to raise the proletariat to the position of ruling class to win the battle of democracy.

The proletariat will use its political supremacy to wrest, by degree, all capital from the bourgeoisie, to centralise all instruments of production in the hands of the State, *i.e.*, of the proletariat organised as the ruling class; and to increase the total productive forces as rapidly as possible....

The Communists disdain to conceal their views and aims. They openly declare that their ends can be attained only by the forcible overthrow of all existing social conditions. Let the ruling classes tremble at

4   https://www.marxists.org/archive/marx/works/1848/communist-manifesto/

a Communistic revolution. The proletarians have nothing to lose but their chains. They have a world to win.

Working Men of All Countries, Unite!

End of Document 2.4

Thus we can say that eventually there were two main strands of radical revolutionary thought in Russia: 1) Populism, which focused on peasants; and 2) **Marxism**, which focused on the working class. Initially, Marx's thought did not seem to be of tremendous relevance to many radicals in Russia. After all, Marx was writing in response to the appearance of a new industrial, capitalist order in the lands in western and central Europe, but in 1848, when the *Communist Manifesto* was written, industrialization was only beginning in Russia. Even in 1867, when Marx completed his most fundamental work, *Capital*, industrialization in Russia was still in its infancy. The working class, or proletariat, remained tiny in comparison to the ocean of peasants that made up Russia's lower classes. The result was that populism continued to be the principal form of radical thought in Russia. This was a radicalism that focused on the peasantry as "the people" and thought in terms of a socialist order that would serve their interests. There was also the hope among Russian radicals that Russia might be able to bypass the miseries of Marx's capitalist stage of development and move directly from the old agrarian order to socialism. From this standpoint, Marx's claim that every society had to go through each stage of historical development—including capitalism—was simply too depressing for many radicals to contemplate, precisely because capitalism in Russia was only *beginning* to appear at the time.[5]

In time, however, Marxism began to seem more relevant. For one, populism did not lead to any successes in destabilizing, let alone overthrowing the tsarist regime. Populists had tried to conduct "agitation and propaganda" among peasants, but peasants had responded with indifference and in some cases had even turned over such agitators to the police. Moreover, as we have seen, populists' turn to terrorism also did not have much success in precipitating revolution. Even when they succeeded in assassinating the emperor in 1881—the head of the entire tsarist system—this did not translate into revolution. Moreover, as time passed, industrialization *did* develop in Russia. As we noted earlier, tsarist leaders were reluctant to embark on such a course but realized that industrialization was necessary for the country to remain competitive with its European rivals. Thus factories appeared in greater numbers in the 1880s and 1890s, and a working class grew as well. True, this proletariat was never large—it made up only a small portion of the population even in 1917—but the fact that it was growing suggested that Marx was right: Russia would have to go through a stage of capitalism like any other society. Thus the failures of populism and the growth of industry combined to make Marxism more attractive to Russian radicals.

Accordingly, Marxist groups began to appear in Russia in the 1880s. The first was the Emancipation of Labor Group, established in 1883, whose members launched a polemical offensive against populism. In their view, the populists were hopeless "utopians" who were wrongly focusing on peasants as potential revolutionary actors. Only the industrial proletariat in Russia could be the force behind a real socialist revolution, they thought. Revolutionaries should therefore focus on that group—the workers—cultivating their consciousness about the need for violent revolution. To be sure, some people managed to maintain both populist and Marxist views simultaneously (both groups wanted revolution and socialism, after all), and there was a good deal of cooperation between the two. But nonetheless certainly by the 1890s we can say that a distinct Russian Marxism, which focused on the urban working class rather than the peasantry, had appeared. Eventually, in 1898, Russian Marxists created the first explicitly Marxist part in Russia: the **Russian Social-Democratic Labor Party (RSDRP)**. As were all political parties before 1905, this one was illegal, which means that its members were constantly subject to arrest, exile, and other forms of repression. It is noteworthy that many of the members of the RSDRP were not

---

5   It is interesting that Marx himself, because he regarded Russia as the bulwark of conservative reaction throughout Europe, strongly supported the terrorist campaign of People's Will in 1879-81.

actually Russian: Poles and Jews were especially prominent in Marxist circles, which was a reflection both of the discrimination that those two groups faced in Russia and of the that fact that Russia was a multiethnic empire, consisting of a wide range of ethnicities, nationalities, and religious groups. Also among the members of the RSDRP was **Vladimir Il'ich Ulianov**, otherwise known as **Lenin** (1870-1924), the central figure of the Russian Revolution. His older brother, Alexander, had been involved in an unsuccessful terrorist attempt on the life of Alexander III and was executed in 1887.

Among the Russian Marxists there were a range of views on revolutionary strategy and organization. For a time, these differences were contained within the one party, but in 1903 the party broke into two factions: the **Bolsheviks** and the **Mensheviks**. There were several reasons for the split, but they were closely related to Lenin's strong views about organization and leadership in the party. In a famous pamphlet entitled *What is to be Done?* (1902), Lenin insisted on the need for "professional revolutionaries" to lead workers to "revolutionary consciousness"—that is, the idea that revolution was necessary and indeed the *only* way for the working class to satisfy its needs and end its misery under industrial capitalism. Marx had proposed that the growing contradictions of capitalism would instill revolutionary consciousness in workers; that is, as their struggles with the bourgeoisie intensified, they would eventually realize that revolution was necessary. Lenin, in contrast, came to the conclusion that this revolutionary consciousness would not appear automatically; rather, in a famous formulation, he contended that left to their own devices workers would attain only "trade-union consciousness"—that is, they might strike for better conditions or higher wages, but they would not by themselves realize that they needed to destroy the capitalist order. Instead, professional revolutionaries were needed to bring this consciousness to the working class. In some sense, Lenin's argument might seem like hair-splitting, but it really concerned how open and democratic the party was to be. Lenin's focus was on a highly disciplined, centralized, and conspiratorial party; his vision was not terribly democratic. Lenin's opponents feared that he and his followers, rather than leading workers, would simply act in their name. Those opponents felt that the party should be an open and democratic one

that helped workers rather that a group of plotters deciding matters for them. As the party split, Lenin's followers became known as Bolsheviks, while their opponents became known as Mensheviks. Both groups were Marxists, but the Mensheviks were arguably the "better" Marxists in the sense that their position was closer to Marx's original one. The Bolsheviks were more flexible and ultimately more impatient and radical. Whereas the Mensheviks worried about trying to make a revolution before the conditions were right, the Bolsheviks had fewer scruples about such things. Thus by 1903 there were in effect two Marxist parties in Russia.

Nor had populism entirely disappeared. In 1901 a new revolutionary party known as the **Socialist Revolutionaries**—or **SRs**—was formed. Although they were familiar with Marx and accepted some of his ideas, the SRs generally drew on the older populist traditions of the 1860s and 1870s. Indeed, some of them even embraced terrorism, and therefore assassinations occurred frequently in the early 20th century.[6] Because they looked to the peasantry—still the country's overwhelming majority—as their constituency, the SRs emerged as an important political group in 1917, although they, too, divided eventually into Left SRs and Right SRs, depending on their degree of radicalism.

For our purposes, then, as Russia entered 1917 we may think in terms of three radical groups: the Bolsheviks and Mensheviks (both Marxists) and the SRs (drawing on populist traditions). Russian liberals, meanwhile, had organized in 1905 into a party known as the **Constitutional Democrats**, or "Kadets." They continued to stand for constitutions, the rule of law, and civil rights, and they occupied a prominent place in the Provisional Government that tried to rule the country in 1917 before the Bolsheviks took power (see the next chapter).

THE REVOLUTION OF 1905: A CONSTITUTIONAL ORDER?

The revolution that finally overthrew the tsarist regime came in 1917, and we will explore that revolution later. But twelve years earlier a "smaller"

---

6   By one estimate, between 1894 and 1917 Russian terrorists killed some 17,000 people (most of them innocent bystanders). Anna Geifman, *Thou Shalt Kill: Revolutionary Terrorism in Russia, 1894-1917* (Princeton, 1995).

revolution occurred, one that had important implications for the last decade of tsarist rule. One historian calls the Revolution of 1905 "the ambiguous revolution," because its results were so inconclusive.[7] On the one hand, the tsarist regime was not overthrown, and by 1907 it had managed to regain its balance and reassert its authority over the country. On the other hand, the regime was forced to make political concessions to the country's population: it permitted the creation of Russia's first popularly elected assembly, the Duma; it proclaimed basic civil rights for the population; and produced a new version of the Fundamental Law that could arguably be regarded as a constitution. In short, the autocracy survived the Revolution of 1905, but it took a different form.

A number of factors contributed to the outbreak of the Revolution of 1905. For one, in the hopes of distracting attention from domestic problems and against the counsel of his more intelligent advisors, Emperor Nicholas II (1894-1917) embarked on a war against Japan in 1904. The supposition was that Russia, as a European country, would easily defeat its Asian rival, which was trying to expand into the same regions of East Asia—Korea and Manchuria—that the Russian coveted. But Japan had been engaged in an extensive program of modernization since 1868 and was therefore able to defeat Russia quite decisively in 1905. (It is a curious fact for our course that Japan introduced a constitution in 1889, whereas Russia did not have one when the war began.) Thus a war that was designed to bolster the tsarist regime instead helped to undermine it.

There were also problems at home. Educated Russians, even moderate ones like liberals, were becoming more and more frustrated by their exclusion from politics. They felt a strong desire to contribute to the country's development and to help solve the country's problems, but the regime continued to treat them like pesky children. In the countryside the population was growing rapidly and there was insufficient land to meet peasants' demand. Peasants also suffered from the remnants of serfdom, which meant that they were not entirely free, while they also had reduced rights compared to other groups in the society and were factually segregated in important ways. In contrast to the

1860s-70s, when populists had agitated among them, peasants were now a good deal more restive and even combustible. Peasant unrest began to appear in parts of the empire already in 1902-03. The cities were also more volatile. Some of them—St. Petersburg, Moscow, Warsaw, Kiev, etc.—had grown quite large with a rapidly growing working class. These workers labored in very difficult conditions, were denied respect from their bosses and foremen, and had no legal right to form unions. Some had also begun to assimilate Marxist ideas, at least on an elementary level. Recall that the regime had been reluctant to promote industrialization because it feared the social instability that might ensue. The situation in the Russian cities by the early 20th century suggests that they had been right to be worried. Finally, many of the country's non-Russians peoples were increasingly dissatisfied with their lack of autonomy and the regime's policy of Russification, which involved the promotion of the Russian language among those who did not otherwise use it. In short, Russia faced numerous problems—both old and new—as it entered the twentieth century. One historian has nicely summarized the situation by remarking, "Russia's entry into the ranks of the industrial powers faced her, at one and the same time, with all of the problems she had inherited from an earlier stage of history as well as those that industrialization itself was creating."[8]

The Revolution of 1905 began in January of that year with the event known as Bloody Sunday. Here factory workers in St. Petersburg, led by a former prison chaplain Father Grigorii Gapon, organized a procession to the Winter Palace (the residence of the tsar) with a petition calling for a wide range of reforms, from constitutional changes and civil rights to an eight-hour workday, workers' insurance, and the right to organize and strike. In effect, these workers were appealing to the tsar to help them, while also vaguely threatening that there would be unrest if he did not. The workers were not able to present the petition, however, as their procession was met with tsarist troops who eventually opened fire on the crowd, killing around 150 people. Tsar Nicholas wrote in his diary that evening (9 January 1905), "A wretched day! In Petersburg there were serious disorders resulting from the desire of workers to make their way to the Winter Palace. Troops were

---

7   Hans Rogger, *Russia in the Age of Modernisation and Revolution, 1881-1917* (New York, 1983).

8   Rogger, *Russia in the Age*, 128.

forced to shoot in various place in the city, there were many killed and injured. Lord, how it is painful and miserable!"[9] Many in Russian society reacted with anger and indignation. Bloody Sunday crystallized discontent throughout much of the society, and even the conservative newspaper *New Times* declared, "It is no longer possible to live in this way."[10]

In subsequent months, unrest developed in various forms. In the countryside, peasants revolted against landlords, burning and looting noble estates, but also organizing and expressing their aspirations in petitions. Strikes engulfed the cities, encompassing not only industrial workers, but also clerical ones, teachers, students, etc. Striking workers began to form councils, or **soviets**, for the purposes of organizing and articulating their demands, which suggested to some radicals that workers were reaching a level of revolutionary consciousness that Marx had predicted. Gradually these various strands of opposition coalesced in a Union of Liberation and a Union of Unions, which called for a constituent assembly to write a new constitution, universal and direct suffrage, and other major reforms. The regime,

for its part, consistently responded with too little too late. For example, in August in 1905, Tsar Nicholas decreed the creation of a consultative assembly (a Duma), which however would only have had the opportunity to advise the tsar, but not any real political power. Almost no one in the opposition considered this to be satisfactory. As the war with Japan went from bad to worse, and as opposition to the regime culminated in a general strike in October of 1905, Nicholas was finally compelled to recognize the need for a more fundamental reform. One of his main advisors, Sergei Witte (1849-1915), remarked that "Russia has outgrown the existing regime and is striving for an order based on civic liberty."[11] Witte accordingly convinced Nicholas II to sign the famous **October Manifesto** creating an assembly, or Duma, with real power and granting basic civil rights to Russia's population.

As you read the October Manifesto think about its constitutional significance. Did it impose limitations on the tsar? Was it possible still to speak of autocracy after the promulgation of the manifesto?

DOCUMENT 2.5

THE OCTOBER MANIFESTO, 1905[12]

17 October 1905

We, Nicholas II, Emperor and Autocrat of All the Russias, Tsar of Poland, Grand Duke of Finland, etc. etc., declare to all our loyal subjects:

The disturbances and unrest in St Petersburg, Moscow and in many other parts of our Empire have filled Our heart with great and profound sorrow. The welfare of the Russian Sovereign is inseparable from the welfare of His people, and national sorrow is His sorrow. The present disturbances could give rise to profound disaffection among the masses, presenting a threat to the unity and integrity of Our State. The oath which We took as Tsar compels Us to use all Our strength, intelligence and authority to put a speedy end to this unrest which is so dangerous for the State. The relevant authorities have been ordered to take measures to deal with direct outbreaks of disorder and violence and to protect people who only want to go about their daily business in peace. However, in view of the need for successful implementation of earlier measures aimed at pacifying the country, we have decided that the work of the higher agencies of government must be coordinated. We have therefore ordered the government to take the following steps in fulfillment of our unbending will:

1. Fundamental civil freedoms will be granted to the population, including real personal inviolability, freedom of conscience, speech, assembly and association.

---

9   *Dnevnik imperatora Nikolaia II, 1890-1906 gg.* (Moscow, 1991), 209.

10   Cited in Rogger, *Russia in the Age*, 209.

11   Cited in Rogger, *Russia in the Age*, 213.

12   Unattributed translation from *Polnoe sobranie zakonov Rossiiskoi Imperii*, 3rd series, vol. XXV/I, no. 26803. Revised (syntax emendations) by Jon Bone.

2. Without halting the elections that have already been scheduled, participation in the Duma will be granted to those classes of the population which are at present deprived of voting powers (insofar as is possible in the short period before its convocation). Further development of a universal franchise will be left to the newly established legislature (i.e., according to the law of August 6, 1905, to the Duma and the Council of State).

3. It is established as an unshakeable rule that no law can come into force without its approval by the State Duma and representatives of the people will be given the opportunity to take real part in the supervision of the legality of authorities appointed by Us.

We call on all true sons of Russia to remember their duty to the homeland, to help put a stop to this unprecedented unrest and, together with this, to devote all their strength to the restoration of peace and quiet in our native land.

Issued at Peterhof on the 17th day of October in the year of Our Lord 1905, in the eleventh year of Our reign.

Original signed by Nicholas II.

End of Document 2.5

By itself, of course, the October Manifesto did not represent a constitution, even if it did have constitutional significance. But shortly after the promulgation of the manifesto, statesmen and legal specialists began to produce a new version of the empire's **Fundamental Law.** A Fundamental Law had existed in Russia since 1832, and no one regarded that as a constitution. The question then becomes whether the revised Fundamental Law in 1906, in conjunction with the October Manifesto, can be regarded as a constitution. Some certainly believe that it was. One historian calls it "Russia's first constitution," while also noting that it was "a highly conservative" one.[13] Yet note how this very "constitution" continued to grant the emperor "supreme autocratic power" (art. 4). Note also how the powers of the new Duma were offset by the power of the more conservative **State Council.** In

short, just as the revolution itself was ambiguous, so too was its constitutional settlement. Here we may note that by the spring of 1906, when the new Fundamental Law were published, the tsarist regime was already beginning to reestablish authority over the country. It would take more than a year to complete that "pacification" of the country, but the Fundamental Law of 1906 reflected the fact that the regime was already in a better position than it had been just a few months earlier, in October of 1905.

As you read through this abridged version of the Fundamental Law of 1906, think about the powers ascribed to the emperor and to other institutions. What kinds of limits are placed on the emperor? How do you think Pobedonostsev would have reacted to the Fundamental Law? How would groups like People's Will and the Russian Marxists?

DOCUMENT 2.6

THE FUNDAMENTAL LAW OF 23 APRIL 1906[14]

1. The Russian State is one and indivisible....

3. The Russian language is the general language of the state, and its use is compulsory in the army, the navy and state and public institutions....

Chapter I. The Essence of the Supreme Autocratic Power

4. The All-Russian Emperor possesses the supreme autocratic power. Not only fear and conscience, but God himself, commands obedience to his authority.

---

13   Paul Bushkovitch, *A Concise History of Russia* (Cambridge, 2012), 285-86.

14   Svod Zakonov Rossiiskoi Imperii, 3rd series, vol. 1, pt. 1 (St Petersburg, 1912), 5-26.

5. The person of the Sovereign Emperor is sacred and inviolable.

6. The same supreme autocratic power belongs to the Sovereign Empress, should the order of succession to the throne pass to a female line...

7. The sovereign emperor exercises power in conjunction with the State Council and the State Duma.

8. The sovereign emperor possesses the initiative in all legislative matters. The Fundamental Laws may be subject to revision in the State Council and State Duma only on His initiative. The sovereign emperor ratifies the laws. No law can come into force without his approval. . . .

9. The Sovereign Emperor approves laws; and without his approval no legislative measure can become law.

10. The Sovereign Emperor possesses the administrative power in its totality throughout the entire Russian state. On the highest level of administration his authority is direct; on subordinate levels of administration, in conformity with the law, he determines the degree of authority of subordinate branches and officials who act in his name and in accordance with his orders.

11. As supreme administrator, the Sovereign Emperor, in conformity with the existing laws, issues decrees for the organization and functioning of diverse branches of state administration as well as directives essential for the execution of the laws.

12 The sovereign emperor takes charge of all the external relations of the Russian State. He determines the direction of Russia's foreign policy. . . .

13. The Sovereign Emperor alone declares war, concludes peace, and negotiates treaties with foreign states.

14 The sovereign emperor is the Commander-in-Chief of the Russian army and navy.

15 The sovereign emperor appoints and dismisses the Chairman the Council of Ministers and individual Ministers....

16. The Sovereign Emperor has the right to coin money and to determine its physical appearance.

17. The Sovereign Emperor appoints and dismisses the Chairman of the Council of Ministers, Ministers, and Chief Administrators of various departments, as well as other officials whose appointment or dismissal has not been determined by law.

18. As supreme administrator the Sovereign Emperor determines the scope of activity of all state officials in accordance with the needs of the state.

19. The Sovereign Emperor grants titles, medals and other state distinctions as well as property rights. He also determines conditions and procedures for gaining titles, medals, and distinctions.

22. Justice is administered in the name of the Sovereign Emperor in courts legally constituted, and its execution is also carried out in the name of His Imperial Majesty.

23. The Sovereign Emperor has the right to pardon the accused, to mitigate the sentence, and even to completely forgive transgressions, including the right to terminate court actions against the guilty and to free them from trial and punishment. Stemming from royal mercy, he also has the right to commute the official penalty and generally to pardon all exceptional cases that are not subject to general laws, provided such actions do not infringe upon civil rights or the legally protected interests of others.

Chapter II. Rights and Obligations of Russian Subjects

28. The defence of the Throne and of the Fatherland is a sacred obligation of every Russian subject. The male population, irrespective of social status, is subject to military service determined by law.

29. Russian subjects are obliged to pay legally instituted taxes and dues and also to perform other obligations determined by law.

30. No one shall be subjected to persecution for a violation of the law except as prescribed by the law.

3I. No one can be detained for investigation otherwise than prescribed by law.

32. No one can be tried and punished other than for criminal acts considered under the existing criminal laws, in force during the perpetration of these acts, provided newly enacted laws do not exclude the perpetrated criminal acts from the list of crimes.

33. The dwelling of every individual is inviolable. Breaking into a dwelling without the consent of the owner and search and seizure are allowed only in accordance with legally instituted procedures.

34. Every Russian subject has the right to freely select his place of dwelling and profession, to accumulate and dispose of property, and to travel abroad without any hindrance. Limits on these rights are determined by special laws.

35. Private property is inviolable. Forcible seizure of immovable property, should state or public need demand such action, is permissible only upon just and decent compensation.

36. Russian subjects have the right to organize meetings that are peaceful, unarmed, and not contrary to the law. The law determines the conditions of meetings, rules governing their termination, as well as limitations on places of meetings.

37. Within the limits determined by law everyone can express his thoughts orally or in writing, as well as distribute these thoughts through publication or other means.

38. Russian subjects have the right to organize societies and unions for purposes not contrary to the law. Conditions for organization of societies and unions, their activity, terms and rules for acquiring legal rights as well as dosing of societies and unions, is determined by law.

39. Russian subjects enjoy freedom of religion. Terms of enjoyment of this freedom are determined by law.

4. Exceptions to the rules outlined in this chapter include localities where martial law is declared or where there exist exceptional conditions that are determined by special laws.

Chapter III. Laws

42. The Russian Empire is governed by firmly established laws that have been properly enacted.

43. Laws are obligatory, without exception, for all Russian subjects and foreigners living within the Russian state.

44. No new law can be enacted without the approval of the State Council and the State Duma, and it shall not be legally binding without the approval of the Sovereign Emperor.

45. Should extraordinary circumstances demand, when the State Duma is not in session, and the introduction of a measure requires a properly constituted legal procedure, the Council of Ministers will submit such a measure directly to the Sovereign Emperor. Such a measure cannot, however, introduce any changes into the Fundamental Laws, or to the organization of the State Council or the State Duma, or to the rules governing elections to the Council or to the Duma. The validity of such a measure is terminated if the responsible minister or the head of a special department fails to introduce appropriate legislation in the State Duma during the first two months of its session upon reconvening, or if the State Duma or the State Council should refuse to enact it into law.

Chapter IV. The State Council, State Duma, and the Scope of Their Activity

56. The Sovereign Emperor, by a decree, annually convenes the session of the State Council and of the State Duma.

57. The Sovereign Emperor determines by a decree the length of the annual session of the State Council and of the State Duma, as well as the interval between the sessions.

58. The State Council is composed of members appointed by His Majesty and of elected members. The total number of appointed members of the Council called by the Emperor to deliberate in the Council's proceedings cannot exceed the total number of the elected members of the Council.

59. The State Duma consists of members elected by the population of the Russian Empire for a period of five years, on the basis of rules governing elections to the Duma.

61. The same person cannot serve simultaneously as a member of the State Council and as a member of the State Duma.

62. The Sovereign Emperor, by a decree, can replace the elected membership of the State Council with new members before its tenure expires. The same decree sets new elections of members of the State Council.

63 The emperor who holds the throne of all Russia cannot profess any religion save the Orthodox. . . .

64. The State Council and the State Duma have equal rights in legislative matters.

68. Those legislative measures that are considered and approved by the State Duma are then submitted to the State Council for its approval. Those legislative measures that have been initiated by the State Council are reviewed by the Council and, upon approval, are submitted to the Duma.

69. Legislative measures that have been rejected either by the State Council or by the State Duma are considered defeated.

70. Those legislative measures that have been initiated either by the State Council or by the State Duma [and approved by both], but which have failed to gain Imperial approval, cannot be resubmitted for legislative consideration during the same session. Those legislative measures that have been initiated by either the State Council or by the State Duma and are rejected by either one of the Chambers, can be resubmitted for legislative consideration during the same session, provided the Emperor agrees to it.

71. Legislative measures that have been initiated in and approved by the State Duma and then by the State Council, and likewise legislative measures initiated and approved by the State Council and then by the State Duma, are submitted by the Chairman of the State Council to the Sovereign Emperor.

81. The Chairman of the Council of Ministers, Ministers, and Heads of various departments, are responsible to the Sovereign Emperor for State administration. Each individual member is responsible for his actions and decisions.

87. If extraordinary circumstances require legislative action whilst the State Duma is in recess, the Council of Ministers may make recommendations direct to the sovereign emperor. Such a measure may not, however, introduce changes in the Fundamental Laws, in the statutes of the State Council and State Duma or in the regulations governing elections to the Council and the Duma. Should such a measure not be introduced into the Duma as a bill within two months from the date of its next meeting . . . it loses force. . . .

End of Document 2.5

By 1907, the Revolution of 1905 was essentially over. For all of its weaknesses, the tsarist regime managed to defeat the revolution in three separate stages. First, it split the opposition by issuing the October Manifesto. Before the manifesto, a huge spectrum of Russian society was mobilized against the regime. The granting of the manifesto satisfied the more conservative segments of the opposition. They ceased attacking the regime and began to think about how to make the most of the parliament and the civil rights that had been granted. More radical forces continued to oppose the regime vigorously, but because the opposition was now divided, it was less effective. This gave the regime the opportunity to regain its balance. Thus when members of the working class began an armed insurrection in December of 1905, the regime was already in a better position to repress it—which it did forcefully. Thus by the end of 1905, the urban revolution had been largely defeated.

Subduing the countryside took a good deal longer—most of 1906. But through the organization of punitive campaigns against insurgent peasants and the creation of military courts to try and rapidly punish insurrectionists, the regime pacified the villages as well. Thus the rural revolution had also been defeated by the end of 1906 or so.

Finally, the regime also managed to tame the parliamentary threat. In organizing elections to the Duma, tsarist statesmen had weighted the votes substantially in favor of the nobility (32.7% of electors), who could be expected to support the regime, and the peasantry (42.3% of electors), who were presumed to be essentially conservative.[15] In fact, in elections from February to April of 1906, peasants elected quite radical delegates to the Duma, and those delegates began agitating for a law that would transfer land from the nobility to the peasantry without compensation. Tsarist leaders thus realized that they would not be able to work with the Duma, and Emperor Nicholas used a legal provision to close the first Duma and call elections

---

15 Town dwellers had 22.5% of the electors and workers only 2.5%.

for a new one. The second elections produced a Duma that was even more radical than the first. It met between February and June of 1907, but the tsar's advisors eventually concluded that it would be impossible to work with this Duma as well. The solution, proposed by Prime Minister **Peter Stolypin** (1862-1911) was to close the second Duma and unilaterally change the electoral law between that and the next Duma. This was a flagrant violation of the Fundamental Law and has therefore been referred to as a "coup."[16] But because the urban and rural revolutions had already been defeated, there was no real force that could prevent the regime from acting in this fashion. The third Duma was accordingly a good deal more conservative than the previous two, even though it still included some oppositional delegates and parties. Thus by the middle of 1907, the political crisis in Russia was essentially over.

Still, there had been important changes. Even if the regime had manipulated the electoral law, the country still had a representative assembly that was elected by some 20-25 million people. Political parties were now legal, as was the establishment of unions among workers. And even though the autocracy continued to rule in an arbitrary fashion in many ways, nonetheless certain basic civil rights had now been secured. Recall earlier (chapter 5) how we noted that the Revolution of 1905 was "ambiguous." This characterization nicely describes the combination of accomplishments and setbacks that came out of the events of 1905-07.

CONCLUSION

As we saw in the previous chapter, the idea of revolution became an important feature of European political thought and action in the 19th century. Gradually, the idea of socialism appeared as a new form of revolutionary ideology in European politics, and by the second half of the century, most European radicals aspired to socialism in one form or another. Revolutionary thought initially took the form of "utopian socialism," which was then largely replaced by Marxism as the industrial capitalist order appeared.

Russian radicals also embraced the ideal of socialism, and their thought took two distinct forms. First was populism, which appeared in the 1860s and focused on the interests of the peasantry, partly because they were the vast majority of the country's population. One the one hand, populists engaged in agitation and propaganda; on the other they embraced terrorism. The greatest success of the terrorists was the assassination of Alexander II in 1881. The second form of Russian radical thought was Marxism, which focused on the working class rather than the peasantry. Marxists believed that capitalism was inevitable, that it was appearing in Russia as well, but that it would also be destroyed eventually by a socialist revolution. The goal of Marxists should thus be to prepare such a revolution.

The tsarist regime found itself in grave danger in 1905, when a series of factors converged to mobilize large segments of the population against it. By October of that year the crisis had reached such a state that that Emperor Nicholas II issued the October Manifesto, granting basic civil rights to the population and creating a new parliament with real powers. The regime also changed the Fundamental Law in order to reflect this new reality. But Nicholas had made these concessions only under great duress, and he sought to undermine them as the regime regained its footing. The results of the Revolution of 1905 were highly ambiguous. The regime had made significant compromises but had also managed to end the revolution and take back some—though by no means all—of what it had granted. It apparently would take a bigger crisis to end the tsarist regime, but as it happened just such a crisis was by then looming on the horizon: World War I.

---

16   See article 45 of the Fundamental Law above.

Further Reading:

Abraham Ascher, *The Revolution of 1905: Authority Restored.* Stanford: Stanford University Press, 1992.

Paul Bushkovitch, *A Concise History of Russia.* Cambridge: Cambridge University Press, 2012.

Anna Geifman, *Thou Shalt Kill: Revolutionary Terrorism in Russia, 1894-1917.* Princeton: Princeton University Press, 1995.

Leszek Kolakowski, *Main Currents of Marxism.* New York: W. W. Norton, 2005.

Hans Rogger, *Russia in the Age of Modernisation and Revolution, 1881-1917.* New York: Longman, 1983.

Marc Szeftel, *The Russian Constitution of April 23, 1906.* Brussels: Librarie Encyclopédique, 1976.

Claudia Verhoeven, *The Odd Man Karakozov: Imperial Russia, Modernity, and the Birth of Terrorism.* Ithaca: Cornell University Press, 2009.

Avrahm Yarmolinsky, *Road to Revolution: A Century of Russian Radicalism.* New York: Macmillan, 1956.

CHAPTER 7

THE REVOLUTIONS OF 1917 & THE NEW COMMUNIST STATE

The Russian Revolution of 1917 was undoubtedly one the most important events of the 20th century. Its result was the destruction of an autocratic regime that had evolved from the 14th century and the overthrow of a dynasty, the Romanovs, that had ruled the country since 1613. The revolution created a communist dictatorship and a new country— Union of Soviet Socialist Republics, the USSR—that played a critical role in the world's history up until its collapse in 1991. The leaders of the new country, the Bolsheviks, engaged in a grand experiment that inspired many people throughout the globe while generating great hostility among others. In a word, it is impossible to understand the 20th century without some comprehension of the Russian Revolution of 1917.

In this chapter we attempt to account for that revolution of 1917. We first consider developments in Russia from around 1907, when the Revolution of 1905 ended, to 1918, when the new rulers of Russia, the Bolsheviks, produced their first constitution and constructed a new "dictatorship of the proletariat." One point should be highlighted immediately: Russia actually had *two revolutions* in 1917 rather than just one. The first brought down the tsarist regime in favor of a new democratic republic under the guidance of a temporary **Provisional Government**. This was the **February Revolution**. That government struggled to deal with the country's many problems, the biggest of which was that Russia, like most of Europe, was in the midst of World War I. In the second revolution the

Bolsheviks overthrew the Provisional Government and established a new communist state unlike anything the world had seen before. This was the **October Revolution**. In effect, the Bolsheviks embarked on a massive experiment in social engineering, whose most remarkable phase was the two decades or so between 1917 and the outbreak of World War II in 1939. Our goals in this chapter will be to explore and understand a) the fall of the tsarist regime in February; b) the factors leading to the Bolsheviks' seizure of power in October; c) the Bolsheviks' initial efforts to create a new communist dictatorship; and d) the place of the first Soviet constitution of 1918 in that process.

WORLD WAR AND THE FAILURE OF THE TSARIST STATE

Historians debate about whether the Russian Empire might have survived had it not been for the **First World War**. On the one hand, important agrarian reforms were introduced by Stolypin, the main figure behind the "coup" of 1907, and perhaps these, along with peasant migration to Siberia, had the potential to solve main elements of the agrarian question. Indeed, Russia seemed in some ways to be weathering the difficult transition from an agrarian order to a modern industrial one as well as other countries had or would, and perhaps after some more years of peace a new social and political order would have emerged. On the other hand, the autocracy continued to resist political reform and, with the assassination of Stolypin in 1911, lost one of its most capable statesmen. By 1912, labor unrest began to increase again, while the rise of a politicized right wing in the country looked ominous as well. In the end, we will never know what might have happened, since the war intervened to set Russia—and all of Europe—on a new and highly destructive course leading to political extremism, strife, and mass killing for the next three decades.

Still, the war itself was hardly a coincidence for Russia. Caught up in a dangerous rivalry with Austria-Hungary over the Balkans in southeastern Europe and faced with threats from neighboring Germany, the tsarist leadership finally decided that it was better to commit to war nobly than to admit diplomatic defeat at the hand of its rivals. Thus when Russia declared war on Germany and Austria-Hungary in late July 1914, its leadership was fully aware of the potential scope of the war to come. As the war spread rapidly to encompass all of the major powers of Europe—from Russia in the east to Great Britain in the west—the continent became engulfed in an unprecedented conflict featuring all of the power of industrialized warfare. Some 35 million people were killed as a result.

Russia entered the war with the largest army in Europe, but one that was not exceptionally modern or well led. The Russian army performed somewhat better than it has often been given credit for, but it had to fight on three separate fronts—against Germany and Austria-Hungary in the west and against the Ottoman Empire in the south. It scored some successes, but a major German offensive in the spring of 1915 occupied Russian Poland and the Baltic region. Russia's economy also faced serious challenges. The country had to devote many of its resources—food, clothing, train cars, machinery, etc.—to the war effort, which means that there was less to be had at home. If there was a certain degree of patriotism when the war began, this waned as the years went by. Winters became especially difficult given the cold, the breakdown of transport, and the lack of food. It is worth underscoring that Russia's rivals, Germany and Austria-Hungary, were managing only a little bit better than Russia itself. In other words, the war imposed great hardships on all Europeans, but it was ultimately Russia that began to collapse first, in February of 1917.

THE FEBRUARY REVOLUTION

Thus as 1917 began, Russia had been fighting a world war for two-and-a-half-years, with all the sacrifice that this entailed and with a significant portion of the empire occupied by German forces. The Revolution of 1905 had ended, but few of the problems that caused it had been solved. Radicals hoped to overthrow and destroy the regime; liberals aspired, at a minimum, to transform it into a constitutional state; and even some conservatives became disenchanted with Nicholas II and his entourage. For his part, Nicholas clung to the myth of the ruler as a saintly and blessed father to his people, which blinded him to the dissatisfaction that was growing. As one historian writes, "Unable to believe that his power was not God-given or that the true Russian people were not as devoted to him as he felt he was to them, he was unable to see coming the storm that swept him and the monarchy away."[1]

The February Revolution grew directly out of the hardships of war. Soldiers in the trenches felt that they were treated less as human beings than as fodder for the opponent's cannons. After more than two years, morale was low. People in the cities were suffering as well. Inflation eroded wages, so that people felt poorer even as they earned the same nominal wage. The war disrupted the labor market, since now many young men, instead of contributing productively to the economy as workers and peasants, were at the front needing food, clothing, and weapons. This created shortages back in the cities, which meant that urban dwellers—frequently women—had to stand in long lines for basic necessities. It thus became more and more difficult both to obtain and to afford food.

It was precisely because of the food issue that the revolution began. Exhausted and frustrated by food shortages, thousands of women textile workers went out onto the street to protest beginning 23 February 1917. In part, they were observing International Women's Day,[2] but the core issue was food. Male workers, many of whom were already

---

1   Mark D. Steinberg, *Voices of Revolution, 1917* (New Haven, 2001), 40.

2   First celebrated in the early 20th century, this was a socialist holiday that focused on equal rights for women, including suffrage (most women in most countries still could not vote). The holiday is celebrated on 8 March, but because Russia used a different calendar at the time, the day fell on 23 February there.

striking for better pay in response to inflation, joined in quickly as well. By 25 February most of the industrial enterprises of the Russian capital, now named **Petrograd**, were shut down. Although the demonstrators remained largely peaceful, many carried makeshift weapons—metal tools, knives, pieces of iron, etc.—and it was clear that they were likely to resist any effort to repress them.

Nicholas himself had become commander of the army in 1915 and was therefore away at the front. As his officials in Petrograd reported on the disturbances, he failed to recognize their seriousness, concluding that a show of force and an order to discontinue the Duma would restore order. However, the soldiers who were called upon to shoot at the demonstrators began to waver. Initially they followed orders to shoot, but they were obviously disturbed by the idea of firing on crowds whose frustrations seemed wholly understandable and worthy of sympathy. By the morning of 27 February, many were in mutiny—they refused to fire on the crowds and instead went over to the side of the demonstrators. Perhaps in peacetime, Nicholas's military advisors would have advocated further repression, but they soon came to the conclusion that Russia would not be able to continue the war against Germany and Austria-Hungary unless some kind of new government were created—one that enjoyed greater legitimacy among the population. In effect, this amounted to a mutiny of Nicholas's own military command, and by 2 March Nicholas concluded that he would have to abdicate—give up the throne that he had occupied since 1894. In effect, one could say that Nicholas was given a choice between Russia and autocracy: would he insist on his autocratic rights, with the result that Russia would go down in defeat, as his generals were now suggesting? Or would he abandon autocracy so that Russia could fight the war more effectively? Given this dilemma, Nicholas chose Russia. He gave up the throne and became a private citizen. Nicholas actually abdicated in favor of his brother, who himself refused the throne. Thus power was not really transferred from Nicholas to anybody (or anything) else, but instead simply dropped. The rest of the story of 1917, writes one historian, "was partly about who would (or could) pick up power and hold on to it."[3]

With political power virtually lying on the street, two political forces emerged to deal with the crisis. The first was a **Provisional Government**, which consisted mostly of liberal leaders associated with the Duma. These leaders were deeply committed to the ideals of legality and legitimacy, and therefore they did not regard themselves as having taken power. Rather, they recognized that someone had to fill the political vacuum that had suddenly appeared, or else there would be chaos and Russia would simply collapse in the face of a German military advance. Thus the Provisional Government was emphatically provisional and viewed itself as temporary. Its principal purpose was to restore and maintain some degree of order and to ensure that Russia not collapse entirely in the context of war. The supposition was that in relatively short order elections would be held for a **Constituent Assembly** that would write a constitution for Russia and resolve all the big questions of the day. What this meant was that the Provisional Government's actions were characterized by much hesitation, as its leaders felt that they were not really authorized to make important decisions. This reticence was to undermine the Provisional Government, making it incapable of preventing the Bolsheviks' seizure of power.

The second political force was the **Petrograd Soviet**. Recall that in the Revolution of 1905, workers' councils, or soviets, had begun to appear in various parts of the country. In 1917, these began to appear again. Their goal was to reflect and promote the interests of workers and other lower-class elements, who did not entirely trust the liberal leaders of the Provisional Government. Soviets also began to appear among soldiers at the front—in order to defend the interests of the rank-and-file with respect to the military officers—and even among peasants in the countryside. A citywide soviet also appeared quickly in the Russian capital and became known, appropriately, as the Petrograd Soviet. Workers and other lower-class elements elected deputies to represent them in the Petrograd Soviet, while the Soviet's leadership consisted primarily of socialist intellectuals—initially they were mainly Mensheviks. One could think of the Soviet as a kind of parliament for the lower classes, with the idea that this institution would ensure that nothing that the Provisional Government did was contrary to the interest of workers, soldiers, and peasants. While leaders of the Petrograd Soviet were socialists, they generally did not believe that Russia was ready for socialism. Recall that Marx proposed that every

---

3   Steinberg, *Voices of Revolution*, citations at 56.

society had to go through *one* revolution to reach the stage of capitalism and a *second* one to get to socialism. The Petrograd Soviet's leaders thought that February was the first revolution (a "bourgeois revolution"), which would establish a republic and introduce extensive democratic reforms and civil rights. A "socialist revolution" would follow later. So the Petrograd Soviet, too, was characterized by considerable hesitation. Its leaders felt that the liberals of the Provisional Government should lead the country for the moment, while the soviets should exert pressure to ensure that lower-class interests were not ignored.

So here was the situation, then: Duma leaders understood that the Soviet could control the crowd in Petrograd and therefore the Russian lower classes as a whole, whereas they could not. They accordingly sought the Soviet's endorsement of their state authority. Leaders of the Petrograd Soviet, for their part, sought mainly to influence the policies of the new government without actually taking responsibility for them. This curious arrangement of the co-existence of the Provisional Government and the Petrograd Soviet became known as **dual power**.

Not everyone was prepared to accept this arrangement, though. Lenin and the Bolsheviks, in particular, proved hostile to it. Like many other revolutionary leaders at the time, Lenin himself was in exile—in Switzerland—when the February Revolution occurred. He was of course eager to return to Russia, but this meant going across either German or Austro-Hungarian territory. The Germans, who generally did everything they could to destabilize their enemies internally, quickly realized that it could be useful to facilitate the return to Russia of revolutionaries like Lenin. They accordingly allowed him to pass across German territory, after which Lenin made his way through Sweden to return in Petrograd in April of 1917. Shortly after his arrival, Lenin provided a radical list of statements that became known as the **April Theses**. In them, Lenin advocated a rapid move towards socialist, and not merely bourgeois, democracy. He thus declared that the Provisional Government should be rejected entirely and all the "falsity of its promises" be exposed; that political power should be transferred from the bourgeoisie to the proletariat as soon as possible; that Russia should seek to establish not a parliamentary republic, but a soviet one—that is, the transfer of all power immediately to the soviets. In short, rather than recognizing the Provisional Government, the lower classes and socialists should seek as quickly as possible to establish a soviet socialist republic.[4] Even some fellow Bolsheviks were surprised by the radicalism of Lenin's pronouncements and his readiness to take power as soon as possible. Still, the Bolsheviks remained a minority even in the Petrograd Soviet, so few were yet prepared to endorse such a radical program.

The Provisional Government could certainly claim some successes in establishing a new and democratic Russia. It quickly sought to realize the ideals of unity, citizenship, and freedom by freeing political prisoners and exiles; proclaiming core freedoms of speech, press, assembly; granting the workers the right to strike; eliminating flogging (corporal punishment), exile to Siberia, and the death penalty; abolishing all forms of discrimination based on nationality or religious belonging; and granting women the right to vote and hold public office. The Provisional Government also began to prepare elections for a Constituent Assembly based on universal, secret, direct, and equal suffrage.[5] There are good reasons for concluding that, for at least a brief time, Russia became the most democratic country in the world.

At the same time, there were many things that the Provisional Government could not do, precisely because it was provisional. Peasants, for example, were eager to acquire land and even began simply to seize it from landlords—without, of course compensating them for it. Were these land seizures legitimate? Should peasants gain immediate access to land? If so, should landowners be compensated? Similarly thorny questions revolved around the war: Should Russia continue to fight the war, now as a new democratic country? Should it fight merely a defensive war, designed to prevent further German advances? Should it launch an offensive to take back the territory that it lost in 1915? Should it sign a peace treaty with the Germans as soon as possible? No less complicated was the national question. Recall that Russia consisted of many ethnic and national groups, not just Russians. Many of those peoples had begun to seek greater autonomy and in a few cases even independence. Should they remain part of Russia? Should Russia grant autonomy or recognize

---

4   The full April Theses are at https://www.marxists.org/archive/lenin/works/1917/apr/04.htm.

5   Steinberg, *Voices of Revolution*, 62.

independence? Would Russia be a federation in order to accommodate these national differences? Workers had big questions, too: Would they be given a greater say in how factories were run? What kinds of rights would they enjoy in the new Russia? Who would actually control and run industry? Finally, there were basic questions about the nature of the new Russian state. Would it be a constitutional monarchy? A republic? Would it be a centralized state or a federation? On all of these questions, the Provisional Government's inclination was to defer to the Constituent Assembly, which would write a new constitution and address these problems. But until such an Assembly could convene, there were no answers. Instead, people were told to wait.

Yet it did not take long for people to become impatient. The war dragged on, and the hardships accumulated. In July of 1917, the Provisional Government ordered a new offensive, but that quickly stalled and began to entail serious human losses—an estimated 200,000 casualties. Army intelligence reports noted that "the influence of Bolshevik ideas is spreading very rapidly [among soldiers]. To this must be added a general weariness, an irritability, and a desire for peace at any price."[6] The army gradually began to disintegrate as soldiers simply decide unilaterally to make their way back home. As noted earlier, peasants simply began taking land from landowners and had no intention of offering any compensation. In their view the land came from God, belonged to those who tilled it, and could not be bought and sold. One peasant wrote in a letter, "Land is the *common and equal legacy of all people* and so cannot be the object of private ownership by individual persons." He added that while confusion about the status of land in the new Russia mounted, "impatience over our landlessness mounts, too."[7] The more distant parts of the Russian Empire, like Finland and Poland, quickly sought independence, but over the course of 1917 even as core a part of the empire as Ukraine began moving towards independence as well. There was a limit to how long Ukrainians would wait for resolution of the national question. As the Provisional Government refrained from addressing these problems—precisely because it *was* provisional—

and as elections to the Constituent Assembly were postponed in the context of the continuing wartime crisis, ordinary people in Russian became more and more impatient.

Moreover, the more moderate socialist parties became contaminated by their association with the Provisional Government. Recall that moderate socialists (the Mensheviks and the more conservative wing of the SRs) believed that Russia was not yet ready for socialism, and that it was best to have power in the hands of the Provisional Government for the time being. They also feared what would happen if, as Russia began to collapse internally, the Germans were to launch a new offensive against Russia. It seemed possible that Germany might defeat Russia and then impose on the country an authoritarian government that would end the revolution. Given these concerns, many socialists felt that the Provisional Government needed to be bolstered for the time being. A major crisis in April of 1917 induced some of the more moderate socialist parties to participate in the Provisional Government in order to bolster its authority and also to shape its policies. Thus several moderate socialists became ministers in the Provisional Government, while **Alexander Kerensky**, a Right SR, became head of the government in July. The result is that to the extent that the Provisional Government proved unsuccessful, moderate socialists were now complicit in those failures.

Meanwhile, the Bolsheviks clearly and forcefully rejected the Provisional Government as "bourgeois" and refused to join its ranks. The Bolsheviks were therefore not associated with the Provisional Government's failures in addressing the main questions of the day. The Bolsheviks also developed simple slogans to express popular aspirations and dissatisfactions. "All power to the soviets!" was one such slogan. "Land, Bread, Peace" was another. Given the impatience, fatigue, and frustration of Russia's lower classes, one can imagine how such slogans would be attractive. Indeed, over the course of 1917 the Bolsheviks gradually became more popular. A growing number of lower-class Russians found their arguments appealing. At the same time, right-wing and conservative groups also became more active, with some convinced that a military dictatorship might be necessary to save Russia from chaos and destruction. Political crises in mid and late summer served primarily to intensify the polarization of Russia and the attraction of more radical solutions

---

6   Robert Weinberg and Laurie Bernstein, *Revolutionary Russia: A History with Documents* (Oxford University Press, 2011), 49.

7   Weinberg and Bernstein, *Revolutionary Russia*, 48 and 49.

to a growing segment of the lower classes.

THE OCTOBER REVOLUTION

Indeed, it was an attempted but unsuccessful coup from the right that moved things rapidly in the Bolsheviks' favor. The precise course of events and the nature of motivations remain unclear, but the coup failed because of the unreliability of the troops called upon to execute it, and because workers in Petrograd organized to resist it. At the same time, the prospect of a right-wing coup that might effectively end the revolution radicalized many in the urban lower classes still further. The Bolsheviks had not actually done very much in resisting the coup, but because they were the most radical party, and because they were not tainted by association with the Provisional Government, popular opinion swung more and more in their favor. The Bolsheviks accordingly became a majority in the Petrograd Soviet by late August (and in the Moscow Soviet by early September).

The big question for the Bolsheviks, then, was whether (and/or when) to attempt an armed insurrection to take power. The Bolshevik leadership was far from united in answering this question. Lenin, then in temporary exile in Finland, argued that the time was right and that the Bolsheviks should prepare such an insurrection. Others in the party thought this would be irresponsible and doubted whether the Bolsheviks would be able to hold onto power alone. Still others wavered or thought that power could be transferred in a quasi-legal or non-violent fashion.

A central issue here was timing. Recall that there were essentially two co-existing institutions exercising political power in an uneasy relationship labeled "dual power": the Provisional Government and the Petrograd Soviet. By the fall of 1917, because of its inability to address the country's pressing problems and its uncertain relationship to the attempted coup, the Provisional Government had lost most of its legitimacy. Its days were probably numbered no matter what the Bolsheviks did. This left the Petrograd Soviet. Without any action on the part of the Bolsheviks, the most likely outcome in 1917 would have been the declaration of "Soviet democracy"—that is, a new socialist republic centered on the Petrograd Soviet. That republic, and the Petrograd Soviet, would have included all

the socialist parties—not only the Bolsheviks, but also the Mensheviks, the SRs, and smaller socialist groups. An **All-Russian Congress of Soviets**—designed to bring representatives from all soviets across the country—was planned for 25 October. It seemed likely that this congress would authorize a full transfer of power to the Petrograd Soviet, thus ending the existence of the Provisional Government.

It was precisely for this reason that Lenin regarded it as crucial that Bolsheviks act before the Congress of Soviets convened, so that the overthrow of the Provisional Government could be presented to the congress as an accomplished fact. He perceived a unique opportunity for the Bolsheviks to take power before the Congress declared the transfer of power from the provisional Government to the soviets. As he wrote already in September, "Having obtained a majority in the Soviet of Workers' and Soldiers' Deputies of both capitals [the Moscow and Petrograd Soviets], the Bolsheviks can and *must* take power into their hands." He continued, "it would be naïve to wait for a 'formal' majority on the side of the Bolsheviks; no revolution ever waits for this…. History will not forgive us if we do not assume power now."[8] Lenin continued that argument in October. "Dear Comrades! Events so clearly indicate the task for us that any delay would be tantamount to a crime…. The Bolsheviks do not have the right to wait for the congress of soviets, they must take *power immediately.*"[9]

The Bolshevik leadership eventually agreed with Lenin, and the insurrection began on 24 October. Bolshevik supporters began to occupy key governmental institutions, took control of the railways and telegraph, and surrounded the Winter Palace, where the Provisional Government was convening. There was little resistance. By the next day (25 October) the Bolshevik coup was essentially over, though the palace was taken—again, without much resistance—only that evening. Even so, as word went out to the provinces, the most common explanation was that the soviets had taken power, not the Bolsheviks as such. The Bolshevik proclamation on 25 October "To the Citizens of Russia" seemed to confirm this picture: "The Provisional Government has been deposed. State power has passed into the hands of the organ of the Petrograd Soviet of Workers'

---

8   Richard Sakwa, *The Rise and Fall of the Soviet Union, 1917-1991* (London, 1999), 45.

9   Sakwa, *Rise and Fall*, 48.

and Soldiers' deputies, the Military Revolutionary Committee, which leads the Petrograd proletariat and garrison." The proclamation likewise declared "the establishment of Soviet power." It did *not* state that the Bolsheviks, specifically, had taken power.[10] But when the Bolsheviks declared the formation of a new government, the Council of People's Commissars (**Sovnarkom**) with only Bolshevik members, it was clear that precisely the Bolsheviks had taken power, and they had no intention of sharing it with any other parties in the Petrograd Soviet.[11]

Let us summarize. Because they refused to compromise with the Provisional Government and the "bourgeoisie," and because they offered the most immediate solutions to Russia's pressing problems (summarized in slogans such as "All power to the soviets" and "Land, Bread, Peace") the Bolsheviks acquired more and more support over the course of 1917. In this sense, one could say that they rode to power on a wave of genuinely popular support. On the other hand, instead of allowing power to pass from the Provisional Government to a united democratic socialist government based on all the parties represented in the soviets, they had seized power for themselves, cutting others out of the deal. For a long time historians have argued about whether the Bolshevik Revolution was a genuinely popular revolution or a classic coup, but the best answer seems to be that there were elements of both. Without broad support in the urban centers, the Bolsheviks could never have taken power. But they also acted in a conspiratorial fashion so as to deny a role in the new government to other socialist parties. Looking more broadly, we should highlight that the Bolsheviks came to power as a minority party. True, they had attained majorities in the Petrograd Soviet by late August. But Petrograd was not Russia, and in the countryside peasants were more inclined to support the SRs than the Bolsheviks. This did not bother the Bolsheviks, however. As the historian Sheila Fitzpatrick writes, "in terms of the mandate to rule, [the Bolsheviks] could and did argue that it was not the population as a whole that they claimed to represent. They had taken power in the name of the working class"—still a small minority of Russia's

population.[12] Marx's colleague Friedrich Engels had once cautioned that a socialist party taking power prematurely might find itself isolated and compelled to create a repressive dictatorship. This, arguably, is the position in which the Bolsheviks now found themselves.

BUILDING THE "DICTATORSHIP OF THE PROLETARIAT"

One might be tempted to think that once the Bolsheviks had taken power in late October of 1917 the revolution was essentially complete. In fact, it was really only starting. It was far from clear what would happen next. Not surprisingly, non-Bolshevik parties were not happy about what the Bolsheviks had done, and they were not prepared to recognize the Bolshevik coup. The Bolshevik seizure had been largely an urban phenomenon, and while this Bolshevik success was replicated in some provincial cities, it did not occur everywhere. The peasantry, moreover, generally supported the SRs rather than the Bolsheviks (though the two parties' programs on land were almost identical), while in some of the non-Russian regions nationalist parties (especially in Ukraine) proved quite strong and thus emerged as alternatives to the Bolsheviks. Non-Bolsheviks accordingly criticized the Bolsheviks in newspaper articles and pamphlets, while those most hostile to the Bolsheviks began thinking about resisting them with force of arms.

Some opponents of the Bolsheviks placed their hopes in the Constituent Assembly. Recall that this assembly was supposed to convene to write a new constitution for Russia, but the elections were constantly postponed because the country was so deeply in crisis. In the event, elections were held only in November of 1917, not long *after* the Bolsheviks had taken power.[13] The results were curious: the Bolsheviks received a full 25% of the popular vote—a good chunk, but far from a majority. The SRs fared the best, receiving around 40%, while the Mensheviks and Kadets picked up smaller portions. The Bolsheviks of course had hoped that the Constituent Assembly

---

10   Sakwa, *Rise and Fall*, 54.

11   In fact for a brief time the Bolshevik government included some Left SRs, but by early 1918 they had left the government.

12   Sheila Fitzpatrick, *The Russian Revolution*, 2nd ed. (Oxford, 1994), 67.

13   Elections had been fully scheduled for 17 September 1917, but the Provisional Government had postponed them again to 12 November, some 2-3 weeks after the Bolshevik seizure of power.

would legitimize their coup (it was for this reason that they allowed the elections to occur), but now they were faced with the clear fact that they were a minority (if a substantial one). In the end, though, the Bolsheviks were revolutionaries and were not going to allow election results to stand in their way. The Constituent Assembly managed to meet for one day (5 January 1918), but when it refused to endorse the program of Bolshevik government, the Bolsheviks simply declared the assembly disbanded on the grounds that it could "only play the role of justifying the struggle of the bourgeois counter-revolution for the overthrow of Soviet power." This dissolution of the assembly was imposed by force, and indeed later that evening two leading Kadet deputies were beaten to death by Bolshevik sailors.[14]

Yet even the Bolsheviks themselves seem to have been uncertain about what the "dictatorship of the proletariat" would mean in practice. Marx himself had not written a great deal about what socialism would actually look like or how it was to be established. There was also an international dimension: the Bolsheviks did not see their revolution as being limited to Russia, but rather as the start of "an all-European revolution." At least for the first several years, their operative assumption was that similar revolutions would occur shortly in other European countries, most importantly in Germany. At one point Lenin declared explicitly, "It is an absolute truth that without a German revolution we are doomed."[15] So the Bolsheviks, like most other revolutionaries, found themselves improvising.

To be sure, they did a few things immediately. First, they issued a "Decree on Peace," directed to people throughout the world, calling for an immediate end to the war. And sure enough, the Bolsheviks began discussions with the German military leadership that resulted in a cease-fire in December of 1917 and a peace treaty at Brest-Litovsk in March of 1918. Although the Bolsheviks were essentially required to acknowledge Russian defeat in World War I, they had at least ended the war. Second, the Bolsheviks issued a decree on land, which abolished, without compensation, "land ownership by the gentry" and transferred lands owned by the nobility, the royal family, and

monasteries to peasant soviets. As we know, peasants had already been seizing land for themselves, so the Bolsheviks were merely legitimizing what was already happening. Next, the Bolsheviks sought to empower workers by promoting "workers' control" in the factories; granted Russia's diverse nationalities "the right to freedom and self-determination"; and abolished all legal distinctions of civic inequality (titles and ranks). At the same time, they began to impose restrictions on their opponents. They shut down many "bourgeois" newspapers, but even some socialist ones that did not agree with the Bolsheviks. They declared the Kadet party to be "a party of enemies of the people" worthy of repression. Building on this idea of "enemies of the people," in December the Bolsheviks created the Cheka, whose full title was the All-Russian Extraordinary Commission for the Struggle against Counter-revolution and Sabotage. This was a secret police organization that was designed to combat the Bolsheviks' enemies.[16] Thus a complex picture emerges: on the one hand the Bolsheviks implemented elements of a social revolution that many regarded favorably; on the other, they set about creating instruments of repression against their opponents and silencing dissent.

The period from the October Revolution to the summer of 1918 thus remained ambiguous and unclear. As the Bolsheviks sought to secure their power, some of their opponents began to assemble forces against them. For example, some members of the disbanded Constituent Assembly, mostly SRs, fled to the Volga region and set up an alternative government there and were able to assemble a military force that took the important city of Kazan in August of 1918. Other opponents gathered around various generals who were prepared to lead military expeditions against the Bolsheviks. By the summer of 1918, a full-fledged civil war had begun, pitting the Bolsheviks on one side (the "Reds") against all opponents willing to take up arms against them on the other (the "Whites"). The first Soviet constitution was produced just as the Russian Civil War was beginning.

To get a better sense of what the Bolsheviks thought they should do with political power once they had it, we can do no better than to consult Vladimir Lenin himself. True, the text below, *State*

---

14   Richard Abraham, "The Constituent Assembly," in Harold Shukman, ed., *The Blackwell Encyclopedia of the Russian Revolution* (New York, 1988), 141.

15   Steinberg, *Voices of Revolution*, 253.

16   Steinberg, *Voices of Revolution*, 255-68 (citations at 256 and 265).

and Revolution, was written before the Bolsheviks took power, in the summer of 1917, when Lenin was in hiding in Finland after an abortive uprising against the Provisional Government in the so-called "July Days." In this context, Lenin had the opportunity to think about the function of the state and thus the purpose of political power. A commentary on the political program of Karl Marx and Friedrich Engels, this text is often regarded as Lenin's central contribution to political theory. At the core of the text was the idea that the "bourgeois" state had to be completely destroyed and replaced by an entirely new revolutionary state. Some commentators have drawn attention to the anti-authoritarian character of this work, in quite sharp contrast to the more disciplinarian orientation of many of his other works. As you read, think about Lenin's definition of the state (which he conveniently provides in the first sentence of the selection). Why do states exist? What does Lenin regard as being necessary for the overthrow of the bourgeoisie? Does Lenin expect that the bourgeoisie will resist their own overthrow? What will the proletariat need in order to deal with the bourgeoisie? Finally, consider the ways in which Lenin's conceptions of the state are visible in the constitution of the RSFSR in 1918, as described in the reading that follows.

DOCUMENT 2.7

VLADIMIR LENIN, *STATE AND REVOLUTION* (1917)

The state is a product and a manifestation of the *irreconcilability* of class antagonisms. The state arises where, when and insofar as class antagonism objectively *cannot* be reconciled. And, conversely, the existence of the state proves that the class antagonisms are irreconcilable....

The theory of Marx and Engels of the inevitability of a violent revolution refers to the bourgeois state. The latter *cannot* be superseded by the proletarian state (the dictatorship of the proletariat) through the process of "withering away", but, as a general rule, only through a violent revolution. The panegyric Engels sang in its honor, and which fully corresponds to Marx's repeated statements (see the concluding passages of The *Poverty of Philosophy* and the *Communist Manifesto*, with their proud and open proclamation of the inevitability of a violent revolution; see what Marx wrote nearly 30 years later, in criticizing the Gotha Program of 1875, when he mercilessly castigated the opportunist character of that program) — this panegyric is by no means a mere "impulse", a mere declamation or a polemical sally. The necessity of systematically imbuing the masses with *this* and precisely this view of violent revolution lies at the root of the *entire* theory of Marx and Engels....

The supersession of the bourgeois state by the proletarian state is impossible without a violent revolution. The abolition of the proletarian state, i.e., of the state in general, is impossible except through the process of "withering away"....

The overthrow of bourgeois rule can be accomplished only by the proletariat, as the particular class whose economic conditions of existence prepare it for this task and provide it with the possibility and the power to reform it. While the bourgeois breaks up and disintegrates the peasantry and all the petty bourgeois strata, it welds together, unites and organizes the proletariat. Only the proletariat—by virtue of the economic role it plays in large-scale production—is capable of being the leader of *all* the toiling and exploited masses, whom the bourgeois exploits, oppresses and crushes often not less, but more, than it does the proletarians, but who are incapable of waging an *independent* struggle for their emancipation.

The teaching on the class struggle, when applied by Marx to the question of the state and of the socialist revolution, leads of necessity to the recognition of the *political rule* of the proletariat, of its dictatorship, i. e., of power shared with none and relying directly upon the armed force of the masses. The overthrow of the bourgeois, can be achieved only by the proletariat becoming transformed into the *ruling class*, capable of crushing the inevitable and desperate resistance of the bourgeois, and of organizing *all* the toiling and exploited masses for the new economic order.

The proletariat needs state power, the centralized organization of force, the organization of violence, both to crush the resistance of the exploiters and to *lead* the enormous mass of the population—the peasantry, the petty bourgeois, the semiproletarians—in the work of organizing socialist economy.

By educating the worker's party, Marxism educates the vanguard of the proletariat which is capable of assuming power and *of leading the whole people* to Socialism, of directing and organizing the new order, of being the teacher, the guide, the leader of all the toilers and exploited in the task of building up their social life without the bourgeoisie and against the bourgeoisie....

... Forward development, i.e., towards communism, proceeds through the dictatorship of the proletariat, and cannot do otherwise, for the *resistance* of the capitalist exploiters cannot be *broken* by anyone else or in any other way.

And the dictatorship of the proletariat, i.e., the organization of the vanguard of the oppressed ruling class for the purpose of suppressing the oppressors, cannot result merely in an expansion of democracy. *Simultaneously* with an immense expansion of democracy, which *for the first time* becomes a democracy for the poor, democracy for the people, and not democracy for the moneybags, the dictatorship of the proletariat imposes a series of restrictions on the freedom of the oppressors, the exploiters, the capitalists. We must suppress them in order to free humanity from wage slavery, their resistance must be crushed by force; it is clear that where there is suppression, where there is violence, there is no freedom and no democracy....

Only in communist society, when the resistance of the capitalists has been completely crushed, when the capitalists have disappeared, when there are no classes (ie., when there is no difference between the members of society as regards their relation to the social means of production), *only* then "the state . . . ceases to exists," and it *"becomes impossible to speak of freedom."* Only then will there become possible and be realized a truly complete democracy, democracy without any exceptions whatever. And only then will democracy begin to *wither away*, owing to the simple fact that, freed from capitalist slavery, from the untold horrors, savagery, absurdities and infamies of capitalist exploitation, people will gradually *become accustomed* to observing the elementary rules of social intercourse that have been known for centuries and repeated for thousands of years in all copybook maxims; they will become accustomed to observing them without force, without compulsion, without subordination, *without the special apparatus* for compulsion which is called the state...

Only communism makes the state absolutely unnecessary, for there is *nobody* to be suppressed—"nobody" in the sense of a *class*, in the sense of a systematic struggle against a definite section of the population. We are not utopians, and do not in the least deny the possibility and inevitability of excesses. But, in the first place, no special machine, no special apparatus of suppression is needed for this; this will be done by the armed people itself, as simply and as readily as any crowd of civilized people, even in modern society, interferes to put a stop to a scuffle or to prevent a woman from being assaulted. And, secondly, we know that the fundamental social cause of excesses, which consist in the violation of the rules of social intercourse, is the exploitation of the masses, their want and their poverty. With the removal of this chief cause, excesses will inevitably begin to *"wither away."* We do not know how quickly and in what succession, but we know that they will wither away. With their withering away the state will also *wither away*....

End of document 2.6

It is a curious thing that not long after taking power the Bolsheviks began the process of producing a constitution for the new republic, which was formally named the **Russian Soviet Federated Socialist Republic,** or the **RSFSR.** The Bolsheviks faced a grave and continuing crisis the first few months, and they were in any event revolutionaries who had no particular concern for legality and legal forms. And yet although the principal leaders of the revolution took little part in making the constitution, the party leadership nonetheless decided in early April of 1918 to form a commission to draft a constitution. Few historians have devoted a great deal of attention to this first Soviet constitution,

but one who did was **Edward H. Carr** (1892-1982), a British scholar who wrote one of the best early histories of the Russian Revolution.[17] Carr describes the process of the constitution's making as well as many of its main attributes. As you read, you might ask: How important was the constitution to the Bolsheviks? What were the constitution's main features? How was the process of constitution-making in the RSFSR similar to or different from the process in the case of the United States?

---

17   The chapter reproduced below is from Edward Hallett Carr, *The Bolshevik Revolution, 1917-1923,* vol. 1 (New York, 1951), 125-50.

READING 2.1

EDWARD H. CARR, "THE CONSTITUTION OF THE RSFSR"

The Constitution Of The REFSR

The period of the drafting of the constitution was one of grave and continuous crises both in economic and in external policy, which threatened the existence of the regime and left little leisure for smaller preoccupations. The republic for which the constitution was being drafted was still regarded by its rulers as a brief transitional stage on the way to a world-wide socialist republic or federation of republics. The constitution was scarcely expected to last as a working instrument.

In these circumstances it is not surprising that the principal leaders themselves took no personal part in the work. The revision of the party programme, much discussed at this time though not in fact undertaken till a year later, occupied far more attention in party circles. Lenin's copious speeches and writings of these months will be searched in vain for any reference to constitution-making. It was the period of the Brest-Litovsk crisis and of the hurried transfer of the capital from Petrograd to Moscow. For more than two months, apart from several draft constitutions prepared in the commissariats of Internal Affairs and of Justice and elsewhere, no progress was made; and nothing was ready for the fourth All-Russian Congress of Soviets when it met in March. Then on April 1, 1918, VTsIK decided after a short debate to create a commission to draft a constitution. The commission worked for three months and produced an agreed text. The result of its labours was published on July 3, 1918, the same day on which it was submitted for approval to the central committee of the party as a preliminary to its presentation to the fifth All-Russian Congress of Soviets.

The constitution began with general principles. The first four chapters recited textually the Declaration of Rights of the Toiling and Exploited People adopted by the third Ail-Russian Congress of Soviets. Chapter 5 enunciated a series of "general propositions", including the federal character of the republic; the separation of church from state and school from church; freedom of speech, opinion and assembly for the workers, assured by placing at their disposal the technical means of producing papers, pamphlets and books as well as premises for meetings; the obligation for all citizens to work on the principle "he that does not work, neither shall he eat"; the obligation for all workers of military service in defence of the republic; the right of citizenship for all workers living on Russian territory and of asylum for foreigners persecuted on the ground of political or religious offences; and the abolition of all discrimination on grounds of race or nationality. The constitution then turned to practical arrangements. Chapters 6 to 8 dealt with organization at the centre. The supreme power was the All-Russian Congress of Soviets, composed of representatives of city Soviets on the basis of one deputy to every 25,000 voters and of provincial Soviets on the basis of one deputy to every 125,000 inhabitants. The All-Russian Congress elected the All-Russian Central Executive Committee (VTsIK) of not more than 200 members which exercised all powers of the congress when the congress was not in session. VTsIK appointed the Council of Peoples' Commissars (Sovnarkom), whose function was the "general administration of the affairs of the RSFSR", but also extended to the issuing of "decrees, orders and instructions". The ninth chapter defined the functions of the All-Russian Congress and of VTsIK, while chapters 10 to 12 related to the organization of regional, provincial, county and district congresses of Soviets and to the formation of city and village Soviets. Chapter 13 confined the franchise to those who "earn their living by production or socially useful labour", soldiers and disabled persons, specifically excluding persons who employ hired labour, *rentiers,* private traders, monks and priests, and officials and agents of the former police. The remaining articles were concerned with routine matters of detail.

The making of constitutions is normally a battlefield of contending purposes, and the finished product bears on its face more or less obvious scars of the conflict. The controversy which lay behind the making of the first constitution of the RSFSR took three forms which were often barely distinguishable. It was a conflict between those who sought a weakening and those who sought a strengthening of state power; between those who desired a dispersal of power and initiative through local authorities and those who desired a concentration of authority and discipline at the centre; and between those who sought to make federalism effective and those who, under whatever guise, sought to establish the "one and indivisible" republic.

The Bolshevik doctrine of the state was entangled in a contradiction already inherent in Marxist teaching. Marx and Engels accepted to the full the traditional socialist hostility to the oppressive state, culminating in the belief that the state would die away altogether in conditions of socialism; at the same time they recognized the need to establish a powerful state machine to consummate and establish the victory of the revolution through the dictatorship of the proletariat. Lenin, who on the eve of the revolution devoted one of his ablest writings, under the title *State and Revolution,* to an analysis of the Marxist doctrine of the state, met the dilemma by regarding the dictatorship of the proletariat as a temporary expedient, necessary so long as the remnants of bourgeois power had not yet been eradicated, but destined, like any other form of state, to die away when the final goal of communism is achieved. The Bolshevik leaders were thus able, while maintaining the deeply rooted socialist tradition of hostility to the state, to defend as a transitional measure that strengthening of state power, the paramount necessity of which became increasingly obvious in the dark winter of 1917-1918, and the still darker summer of 1918.

The distrust of the state and the opposition to bourgeois parliamentarianism which lay at the root of Marxist theory drove many even of the Bolsheviks in the direction of syndicalism; and the Left SRs had marked syndicalist leanings. So long as bourgeois democracy was a living tradition, Bolsheviks and syndicalists could find a certain amount of common ground in denouncing it. Both regarded the "citizen" of bourgeois democracy as an atomized abstraction, and treated man as essentially a member of a class of producers. It was not therefore surprising that the strongest assaults on the conception of a powerful Soviet state should have had a syndicalist complexion.

In the final debate on the constitution in the fifth All-Russian Congress of Soviets one speaker wished to discard the terms "federation" and "republic" as smacking of the old discarded conception of the state and to call the new entity the "All-Russian Workers' Commune."

These syndicalist aberrations led to the intervention of Stalin, who presented a set of theses to the drafting commission and secured their adoption by a majority vote as the basis of its work. They contained a reminder that "the plan of the constitution now being worked out by the commission must be temporary, being designed for the period of transition from the bourgeois to the socialist order", and that it must therefore take account of "questions of the dictatorship of the proletariat and the poor peasantry, of the organization of power as an expression of this dictatorship, etc. — questions which have no relation to an established socialist order where there will be no classes or apparatus of power".[3] The dying away of the state remained as an ultimate ideal. But in the intervening period the state form of the Socialist Soviet Republic was to conform to a pattern of territorial sovereignty familiar in the capitalist world. Article 9 of the finished constitution skilfully combined a recognition of the transitional character of Soviet state power with a reminder that, while it lasted, it must be strong:

> The principal aim of the constitution of the RSFSR, which is designed for the present transition period, consists in the establishment of the dictatorship of the urban and rural proletariat and the poorest peasantry in the form of a strong all-Russian Soviet power for the purpose of the complete crushing of the bourgeoisie, the abolition of the exploitation of man by man and the establishment of socialism, under which there will be neither division into classes nor state power.

Since, however, "the establishment of socialism" could be conceived only as an international event, the Russian federation was merely the first unit of an eventual world federation of socialist republics. In this sense, too, it marked a "transition period".

The underlying clash between the conception of a state in transition towards its own eventual dying away and a dictatorship of the proletariat powerful enough to crush bourgeois opposition was also reflected in the struggle between local self-government and centralization. The peculiarity of the Soviet structure lay in the fact that it was built up round Soviets which had already taken shape and acquired some degree of organization before they became constitutional organs of state power. It was emphasized again and again that the constitution merely registered forms spontaneously evolved by the masses themselves. In the words of the *rapporteur* to the fifth All-Russian Congress of Soviets, it "was realized in practice long before it was written down on paper". The Soviets were initially, and in part always remained, loose and informal assemblies without clearly defined functions. The All-Russian Congress of Soviets was composed of delegates from either provincial or regional congresses and from the largest city Soviets which were outside the lower stages of the congress system. The local Soviet, urban or rural, was the supposed source of power, the congresses of Soviets at different levels and the All-Russian Congress of Soviets at the summit being emanations from it. The very informality of the system was regarded by Lenin as its main recommendation :

All bureaucratic formalities and limitations disappear from the elections, and the masses themselves determine the ordering and timing of the elections with free right of recall of those elected.

The Soviets constituted, a "new kind of state", free from the obnoxious characteristics of the old bureaucratic state and designed to replace it. " All power on the spot ", ran the proclamation of the second All-Russian Congress of Soviets at the moment of the revolution, "passes to the Soviets of Workers', Soldiers' and Peasants' Deputies, who must ensure true revolutionary order."

This idealized conception of authority did not survive the test of experience. The very spontaneity of the movement which had created Soviets in factory and village up and down the country meant that their independent acts were irregular, uncoordinated and disruptive of orderly administration.

In the first half of 1918, when the constitution of the RSFSR was in the making, signs of a general breakdown and dispersal of authority were manifest all over Russia. Lenin himself might pretend to make light of what happened when "some local Soviet sets up an independent republic" and call this "a disease of growth" and a "quite natural phenomenon of the transition from Tsarist Russia to the Russia of united Soviet organizations". But it was not seriously possible to ignore the necessity of restoring some kind of effective central authority if the country was to survive the difficulties crowding in on it from all sides.

The conditions of the moment therefore favoured those who in the drafting commission pleaded the cause of centralization. The initial debate turned on the question whether to begin by defining the powers of the local Soviets or those of the central organs. Stalin is said to have turned the discussion — it is not quite clear how — by invoking the federal principle. A significant verbal antithesis between article 10 and article 12 of the finished constitution may reflect the keenness of the debate. According to the one, "all authority within the territory of the RSFSR is vested in the entire working population organized in urban and rural Soviets"; according to the other, "supreme authority in the RSFSR is vested in the All-Russian Congress of Soviets and, in the interval between congresses, in VTsIK". But the same formal antithesis between the derivation of authority from below and the exercise of authority from above is implicit in any constitution claiming to rest on a basis of popular sovereignty ; and the text of the constitution left no room for doubt. According to the instruction of the third All-Russian Congress of Soviets, "local matters "were to be" decided exclusively by the local Soviets", and the central authorities were to be left to control the execution of "the fundamental principles of the federation "as well as of" measures of national importance". The way in which this instruction was carried out in the final text was decisive. A long and comprehensive enumeration of seventeen "questions of national importance" falling within the competence of the All-Russian Congress of Soviets and of VTsIK was framed in such a way as to be illustrative rather than exhaustive, and followed by the precautionary rider that "in addition to the above-mentioned questions the All-Russian Congress of Soviets and VTsIK may decide on any other matter which they deem within their jurisdiction". This rider was the nearest thing in the constitution to an allocation of residuary powers.

A later chapter of the constitution defined in general terms the tasks of the local Soviets and the regional, provincial, county and district congresses of Soviets with their executive committees. These were:

a.   the carrying into effect of all resolutions of the corresponding higher organs of Soviet power;

b.   the taking of all measures to improve the territory in question culturally and economically;

c.   the settlement of all questions having a purely local significance;.

d.   the unification of all Soviet activity within the territory in question.

The effect of the last provision was to encourage the Soviets to absorb pre-revolutionary organs of local government and to transform themselves into local government organs of the normal pattern. The budgetary chapter of the constitution, which was a subject of controversy between the People's Commissariats of Internal Affairs and of Finance, contributed to the same result. A decree passed while the drafting commission was at work prohibited local Soviets from levying taxation on local organs of the central commissariats serving general state needs. The constitution recognized the right of local Soviets to raise "taxes and levies exclusively for the needs of the local economy". But all local revenue and expenditure were brought under direct or indirect central control, the budgets of the minor Soviets being reviewed by the provincial or regional Soviets or their executive committees, the budgets of the city, provincial and regional Soviets by the All-Russian Congress of Soviets or by VTsIK. What was in effect a monopoly of finance was enjoyed by the central government; and the granting of credits and subsidies was a powerful means of bringing local Soviets under the supervising authority of the People's Commissariat of Internal Affairs.

The Soviets were thus firmly fitted into their place in the constitutional structure. On the one hand, they were the formal source of authority and the electoral colleges by which, through several intermediate stages, the delegates to the supreme All-Russian Congress of Soviets were chosen. On the other hand, they were organs of local government enjoying a large measure of local initiative, but subject in all their functions to ultimate control, through the same intermediate levels of authority, by the organs of the central government. It was this second and novel aspect of their position which at first gave some trouble. In June 1918 the interpretation of the slogan "all power to the Soviets" as meaning "all power to the local Soviets" was pronounced by an authoritative commentator to be "harmful" and "a thing of the past". But the indiscipline of the local Soviets died hard. Six months later it was still necessary to exhort them to "execute without demur and with strict accuracy all decisions and orders of the central authorities".

The very notion of a constitutional act implied in western thought a law to which the state itself was subject; this conception was incompatible with a doctrine which regarded law as a creation of the state. Most constitutions of the western world had been based on the assumption that the power of the state was something which required to be limited and circumscribed by legal enactment in order to prevent abuse. Constitutions were wrung from reluctant monarchs; federations were formed by units determined to allow the smallest possible encroachments on their authority by the federal government. In bourgeois constitutions such limitations might admittedly have some value as affording the workers a certain protection against the bourgeois state. But no such compromises had any place in the Soviet constitution. In Stalin's words, "it came into being not as a result of a deal with the bourgeoisie, but as a result of a victorious revolution". It was the expression not of any balance or bargain between conflicting forces, but of the dictatorship of the proletariat. The absolute character of Bolshevik theory was represented in the phrase "the autocracy of the people" — a sort of parody on the title of the Tsar as "autocrat" (*samoderzhavets*) —which figured prominently in the party programme of 1903 and was long current in party circles. Every state and every government was an instrument of the supremacy of a ruling class. The dictatorship of the proletariat, like every other form of state, was in Lenin's phrase "a special kind of cudgel, nothing else"; its purpose was to beat down and crush the exploiting classes. It followed that the powers conferred on this state by the constitution were in their essence unlimited, undivided and absolute.

It was a deduction from this view that the Soviet constitution involved no recognition of "constitutional safeguards" or of rights of individual citizens against the state. The Declaration of Rights of the Toiling and Exploited People was not a declaration of rights in the conventional sense; it was the announcement of a social and economic policy. This was perfectly logical. Marxism rejected the bourgeois view that the freedom of the individual could be guaranteed by the non-intervention of the state in his activities; such freedom in conditions of class rule remained formal and ineffective. To bring true freedom to the workers positive action was required. Thus under the constitution of the RSFSR freedom of conscience was secured to the workers by the separation of church from state, and of school from church; freedom of opinion by assuring to the workers "all technical and material means for the publication of newspapers, pamphlets, books and all other printed works", and for their distribution throughout the country; freedom of assembly by putting at the disposal of the workers "all premises suitable for holding popular meetings with equipment, lighting and heating"; access to knowledge by "full, universal and free education". The freedom of the worker was to be asserted, not against the state, but through the action of the state. What the constitution provided was the promise and guarantee of this action. The notion of an antithesis between individual and state was the natural assumption of a class society. The interest of the individual worker was the interest of the working class as a whole; it would have been illogical and incongruous to set him in opposition to the workers' state.

It followed also that the constitution did not recognize any formal equality of rights. No such tradition existed in Russian constitutional practice. The subjects of the Tsars had been divided into five legally established "estates", each enjoying a different legal status. A decree of November 10/23, 1917, abolished these distinctions and created a single legal category of citizens. But so long as economic classes existed in fact, equality between individual members of unequal classes, such as was recognized in bourgeois-democratic constitutions, remained, according to Bolshevik doctrine, essentially unreal. Equality between individuals could become real only in the classless society. The purpose of the dictatorship of the proletariat was not to establish formal equality between individual members of the bourgeoisie and of the working classes but to destroy the bourgeoisie as a class. The Soviets, which were the embodiment of that dictatorship, were class organs of the workers and peasants. Only workers and peasants were recruited into the Red Army. The rights accorded by the constitution were thus logically accorded to "the toilers" or "the working class and the poor peasantry" — and to them alone. The statement of "general principles" specifically justified discrimination:

> In the general interest of the working class the RSFSR deprives individuals or separate groups of any privileges which may be used by them to the detriment of the socialist revolution.

Hence no validity was conceded to such principles of bourgeois democracy as "one man, one vote" ; and the franchise "ceases to be a right and is transformed into a social function of the electors". The constitution of the RSFSR excluded from the franchise "those who employ others for the sake of profit", "those who live on income not arising from their own labour", "private business men" and "monks and priests", as well as criminals and imbeciles. The decision not to exclude professional men and intellectuals from the franchise was much contested, and was inspired, as a commentator remarks, "not by considerations of so-called social justice, and still less by sentimental motives", but by considerations of practical utility. The discriminatory franchise remained in force until 1936.

A more complicated example of discrimination was the difference between the voting rules in town and country for the All-Russian Congress of Soviets. In the cities the number of delegates to the congress was fixed at one for every 25,000 *electors,* in the country at one for every 125,000 *inhabitants.* The difference had its historical origin. Lenin spoke of "the inequality of workers and peasants" under the constitution, and justified it by its origin in the history of the Soviets. The party programme adopted in 1919 specifically noted that "our Soviet constitution" reflected the leading role of the urban worker in the revolution "by retaining a certain preference for the industrial proletariat in comparison with the more dispersed petty-bourgeois masses in the country". Such issues were always to be considered from the empirical standpoint, not from that of formal or abstract equality. The more highly developed class-consciousness of the urban workers and, consequently, their greater effectiveness in the struggle against the bourgeoisie entitled them to a privileged franchise in the revolutionary state.

The absolute character of state power meant that this power was not only unlimited but indivisible. Marx, in an early work, described the familiar constitutional doctrine of the "separation of powers" as the product of an age in which "the royal power, the aristocracy and bourgeoisie are struggling for supremacy", elevated into an "eternal law". But such distinctions would be swept away in a socialist revolution. Marx praised the Paris commune for having been "not a parliamentary but a working corporation which at one and the same time legislated and executed the laws", Lenin regarded the separation of executive from legislative as a specific characteristic of parliamentarianism, their fusion as a specific merit of the Soviet system. Under the dictatorship of the proletariat the organs of state power were merely different instruments wielded by or on behalf of the workers for the achievement of the same purpose. The issue was stated at the time of the drafting of the constitution by Reisner, the spokesman of the People's Commissariat of Justice :

> The separation of powers into legislative, executive and judicial... corresponds to the structure of the bourgeois state where the principal task is the balancing of the main political forces, i.e. the possessing classes on the one hand and the toiling masses on the other. Being inevitably by its nature a compromise between exploiters and exploited, the bourgeois state has to balance and divide power....

> The Russian socialist republic has no interest in any division or balancing of political forces for the simple reason that it bases itself on the domination of one all-embracing political force, i.e. the Russian proletariat and the peasant masses. This political force is engaged in the realization of a single end, the establishment of a socialist order, and this heroic struggle requires unity and concentration of power rather than division.

It was therefore logical that the constitution of the RSFSR should recognize no separation of legislative and executive functions. The favourite comparison of VTsIK with Parliament and of Sovnarkom with the Cabinet ignores the absence of any distinction, either in the terms or in the working of the constitution, between the function of the two bodies, which were equally legislative and executive : indeed, there was logic in a proposal made during the discussions on the constitution for the fusion of the two bodies. Equally little justification could be found in constitutional theory for a separate and independent judiciary as for a separate and independent executive. The constitution of the RSFSR made no specific provision at all for the exercise of the judicial function ; and the direct organization and control of the judiciary by the People's Commissariat of Justice clearly marked its subordination to the executive. Every function of government was one; it should be exercised for a single purpose by a single undivided authority.

So acute an observer of political realities as Lenin could not fail to see in the concentration of power at the centre a threat to the principle of authority emanating "from below" and an encouragement to the endemic evil of bureaucracy.

What he believed was that the centralization of authority carried with it its own antidote. The effect of the fusion of legislative and executive functions would mean the disappearance of the professional administrator as differentiated and divorced from the elected legislator. The advantage of the fusion would be "to unite in the persons of the elected representatives of the people both legislative and executive functions" — a combination which was the essence of " direct democracy". The revised party programme of 1919 included among "the negative sides of parliamentarianism" not only "the separation of the legislative and executive powers", but "the divorce of representative institutions from the masses". The Soviets seemed to Lenin to embody the notion of the masses of workers and peasants legislating for themselves, carrying out their own decisions, and administering their own affairs ; and this highly idealized picture of "direct democracy" helped to mask the increasingly stubborn reality of an immense accretion of bureaucratic power at the centre. But here, too, the ultimate sanction rested with the party, whose authority could always be invoked to remedy constitutional shortcomings.

The practical working of a constitution commonly depends not only on the principles inspiring its framers or on the rules laid down by them, but even more on the political conditions in which it is brought into operation. The changes which occurred in Soviet Russia during the preparation of the constitution were the continuation of a process which had been at work since the inception of the regime. But they were significant and decisive. When the main principles of the future constitution were enunciated by the third All-Russian Congress of Soviets after the dispersal of the Constituent Assembly in January 1918, the government was a coalition of Bolsheviks and Left SRs. When the drafting commission met in April, the Left SRs, though they had left the government, remained in the Soviets and were represented in the commission. When the fifth All-Russian Congress of Soviets finally approved the constitution in July 1918, the Left SRs had just been expelled and outlawed and the civil war had begun. The growth of the one-party state and the impact of the civil war, which for the next two years put the survival of the republic in almost daily jeopardy, destroyed the optimistic foundations on which the constitution had been built, and threw into the shade most of the controversies which had occupied the drafting commission. The needs of the army in the field and of security at home created an atmosphere inimical to constitutional niceties. The experience of much early Soviet legislation revealed a broad gulf between idealistic principles and the stern realities of practice. If this was also true of the constitution of the RSFSR, the circumstances of its birth went far to explain the rift.

The draft constitution was examined on July 3, 1918, by the central committee of the party, which made a few minor amendments. On Lenin's proposal the Declaration of Rights of the Toiling and Exploited People was incorporated in the constitution as a preamble. This done, the draft was presented to the fifth All-Russian Congress of Soviets. The congress was interrupted for three days by the serious crisis arising from the murder of the German ambassador, Mirbach. Then, on July 10, 1918, it listened to an exposition of the new constitution by Steklov and endorsed it unanimously. It came into force on its official publication in *Izvestiya* of July 19, 1918, as the "Constitution (Fundamental Law) of the Russian Socialist Federal Soviet Republic ".

End of Reading 2.1

Carr provides a good overview of the constitution, but nothing can replacement the sheer joy and excitement of reading portions of that document itself, which are provided as document 2.8. Indeed, the Constitution of the RSFSR offers valuable insights into the young Soviet state. We might begin by considering the extent to which Lenin's vision of the state was reflected in the 1918 constitution. How are class distinctions evident in the constitution? Are there other characteristics of the Constitution of the RSFSR that you find unusual? In what ways is it distinct form or similar to the US Constitution?

THE CONSTITUTION OF THE RSFSR[18]

The Declaration of Rights of the Working and Exploited People, approved by the Third All-Russia Congress of Soviets in January 1918, together with the constitution of the Soviet Republic approved by the Fifth Congress, make up the single fundamental law of the Russian Socialist Federative Soviet Republic.

This fundamental law becomes effective from the moment of its publication in final form in *News of the All-Russian Central Executive Committee*. It shall be published by all local organs of Soviet government and prominently displayed in all Soviet institutions.

The Fifth Congress instructs the People's Commissariat for Public Education to introduce in all schools and other educational establishments of the Russian Republic, without exception, the study of the basic provisions of the present constitution, as well as their explanation and interpretation.

CHAPTER ONE

Article 1. Russia is hereby proclaimed a Republic of Soviets of Workers', Soldiers' and Peasants' Deputies. All power, centrally and locally, is vested in these Soviets.

Article 2. The Russian Soviet Republic is established on the principle of a free union of free nations, as a federation of Soviet national republics.

CHAPTER TWO

Article 3. Its fundamental aim being abolition of all exploitation of man by man, complete elimination of the division of society into classes, merciless suppression of the exploiters, socialist organization of society, and victory of socialism in all countries, the Third All-Russia Congress of Soviets of Workers', Soldiers' and Peasants' Deputies further resolves:

a. Pursuant to the socialization of land, private land ownership is hereby abolished, and all land is proclaimed the property of the entire people and turned over to the working people without any redemption, on the principles of egalitarian land tenure.

b. All forests, mineral wealth and waters of national importance, as well as all live and dead stock, model estates and agricultural enterprises are proclaimed the property of the nation.

c. The Soviet laws on workers' control and on the Supreme Economic Council are hereby confirmed in order to guarantee the power of the working people over the exploiters and as a first step towards the complete conversion of factories, mines, railways and other means of production and transportation into the property of the Soviet Workers' and Peasants' Republic.

d. The Third Congress of Soviets regards as a first blow at international banking, financial capital, the Soviet law on the annulment of loans negotiated by the governments of the tsar, the landlords and the bourgeoisie and expresses confidence that Soviet power will be advancing steadfastly along this road until the complete victory of an international workers' uprising against the rule of capital.

e. To ensure the sovereign power of the working people and to rule out any possibility of restoration of the power of the exploiters, the arming of the working people, the creation of a socialist Red Army of workers and peasants, and the complete disarming of the propertied classes are hereby decreed.

CHAPTER THREE

Article 4. Expressing firm determination to wrest mankind from the clutches of finance capital and imperialism, which have in this most criminal of wars drenched the world in blood, the Third Congress of Soviets unreservedly endorses Soviet policy of denouncing the secret treaties, organizing most extensive fraternization with the workers and peasants of the combatant armies and achieving at all costs by revolutionary means a democratic peace for the working people, without annexations of indemnities, on the basis of free self-determination of nations.

---

18   The full constitution can be accessed at http://www.departments.bucknell.edu/russian/const/18cons01.html or http://www.marxists.org/history/ussr/government/constitution/1918/.

Article 5. With the same aim in view, the Third Congress of Soviets insists on a complete break with the barbarous policy of bourgeois civilization, which has built the prosperity of the exploiters in a few chosen nations through the enslavement of hundreds of millions of working people in Asia, in the colonies in general, and in small countries.

Article 6. The Third Congress of Soviets supports the policy of the Council of People's Commissars which has proclaimed the complete independence of Finland, commenced the withdrawal of troops from Persia, and proclaimed freedom of self-determination for Armenia.

CHAPTER FOUR

Article 7. The Third All-Russia Congress of Soviets holds that now, in the hour of the people's resolute struggle against the exploiters, there should be no room for exploiters in any governmental agency. Power must belong fully and exclusively to the working people and their plenipotentiary representatives - the Soviets of Workers', Soldiers' and Peasants' Deputies.

Article 8. At the same time, endeavoring to create a genuinely free and voluntary, and therefore all the more firm and stable, union of the working classes of all the nations of Russia, the Third Congress of Soviets confines itself to promulgating the fundamental principles of a federation of Soviet republics of Russia, leaving it to the workers and peasants of each nation to decide independently at their own representative congresses of soviets whether they wish to participate in the federal government and in the other federal Soviet institutions, and on what terms.

CHAPTER FIVE

Article 9. The main objective of the constitution of the Russian Socialist Federative Soviet Republic, designed for the present transitional period, is to establish the dictatorship of the urban and rural proletariat and the poorest peasantry in the form of a powerful All-Russia Soviet Government, with a view to completely suppressing the bourgeoisie, abolishing exploitation of man by man, and establishing socialism, under which there will be neither division into classes nor state power.

Article 10. The Russian Republic is a free socialist society of all the working people of Russia. All power in the Russian Socialist Federative Soviet Republic belongs to the entire working population of the country united in urban and rural soviets.

Article 11. The soviets of regions with a distinct mode of living and national composition can unite in autonomous regional unions at the head of which, as at the head of all regional unions that can be eventually formed, stand regional congresses of Soviets and their executive agencies.

These autonomous regional unions form, on a federal basis, component parts of the Russian Socialist Federative Soviet Republic.

Article 12. Supreme power in the Russian Socialist Federative Soviet Republic is exercised by the All-Russia Congress of Soviets, and in the intervals between Congresses by the All-Russia Central Executive Committee.

Article 13. In order to ensure genuine freedom of conscience for the working people, the church is separated from the State, and the school from the church: and freedom of religious and anti-religious propaganda is recognized for all citizens.

Article 14. In order to ensure genuine freedom of expression for the working people, the Russian Socialist Federative Soviet Republic abolishes the dependence of the press on capital, and places at the disposal of the working class and the poor peasantry all the technical and material requisites for the publication of newspapers, pamphlets, books and all other printed matter, and guarantees their unhindered circulation throughout the country.

Article 15. In order to ensure genuine freedom of assembly for the working people, the Russian Socialist Federative Soviet Republic, recognizing the right of citizens of the Soviet Republic freely to hold assemblies, meetings, processions, etc., places at the disposal of the working class and the poor peasantry all buildings suitable for the holding of public gatherings, complete with furnishing, lighting and heating.

Article 16. In order to ensure genuine freedom of association for the working people, the Russian Socialist Federative Soviet Republic, having destroyed the economic and political rule of the propertied classes and thereby removed all the obstacles which heretofore, in bourgeois society, prevented the workers and peasants from enjoying freedom of organization and action, renders material and all other assistance to the workers and poorest peasants for purposes of their association and organization.

Article 17. In order to ensure access to knowledge for the working people, the Russian Socialist Federative Soviet Republic makes its aim to give the workers and poorest peasants complete all-round and free education.

Article 18. The Russian Socialist Federative Soviet Republic declares labor to be the duty of all citizens of the Republic, and proclaims the slogan: 'He who does not work, neither shall he eat!'

Article 19. In order to safeguard the gains of the great workers' and peasants' revolution, the Russian Socialist Federative Republic declares defence of the socialist Fatherland to be the duty of all the citizens of the Republic and introduces universal military service. The honorable right of bearing arms in defence of the revolution is granted only to working people; non-working elements are enlisted for other military duties.

Article 20. Proceeding from the principle of solidarity of the working people of all nations, the Russian Socialist Federative Soviet Republic grants full political rights of Russian citizens to foreigners residing in the territory of the Russian Republic for purposes of employment, and belonging to the working class or to the peasantry not employing the labour of others: and it empowers the local Soviets to grant to such foreigners, without any cumbersome formalities, Russian citizenship rights.

Article 21. The Russian Socialist Federative Soviet Republic grants the right of asylum to all foreigners subjected to persecution for political and religious crimes.

Article 22. The Russian Socialist Federative Soviet Republic, recognizing the equality of rights of all citizens, irrespective of their race or nationality, declares the establishment or toleration on this basis of any privileges or advantages, or any oppression of national minorities or restriction of their equality, to be contraventions of the fundamental laws of the Republic.

Article 23. Guided by the interests of the working class as a whole, the Russian Socialist Federative Soviet Republic deprives individuals and groups of rights which they utilize to the detriment of the socialist revolution.

CHAPTER THIRTEEN

Article 64. The right to elect and to be elected to soviets is enjoyed, irrespective of religion, nationality, sex, domicile, etc. by the following citizens of the Russian Socialist Federative Soviet Republic who have reached the age of eighteen by polling day:

a.   All those who earn a living by productive and socially useful labour (as well as persons engaged in housekeeping which enables the former to work productively), viz. wage and salaried workers of all groups and categories engaged in industry, trade, agriculture, etc. and peasants and Cossack farmers who do not employ hired labour for profit;

b.   Soldiers of the Soviet army and navy;

c.   Citizens belonging to categories listed in Paragraphs (a) and (b) of the present article who have been to any degree incapacitated.

   NOTE 1. The local soviets may, subject to approval by the central authority, lower the age limit established in the present article.

   NOTE 2. As far as resident foreigners are concerned, active and passive suffrage is enjoyed by persons indicated in **Article 20** (Part Two, Chapter V).

Article 65. The right to elect and to be elected is denied to the following persons, even if they belong to one of the categories listed above:

a.   Persons who employ hired labour for profit;

b.   Persons living on unearned income, such as interest on capital, profits from enterprises, receipts from property, etc.;

c.   Private traders and commercial middle-men;

d.   Monks and ministers of religion;

e.   Employees and agents of the former police, the special corps of gendarmerie and the secret political police department, as well as members of the former imperial family;

f.   Persons declared insane by legal proceeding, as well as persons in ward;

g.   Persons condemned for pecuniary and infamous crimes to terms established by law or by a court decision.

CHAPTER SIXTEEN

Article 79. The main objective of the fiscal policy of the Russian Socialist Federative Soviet Republic in the current transitional period of the dictatorship of the working people is expropriation of the bourgeoisie and preparation of conditions for the universal equality of the citizens of the Republic in the sphere of production and distribution of values. It is therefore aimed at placing at the disposal of the organs of Soviet power all the means necessary for satisfying the local and national needs of the Soviet Republic, in the pursuit of which tasks it will not stop at invading the sphere of the right of private ownership.

CHAPTER SEVENTEEN

Article 89. The Arms of the Russian Socialist Federative Soviet Republic consist of a sickle and a hammer with their handles crossed, pointing downwards, gold upon a red field in the sun's rays, and surrounded by a wreath of ears of grain, with the inscriptions:

a.   'Russian Socialist Federative Soviet Republic', and

b.   'Proletarians of all Countries, Unite!'

Article 90. The flag and ensign of the Russian Socialist Federative Soviet Republic is of red cloth with the gold letters 'RSFSR' or the words 'Russian Socialist Federative Soviet Republic' in the left upper corner near the staff.

Adopted by the Fifth All-Russia Congress of Soviets, 10 July 1918.

End of Document 2.8

Further Reading:

Edward Hallett Carr, *The Bolshevik Revolution, 1917-1923*, vol. 1. New York: Macmillan, 1951.

Sheila Fitzpatrick, *The Russian Revolution*, 2nd ed. Oxford: Oxford University Press, 1994.

Michael T. Florinsky, *Russia: A History and an Interpretation*, vol. 2. New York: Macmillan, 1953.

Richard Sakwa, *The Rise and Fall of the Soviet Union, 1917-1991*. London: Routledge, 1999.

Josh Sanborn, *Imperial Apocalypse: The Great War and the Destruction of the Russian Empire*. Oxford: Oxford University Press, 2014.

Mark D. Steinberg, *Voices of Revolution, 1917*. New Haven: Yale University Press, 2001.

Robert Weinberg and Laurie Bernstein, *Revolutionary Russia: A History with Documents*. Oxford: Oxford University Press, 2011.

CHAPTER 8

THE CIVIL WAR AND THE CREATION OF THE USSR

By the time the Bolsheviks approved the constitution of the USSR in July of 1918, the country was already in a civil war. As we noted earlier, various forces hostile to the Bolsheviks, especially on the periphery of the country, had taken up arms against the new regime and sought to dislodge them. Even foreign powers—Russia's allies during the war—intervened in the country's affairs, creating Bolshevik fears of "capitalist encirclement" for decades thereafter. The result was that the Bolsheviks had to fight for their very existence, and most of their decisions in the years 1918-20 were taken in the context of extreme crisis and with the goal of the very survival of their regime.

By early 1921, however, the Bolsheviks had vanquished their ideological enemies within Russia. But as they had done so they were forced to confront the question of where the borders of the new country should be. How much of the old Russian Empire should the Bolsheviks attempt to include in the new country? And as they moved into non-Russian areas, would the populations there be sympathetic to Bolshevism, or would they reject it simply as a new form of Russian rule? In other words, how would the Bolsheviks deal with the **national question**—the problem of what to do about non-Russian minorities in Russia—which had proved so vexing on the eve of the war and during the revolution?

In this chapter we investigate a cluster of issues connected to the national question. We first of all focus on the Bolsheviks' experience in the Civil War, exploring above all how it shaped the young Bolshevik regime and made it more authoritarian

than it might have been otherwise. We next consider the specific ways in which the Bolsheviks tried to resolve the national question. Having come to power focusing on *class* (recall that class struggle was a core concept for Marxists), the Bolsheviks suddenly found themselves having to resolve this problem, which proved unusually complicated. The Bolsheviks' eventual solution was to create an entirely new kind of state—the **Union of Soviet Socialist Republics**, or USSR—which entailed a strange combination of conquest and concessions to national minorities. In its policies towards non-Russian groups, the USSR became an **"affirmative action empire,"** as the reading at the end of this chapter suggests.

THE CIVIL WAR AND ITS EFFECTS

The Civil War had an enormous impact on the young Soviet republic. It polarized society into Reds and Whites. It legitimated violence as a solution to political problems. It devastated the economy, stopping industry almost completely and driving many city dwellers back into the countryside in search of food. In a distinct irony, the proletariat was even *smaller* at the end of the war than it had been before, since so many workers either made their way back to their home villages or into the Red Army to fight the war (where many died). The Civil War also militarized the Bolsheviks, by increasing their willingness to resort to coercion and violence in solving their problems and dealing with their opponents. At the same time, we should remember that the Bolsheviks had consciously seized power as a minority party; staying in power was bound to require an authoritarian approach. Sheila Fitzpatrick, a leading historian of revolutionary Russia, nicely summarizes the ways in which the Bolsheviks made themselves more authoritarian by essentially inviting a civil war: "The Civil War was not an unforeseeable act of God for which the Bolsheviks were in no way responsible. On the contrary, the Bolsheviks had associated themselves with armed confrontation and violence in the months between February and October 1917; and, as the Bolshevik leaders knew perfectly well before the event, their October *coup* was seen by many as an outright provocation to civil war. The Civil War certainly gave the new regime a baptism by fire, and thereby influenced its future development. But it was the kind of baptism the Bolsheviks had risked, and may even have sought."[1]

Since the Whites initially controlled broad portions of the south, Siberia, and other regions, it seemed for a time like the Bolsheviks were doomed to defeat. But they had several important advantages. The White armies were largely separated from one another, which made it hard to coordinate and act in a unified fashion. The Bolsheviks, on the other hand, controlled the center of the country, including much of its industry and the rail networks centered in Moscow. The Bolsheviks also proved effective at building a new Red Army, under the leadership of **Leon Trotsky**, and also drawing some 50,000 officers of the old tsarist army into this new force to provide military expertise and leadership. The Red Army proved effective at conscripting a large number of workers and peasants into its ranks. For the most part, peasants had no love for either the Reds or the Whites and in some cases created their own military formations to fight against both of them. But when a choice needed to be made, the Bolsheviks were more attractive than the Whites, since at least they had authorized the peasant seizure of land shortly after coming to power. All of these factors help to explain how the Bolsheviks emerged victorious in the Civil War by 1921.

In order to secure that victory, the Bolsheviks needed to be brutal and authoritarian. That they were prepared to use violence, coercion, and terror was clear enough. Recall that Lenin had defined the state—and by extension the army—as an instrument of class rule, "a special kind of cudgel" with which to beat the class enemy.[2] In the context of war, the Bolsheviks regarded as a "class enemy" virtually anyone who resisted them. They also asserted more and more control over the economy, for example by nationalizing factories, railways, enterprises, etc.[3] It is hard to tell whether they did this primarily because they were communists—who after all were supposed to be enemies of private property—or because it was the only way to keep factories running in the context of wartime chaos. But at a minimum we can say that the Civil War drove the Bolsheviks to extend the sphere of centralized government control over the economy a good deal faster and further than they had originally intended. By late 1920 the Bolsheviks had asserted control over the most of the economy and had created a monopoly over the grain trade to ensure the flow of foodstuffs from the countryside to the city. This in turn required compelling peasants to sell grain to the Bolsheviks at fixed prices and to shoot them if they refused. They also asserted greater discipline over workers in factories in order to ensure that they provided the needed goods for the war effort against the Whites. This cluster of coercive policies became known later as **War Communism**. Meanwhile, the Communist Party became ever more important than state institutions.[4]

Thus the Bolsheviks triumphed in the Civil War, but the country was now in a dreadful state. After some seven years of world war and civil war, Russia resembled—in Lenin's apt comparison—a man who had been beaten within an inch of his life. The new Bolshevik state had become highly authoritarian in the war, leaving an imprint that would remain on the country for decades thereafter.

THE NATIONAL QUESTION AND THE USSR

To understand the national question, we need to backtrack a bit into the tsarist period. Recall that

---

1   Sheila Fitzpatrick, *The Russian Revolution*, 2nd ed. (Oxford, 1994), 72.

2   Lenin as cited in Edward Hallett Carr, *The Bolshevik Revolution, 1917-1923*, vol. 1 (New York, 1951), 141.

3   "To nationalize" in this context has the distinct meaning "to transfer (a major branch of industry or commerce) from private to state ownership or control" (Oxford English Dictionary).

4   The discussion here is based on Fitzpatrick, *Russian Revolution*, 67-92.

Russia was a multinational empire consisting of a large number of different peoples. The principality of Moscow had appeared among people we would now regard as Russian, but as the country expanded and became the Russian Empire, it incorporated various other groups. By the time of the Bolshevik Revolution, the largest groups were Slavic peoples (Russians, Ukrainians, Belarusians, Poles), Turkic peoples (Tatars, Bashkirs, Azeris, Kazakhs, Uzbeks, Turkmens, etc.); Finnic peoples (Finns, Estonians, Maris, Udmurts, and Mordvins), and many other nationalities: Armenians, Georgians, Chechens Germans, Latvians, Lithuanians, Jews, etc. There were in fact well over a hundred such national groups, each with its own language and culture.

For much of Russian history before 1900, social and religious distinctions had been more important than national ones. People had different rights and obligations based on the social group to which they belonged and the faith that they confessed. This arrangement worked reasonably well for a pre-modern empire. It allowed the empire to incorporate local elites into its own elite as the country expanded, which helped to make those local elites loyal to their new ruler. They were often willing to accept incorporation into the Russian Empire because their own privileges were protected, and in many cases they continued to predominate in the local society much as they had before. Loyalty was directed to the dynasty—to the ruler—rather than to abstractions such as "the nation." As long as the empire also provided a basic level of religious toleration, so as not to violate the culture and traditions of non-dominant religious communities, the empire could function reasonably well.

However, the late 19th and early 20th centuries were an age of nationalism. The French Revolution in 1789 had located sovereignty in "the nation," much like the American Revolution had located it in "the people." Indeed, because France was a largely homogeneous country—especially compared to a country like Russia—locating sovereignty in the nation and the people was pretty much the same thing. But as one went further east in Europe, one encountered large multinational empires like Russia. As people there began to think about national sovereignty—the idea that the nation is sovereign—it seemed to some of them that in order to be sovereign their ethnic group might need to break away from large empires and create their own country. In Russia, most non-Russian people had not yet reached this

conclusion by 1900, and thus most of them thought in terms of more cultural rights and perhaps a degree of autonomy. They simply sought space to be able to develop their own cultures and languages, at least in the parts of the country where they predominated. An exception to this statement were the Poles and, to a lesser degree, the Finns. The Poles had had their own country until 1795, when it was swallowed up by Russia, Austria, and Prussia. Over the generations, Poles cultivated a historical memory of independence and hoped to be able to resurrect the country at some point in the future. They revolted against Russian rule in 1830-31 partly for this reason and then again 1863-64, though in both cases the revolts were suppressed by tsarist forces.[5] Finland had been part of Sweden before annexation by Russia in 1809, but because its institutions and ways of life were so distinct, and because Russians were only a tiny minority in Finland, Finns began to think more about greater autonomy and even independence in the early 20th century.

Tsarist rulers were of course concerned about these aspirations for autonomy and began to fear what they called "separatism"—that is, the supposed aspiration of non-Russians to break away from the Empire. Tsarist rulers also saw that some degree of national unification would help to strengthen the country by spreading a common language and a shared culture across the country's diverse population. For these two reasons—to counter non-Russian nationalism and to unite the country more thoroughly—the tsarist autocracy promoted **Russification**, especially in the 1880s-90s. "Russification" in this case meant the promotion of the Russian language among non-Russian peoples and efforts to promote a single shared culture, which was in large measure Russian culture. For the most part, tsarist leaders did not really hope to "convert" non-Russian peoples into Russians, at least not in the short term. Rather, they wanted to bind the diverse population of the country together and allow rulers to mobilize the country's human resources more effectively. As with industrialization, the assumption was that these efforts were needed to ensure the country's competitiveness on the world stage. Not surprisingly, non-Russians sometimes resented these efforts at Russification, which they saw as destructive of their own culture and

---

5   As a result of the first revolt, the constitution of the Kingdom of Poland (see chapter 5) was abrogated.

language. So a fraught situation appeared: tsarist rulers felt that they had no choice but to promote some kind of cultural unification of the country, whereas non-Russians—first of all Poles, but then others as well—wanted essentially the opposite: the opportunity to develop their culture and language without the state's interference.

The Bolsheviks inherited this fundamental contradiction, and in large measure they were unprepared to deal with it. True, the Bolsheviks had given some thought to the national question even before World War I, because they recognized the power of nationalism. **Joseph Stalin**, who would later become the dictator of the USSR, even wrote an entire book in 1913 called *Marxism and the National Question.* However, the national question was not the principal focus of the Bolsheviks, who believed that *class*—not nationality—represented the main principle of division in human societies. Recall the first words of Marx's *Communist Manifesto* of 1848: "The history of all hitherto existing society is the history of class struggles." The Bolsheviks also believed that if they could solve the problem of class struggle by making a violent revolution that would introduce socialism, then the national question would essentially solve itself. Class was primary, in short, while nationality was only secondary. Thus aside from a few slogans that were designed to appeal to non-Russians but did not really offer much concrete, the Bolsheviks did not pay a great deal of attention to national issues. Moreover, the Bolsheviks actually opposed the principle of **federalism,** because they presumed that it would dilute the working class and divert attention away from class struggle. In March of 1917, Stalin wrote an article entitled "Against Federalism," in which he asserted that "federalism in Russia does not and cannot solve the national question," but instead "merely confuses it and complicates it."[6] So in 1917, the Bolsheviks really envisioned only two possible outcomes for non-Russian peoples: either full independence and separation from the rest of Russia, on the one hand, or inclusion in a unitary socialist state, on the other. Poland and Finland seemed to fall into the first category,[7] but the future of other parts of the Russian Empire was less clear.

Once they had taken power, the Bolsheviks had to deal with the national question directly, rather than merely dismissing it as less important than the question of class. The situation was complicated significantly by the fact that the Germans were occupying parts of the tsarist empire, and the Bolsheviks had to negotiate with Germany in order to secure peace. Recall that in 1915 the Germans had begun a major offensive against Russia that penetrated deep into the Russian Empire itself. Russia thus lost control over Poland, Lithuania, parts of Belarus, and a good portion of Latvia. As Russia experienced revolution in 1917, the situation became even worse, with the Germans putting ever greater pressure first on the Provisional Government and then, after October, on the Bolsheviks. The Germans themselves were fighting a war on two fronts, and so their major goal was to knock Russia out of the war and then concentrate all of their forces on the western front so as to defeat Britain and France. A secondary goal was to deprive Russia, especially after the Bolshevik Revolution, of as much territory as possible—for two major reasons. First, since the German military leadership was deeply conservative, it wanted to keep the Bolsheviks as far away from Germany as possible so as to prevent any revolutionary contamination. Second, because Germany and Austria-Hungary were facing serious food supply problems of their own, they were looking for grain and other foodstuffs wherever they could find it. They reckoned that if they could pry the western portions of the old Russian Empire away from the Bolsheviks, they would gain access to its agricultural produce and be able to feed their own populations so as to prevent their own collapse. The Bolsheviks, for their part, had come to power with "Peace" as one of their slogans, and since the Russian army was disintegrating, they really had little choice but to accept the terms that the Germans set at the city of Brest-Litovsk.

Peace negotiations were conducted in Brest-Litovsk from January to March of 1918. The Bolsheviks were especially reluctant to recognize the loss of Ukraine, but the Germans were determined to secure its nominal independence from Russia, with the idea that Germany would be able to dominate the country and acquire its foodstuffs. The Bolshevik delegation initially tried to stall as a way of resisting the German demands, but when the Germans began marching on Petrograd—it was precisely then that

---

6   Stalin as cited in Carr, *Bolshevik Revolution,* 137.

7   Recall that these were the only two parts of the Russian Empire with respect to which the tsars had ever recognized a constitution.

the Bolsheviks moved the capital to Moscow to have it further from danger—the Bolsheviks realized that they had no choice but to sign the draconian **Treaty of Brest-Litovsk.** By that treaty, the new Bolshevik state signed away a huge portion of the old Russian Empire, where a series new countries—Poland, Finland, Ukraine, Lithuania, Latvia, Estonia—now appeared, all of them allied with Germany or under German military domination.

This was the context as the Bolsheviks prepared their first constitution discussed in the previous chapter. To understand the place of Soviet-style federalism for that constitution, we can do little better than to turn to Edward Carr again.

READING 2.2

EDWARD H. CARR, "THE CONSTITUTION OF THE RSFSR"

The relationship—between the federal and the unitary state—was not explicitly raised in the debates on the constitution, but was implicit in discussions of the interpretation to be given to the term "federal" in the title of the RSFSR. The words "federal" and "federation", while having a precise meaning in constitutional law, are politically neutral in colour. It was the tradition of the French revolution which influenced nineteenth-century socialist views of "federation". In his address of 1850 to the Communist League Marx had written that, while German bourgeois democrats supported federation and sought to weaken the central power by strengthening the independence of the regions, "the workers must use their influence not only for the one and indivisible German republic, but for a decisive centralization of force within it in the hands of the state power". Engels at the very end of his life, attacking the system of "petty states" under the federal constitutions of Germany and Switzerland, held that "the proletariat can make use only of the form of the one and indivisible republic". On the other hand, Proudhon and the anarchists, invoking the other aspect of the French revolutionary tradition, freely used the words "federal" and "federation" without constitutional precision, but with a strong flavour of emotional approval, to indicate a loose voluntary association of local units — the antithesis of the strong and centralized state.

Marxist objections to federalism were inherited by Lenin and the Bolsheviks, and were reinforced by the long struggle with the Jewish Bund, which, following the precedent of Austrian social-democracy, wished to introduce the federal principle into the organization of the party. Even later, when prejudices against a federal constitution for the state had been overcome, Bolshevism never wavered in its insistence on a unitary, centralized Russian communist party. But at the outset objections to federalism were as rigidly maintained in state as in party organization. In 1903 Armenian social-democrats were rebuked by Lenin for advocating a federal Russian republic. In 1913 Lenin noted that "Marxists are, of course, hostile to federation and decentralization" (he evidently drew no clear distinction between them) on the ground that "capitalism for its development demands as large and as highly centralized states as possible"; and in a letter of the same year he declared himself "against federation in principle", adding that it "weakens the economic link and is an unsuitable form for a single state". The argument was not constitutional but practical. Federation meant decentralization; the unitary state was praised as the instrument of centralization.

Like other political principles, opposition to federation was for Lenin never an absolute rule. It had, for instance, to be weighed against the principle of national self-determination.

The party tradition continued, however, to be strongly weighted against federation. Stalin in an article of March 1917 *Against Federalism* declared that the trend was everywhere towards centralization.

> Is it not clear [he concluded] that federalism in Russia does not and cannot solve the national question, that it merely confuses and complicates it with quixotic ambitions to turn back the wheel of history?

Party orthodoxy was modified only by the victory of the revolution. In the first place, the Soviet system, purporting to follow the precedent of the Paris commune and professedly based on the voluntary organization of local organs to form a central authority, was the very essence of what nineteenth-century socialist writers had meant by federalism. Secondly, federation was the one political concept which could be invoked to satisfy the aspirations of the former dependent nations of the Tsarist empire and at the same time retain them within a Soviet framework; once the right of national self-determination had been proclaimed, federalism became an indispensable corollary—or antidote. The turning-point coincided with Lenin's *State and Revolution,* written on the eve of the October revolution. Engels in the criticism of the Erfurt programme, in which he had declared so bluntly for the "one and indivisible republic", had none the less admitted that "in England, where four nations live on two islands", federation would be "a step forward". Lenin, quoting this passage, described federation as "an exception and a hindrance to development" which may yet be "a 'step forward' in certain special conditions". And "among these special conditions the national question appears prominently". But the discussion that followed made it clear that the issue of federal or unitary state was still for Lenin a question not of constitutional form, but of the decentralization or centralization of power; and it was significant that this qualified conversion to federation occurred in a work in which he was largely concerned with the dying away of the state.

Such was the background of the federal aspects of Soviet constitution-making. The Declaration of Rights of the Toiling and Exploited People, drafted by VTsIK and presented by way of ultimatum to the Constituent Assembly, proclaimed the Russian Soviet republic as "a federation of national Soviet republics"; and, after the dissolution of the Constituent Assembly, the third All-Russian Congress of Soviets instructed VTsIK to draft" the fundamental principles of the constitution of the Russian Federal Republic". The use of the term was doubtless due in part to its popular appeal. It even gave encouragement to syndicalist visions of a "federation of social-economic organizations". But the position was made clear in a statement by Stalin which was published in *Pravda* on April 3 and 4, 1918, while the drafting commission was at work. The Soviet federation did not represent, like the Swiss or American federations, a union of territories divided only by geographical environment or by historical accident; it was "a union of historically distinct territories differentiated by a special way of life, as well as by their national composition". Whereas, moreover, bourgeois federation was "a transitional stage from independence to imperialist unification", Soviet federation represented a transition, to be achieved "with the lapse of time", from "forced unification" under the Tsars to "the voluntary and fraternal union of the working masses of all nations and peoples of Russia". The ultimate goal was "the future *socialist* unitarism". On Stalin's motion a resolution in similar terms was adopted by the drafting commission as the basis of its work. What clearly emerged was the view of federation not as a good in itself (that would have been too much at variance with established party doctrine), but as a convenient transitional stage, necessitated by the particular conditions of the national question in Russia, to something better. This view was confirmed by the party programme, adopted a year later, which described "a federal union of states organized on the Soviet model "as" one of the transitional forms to complete unity".

These uncertainties were reflected in the curious fact that, while the RSFSR was freely referred to as a federation, and while the word "federal" appeared in its title and in the initial chapters of the constitution devoted to general principles, the word nowhere recurred in the body of the constitution. The extent and composition of the federation, as well as much of its constitutional machinery, were undefined. This was easily explicable by the precarious conditions in which the constitution was drafted. In the spring and early summer of 1918 German armies were in occupation of the former Baltic provinces, of most of White Russia and of the whole Ukraine, and had penetrated even into the northern Caucasus and into Transcaucasia, where Baku stood out as a solitary islet of Bolshevik power. A Bolshevik Turkestan was isolated from all communication with Europe. Siberia, where Bolshevik authority seemed at one moment to be slowly consolidating itself, was completely cut off after May 1918 by the revolt of the Czech legions, which also led to the establishment of an anti-Bolshevik government on the Volga. In these circumstances nearly everything in the constitution necessarily remained provisional. The Declaration of Rights of the Toiling and Exploited People had left

> to the workers and peasants of each nationality the right to make an independent decision, at their own plenipotentiary congress of Soviets, whether they desire, and, if so, on what basis, to participate in the federal government and in other Soviet institutions.

The resolution of the third All-Russian Congress of Soviets on the drafting of the constitution provided that "the order of participation of individual republics and separate regions in the federal government" should be determined when the republics and regions were eventually constituted. But this had not yet occurred; and a constitution could not well be made for a federation of indeterminate or non-existent units. What was in fact created in 1918 was a Russian republic of undefined territorial extent. Room was made in the general provisions of the constitution for the incorporation in it of "autonomous regions"; and it was laid down in article 11 of the constitution that the highest organs of an autonomous region, its congress of Soviets and executive committee, would have the same rank and status as the regional congress of Soviets and executive committee of any other region, Russian or non-Russian, of the RSFSR. In other words, federation was treated in the constitution, as in the earlier writings of Lenin and Stalin, as equivalent to decentralization. It was a matter of administrative organization rather than of the essential character of the constitution. The party resolution of 1913 on the national question had failed to distinguish between "broad regional autonomy" and "democratic local self-government"; their identity was still assumed in Bolshevik thought. Of specifically federal machinery, as distinct from the division of powers between central and local organs of government, the constitution of 1918 contained no trace whatever. These arrangements may have been well enough designed to secure a reasonable degree of local self-government for national groups without endangering the essential unity of the RSFSR. But they were not federal in a constitutional sense.

End of Reading 2.2

Thus the Bolsheviks, as they prepared the constitution, realized that they had to make some concession to non-Russian nationalism if they were ever to gain territories like Ukraine back again. Offering non-Russians a federation—a less centralized state—was one way to do this. Federation would not give territories like Ukraine full independence, as some Ukrainian nationalists wanted, but it would give them a degree of autonomy and self-determination. It is important to emphasize that the Bolsheviks had not been converted to the idea of federalism as a good in itself—they believed too strongly in the need for a centralized, unitary state for that—but they did recognize federalism as a convenient transitional stage given the conditions in which they found themselves. Thus article 2 of the constitution stated, "The Russian Soviet Republic is established on the principle of a free union of free nations, as a federation of Soviet national republics." The Bolsheviks did not have a lot to say at this point about what Soviet federalism would actually entail. And thus Soviet Russia became a federal republic, but without the idea of "federalism" having much specific content or meaning.

Things began to take more concrete shape as Germany lost the war in the west and as the Civil War progressed. By November of 1918 Germany had been forced to seek an armistice with Britain, France, and the United States and had thus lost the war. The Bolsheviks used the occasion to repudiate the Treaty of Brest-Litovsk, which cleared the way for the new Soviet Russia to claim the lost territories again. At the end of 1918 the Bolsheviks were still in no position to do this, as they were only six months or so into their Civil War against the Whites. But gradually, as the Bolsheviks defeated their White opponents, they began to move into non-Russian territories such as Ukraine. And as they did so, they realized that "federalism" represented a good slogan

for attracting Ukrainians and others to the Bolshevik cause. To insist on a centralized, unitary state would likely have alienated Ukrainians. But offering them their own republic within a larger Soviet state would help to secure their acceptance of Soviet rule.

The idea of federalism proved similarly useful to the Bolsheviks in the east of the country. In 1919, at one of the darker moments of the Civil War for the Bolsheviks, Lenin and his comrades realized that granting forms of federalism could earn them allies in their struggle. The **Bashkirs**, a semi-nomadic Turkic people with a capable fight force, initially supported White forces operating out of western Siberia. At a critical point, the Bolsheviks approached the Bashkir leadership and offered them their own autonomous republic within the RSFSR if they switched sides and fought against the Whites. Since the Whites were not offering such a republic, the Bashkirs changed sides and joined the Bolsheviks. This was followed by the proliferation of other autonomous national units within RSFSR for Tatars, Chuvash, and other ethnic groups. In short, in order both to gain allies during the Civil War and to facilitate the reincorporation of territories that had enjoyed a brief period of independence after 1917, the Bolsheviks found themselves creating republics based on the national principle. Eventually, these republics would be assembled into the USSR.

The Bolsheviks were not able to reconstitute the old Russian Empire completely. They were prepared to recognize the independence of Finland and Poland, while the Baltic states—Estonia, Latvia, and Lithuania—also became independent. For the most part Soviet Russia was able to establish borders with these new states without too much conflict, although in the case of Poland it took yet another war (1920-21), because both countries claimed the same territory.[8] The lands of the south Caucuses—Azerbaijan, Georgia, and Armenia—had enjoyed almost three years of independence (1918-21), but Bolshevik forces were able to conquer this area as well, while also granting national republics to the ethnic groups there. It took a bit longer to reincorporate Central Asia into the new Soviet state, but by the mid-1920s the Bolsheviks had extended their control essentially as far as the tsars had before them, eventually creating national republics for Kazakhs, Uzbeks, Tajiks, Turkmens, and Kyrgyz.

Thus in its territorial extent, the new Soviet country looked quite similar to the old Russian Empire—minus Finland, Poland, and the Baltic region. But it took a very different form. Instead of a multinational empire ruled by a tsar and his bureaucracy, the Bolsheviks created a union of national territorial units—**the Union of Soviet Socialist Republics**, or **USSR**. Almost every republic was identified with a particular ethnic or national group—a Russian Republic, a Ukrainian Republic, a Georgian Republic, etc. But even if the USSR took the form of a "union" or a "federation" of national republics, nonetheless the country factually remained a centralized state. This was because even while the structures of the state were formally decentralized in the form of national republics, the Communist Party—in which the real decisions for the country were being made—remained highly centralized in Moscow. The result was that the Bolsheviks created a kind of pseudo-federalism: a country that took the form of a federation but actually retained the characteristics of a centralized state.

To better understand the strange character of the USSR in this regard, we turn to two texts. The first is the **Constitution of 1924**, which describes the structure of the USSR in somewhat greater detail. Like the RSFSR constitution of 1918, the constitution of 1924 essentially regularized a situation that had *already* come into being factually. The constitution of 1924 took the form of a treaty, ostensibly among a set of independent socialist republics (including the RSFSR), which established a federation or union. The "Declaration" section of the text explains how this Soviet solution to the nationalities problem was supposedly superior to the solutions offered by the "bourgeois state."

DOCUMENT 2.9

CONSTITUTION OF THE USSR (1924)[9]

PART I: DECLARATION

Since the foundation of the Soviet Republics, the states of the world have been divided into two camps: the camp of capitalism and the camp of socialism. There, in the camp of capitalism: national hate and inequality, colonial slavery and chauvinism, national oppression and massacres, brutalities and imperialistic wars. Here, in the camp of socialism: reciprocal confidence and peace, national liberty and equality, the pacific co-existence and fraternal collaboration of peoples. The attempts made by the capitalistic world during the past ten years to decide the question of nationalities by bringing together the principle of the free development of peoples with a system of exploitation of man by man have been fruitless. In addition, the number of national conflicts becomes more and more confusing, even menacing the capitalist regime. The bourgeoisie has proven itself incapable of realizing a harmonious collaboration of the peoples. It is only in the camp of the Soviets, only under the conditions of the dictatorship of the proletariat that has grouped around itself the majority of the people, that it has been possible to eliminate the oppression of nationalities, to create an atmosphere of mutual confidence and to establish the basis of a fraternal collaboration of peoples. It is only thanks to these circumstances that the Soviet Republics have succeeded in repulsing the imperialist attacks both internally and externally. It is only thanks to them that the Soviet Republics have succeeded in satisfactorily ending a civil war, in assuring their existence and in dedicating themselves to pacific economic reconstruction. But the years of the war have not passed without leaving their trace. The devastated fields, the closed factories, the forces of production destroyed and the economic resources exhausted, this heritage

---

8   Poland's claims were historical—the territory in question had been Polish before 1772. The Bolsheviks' claims were ethnic—the territory was inhabited primarily by Ukrainians and Belarusians.

9   A full text can be found at http://users.cyberone.com.au/myers/ussr1924.html, as well as in Rex A. Wade, ed., *Documents of Soviet History, vol. 3 Lenin's Heirs* 1923-1925 (Gulf Breeze, Fl., 1995).

of the war renders insufficient the isolated economic efforts of the several Republics. National economic reestablishment is impossible as long as the Republics remain separated. On the other hand, the instability of the international situation and the danger of new attacks make inevitable the creation of a united front of the Soviet Republics in the presence of capitalist surroundings. Finally, the very structure of Soviet power, international by nature of class, pushes the masses of workers of the Soviet Republics to unite in one socialist family. All these considerations insistently demand the union of the Soviet Republics into one federated state capable of guaranteeing external security, economic prosperity internally, and the free national development of peoples. The will of the peoples of the Soviet Republics recently assembled in Congress, where they decided unanimously to form the "Union of Socialist Soviet Republics," is a sure guarantee that this Union is a free federation of peoples equal in rights, that the right to freely withdraw from the Union is assured to each Republic, that access to the Union is open to all Republics already existing as well as those that may be born in the future, that the new federal state will be the worthy crowning of the principles laid down as early as October 1917 of the pacific co-existence and fraternal collaboration of peoples, that it will serve as a bulwark against the capitalist world and mark a new decisive step towards the union of workers of all countries in one world-wide Socialist Soviet Republic.

PART II: TREATY

The Russian Socialist Federal Soviet Republic, the Socialist Soviet Republic of Ukraine, the Socialist Soviet Republic of White Russia, and the Socialist Soviet Republic of Transcaucasia (including the Socialist Soviet Republic of Azerbaijan, the Socialist Soviet Republic of Georgia, and the Socialist Soviet Republic of Armenia) unite themselves in one federal state – "The Union of Socialist Soviet Republics."

Chapter I. Attributions of the Supreme Organs of Power of the Union

Article 1. The Union of Socialist Soviet Republics through its supreme organs has the following powers: (a) To represent the Union in its international relations; to conclude all diplomatic relations; to conclude treaties, political and otherwise, with other States; (b) to modify the exterior frontiers of the Union, as well as to regulate questions concerning the modification of frontiers between the member Republics; (c) to conclude treaties concerning the reception of new Republics into the Union; (d) to declare war and to conclude peace; (e) to conclude internal and external loans of the Union and to authorize internal and external loans of the member Republics; (f) to ratify international treaties; (g) to direct commerce with foreign countries and to determine the system of internal commerce; (h) to establish the basic principles and the general plan of the national economy of the Union; to define the domains of industry and industrial enterprises that are of federal interest; to conclude treaties of concession both federal and in the name of the member Republics; (i) to direct transportation and the postal and telegraph services; (j) to organize and direct the armed forces of the Union; (k) to approve the budget of the federal state which includes the budgets of the member Republics; to establish duties and federal revenues, making additions and reductions in order to balance the member Republics' budgets; to authorize duties and supplementary taxes to meet the member Republics' budgets; (l) to establish a uniform system of money and credit; (m) to establish general principles of exploitation and use of the earth, as well as those of the sub-soil, the forests, and the waters of the territories of the Union; (n) to establish federal legislation on the emigration from the territory of one of the Republics to the territory of another and to set up a fund for such emigration; (o) to establish principles of the judicial organization and procedure, as well as civil and criminal legislation for the Union; (p) to establish the fundamental laws regarding work; (q) to establish the general principles regarding public instruction; (r) to establish the general measures regarding public hygiene; (s) to establish a standard system of weights and measures; (t) to organize federal statistics; (u) to fix the fundamental legislation regarding federal nationality, with reference to the rights of foreigners; (v) to exercise the right of amnesty in all territories of the Union; (w) to abrogate the acts of the Congresses of the Soviets and the Central Executive Committees of the member Republics contrary to the present Constitution; (x) to arbitrate litigious questions between the member Republics.

Article 2. The approval and modification of the fundamental principles of the present Constitution belong exclusively to the Congress of Soviets of the Union of Socialist Soviet Republics.

CHAPTER II: Sovereign Rights of the Member Republics

Article 3. The sovereignty of the member Republics is limited only in the matters indicated in the present Constitution, as coming within the competence of the Union. Outside of those limits, each member Republic exerts its public powers independently; the U.S.S.R. protects the rights of the member Republics.

Article 4. Each one of the member Republics retains the right to freely withdraw from the Union.

Article 5. The member Republics will make changes in their Constitutions to conform with the present Constitution.

Article 6. The territory of the member Republics cannot be modified without their consent; also, any limitation or modification or suppression of Article 4 must have the approval of all the member Republics of the Union.

Article 7. Just one federal nationality is established for the citizens of the member Republics.

CHAPTER III: Congress of Soviets of the Union

Article 8. The supreme organ of power of the U.S.S.R. is the Congress of Soviets, and, in the recesses of the Congress of Soviets – the Central Executive Committee of the U.S.S.R. which is composed of the Federal Soviet and the Soviet of Nationalities.

Article 9. The Congress of Soviets of the U.S.S.R. is composed of representatives of the city and town Soviets on the basis of one deputy per 25,000 electors, and of representatives of the provincial Congresses of Soviets on the basis of one deputy per 125,000 inhabitants.

CHAPTER IV: The Central Executive Committee of the Union

Article 13. The Central Executive Committee of the U.S.S.R. is composed of the Federal Soviet and the Soviet of Nationalities.

Article 14. The Congress of Soviets of the U.S.S.R. elects the Federal Soviet from among the representatives of the member Republics in proportion to the population of each one to make a grand total of 371 members.

Article 15. The Soviet of Nationalities is composed of representatives of the member Republics and associated autonomous Republics of the R.S.F.S.R. on the basis of five representatives for each member Republic, and one representative for each associated autonomous Republic....

CHAPTER XI: The Unified Political Administration of State

Article 61. With the goal of unifying the revolutionary efforts of the member Republics in their struggle against political and economic counter-revolution, spying and banditry, there shall be created under the jurisdiction of the C.P.C. of the U.S.S.R., a Unified State Political Administration (O.G.P.U.) of which the President shall be a consulting member of the C.P.C. of the U.S.S.R.

Article 62. The O.G.P.U. of the U.S.S.R. directs the activities of the local organs of O.G.P.U. through its delegates under the jurisdiction of the C.P.C. of the member Republics, acting in virtue of a special ruling sanctioned through legislative channels.

CHAPTER XI: Arms, Flag and Capital of the Union

Article 70. The insignia of the State of the U.S.S.R. is composed of a sickle and a hammer on an earthly globe, surrounded by sun rays and framed with wheat stalks, with an inscription in the six languages mentioned in Article 34: "Proletarians of all countries, unite!" Above the insignia, there shall be a five pointed star.

Article 71. The flag of the State of the U.S.S.R. shall be in red or vermillion cloth with the arms of the Union.

Article 72. The Capital of the U.S.S.R. is Moscow.

End of document 2.7

The Constitution of 1924 gives a sense of how the USSR was to be structured formally, but this represents only part of the way in which the Bolsheviks addressed the national question in Russia. The reading below, by Terry Martin of Harvard University, seeks to explain the logic of Soviet policy on the national question as it emerged in the crucial years of 1919-23. Martin offers an interesting argument for why the USSR should be considered an "affirmative action empire." Why does he use this term? In what ways was the USSR an empire, and in what fashion did it promote "affirmative action"? What does "affirmative action" mean in this Soviet context? Does it seem that the Bolsheviks had found a viable solution to the national question?

READING 2.3

AN AFFIRMATIVE-ACTION EMPIRE: THE EMERGENCE OF THE SOVIET NATIONALITIES POLICY, 1919-1923[10]

Terry Martin

When the Bolsheviks seized power in October 1917, they did not possess a coherent nationalities policy. They had only a slogan, which they shared with Woodrow Wilson, of the right of all peoples to self-determination. This slogan, however was designed to recruit ethnic support for the revolution, not to provide a model for the governing of a multiethnic state. The strength of nationalism as a mobilizing force during the revolution and civil war greatly surprised and disturbed the Bolsheviks They expected nationalism in Poland and Finland, but the numerous nationalist movements that sprung up across most of the former Russian empire were not expected. In particular, the strong nationalist movement in Ukraine, which most Bolsheviks felt differed little from Russia, was particularly unnerving. This direct confrontation with nationalism compelled the Bolsheviks to formulate a new nationalities policy.

The Logic Of The Soviet Nationalities Policy

Nationalities policy was not on the agenda when the Eighth Communist Party Congress convened in March 1919. However, during a discussion of the Party Program, a polemic arose over the Bolsheviks' traditional support for the right of national self-determination. Piatakov argued that "during a sufficiently large and torturous experience in the borderlands, the slogan of the right of nations to self-determination has shown itself in practice, during the social revolution, as a slogan uniting all counterrevolutionary forces." Once the proletariat had seized power, Piatakov maintained, national self-determination became irrelevant: "it's just a diplomatic game, or worse than a game if we take it seriously. Piatakov was supported by Bukharin, who argued that the right to sell-determination could only be invested in the proletariat, not in "some fictitious so-called 'national will.'"

Lenin had clashed with Piatakov and others on this issue both before and during the revolution, and he answered this new challenge with characteristic vigor. Nationalism had united all counterrevolutionary forces, Lenin readily agreed, but it had also attracted the Bolsheviks' class allies. The Finnish bourgeoisie had successfully "deceived the working masses that the Muscovites *(Moskvaly)*, chauvinists, Great Russians want[ed] to oppress the Finns." Arguments such as Piatakov's served to increase that fear and therefore strengthen national resistance. It was only "thanks to our acknowledgement of [the Finns'] right to self-determination that the process of [class] differentiation was eased there." Nationalism was fueled by historic distrust: "the working masses of other nations were full of distrust *(nedovcrie)* toward Great Russia, as a kulak and oppressor nation." Only the right to self-determination could overcome that distrust, Lenin argued, but Piatakov's policy would instead make the party the heir to Tsarist chauvinism: scratch any Communist and you find a Great Russian chauvinist... He sits in many of us and we must fight him."

The congress supported Lenin's position and retained the right of national self-determination. Of course, the majority of the former Russian empires nationalities were forced to exercise that right within the confines of the Soviet Union The period from 1919 to 1923, therefore, was devoted to working out what exactly non-Russian "national self-determination" could mean in the context of a unitary Soviet state. The result was the Soviet nationalities policy: a strategy aimed at disarming nationalism by granting the forms of nationhood. This policy was based on a diagnosis of nationalism worked out largely by Lenin and Stalin. Lenin addressed the national question repeatedly from 1912 to 1916, when he formulated and defended the slogan of self-determination, and again from 1919 to 1922, after the alarming success of nationalist movements during the civil war. Stalin was the Bolsheviks' acknowledged "master of the nationalities question": author of their standard prerevolutionary text—*Marxism and the Nationalities*

---

10   The text here is from Roland Grigor Suny, ed., The Structure of Soviet History: *Essays and Documents*, 2nd. Ed. (Oxford, 2012), 97-107

Question, Commissar of Nationalities from 1917 to 1924, and official spokesman on the national question at party congresses. Lenin and Stalin were in fundamental agreement on both the logical rationale and the essential aspects of this new policy, though they came into conflict in 1922 over important issues of implementation.

Their diagnosis of the nationalities problem rested on three premises. First, the point on which Piatakov and Lenin agreed, nationalism was a uniquely dangerous mobilizing ideology because it had the potential to forge an all-class alliance for national goals. Lenin called nationalism a "bourgeois trick," but recognized that like the hedgehog's, it was a good one. It worked because it presented legitimate social grievances in a national form. At the Twelfth Party Congress in 1923, Bukharin, now a fervid defender of the party's nationalities policy, noted that "when we tax [the non-Russian peasantry], their discontent takes on a national form, is given a national interpretation, which is then exploited by our opponents." Ernest Gellner parodied this argument as the "Wrong-Address Theory" of nationalism: "Just as extreme Shi'ite Muslims hold that Archangel Gabriel made a mistake, delivering the Message to Mohammed when it was intended for Ali, so Marxists basically like to think that the spirit of history or human consciousness made a terrible boob. The wakening message was intended for *classes,* but by some terrible postal error was delivered to *nations.*"

The Bolsheviks viewed nationalism, then, as a masking ideology. Masking metaphors recur again and again in their discourse about nationality. Stalin was particularly fond of them: "the national flag is sewn on only to deceive the masses, as a popular flag, a convenience for covering up (*dlia prykrytie*) the counterrevolutionary plans of the national bourgeoisie." "If bourgeois circles attempt to give a national tint (*natsional'naia okraska*) to [our] conflicts, then it is only because it is convenient to hide their battle for power behind a national costume." This interpretation of nationalism as a masking ideology helps explain why the Bolsheviks remained highly suspicious of national self-expression, even after they adopted a policy explicitly designed to encourage it. For example in 1934, in justifying a wave of national repression, Stalin characteristically invoked a masking metaphor: "The remnants of capitalism in the people's consciousness are much more dynamic in the sphere of nationality than in any other area. This is because they can mask themselves so well in a national costume."

This understanding of nationalism led Piatakov to support the only apparently logical response: attack nationalism as a counterrevolutionary ideology and nationality itself as a reactionary remnant of the capitalist era. Lenin and Stalin, however, drew the exact opposite conclusion. They reasoned as follows: By granting the forms of nationhood, the Soviet state could split the above-class national alliance for statehood. Class divisions, then, would naturally emerge, which would allow the Soviet government to recruit proletarian and peasant support for their socialist agenda. Lenin argued that Finnish independence had intensified, not reduced, class conflict. National self-determination would have the same consequences within the Soviet Union. Likewise, Stalin insisted it was necessary to "take" autonomy away from [the national bourgeoisie], having first cleansed it of its bourgeois filth and transformed it from bourgeois into Soviet autonomy." A belief gradually emerged, then, that the above-class appeal of nationalism could be disarmed by granting the forms of nationhood.

This conclusion was buttressed by a second premise: National consciousness was an unavoidable historic phase that all peoples must pass through on the way to internationalism. In their prerevolutionary writing, Lenin and Stalin argued that nationality emerged only with the onset of capitalism and was itself a consequence of capitalist production. It was not an essential or permanent attribute of mankind. Piatikov understandably interpreted this as meaning that under socialism nationality would be irrelevant and therefore should be granted no special status. However, both Lenin and Stalin insisted that nationality would persist for a long time even under socialism. In fact, national self-awareness would initially increase. Already in 1916, Lenin stated that "mankind can proceed towards the complete freedom of all oppressed nations." Stalin later explicated this paradox as follows: "We are undertaking the maximum development of national culture, so that it will exhaust itself completely and thereby create the base for the organization of international socialist culture."

Two factors appear to have combined to create this sense of the inevitability of a national stage of development. First, the collapse of the Austro-Hungarian empire and, second, the surprisingly strong nationalist movements of 1917 to 1921 within the former Russian empire, which greatly increased the Bolsheviks' respect for the power and ubiquity of nationalism. Stalin was particularly impressed by the process of national succession in the formerly German cities of Austro-Hungary. At the 1921 party congress, he pointed out that just fifty years ago, all cities in Hungary were predominately German, but had now become Hungarian. Likewise, he maintained, all Russian cities in Ukraine and Belorussia would "inevitably" be nationalized. Opposing this was futile: "It is impossible to go against history (*nel'zia itti protiv istorii*)." Elsewhere Stalin called this pattern "a general law of national development in the entire world." National consolidation, then was unavoidable even under socialism.

Moreover, this national stage of development took on a more positive connotation as it became associated not only with capitalism, but with modernization in general. In his rebuttal of Piatakov and Bukharin, citing the example of the Bashkirs, Lenin stated that "one must await the development of a given nation, the differentiation of proletariat from bourgeois elements, which is unavoidable... the path from the medieval to bourgeois democracy, or from bourgeois to proletarian democracy. This is an absolutely unavoidable path." As Lenin focused Bolshevik attention on the Soviet Union's eastern, "backward" nationalities, the consolidation of nationhood became associated with historical progress. This trend reached its climax during the Cultural Revolution, when Soviet propaganda would boast that in the Far North, the thousand-year process of national formation had been telescoped into a mere decade. The formation of nations, then, came to be seen as both an unavoidable and positive stage in the modernization of the Soviet Union.

A third and final premise asserted that non-Russian nationalism was primarily a response to tsarist oppression and was motivated by an historically justifiable distrust (*nedoverie*) of the Great Russians. This argument was pressed most forcefully by Lenin, who already in 1914 had attacked Rosa Luxembourg's denial of the right of separation as "objectively aiding the Black Hundred Great Russians.... Absorbed by the fight with nationalism in Poland, Rosa Luxembourg forgot about the nationalism of the Great Russians, though it is exactly this nationalism that is the most dangerous of all." The nationalism of the oppressed, Lenin maintained, had a "democratic content" which must be supported, while the nationalism of the oppressor had no redeeming feature. He ended with the slogan: "fight against all nationalisms and, first of all, against Great Russian nationalism."

Bolshevik conduct between 1917 and 1919 convinced Lenin that the All-Russian Communist party had inherited the psychology of Great Power chauvinism from the tsarist regime. In non-Russian regions, the Bolshevik party, relying almost exclusively on the minority Russian proletariat and colonists, had frequently adopted an overtly chauvinist attitude toward the local population. This attitude alarmed Lenin and prompted his harsh words for Piatakov in March 1919, as Piatakov had supported an anti-Ukrainian line in Kiev. In December 1919, Lenin again launched a fierce denunciation of Bolshevik chauvinism in Ukraine. His anger climaxed during the notorious Georgian affair of 1922, when he denounced Dzerzhinskii, Stalin, and Ordzhonikidze as Great Russian chauvinists. (Russified natives, he maintained, were often the worst chauvinists.) Bolshevik chauvinism inspired Lenin to coin the term *"rusotiapstvo"* (mindless Russian chauvinism), which then entered the Bolshevik lexicon and became an invaluable weapon in the national republics' rhetorical arsenals.

Lenin's concern over Great Russian chauvinism led to the establishment of a crucial principle of the Soviet nationalities policy. In December 1922, he reiterated his 1914 position with an admonition that one must "distinguish between the nationalism of oppressor nations and the nationalism of oppressed nations, the nationalism of large nations and the nationalism of small nations ... in relation to the second nationalism, in almost all historical practice, we nationals of the large nations are guilty, because of an infinite amount of violence [committed]." This concept entered formulaic Bolshevik rhetoric as the distinction between offensive (*nastupitelnyi*) Great Power nationalism and defensive (*oboronitelnyi*) local nationalism, the latter being accepted as a justifiable response to the former. This belief in turn led to the establishment of the important "Principle of the Greater Danger": namely, that Great Power (or Great Russian) chauvinism was a greater danger than local nationalism.

Lenin's extremely categorical expression of this principle led to one of his two differences of opinion with Stalin over nationalities policy in late 1922. They also disagreed about the structure of the Soviet Union.... . Stalin had supported the Principle of the Greater Danger prior to 1922-23, reiterated his support in 1923, and supervised a nationalities policy based on that principle from 1923 through 1934. Nevertheless, Stalin was uncomfortable with the insistence that *all* local nationalism could be explained as a response to Great Power chauvinism. Based on his experience in Georgia, Stalin insisted that Georgian nationalism was also characterized by Great Power exploitation of their Ossetine and Abkhaz minorities. Stalin, therefore, always paired his attacks on Great Russian chauvinism with a complementary attack on the lesser danger of local nationalism. This difference in emphasis led Stalin, in September 1922, to jocularly accuse Lenin of "national liberalism." This difference of emphasis was also evident in Lenin and Stalin's terminology.

Lenin always referred to Russian nationalism as Great Power chauvinism, which distinguished it from other nationalisms, while Stalin preferred the term Great Russian chauvinism. Still, this was a difference in emphasis, not content. Stalin consistently supported the Principle of the Greater Danger.

These three premises, then, combined to form the theoretical rationale for the nationalities policy that Lenin and Stalin successfully imposed on the Bolshevik party through a series of resolutions at the 1919, 1921, and 1923 party congresses. Their reasoning can be summarized as follows. Nationalism is a masking ideology that leads legitimate class interests to be expressed, not in an appropriate class-based socialist movement, but rather in the form of an above-class national movement. National identity is not a primordial quality, but rather an unavoidable by-product of the modern capitalist *and* early socialist world, which must be passed through before a mature international socialist world can come into being.

Because national identity *is* a real phenomenon in the modern world, the nationalism of the oppressed non-Russian peoples expresses not only masked class protest, but also legitimate national grievances against the oppressive Great Power chauvinism of the dominant Russian nationality. Neither nationalism nor national identity, therefore, can be unequivocally condemned as reactionary. *Some* national claims—those confined to the realm of national form—are in fact legitimate and must be granted to split the above-class national alliance. Such a policy will speed the emergence of class cleavages, and so allow the party to recruit non-Russian proletarian and peasant support for its socialist agenda. Nationalism will be disarmed by granting the forms of nationhood.

I have thus far ignored one other factor, foreign policy concerns, that did play a role in the formation of the Soviet nationalities policy. Already in November 1917, Lenin and Stalin issued an "Appeal to all Muslim Toilers of Russia and the East," which promised to end imperial exploitation within the former Russian empire and called on Muslims outside Russia to overthrow their colonial masters. This link between domestic nationalities policy and foreign policy goals in the East was quite common during the civil war period. After the Treaty of Riga fixed the Soviet-Polish border in 1921, this concern shifted westward. The Soviet Union's western border now cut through the ethnographic territory of Finns, Belo-russians, Ukrainians, and Rumanians, and it was hoped that a generous treatment of those nationalities would attract support from their ethnic brethren in neighboring countries. This foreign policy goal, however, was never the primary motivation of the Soviet nationalities policy. It was seen as an exploitable benefit of a domestically driven policy that affected the intensity of implementation in sensitive regions, but not the content of the policy itself.

The Content of the Soviet Nationalities Policy

An authoritative account of the actual content of the Soviet nationalities policy was finally delineated in resolutions passed at the Twelfth Party Congress in April 1923 and a special TsK conference on nationalities policy in June 1923. These two resolutions, along with Stalin's speeches in defence of them, became the standard Bolshevik proof texts for nationalities policy and remained so throughout the Stalinist era. Prior to April 1923, nationalities policy had been debated repeatedly at important party meetings. After June 1923, this public debate ceased The 1923 resolutions affirmed that the Soviet state would maximally support those forms of nationhood that did not conflict with a unitary central state. This meant a commitment to support the following national forms: national territories, national cultures, national languages, and national elites.

National territories had in fact already been formed for all the large Soviet nationalities. The 1923 resolutions merely reaffirmed their existence and denounced all plans to abolish them.... The 1923 resolutions also reiterated the party's recognition of distinct national cultures and pledged central state support for their maximal development.... The primary focus of the 1923 resolutions was on national languages and national elites. In each national territory, the language of the titular nationality was to be established as the official state language National elites were to be trained and promoted into positions of leadership in the party, government, industry, and schools of each national territory. Although these policies had been articulated as early as 1920, and officially sanctioned at the 1921 party congress, next to nothing had actually been accomplished. These two policies came to be called *korenizatsiia*....

Korenizatsiia is best translated as indigenization. It is not derived directly from the stem *koren-* ("root"-with the meaning "rooting"), but from its adjectival form *korennyi* as used in the phrase *korennyi narod* (indigenous people). The coining of the word *korenizatsiia* was part of the Bolsheviks' decolonizing rhetoric which systematically favored the claims of indigenous peoples over "newly arrived' elements" (*prishlye elementy*)....

The 1923 resolutions established *korenizatsiia* as the most urgent item on the Soviet nationalities policy agenda. In keeping with the Bolshevik interpretation of nationalism, *korenizatsiia* was presented in psychological terms It would make Soviet power seem "native" *(rodnoi)*, "intimate" *(blizkii)* "popular"*'(narodnoi)*, "comprehensible" *(poniatnyi)*. It, would address the positive psychological needs of nationalism: "The [non-Russian] masses would see that Soviet power and her organs are the affair of their own efforts, the embodiment of their desires." It would likewise disarm nationalisms negative psychological anxiety: "Soviet power, which up to the present time [April 1923] has remained Russian power, [would be made] not only Russian but international, and become native *(rodnoi)* for the peasantry of the formerly oppressed nationalities." Native languages would make Soviet power comprehensible Native cadres who understood "the way of life, customs, and habits of the local population" would make Soviet power seem indigenous rather than an exler-nal Russian imposition.

...Soviet nationalities policy.... did not involve federation. In 1923, Ukraine, led by Khristian Rakovskii, pressed very aggressively for the devolution of meaningful federal powers to the national republics. Stalin rebuffed Rakovskii's proposals scornfully as amounting to confederation. Although the 1922-23 constitutional settlement was called a federation, it in fact concentrated all decisionmaking power in the center. National republics were granted no more powers than Russian provinces. Prior to June 1917, both Lenin and Stalin denounced federation and advocated a unitary state with "oblast autonomy" for national regions. This meant the formation of national administrative units and the selective use of national languages in government and education. In June 1917, Lenin abruptly rehabilitated the term federation, but used it to describe what amounted to a much more ambitious version of oblast autonomy. As Stalin noted coyly in 1924, federation "turned out to be not so nearly in contradiction with the goal of economic unification as it might have seemed earlier." Soviet federation did not mean devolution of political power, but rather the promotion of national forms: national territories, cultures, elites, and languages.

Economic equalization occupied a much more ambiguous place in the Soviet nationalities policy. The 1923 resolutions called for measures to overcome "the real economic and cultural inequality of the Soviet Union's nationalities." One economic measure proposed was transferring factories from the Russian heartland to eastern national regions. This policy was adopted but then almost immediately discontinued. This proved typical of economic equalization programs. In contrast to cultural and national equalization, there were almost no bureaucratic institutions to supervise and implement economic equalization. Economic equalization programs belonged to an all-Union economic policy sphere, where they had to compete with other economic goals, rather than a privileged nationalities policy sphere. National republics could and often successfully did use the 1923 resolutions and their "backward" national status to lobby ail-Union agencies for privileged economic investment. However, they could make no absolute claim to investment based on nationalities policy. One prominent exception to this rule in the 1920s was the preferential redistribution of land in favor of titular nationalities, which did become a systematic part of the Soviet nationalities policy.

An Affirmative-Action Empire

If the Soviet Union cannot accurately be described as a federation, then how should it be categorized? Its distinctive feature was the systematic support of national forms: territory, culture, language, and elites. These were not original choices. They are the primary domestic concerns of most newly formed nation-states. In Georgia and Armenia, for instance, the Soviet government boasted that it had deepened the national work begun by the governments it deposed in 1920-21. Soviet policy was original in that it supported the national forms of minorities rather than majorities. It decisively rejected the model of the nation-state and replaced it with a plurality of nation-like republics. The Bolsheviks attempted to fuse the nationalist's demand of national territory, culture, language, and elites, with the socialist's demand for an economically and politically unitary state. In this sense, we might call the Bolsheviks international nationalists.

To develop this idea, I compare Soviet practice with Miroslav Hroch's famous three-phase model for the development of nationalism among the "small" stateless peoples of Eastern Europe: first, elite nonpolitical interest in folklore and popular culture (phase A); second, the consolidation of a nationalist elite committed to the formation of a nation-state (phase B); third, the emergence of a nationalist movement with mass popular support (phase C). Hroch largely ignored the existing multiethnic state, reflexively assuming it would oppose these developments. The Soviet state, instead, literally seized leadership over all three phases: the articulation of a national culture, the formation of national elites, and the propagation of mass national consciousness. It went still further and initiated even "Phase D" (my term now, not Hroch's) measures typical of newly formed nation-states: establishing a new language of state and a new governing elite. To use more familiar Bolshevik terminology, the party became the vanguard of non-Russian nationalism. Just as party leadership was needed to lead the proletariat beyond trade-union consciousness to revolution; the party could also guide national movements beyond bourgeois nationalism to Soviet international nationalism.

This policy represented a dramatic shift from 1913, when Lenin argued that the party should only support ending all national discrimination and warned that "the proletariat cannot go further [than this] in the support of nationalism, for going further means the 'positive' (*pazitivnaia*) affirmative action (*polozhitel'naia deiatel'nost'*) of the bourgeoisie which aims at strengthening nationalism." In the same spirit, Zinoviev told a Ukrainian audience in 1920 "that languages should develop freely. In the end, after a period of years, the language with the greater roots, greater life and greater culture will triumph." Dmitrii Lebed, Secretary of the Ukrainian TsK, called this theory "The Battle of Two Cultures" in which, "given a party policy of neutrality, the victory of the Russian language will be guaranteed due to its historic role in the epoch of capitalism."

By the 1923 party congress, neutrality had become anathema. Zinoviev himself now stated, "We should first of all reject the 'theory' of neutralism. We cannot adopt the point of view of neutralism ... we should help [the non-Russians] create their own schools, should help them create their own administration in their native languages... Communists [should not] stand to the side and think up the clever phrase 'neutrality?' Neutrality, Zinoviev insisted, was simply a cover for Great Russian chauvinism.

The 1923 resolutions supported this position. Not only was Piatakov's call for a positive fight against nationalism denounced as Great Power chauvinism, so was Lenin's prerevolutionary policy of neutrality. Lebed's "Battle of Two Cultures" was condemned in 1923 as was a similar "leftist" position in Tatarstan and Crimea.

The Communist party had now embraced Lenin's "positive affirmative action of the bourgeoisie." However, as the Hroch comparison illustrated, Soviet affirmative action supported national minorities, not majorities. The Bolsheviks now scorned bourgeois governments for supporting only formal "legal equality," instead of taking positive action to achieve "actual (*fakticheskoe*) equality." This extreme suspicion of neutrality explains one of the most striking features of the Soviet nationalities policy: its resolute hostility to even voluntary assimilation. Neutrality meant voluntary assimilation due to the historic strength of Russian national culture. Positive action, therefore, was needed to defend non-Russian national culture against this unjust fate. No one denounced neutrality and assimilation more categorically than Stalin:

> We are undertaking a policy of the maximum development of national culture... It would be an error if anyone thought that in relation to the development of the national cultures of the backward nationalities, central workers should maintain a policy of neutrality—'O.K. fine, national culture is developing, let it develop, that's not our business.' Such a point of view would be incorrect. We stand for a protective (*pokrovitel'stvenniu polhiku*) policy in relation to the development of the national culture of the backward nationalities. I emphasize this so that [it will] be understood that we are not indifferent, but actively protecting (*pokrovitel'stvuiushchie*) the development of national culture.

Of course, positive action on behalf of one nationality implies negative action toward others. In the Soviet case, where all non-Russians were to be favored, Russians alone bore the brunt of positive discrimination. Bukharin stated this tact bluntly: "As the former Great Power nation, we should indulge the nationalist aspirations [of the non-Russians] and place ourselves in an unequal position, in the sense of making still greater concessions to the national current. Only by such a policy, when we place ourselves artificially in a position lower in comparisons with others, only by such a price can we purchase for ourselves the trust of the formerly oppressed nations." Stalin, who was more sensitive to Russian feelings, rebuked Bukharin for the crudeness of his statement, but did not and could not dispute its content. As we shall see, Soviet policy did indeed call for Russian sacrifice in the realm of nationalities policy: Majority Russian territory was granted to non-Russian republics; Russians had to accept extensive affirmative-action programs for non-Russians; they were asked to learn non-Russian languages; and traditional Russian culture was stigmatized as the culture of oppression.

New phenomena merit new terminology. As a national entity, I believe the Soviet Union can best be described as an Affirmative-Action Empire. I am, of course, borrowing the contemporary American term for policies that give preference to members of ethnic groups that have suffered from past discrimination. Such policies are common internationally and go by various names: compensatory discrimination, preferential policies, positive action, affirmative discrimination. I prefer the term Affirmative Action because, as the above paragraphs have shown, it describes precisely the Soviet policy choice: affirmative action *(polozhitel'naia deiatel'nost')* instead of neutrality. The Soviet Union was the first country in world history to establish affirmative-action programs for national minorities and no country has yet approached the vast scale of Soviet affirmative action. The Soviet Union also adopted even more extensive class-based affirmative-action programs and considerably less assertive gender-based programs. As a result, the vast majority of Soviet citizens were eligible for some sort of preferential treatment. Affirmative action permeated the early Soviet Union and was one of its defining features.

However, the existence of such programs alone does not justify calling the Soviet Union an Affirmative-Action Empire, because I am proposing this term as an ideal-type to distinguish the Soviet Union *as a national entity* from alternative ideal-types: nation-state, city-state, federation, confederation, empire. I am using affirmative action here to refer not only to programs on behalf of members of a given ethnic group, but primarily to Soviet state support for the national forms of those ethnic groups. As noted in the Hroch comparison above, the Communist party assumed leadership over the usual process of national formation, and took positive action to construct Soviet international nations (nations in form not content) that would be content to be part of a unitary Soviet state. Positive support of the forms of nationhood was the essence of Soviet nationalities policy. The formation of the Soviet Union in 1922-23 established the territorial form of nationhood, not a federation of autonomous national territories. Therefore, the constitutional form of the Soviet Union was itself an act of affirmative action....

...Modern empires, however, are not usually associated with affirmative action. They were typically divided into a center and periphery with different legal, political, and economic norms. The Soviet Union was a unitary state. In modern empires, the periphery was economically exploited by the center. This was not at all the case in the Soviet Union. Most importantly modern empires had a privileged state-bearing people (Lenin's Great Power Nation), with whom the empire was identified and whose interests the empire served. The Soviet Union explicitly renounced the idea of a state-bearing people. Despite this fact, in an important sense the Russians did remain the Soviet Union's state-bearing people. Only the Russians were not granted their own territory and their own Communist party. Instead, the party asked the Russians to accept a formally unequal *national* status to further the cohesion of the multinational state. The hierarchical distinction between state-bearing and colonial peoples was thus reproduced, but reversed, as the new distinction between the formerly oppressed nationalities and the former Great Power nation.

...In Hroch's model, the imperial state acts only negatively (and futilely) to prevent the emergence of national movements. The Soviet state instead adopted the opposite strategy. It acted positively in support of this decolonizing movement with the aim of co-opting and diverting it away from the goal of independent statehood. Soviet affirmative action, (then, was a radical strategy for imperial maintenance. As the state-bearing people, Russians were now literally asked to bear the burden of empire by suppressing their national interests and identifying with a nonnational Affirmative Action Empire. Had Lenin lived to write a theoretical account of his creation, he might have called it: *The Soviet Union, as the Highest Stage of Imperialism.*

End of Reading 2.3

Further Reading:

Edward Hallett Carr, *The Bolshevik Revolution, 1917-1923*, vol. 1 New York: MacMillan, 1951.

Sheila Fitzpatrick, *The Russian Revolution*, 2nd ed. Oxford: Oxford University Press, 1994.

Terry Martin, *The Affirmative Action Empire: Nations and Nationalism in the Soviet Union, 1923-1939*. Ithaca: Cornell University Press.

Ronald Grigor Suny, *The Soviet Experiment: Russia, the USSR, and the Succesor States*. New York: Oxford University Press, 1998.

CHAPTER 9

THE STALIN REVOLUTION AND THE CONSTITUTION OF 1936

With the creation of the USSR in 1922 and its elaboration in the Constitution of 1924, it might seem as though there was no more need for constitutional change. After all, the USSR continued to exist up until 1991, and the Bolsheviks—or the Communist Party—remained in power throughout that whole period. But even though the situation was finally stabilizing in the early 1920s as the country came out of some seven years of world war and civil war, the USSR was to undergo another radical transformation starting at the end of the 1920s. This transformation was closely associated with Joseph Stalin, and it is therefore sometimes called **"the Stalin revolution"** or the "revolution from above." It was not literally a revolution in the political sense of the term, but the country was nonetheless transformed profoundly. This in turn created a set of new political and social conditions that served as the backdrop for a new **constitution of 1936**, sometimes called the Stalin Constitution.

What was the nature of this transformation? In a political sense, it entailed the establishment of a one-man dictatorship under Stalin and the elimination of any and all political rivals. In the social and economic sphere there were three main dimensions to the Stalin Revolution: massive and rapid industrialization, collectivization of the peasantry, and a "cultural revolution" against the regime's (supposed) class enemies. We shall discuss these developments in greater detail below, but for the moment let us emphasize that the new constitution was designed to reflect and codify the massive changes that occurred within the country beginning in about 1928.

The situation was also changing in the broader international sphere. Recall that the Bolsheviks had come to power on the assumption that theirs, the Bolshevik Revolution, was the beginning of worldwide revolution. Despite some revolutionary stirrings in countries like Hungary, Germany, and Italy, in no other country did a Bolshevik-style revolution bring communists to power for more than six months. This meant that by the time the Civil War had ended, and certainly by 1923-24, it was clear that for the moment at least, the USSR would be the only Marxist country and would have to try to build socialism on its own. Indeed, the Bolsheviks were well aware that the other countries of Europe were hostile to the USSR. And as Europe entered the 1930s, things only became worse. The Great Depression affected Europe much as it did the United States, and in this context a strongly anti-Bolshevik party—the **Nazis**—came to power in Germany in January of 1933. The Nazis and their leader, Adolf Hitler, made no secret of their hostility towards Russia and the Bolsheviks, and many in the USSR had to think more seriously about the possibility of having to fight a war against Germany. Curiously, this circumstance helped to shape the character of the Soviet constitution of 1936.

In this chapter we seek to contextualize the making of the 1936 constitution by analyzing each of these issues in greater depth, while also consulting both a speech by Stalin himself on the constitution and an analysis of how Stalin's regime tried to promote awareness of the constitution among the Soviet population. We start by briefly considering the **New Economic Policy** (NEP), which framed the Soviet experience for much of the 1920s and also served as the departure point for the Stalin Revolution beginning around 1928. We next consider the political struggle over the course of the 1920s and the consequences for the future of NEP. We will see that by the late 1920s, Stalin had decided to embark on another revolutionary offensive that signified the end of NEP. Thereafter we turn to the Stalin Revolution itself, focusing on its three main components—**rapid industrialization, collectivization**, and **cultural revolution**—in order to understand the remarkable transformation that had occurred in the country by the mid 1930s. We finally consider the regime's apparent turn away from revolutionary radicalism by the mid-1930s and consider how the constitution of 1936 related to this development.

THE NEW ECONOMIC POLICY

By early 1921, the Bolsheviks had won the Civil War. But as they secured this victory, the situation in the country was still dire. On the broader European scene, the international revolution that the Bolsheviks had expected did not occur. True, there was an attempted revolution in Germany in January of 1919, and later that same year a Bolshevik-style government managed to hold onto power for a full six months in Hungary. But both of these revolutions had collapsed by the end of 1919, and as the situation in Europe began gradually to stabilize after World War I, the Bolsheviks found themselves standing alone as the only socialist country in the world. Internally, the challenges of the World War and the policies of War Communism during the Civil War had left the country devastated and in chaos. Because of losses in the Civil War and the return of many workers to the villages, the industrial proletariat—the class in whose name the Bolsheviks claimed to rule—was reduced in number from 3.6 million in 1917 to a mere 1.5 million in 1920. Subject to harsh policies of requisitioning, by which the Bolsheviks took grain from the villages at prices that they themselves dictated, peasants were sullen and angry, and indeed a number of peasant revolts against the Bolsheviks suggested that the Communist Party

would have to change course. A terrible famine spread through parts of the country in 1921-22, producing even cases of cannibalism in the areas most deeply affected. Most strikingly, the sailors at the Kronstadt naval base, who had supported the Bolsheviks at several key points over the course of the revolution and Civil War, now revolted openly against Lenin's regime. The Party suppressed the rebellion with force, thereby turning its guns on the revolutionary proletariat itself for the first time. The Bolsheviks were inclined to argue that all of their harsh policies during the Civil War had been necessary for them to stay in power—and perhaps they were right—but it was clear by the spring of 1921 that the Bolsheviks needed a new set of policies in order to revive the economy. As Lenin remarked, "We were forced to resort to 'War Communism' by war and ruin. It was not, nor could it be, a policy that corresponded to the economic tasks of the proletariat. It was a temporary measure."[1]

The new approach was appropriately labeled the New Economic Policy, or NEP. As Sheila Fitzpatrick has written, "It was an improvised response to desperate economic circumstances," and its "beneficial impact on the economy was swift and dramatic."[2] In almost all areas of production the country had achieved pre-war levels by 1926. In certain ways it was a profound reversal of the practices that made up War Communism. The state maintained control over what the Bolsheviks called the "commanding heights" of the economy—for example, banking, communications, major enterprises and large-scale industry—but otherwise the drive for nationalization was reversed: the private sector was allowed to re-emerge, and the state replaced grain requisitioning from the peasants by a tax (initially in produce—grain—and then in money). This meant that as long as peasants paid their tax, they could sell any surplus that they produced on the market. As Lenin remarked in April of 1921, "The most urgent thing at the present time is to take measures that will immediately increase the productive forces of peasant farming."[3] This in turn created space for the legalization of private trade and thus the appearance of a class of middlemen

---

1   Richard Sakwa, *The Rise and Fall of the Soviet Union, 1917-1991* (London, 1999), 129.

2   Sheila Fitzpatrick, *The Russian Revolution*, 2nd ed. (Oxford, 1994), 95.

3   Sakwa, *The Rise and Fall*, 128.

shuttling between the countryside and the city with grain—the so-called "nepmen." Retail shops and restaurants opened again in the cities, and to some extent the USSR began to resemble Russia before the Bolshevik Revolution. Living standards increased as industrial production recovered, and the artistic scene featured a vibrant utopian experimentalism. In short, the Bolsheviks found themselves acquiescing in the partial restoration of capitalism as a matter of necessity. NEP was above all a concession to the peasantry, who were now given incentives to produce and even told: "enrich yourselves."

At the same time, the Bolsheviks eliminated any last traces of political dissent in the country. Lenin was clear that NEP represented a retreat, and—extending the military metaphor—he emphasized that it was especially in retreat that an army needed strict discipline. Thus factions in the Party were banned, and a trial of remaining Right SR's made clear that the Bolsheviks would use "show trials" against their opponents. In the fall of 1921 the Bolsheviks, concerned that the Communist Party had been infiltrated with "careerists" and "class enemies," conducted a full-scale purge of its ranks. It required every party member to appear before a purge commission and justify his revolutionary credentials. Roughly a quarter of the party membership was deemed unworthy and thus expelled from the party. In short, if the NEP saw liberalization in the economic sphere, it featured further tightening in the political one.

Extending that point we can say that NEP was paradoxical in almost every way. The USSR was a workers' state in a largely peasant land. It was supposedly socialist, but with a significant capitalist sector, featuring numerous traders, peddlers, and retailers. It was an authoritarian state that had only a limited presence in the countryside. It was a regime waiting for worldwide revolution, but forced to promote the building of "socialism in one country"—i.e., to create a socialist order without external help. It was a country that emphasized the importance of class, but had a nationalities policy that recognized and promoted national and ethnic difference. It was, in short, a deep compromise between radical Bolshevik visions and the traditional, agrarian reality of Russia. It should not surprise us that some eager Bolsheviks were profoundly uneasy with these paradoxes and with the compromises that the party had been compelled to make. Some were prepared to be patient, but

others were eager to take the next big step in creating a socialist utopia. After all, Lenin himself had said in 1922 that the Bolsheviks were indeed retreating by introducing NEP, "but we are doing so, after first retreating, to take a running start and make a bigger leap forward."[4] Impatient communists wanted to know when the country would make that leap. Joseph Stalin would provide the answer, though he first of all had to secure political power for himself.

THE POLITICAL STRUGGLE AND THE FATE OF NEP

Lenin suffered his first stroke already in 1922, and as time progressed he became incapacitated further. In January of 1924 he died, and Petrograd was renamed Leningrad shortly thereafter in his honor. His body was embalmed and placed in a newly constructed mausoleum on Red Square where one can still see him today. Lenin had undoubtedly been the leader of the Bolsheviks, but at the same time the Communist Party had developed a tradition of collective leadership. This meant that the key decisions were made by a small group at the center of the party, and that Lenin, though he most often got his way, did not always win the argument. As Lenin approached death, real power came to rest in the party's Politburo, which consisted of six people aside from Lenin himself. Although the party committed itself to collective leadership, there soon began an intense struggle for power behind the scenes.

The struggle continued for the better part of the 1920s, during the period of NEP. There were different factions and alliances that developed and then shifted, and these make for great political drama. For our purposes, it is enough to say that Stalin allied with one group that was slightly less radical in order to prevail over Leon Trotsky, another leading Bolshevik, and then allied with another group to oust his previous allies. Stalin was less charismatic and intellectually impressive than some of his rivals, but he was an excellent backroom politician. Using his position as General Secretary of the party, he was able to fill key spots in the party leadership with people loyal to him. This gave him tremendous leverage against his opponents and thus permitted him to emerge as the central figure in the party by the late 1920s. As he consolidated

---

4   Sakwa, *The Rise and Fall*, 130.

his power further, he became the country's dictator. By the 1930s there was a full-blown cult of Stalin, according to which Stalin was worthy of the highest possible praise for all of the great things that the USSR had accomplished. For example, in 1935 the Soviet writer A. O. Avdienko wrote in praise, "Centuries will pass, and the generations still to come will regard us as the happiest of mortals, as the most fortunate of men, because we lived in the century of centuries, because we were privileged to see Stalin, our inspired leader." Stalin, in his view, "never had an equal in world history."[5] In short, by around 1930 or so, the USSR had become a one-man dictatorship, with no one in a position to challenge Stalin's power and authority.

Among the disagreements that framed the struggle for power in the 1920s was the question of the future of NEP. The New Economic Policy was supposed to have been a temporary retreat, so the question became how to take the next step in the "building of socialism." What precisely the Bolsheviks meant by that expression is something that even they themselves were not entirely sure of. They were certain, though, that it meant transforming Russia into a modern industrial society with factories, railways, cities, machinery, and technology. But how to get there? Could the country progress to "socialism" by continuing with NEP? Or did there need to be a break with NEP?

Of critical significance in this matter was the Bolsheviks' relationship with the peasantry. As noted, NEP represented a concession to peasants as a way of stimulating their production. Moreover, Lenin had written before his death that the success of the revolution depended on an "agreement" between the proletariat and the peasantry — symbolized by the hammer and sickle. But on some basic level, the Bolsheviks knew that the interests of the working class and the peasantry were at odds. Workers were the vanguard of a bright socialist future, whereas peasants represented the past and, the Bolsheviks thought, exhibited "petty bourgeois" inclinations — they were in effect just rural petty bourgeois capitalists. A critical problem was that the Bolsheviks had no way of compelling peasants to part with their agricultural produce. Peasants could choose to market any surplus that they produced (that is, beyond what they needed for themselves) or

they could refuse to do so, either producing less or consuming more. Especially if peasants felt that the cities produced little that they needed, why would they part with their produce? The Bolsheviks faced this problem on a couple of occasions in the 1920s, when peasants refused to market their grain either because they were waiting for prices to rise on their agricultural goods or because they felt there was nothing to purchase with the money they earned from their selling. In general, peasants were simply marketing less — on average only half of what they had marketed on the eve of World War I. During the Civil War, of course, the Bolsheviks had simply demanded that peasants part with their grain with the barrel of a gun, but under NEP Bolsheviks had no way to force them to sell. Meanwhile, industry needed capital for investment. The Bolsheviks could not borrow money abroad — what capitalist would lend money to radical communists who had already refused to pay the debt of the old tsarist regime? So really the peasantry was the only source of capital for investment for the development of industry. But — once again — the Bolsheviks had no way to extract that capital, in the form of grain, from the peasantry.

One can see the dilemma the Bolsheviks faced in the debates that developed in the 1920s. Trotsky, for example, was a major proponent of rapid industrialization who believed that this had to occur at the expense of the peasantry. In 1923 he wrote, "Only the development of industry creates the unshakable basis for the dictatorship of the proletariat." He insisted that heavy industry needed to be restored after the devastation of 1914-21, and that the Bolsheviks needed to promote the spread of electricity and other elements of modernity in the country. Only then, he proposed, "will it become both possible and, indeed, inevitable to alter the relative significance in our economic life of agriculture and industry and to shift the center of gravity from the former to the latter. The Party must work systematically and perseveringly, whatever the sacrifice or labor, to accelerate this process."[6] Others in Trotsky's camp believed that the state needed to strip resources from the countryside, by force if necessary, and use them to support rapid industrialization. They felt that the existence of small-scale peasant farming would strengthen capitalism in the USSR, thus creating a dangerous

---

5   Robert Weinberg and Laurie Bernstein, *Revolutionary Russia: A History with Documents* (Oxford, 2011), 166.

6   Weinberg and Bernstein, *Revolutionary Russia*, 112-13.

counterforce to the Bolsheviks. Opposing Trotsky was Nikolai Bukharin, who proposed a more modest pace of industrialization and the need for a full recovery of agriculture in the country. He worried about the future of the regime if it were to antagonize the peasantry. He thus concluded in 1926 that Trotsky and his supporters "are desirous of putting so severe a pressure upon the peasantry that in our opinion the result would be economically irrational and politically unallowable."[7] He felt that as long as the party controlled the state apparatus and industry, peasants did not represent a major threat to the country, and the Bolsheviks could soon build a socialist industrial society.[8]

When Trotsky was defeated in the political struggle described above, it seemed that the position of Bukharin had prevailed and that NEP would continue. But at the end of 1927 the amount of grain procured by the state to feed the cities dropped significantly. Stalin, who was then becoming the country's unchallenged dictator, was inclined to believe that peasants—and in particular rich ones, known as **kulaks**—were hoarding grain, either in order to obtain better prices or even deliberately to harm the Soviet regime. In this context Stalin seems to have come to the conclusion that the USSR had one of two choices: postpone industrialization or risk a major confrontation with the peasantry. Postponing industrialization was dangerous. The Bolshevik leadership knew that all of Europe was hostile to the USSR, and there were real fears that the country might have to fight a war soon against the capitalist West. How would it fare in such a war if it did not industrialize? Moreover, the industrial recovery of 1921-28 was mostly a matter of restoring pre-war capacity. To take the next step, the country would need to build new factories, not just reactivate old ones. Extracting resources from the countryside was really the only way to obtain the capital for this next stage. By early 1928 Stalin apparently made up his mind. To quote Fitzpatrick, "Stalin intended to industrialize, and if this meant a political confrontation with the countryside, Stalin thought that 'the town'—that is, the urban proletariat and the Soviet regime—would win."[9] More generally, one can point to a sense of disquiet and malaise among

many communists. With its largely independent peasantry, its partial restoration of capitalism, and its continued reliance on "bourgeois specialists" (because the Bolsheviks did not have enough technical expertise of their own), NEP did not seem to many communists to be what the revolution had sought to achieve. The mood in the party, writes Fitzpatrick, was not one of satisfaction, but instead "a mood of restlessness, dissatisfaction, and barely subdued belligerence and, especially among party youth, nostalgia for the old heroic days of the Civil War."[10] In short, the decision to initiate a new, dramatic stage in the building of socialism depended not only on the vision of Stalin himself, as important as that was, but also on sentiments among broader segments of the party.

THE STALIN REVOLUTION

Stalin's revolution consisted of four main components, all of which were fundamentally interconnected. The first was the creation of a one-man dictatorship culminating in a remarkable personality cult. The second and third components were collectivization and rapid industrialization, which were fundamentally linked. The fourth component was a "cultural revolution" which took the form of a class war, directed by Stalin and pitting people of proletarian origin against the remnants of the "bourgeoisie," many of whom still occupied prominent positions as engineers and other professionals because they had education and expertise. Since we already addressed the first of the four components above, let us look at the other three in more detail here.

The collectivization of agriculture in the USSR grew directly out of the grain procurement crisis that appeared in 1927-28. Unable to extract grain from peasants on favorable terms, many Bolsheviks became impatient and also worried that perhaps "kulaks" were developing into a powerful class that could thwart Bolshevik plans with ever greater effectiveness. Stalin accordingly organized an expedition into the Urals and Siberia to extract grain from peasants by forceful measures, and the expedition returned in railcars loaded with grain. This kind of coercion represented a short-term solution to the problem. The long-term solution

---

7   Weinberg and Bernstein, *Revolutionary Russia,* 114.

8   Paul Bushkovitch, *A Concise History of Russia* (Cambridge, 2012), 322-23.

9   Fitzpatrick, *Russian Revolution,* 116.

10   Fitzpatrick, *Russian Revolution,* 118-19.

was for the state to intervene aggressively in the agricultural sector and to collectivize the peasantry by forcing them into large collective farms (or kolkhozes) that would ensure a reliable source of grain for the cities, the Red Army, and for export as a way of earning foreign capital for investment in industry. Peasants would lose control over the farming process, as well as ownership of their animals, land, and tools, and would instead pool their property in collective farms that would be overseen by managers who would answer directly to the state and the party. This signaled an end to traditional peasant farming and to the market mechanisms that had existed under NEP. It also entailed an attack on peasant traditions, especially religion, which the Bolsheviks regarded as an archaic holdover from the past. In many ways, the project of collectivization represented an assault on virtually all aspects of peasant life in the USSR, and in this sense—although the Bolsheviks did not express matters in these terms—it represented a civil war of the regime against its own peasantry, still the majority of the population. In particular collectivization was an attack on the kulaks, who of course could be expected to resist Bolshevik plans with particular force. One of the campaign's slogans thus declared that kulaks needed to be "liquidated as a class." The party had committed itself to wholesale collectivization by the end of 1929, convinced not only that this would fuel the country's industrialization, but also that collective agriculture was most consistent with the ideals of socialism.

To understand the party's thinking, we can do no better than to listen to the words of Stalin himself. In a speech in 1929 he asked rhetorically: could the USSR advance its industry at an accelerated rate while having to rely "on an agricultural base, such as is provided by small peasant framing, which is incapable of expanded reproduction"? Obviously not. Could the work of "socialist construction" for any length of time be based simultaneously on "the most large-scale and concentrated Socialist industry" and on "the most scattered and backward, small-commodity peasant farming"? The answer was clearly no. What, then, was the solution, Stalin asked? "The solution lies in enlarging the agricultural units, in making agriculture capable of accumulation, of expanded reproduction, and in thus changing the base of our national economy." And how was this to be done? The socialist way to do this, declared Stalin, was to amalgamate small peasant farms "into large collective farms, technically and scientifically equipped," and to squeeze the "capitalist elements" out of agriculture. Previously, under NEP, the Bolsheviks had not been able to do this. "Now we are able to carry on a determined offensive against the kulaks, to break their resistance, to eliminate them as a class." Now, Stalin continued, "The expropriation of the kulaks is an integral part to the formation and development of collective farms."[11] Hooray.

The Bolshevik assumption was that they would be able to foster a "class war" by mobilizing poorer peasants against kulaks. In the event, most peasants resisted collectivization, with the result that many of them, regardless of their actual wealth, were labeled "kulaks." Likewise, despite party activists' attempts to promote a voluntary movement of peasants in favor of collectivization, their efforts actually produced outrage and chaos in the villages. Peasants refused to hand over their animals to collective farms, choosing instead to slaughter them immediately in order to be able to sell the meat. Peasants beat or shot at party officials trying to engineer collectivization. Peasant women wailed, complained and hurled insults at party activists. "Expropriated" kulaks sometimes terrorized the village by night. Many kolkhoz members absconded from the collective farms and made their way to cities and industrial sites, where labor was needed. Convinced that kulaks were hoarding grain, party activists became ruthless in confiscating goods from peasants. One such activist, Lev Kopelev, described the experience later in life. "I was convinced that we were warriors on an invisible front, fighting against kulak sabotage for the grain which was needed by the country." He described the "highest measure of coercion" that was deployed against the hard-core holdouts. A team, he described, "would search the hut, barn, yard, and take away all the stores of seed, lead away the cow, the horses, the pigs." In some cases the team would leave behind some food for the family, but stricter ones would make a "clean sweep," taking all food, all livestock, and all valuables. "The women howled hysterically, clinging to the bags" of grain, insisting that this was all they had to feed their children. "I heard the children echoing them with screams, choking, coughing with screams. And I saw the looks of the men: frightened, pleading, hateful, dully impassive,

---

11   Weinberg and Bernstein, *Revolutionary Russia*, 126-127.

extinguished with despair or flaring up with half-mad, daring ferocity." Kopelev described his own mentality at the time, which allowed him not only to endure all of this but to believe that it was right: "It was excruciating to see and hear all this. And even worse to take part in it…. And I persuaded myself, explained to myself: I mustn't give in to debilitating pity. We were realizing historical necessity. We were performing our revolutionary duty. We were obtaining grain for the socialist fatherland."[12]

Stalin's regime proved remarkably ruthless in extracting grain from the new collective farms by setting high delivery quotas. In some cases it even took seed grain, thus depriving peasants of the possibility of even planting the next year's crops. In certain places—Ukraine, Kazakhstan, the North Caucasus—this produced famine in the winter of 1932-33, which killed as many as seven million people. In Ukraine, especially, many today regard the famine as a genocidal act of Stalin's regime, an attempt to eliminate the Ukrainian people. This was undoubtedly the most frightening part of collectivization. But by the mid-1930s the party had achieved a kind of success. Millions had been "dekulakized." Collective farms had been established in much of the country. Admittedly at great cost, the regime had won its civil war against the peasantry, and could now more or less guarantee a flow of grain from the countryside to the cities at low, non-negotiable prices. Still, peasants remained angry and withdrawn, and they regarded collectivization, with some foundation, as a return to serfdom. The regime had to invest more in the agricultural sector than it had originally intended, while it also had to allow peasants to retain small private plots by their homes, which actually proved to be the most productive sector of Soviet agriculture and allowed peasants to skimp on their work for the collective farms. In short, the regime had won the struggle, but at a very high price and only by making some concessions to peasants.

Collectivization provided the material foundations for industrialization, which was the main goal of Stalin's revolution. Stalin made the case that the USSR had no choice but to industrialize quickly or to fall fatally behind the capitalist powers and eventually to be beaten. In response to those who called for a slowing of the tempo, Stalin responded vigorously: "No, comrades, it is not possible! The tempo must not be reduced! On the contrary, we must increase it as much as is within our powers and possibilities." Stalin recounted all the time that "old Russia" had been beaten for her "backwardness"—by the Mongols, by the Poles, by the Japanese, by the British and French capitalists, etc. "Do you want our socialist fatherland to be beaten and to lose its independence? If you do not want this you must put an end to its backwardness in the shortest possible time and develop a genuine Bolshevik tempo in building up its socialist system of economy. There is no other way… We are fifty or a hundred years behind the advanced countries. We must make good this distance in ten years. Either we do it or they crush us."[13] Stalin left little room for argument.

The result was that the country saw an extraordinary explosion of industrial development—the construction of new factories, dams, mines, and even cities on a fantastical scale. In 1928 Stalin issued a Five-Year Plan, according to which the entire economy would be directed by the state. The Plan set impossibly high targets—e.g., annual increases of industrial production on the order of 20% annually—and then enjoined the population to "fulfill the Five-Year Plan in Four" (as one slogan declared). The state accordingly took almost complete control of the industrial economy, trade, and distribution and subordinated all of it to centralized planning. The first five-year plan represented a fundamental break with the past and a great turning point in the "building of socialism." Construction sites were everywhere, and huge projects were indeed completed in record time. No doubt, there was much coercion—for example, prison labor was exploited ruthlessly on several major projects—and a great deal of sacrifice on the part of the Soviet people. Many died in industrial accidents, since safety was not a priority for the regime. But even if it was inefficient and costly, there was real industrial growth in the 1930s, and it is hard to imagine that the USSR could have defeated Nazi Germany in 1941-45 had it not been for the developments of the previous decade.

The last component of the Stalin Revolution was "cultural revolution," which took the form of a class war. After 1917 the Bolsheviks had been compelled to rely on various "specialists"—engineers, doctors, professors, etc.—who were

---

neither of proletarian origin nor Bolsheviks by political conviction. This was necessary because these specialists had skills and expertise that the Bolsheviks needed, and the specialists, for their part, needed to feed themselves and their families and were not necessarily hostile to the revolution. This reliance on what the Bolsheviks called "bourgeois specialists" was yet another of the compromises that seemed unavoidable during NEP but that also aggravated ardent communists. Gradually, over the course of the 1920s, communists and workers received more education and seemed to be in a position now to replace the "bourgeois specialists." So here was yet another group that, by the late 1920s, was eager for a break from the past, since it was clear that they were likely to benefit from an attack on the "bourgeois specialists." When in March of 1928 Stalin initiated a trial against several engineers in the Shakhty region of Ukraine for deliberate sabotage and conspiracy with foreign powers, this was a sign to attack the "bourgeois specialists" and to replace them with communists or people of proletarian origin. This campaign probably made the industrial campaign more difficult, since it removed some of the most qualified people at precisely the point when industrialization was accelerating radically. But it also had the effect of putting in place a new Soviet elite, which owed its position and privileges precisely to Stalin and the new order. These people would of course be unlikely to question Stalin and his policies and would serve therefore to stabilize his rule. As Fitzpatrick recounts, "From Stalin's standpoint, one of the greatest achievements of the Revolution had been the creation of a 'new Soviet intelligentsia' (which in essence meant a new managerial and professional elite), recruited from the working class and the peasantry. The Soviet regime no longer had to depend on holdovers from the old elites, whose loyalty would always be dubious, but could now rely on its own elite of home-grown 'leading cadres and specialists,' men who owed their promotion and careers to the Revolution and could be relied on to be completely loyal to it (and to Stalin)."[14]

STABILIZATION IN THE MID-1930S

By the mid-1930s, then, the USSR had undergone a tremendous transformation as compared to the last years of NEP. Stalin was now fully in control as the unquestioned dictator of the country. Peasants had been largely collectivized, if at great cost. The country had taken a huge step forward in its industrial development. And the old "bourgeois" elite had been replaced by a new communist or "proletarian" one. By the mid-1930s, Stalin decided that he needed above all to consolidate this transformation and to stabilize the country as much as possible. The Constitution of 1936 should be seen in this context.

In important ways Stalin was faced with the task of ending the revolution, which raises important general questions. At what point can one say that a revolution is over? At what point can a regime with revolutionary origins claim that the main tasks have been achieved? Stalin's answer, in part, was simply to declare victory. The country really *had* been transformed by the mid-1930s, so there was certainly some basis for this claim. The rhetoric of "victory" was accordingly prominent in the mid-1930s—for example, the 17th Party Congress in 1934 was titled "The Congress of the Victors"—while a slogan of 1935 declared, "Life has become more joyful, comrades!" Stalin correspondingly began to emphasize the virtues of order, moderation, stability, and predictability in Soviet life—the revolution's goals had been achieved, he seemed to be saying, so there was no longer any need to rock the boat. As we shall see in the speech below, Stalin likewise declared, "Our Soviet society has already, in the main, succeeded in achieving Socialism." True, the Bolsheviks had always been a bit unclear about what "socialism" meant, and some were undoubtedly surprised to learn that the USSR in 1936 was already there. One key question pertained to the state, which was supposed to "whither away" under socialism. Yet anybody with eyes could see that the state was still very much in existence, probably stronger than it ever had been. Stalin squared the circle by proposing that only in the next stage—"communism"—would the state actually "whither away." As long as the USSR remained the only country in which a socialist revolution had occurred, the socialism of the 1930s was as far as things could go. Class struggle had disappeared, he claimed, given that the kulaks and bourgeoisie had been defeated. This victory also meant that now all Soviet citizens could have equal rights—there was no longer a class enemy to be deprived of rights. The "dictatorship of the proletariat" was effectively ending.

---

14   Fitzpatrick, *Russian Revolution*, 156.

Stalin's claims were certainly not without foundation, as we have suggested. But they could also be contested. To declare the revolution "won" and to focus on order and stability was at least partially to repudiate revolutionary ideology and practice. To provide privileges to the new "proletarian intelligentsia" was also to accept elements of hierarchy and inequality based on education, occupation, and status. Providing material incentives to individual workers for greater work also seemed to represent a step away from equality and solidarity among workers. There were other signs of a distinct conservatism in Stalinist society now. Abortion was outlawed in 1936, which arguably limited prospects for women's emancipation in Soviet society by emphasizing motherhood; divorce became more difficult to obtain as well. Soviet culture became more conservative and pedantic. Higher education was reorganized to appear more like its tsarist predecessor. Soviet schools emphasized history, which they had previously ignored, partly in order to foster patriotism—clearly a traditional value. Pointing to these kinds of developments, Trotsky, now in exile, criticized Stalin's USSR in a famous work of 1937 called *The Revolution Betrayed*, though Stalin had him assassinated in 1940—with an ice axe, no less. Some historians have seen the mid-1930s as a "great retreat" from the values of the revolution, a turn towards conservatism and stability with a layer of revolutionary ideology over it.[15]

No doubt, debate on this score will continue. For us, the critical thing is to be aware of this general context as we consider two texts on the Constitution of 1936 itself. One of these is a speech by Stalin, "On the Draft Constitution," in which the dictator justifies the need for a new constitution by pointing to all the changes since 1924, and also anticipates certain questions that the Soviet people might want to ask about the draft. This speech was part of a process by which Stalin wished to involve the population of the country in the making of the constitution. Of course, he did not really want the people to shape the content of the constitution (unless they agreed with Stalin completely), but he did wish to create the semblance of a democratic process. As you read, consider the image of the USSR that Stalin wanted to portray to the country's own citizens and even abroad, as well as the arguments about that the USSR had already achieved and what remained to be done.

DOCUMENT 2.10

JOSEPH STALIN, "ON THE DRAFT CONSTITUTION" (1936)[16]

Changes in the Life of the USSR in the Period from 1924 to 1936

What are the changes in the life of the USSR that have been brought about in the period from 1924 to 1936 and which the Constitution Commission was to reflect in its Draft Constitution?

What is the essence of these changes? What was the situation in 1924? At that time we were in the first period of the New Economic Policy, the beginning of NEP, the period of a certain revival of capitalism; now, however, we are in the last period of NEP, the end of NEP, the period of the complete liquidation of capitalism in all spheres of the national economy.

And what does this mean? It means that the exploitation of man has been abolished, eliminated, while the Socialist ownership of the implements and means of production has been established as the unshakable foundation of our Soviet society. [Prolonged applause.]

As a result of all these changes in the sphere of the national economy of the USSR, we now have a new, Socialist economy, which knows neither crises nor unemployment, which knows neither poverty nor ruin, and which provides our citizens with every opportunity to lead a prosperous and cultured life.

---

15   Fitzpatrick provides an excellent balance sheet juxtaposing arguments for "revolution accomplished" with those for "revolution betrayed," in *Russian Revolution*, 150-63.

16   Source: *J. V. Stalin on the Draft Constitution of the U.S.S.R.* (Moscow, 1936; Syndey, 1942). The speech can also be found at https://www.marxists.org/reference/archive/stalin/works/1936/11/25.htm.

In conformity with these changes in the economic life of the USSR, the class structure of our society has also changed. The landlord class, as you know, had already been eliminated as a result of the victorious conclusion of the civil war. As for the other exploiting classes, they have shared the fate of the landlord class. The capitalist class in the sphere of industry has ceased to exist. The kulak class in the sphere of agriculture has ceased to exist. And the merchants and profiteers in the sphere of trade have ceased to exist. Thus all the exploiting classes have now been eliminated.

There remains the working class. There remains the peasant class. There remains the intelligentsia. But it would be a mistake to think that these social groups have undergone no change during this period, that they have remained the same as they were, say, in the period of capitalism.

Take, for example, the working class of the USSR. By force of habit, it is often called the proletariat. But what is the proletariat? The proletariat is a class bereft of the instruments and means of production, under an economic system in which the instruments and means of production have been taken for the capitalists and transferred to the state, of which the leading force is the working class. Consequently, there is no longer a capitalist class which would exploit the working class... This being the case, can our working class be called the proletariat? Clearly, it cannot... And what does this mean? This means that the proletariat of the USSR has been transformed into an entirely new class, into the working class of the USSR, which has abolished the capitalist economic system, which has established the Socialist ownership of the instruments and means of production and is directing Soviet society along the road to Communism.... Let us pass on to the question of the peasantry... In our country there are no longer any landlords and kulaks, merchants and usurers who could exploit the peasants. Consequently, our peasantry is a peasantry emancipated from exploitation. Further. Our Soviet peasantry, in its overwhelming majority is a collective farm peasantry, i.e., it bases its work and wealth not on individual labor and on backward technical equipment, but on collective labor and up-to-date technical equipment. Finally, the economy of our peasantry is based not on private property, but on collective property, which has grown up on the basis of collective labor.

Lastly, let us pass on to the question of the intelligentsia, to the question of engineers and technicians, of workers on the cultural front, of employees in general, and so on. The intelligentsia, too, has undergone great changes during this period. It is no longer the old hidebound intelligentsia which tried to place itself above classes, but which actually, for the most part, served the landlords and the capitalists. Our Soviet intelligentsia is an entirely new intelligentsia, bound up by its very roots with the working class and the peasantry. In the first place, the composition of the intelligentsia has changed. People who come from the aristocracy and the bourgeoisie constitute but a small percentage of our Soviet intelligentsia; 80 to 90 per cent of the Soviet intelligentsia are people who have come from the working class, from the peasantry, or from other strata of the working population. Finally, the very nature of the activities of the intelligentsia has changed. Formerly it had to serve the wealthy classes, for it had no alternative. Today it must serve the people, for there are no longer any exploiting classes. And that is precisely why it is now an equal member of Soviet society, in which, side by side with the workers and peasants, pulling together with them, it is engaged in building the new, classless, Socialist society.

What do these changes signify? Firstly, they signify that the dividing lines between the working class and the peasantry, and between these classes and the intelligentsia, are being obliterated, and that the old class exclusiveness is disappearing. This means that the distance between these social groups is steadily diminishing. Secondly, they signify that the economic contradictions between these social groups are declining, are becoming obliterated. And lastly, they signify that the political contradictions between them are also declining and, becoming obliterated. Such is the position in regard to the changes in the class structure of the USSR.

The Principal Specific Features of the Draft Constitution

How are all these changes in the life of the USSR reflected in the draft of the new Constitution? ... In drafting the new Constitution, the Constitution Commission proceeded from the proposition that a constitution must not be confused with a program... Whereas a program speaks of that which does not yet exist, of that which has yet to be achieved and won in the future, a constitution, on the contrary, must speak of that which already exists, -of that which has already been achieved and won now, at the present time. A Program deals mainly with the future, a constitution with the present.

Two examples by way of illustration. Our Soviet society has already, in the main, succeeded in achieving Socialism; it has created a Socialist system, i.e., it has brought about what Marxists in other words call the first or lower, phase of Communism, Hence, in the main, we have already achieved the first phase of Communism, Socialism. The fundamental principle of this phase of Communism is, as you know, the formula: From each according to his abilities, to each according to his work." Should our constitution reflect this fact, the fact that Socialism has been achieved? Should it be based on this achievement? Unquestionably, it should. It should, because for the USSR. Socialism is something already achieved and won.

But Soviet society has not yet reached the higher phase of Communism, in which the ruling principle will be the formula: "From each according to his abilities, to each according to his needs!; although it sets itself the aim of achieving the higher phase of Communism in the future. Can our Constitution be based on the higher phase of Communism, which does not yet exist and which has still to be achieved? No, it cannot, because for the USSR the higher phase of Communism is something that has not yet been realized, and which has to be realized in the future. It cannot, if it is not to be converted into a program or a declaration of future achievements.

Such are the limits of our Constitution at the present historical moment.

Further. The constitutions of bourgeois countries usually proceed from the conviction that the capitalist system is immutable. Unlike these, the draft of the new Constitution of the USSR proceeds from the, fact that the capitalist system has been liquidated, and that the Socialist system has triumphed in the USSR....

Further. Bourgeois constitutions tacitly proceed from the premise that society consists of antagonistic classes, of classes which own wealth and classes which do not own wealth.... Unlike bourgeois constitutions, the draft of the new Constitution of the USSR proceeds from the fact that there are no longer any antagonistic classes in society; that society consists of two friendly classes, of workers and peasants; that it is these classes, the laboring classes, that are in power; that the guidance of society by the state (the dictatorship) is in the hands of the working class, the most advanced class in society; that a constitution is needed for the purpose of consolidating a social order desired by and beneficial to the working people....

Further. Bourgeois constitutions tacitly proceed from the premise that nations and races cannot have equal rights, that there are nations with full rights and nations without full rights, and that in addition, there is a third category of nations or races for example in the colonies, which have even fewer rights than the nations without full rights. This means that, at bottom, all these constitutions are nationalistic, i.e., constitutions of ruling nations. Unlike these constitutions, the draft of the new Constitution of the USSR is, on the contrary, profoundly internationalist. It proceeds from the proposition that all nations and races have equal rights. It proceeds from the fact that neither difference in color or language, cultural level, or level of political development, nor any other difference between nations and races, can serve as grounds for justifying national inequality of rights....

The fifth specific feature of the draft of the new Constitution is its consistent and thorough going democratism. From the standpoint of democratism bourgeois constitutions may be divided into two groups: One group of constitutions openly denies, or actually nullifies, the equality of rights of citizens and democratic liberties. The other group of constitutions readily accepts, and even advertises, democratic principles, but at the same time it makes reservations and provides for restrictions which utterly mutilate these democratic rights and liberties....

What distinguishes the draft of the new Constitution of the USSR is the fact that it is free from such reservations and restrictions.... For it, all citizens have equal rights. It is not property status, not national origin, not sex, nor office, but personal ability and personal labor, that determines the position of every citizen in society.

Lastly, there is still one more specific feature of the draft of the new Constitution. Bourgeois constitutions usually confine themselves to stating the formal rights of citizens, without bothering about the conditions for the exercise of these rights, about the opportunity of exercising them, about the means by which they can be exercised.

What distinguishes the draft of the new Constitution is the fact that it does not confine itself to stating the formal rights of citizens, but stresses the guarantees of these rights the means by which these rights can be exercised. It does not merely proclaim equality of rights for citizens, but ensures it by giving legislative embodiment to the fact that the regime of exploitation has been abolished, to the fact that the citizens have been emancipated from all exploitation. It does not merely proclaim the right to work, but ensures it by giving legislative embodiment to the fact that there are no crises in Soviet society, and that unemployment has been abolished. It does not merely proclaim democratic liberties, but legislatively ensures them by providing definite material resources.

Bourgeois Criticism of the Draft Constitution

[As concerns political parties, we say the following:] A party is a part of a class, its most advanced part. Several parties, and, consequently, freedom for parties, can exist only in a society in which there are antagonistic classes whose interests are mutually hostile and irreconcilable—in which there are, say, capitalists and workers, landlords and peasants, kulaks and poor peasants, etc. But in the USSR there are no longer such classes as the capitalists, the landlords, the kulaks, etc. In the USSR there are only two classes, workers and peasants, whose interests—far from being mutually hostile—are, on the contrary, friendly. Hence, there is no ground in the USSR for the existence of several parties, and, consequently, for freedom for these parties. In the USSR there is ground only for one party, the Communist Party. In the USSR only one party can exist, the Communist Party, which courageously defends the interests of the workers and peasants to the very end...

They talk of democracy. But what is democracy? Democracy in capitalist countries, where there are antagonistic classes, is, in the last analysis, democracy for the strong, democracy for the propertied minority. In the USSR, on the contrary democracy is democracy for the working people, i.e., democracy for all....

Amendments and Addenda to the Draft Constitution

[Some are proposing] an amendment to Article 17 of the Draft Constitution. The amendment proposes that we completely delete from the Constitution Article 17, which reserves to the Union Republics the rights of free secession from the USSR. I think that this proposal is a wrong one and therefore should not be adopted by the Congress. The USSR is a voluntary union of Union Republics with equal rights. To delete from the Constitution the article providing for the right of free secession from the USSR would be to violate the voluntary character of this union. Can we agree to this step? I think that we cannot and should not agree to it. It is said that there is not a single republic in the USSR that would want to secede from the USSR, and that therefore Article 17 is of no practical importance. It is, of course, true that there is not a single republic that would want to secede from the USSR. But this does not in the least mean that we should not fix in the Constitution the right of Union Republics freely to secede from the USSR....

Finally, there is one other amendment of a more or less material character. I am referring to an amendment to Article 135 of the Draft Constitution. It proposes that ministers of religion, former White Guards, all the former rich, and persons not engaged in socially useful occupations be disfranchised, or, at all events, that the franchise of people in this category be restricted to the right to elect, but not to be elected. I think that this amendment should be likewise be rejected. The Soviet government disfranchised the non-working and exploiting elements not for all time, but temporarily, up to a certain period. There was a time when these elements waged open war against the people and actively resisted the Soviet laws. The Soviet law depriving them of the franchise was the Soviet government's reply to this resistance. Quite some time has elapsed since then. During this period we have succeeded in abolishing the exploiting classes, and the Soviet government has become an invincible force. Has not the time arrived for us to revise this law? I think the time has arrived.

End of Document 2.10

In introducing Stalin's speech, we noted that the dictator was very much concerned with rituals of democracy—making the Soviet system *seem* open and democratic even when it was not. Partly this was a matter of bolstering the legitimacy of the regime internally. Like any ruler, Stalin wished to legitimize his rule and the social and political order over which he reigned. Partly the concern was an external one as well. As we noted in the introduction, by January of 1933 the Nazis had come to power in Germany in January of 1933. It was not immediately clear what this would mean for the USSR and the rest of the world, but by 1936 or so Nazi Germany began to appear more and more dangerous—to the USSR in particular. The Nazis were openly hostile to Marxism—to Bolshevism, specifically—and thus to the USSR. Stalin began more and more to fear the prospect of a war against Germany. A key concern was that the other western powers, such as Britain and France, might themselves be so hostile to the USSR that they would not help the country against Germany. Worse still, if fascism were to spread to other countries, all of Europe might unite against the USSR. Stalin therefore felt that he had to make the USSR look more democratic, more stable—in a word, more "normal"—than it had in the past to people in other countries. This was another reason for both the conservatism of the 1930s and for the constitution itself. The constitution was designed to make the USSR look more like other countries, with the idea that other countries would be more likely to help it in a war against fascism and the

Nazis. Rituals of democracy were designed to help in this regard as well.

In the chapter below, the historian Karen Petrone describes some of the rituals of democracy connected to the constitution of 1936. As the speech above suggests, Stalin was eager to make it appear as if there was a large, countrywide conservation about the constitution that would bolster the democratic credentials of the USSR. Petrone shows the ways in which the regime's efforts to shape the discussion were successful, but also how it was hard to control that discussion completely. The text nicely shows that for all of his accumulated power, Stalin could not actually control everything. Ordinary people could interpret the constitution and its meaning in their own ways.

READING 2.4

KAREN PETRONE, "CELEBRATING CIVIC PARTICIPATION: THE STALIN CONSTITUTION AS RITUAL OF DEMOCRACY"[17]

…Since the Party focused its limited agitational energies in the 1930s on production issues and on raising the consciousness of those in its ranks, the political education of the rest of the population suffered relative neglect. In this context, the "nationwide discussion" of a draft constitution, the promulgation of the constitution, and the preparation for elections to newly created legislative organs played especially significant roles in educating the general population about how they should participate in Soviet political life. The Soviet government mobilized its citizens to participate in civic rituals of democracy at the same time that it denied them basic civil rights.

In February 1935, Stalin decided to amend the constitution of the USSR that had been promulgated in 1924. The draft of the new constitution, which was unveiled in June 1936, resembled the constitutions of Western Europe and the United States in that it guaranteed the citizens of the Soviet Union universal suffrage and basic civil rights. The constitution also restored the right to vote to so-called class enemies such as priests and kulaks. The Central Executive Committee of the USSR called for a "nationwide discussion" of the draft constitution so that Soviet citizens could propose changes. After several months of nationwide discussion, the Eighth Extraordinary Congress of Soviets approved the new constitution on December 5, 1936. This constitution included forty-eight corrections that had been collected during discussions with the population…

Since the civil rights guaranteed in the constitution existed on paper only, most analysts have treated the constitution of 1936 as a propaganda ploy to prove to the West that the Soviet Union was a democracy…. Whatever Stalin's political intentions were, the public celebration of the constitution and elections introduced a new political discourse within which Soviet cadres and citizens could articulate their goals and aspirations.

By creating a public discourse of democracy and participation, the Soviet government provided a space for the discussion of political issues such as equality, justice, and civil rights and a new language with which to discuss them. Given the political pressure exerted on Soviet cadres and citizens, it is hardly a surprise that this discussion was comprised primarily of statements of support for the Soviet state. This state-sponsored invitation to talk about politics also elicited a variety of unanticipated responses, however, including protest against state policies both for being too "liberal" and too restrictive? As Sheila Fitzpatrick has pointed out, Stalin never again repeated this invitation to the population to participate in open political discussion….

Because of its rhetoric of democracy, justice, and equality, and its enumeration of specific economic rights, the Stalin constitution of 1936 caught the interest of many Soviet citizens. An August 1936 report from the Agitation and Propaganda Department of the Central Committee noted disapprovingly that in Kursk Region "in a great number of instances, collective farmers began reading and discussing the draft constitution themselves, without waiting for the Party organizations." Central officials considered discussion of the constitution not directed by local Party leaders to be undesirable because it would enable peasants to construct independent interpretations of the constitution and publicly articulate them. Even when Soviet officials guided the reading of the constitution, the experience, in the words of a cultural official from Leningrad Region, "put an enormous number of political questions before the collective farmers that had never been put in front of them before." This expansion of the peasants' political language enabled them to think and talk about their lives in new ways.

A New Audience

The audience envisioned by the Soviet state for the constitution and election campaigns was far wider than that of other Soviet holidays. The Soviet government aimed to mobilize every adult Soviet citizen to participate in these campaigns, and the Central Committee kept detailed statistics on the number of citizens who took part. These statistics about the number of participants in the nationwide discussion of the constitution are inconsistent, however, ranging between 36 million to 75 million people, or between 40 to 80 percent of the adult population…These extremely high figures reflect local officials' desires to prove their efficiency and loyalty to the state rather than concrete realities, and in some districts the turnout was 10 to 15 percent lower. Nevertheless, in 1936, Party and government officials were repeatedly directed to mobilize their constituencies to discuss the constitution and their efforts were monitored by the central government….

In the fall of 1936, the Central Executive Committee collected bimonthly reports about the course of the discussion of the constitution in all parts of the Soviet Union. These documents suggest that constitution discourse reached the greatest number of people in the Russian Republic where, by November 1, 1936, 160,092 meetings about the constitution attended by 12,702, 508 workers and peasants were reported to have been held. An October 15, 1936, report to the Central Committee of the Communist Party claimed that over 70 percent of the voters in Moldavia and over 2 million people in Kiev Region had discussed the constitution. This report also indicated that the campaign was not going as well in Tadzhikistan, where discussions had only reached as far as district centers. Like all Soviet political campaigns, the constitution campaign weakened as it spread from the center to the periphery.

Central authorities continued to press for the study of the constitution in factories and collective farms after it was ratified in December 1936. Stalin's speech to the Eighth Extraordinary Congress of Soviets became the most important political document associated with the constitution. In August 1937, the government ordered that this speech be reproduced in 20 million printed copies and on 5 million phonograph records. While it is unlikely that this number of copies ever reached the population, it is clear that the political ideas expressed in Stalin's speech were intended to achieve an extremely wide currency and extend the constitution campaign.

Party organizations continued to monitor and promote study of the constitution in the early months of 1937. In July 1937, the government published election laws for the Supreme Soviet elections and new efforts were made to promote the study of these laws along with the constitution. During the celebration of the Twentieth Anniversary of the October Revolution, the constitution was heralded as the embodiment of the achievements of twenty years of Soviet rule, and in December of 1937 voters were mobilized to show their support of the Soviet state during the elections to the Supreme Soviet. The extension of the celebration of the constitution for eighteen months indicates its importance to the Soviet leadership. Because of the central government's persistent attention to the campaign, constitution discourse was far more widely disseminated than other political agitation.

During the celebration of the constitution and the elections, new segments of the population were targeted for political mobilization. Since virtually all Soviet political education and mobilization occurred at school or in the workplace, there were certain categories of people who were usually beyond the reach of Soviet propagandists. Constitution and election propagandists made a concerted effort to involve the "unorganized" population, including housewives, the elderly, and domestic workers, in Soviet politics. An elderly housewife from the city of Pushkin in Moscow Region announced at a women's meeting about the constitution on September 30, 1936, "Today is a holiday for us housewives because I do not remember another occasion on which they gathered us together to discuss issues." This statement rings truer than most ceremonial speeches made at political meetings because it contained an implicit critique of past propaganda work. Although it is unlikely that the discussion of the constitution and elections actually reached all of the people that the government claimed it to have reached, it certainly placed political questions before segments of the population that had not been addressed in this way before. This appeal to the politically inexperienced or apathetic gave the government the opportunity to gain new support, and it also invited previously silent elements of the population to voice views that may or may not have corresponded with the views of the state.

A New Language

The celebration of the constitution and elections both transformed and expanded Soviet political rhetoric. The constitution transformed Soviet discourse by publicly refuting the notion that class enemies and other "former people" should be denied their civil rights. By extending the right to vote to all Soviet citizens "irrespective of... religious persuasion... social origin, property position and past activities," the constitution destabilized the old conception of "enemy" as one who was already marked and set apart from the community. In his speech to the Congress of Soviets, Stalin suggested that the old enemies had been completely vanquished, citing Lenin's 1919 call for universal suffrage after the "expropriators had been expropriated." But he contradicted himself by acknowledging that the "expropriators" could still pose a threat if they were elected to the Supreme Soviet. Denying any possibility of a loyal opposition, Stalin proclaimed that "if our agitational work is conducted in a Bolshevik manner, then the narod will not allow hostile people into their supreme organs." Only the vigilance of the propagandists and the electorate could prevent enemies from penetrating the Soviet community once more, undermining the elections and the entire Soviet state. By removing the juridical boundary between enemies and the rest of the population, the new political language of the Stalin Constitution allowed for the possibility that enemies could now be found anywhere in the Soviet state, even in the "supreme organs" of government.

The Stalin Constitution also expanded Soviet rhetoric by bringing western conceptions of civil rights to the forefront, guaranteeing freedom of speech, association, the press, and religion and offering protection against arbitrary arrest. It also identified universal, secret, direct, and equal suffrage as a central tenet of Soviet democracy. By emphasizing those parts of the new constitution that resembled the constitutions of the capitalist West, Stalin publicly charted a new political course. When Soviet institutions did not follow this course in practice, Soviet cadres were obliged to publicly promote new political ideals that were constantly contradicted by their own actions.

The promotion of new political goals caused disruptions in the state's public image. For example, when asked, "How can it be that priests will vote?" one chairman of a village soviet in Voronezh Region replied, "They will be deprived of the vote on Election Day," revealing the intention of local officials to subvert the execution of the new law. When confused officials had to steer the population through a new set of political contradictions that they did not understand or had not yet learned to disguise, they sometimes uncovered the arbitrariness of Soviet rule. The confusion of officials and the population revealed aspects of Soviet politics that had previously been excluded from public discourse and provided new ways of thinking about power relations in the Soviet Union.

The Stalin Constitution was not represented by Soviet officials simply as an enumeration of the civil rights and political responsibilities of Soviet citizens. In addition to introducing new and contradictory political language, the discourse of the constitution and election campaigns reflected propagandists' notions about the magic of literacy and writing. Official discussion of the constitution was couched in a quasi-religious discourse of mystery and wonder... Cadres described the constitution as a powerful mystical force that could transform the lives and mentalities of Soviet citizens, bringing them political consciousness, prosperity, and happiness. That the constitution was identified as Stalin's creation enhanced its strength, since cadres represented the words of Stalin, like the words of God, as particularly powerful utterances.

In addition to the constitution, Stalin's speech to the Eighth Extraordinary Congress of Soviets was identified by Soviet propagandists as a particularly powerful text. In this speech, which was broadcast on the radio, filmed, printed, and recorded, Stalin provided a complicated theoretical discussion of the political underpinnings and significance of the constitution. He chronicled the evolution of the class structure of the Soviet Union since 1924 and discussed the relationships of workers, peasants, and the intelligentsia to the state under socialism. He proclaimed the victory of Lenin's nationality policies and explained the differences between Soviet democratism and bourgeois democracy. This dry and rather technical discussion of the constitution was aimed at an audience of politically educated Soviet citizens and the foreign press, and it was not universally appreciated even by this group. One memoirist recalled the reaction of his co-worker, "a pseudo-Young Communist and a fanatical careerist," who proclaimed that Stalin's speech was "nothing special. He talks like a Tatar and doesn't command respect. I didn't like it and I stopped listening somewhere in the middle."

Soviet ideologues described the spoken words of Stalin in an entirely different way; they represented Stalin's speech as a holy communication that spoke directly to every Soviet listener. The chairman of the Moscow City Department of Enlightenment described reactions to the radio broad cast of Stalin's speech: "A small pre-school child says: 'It is so interesting, it is almost as if it is for children.'... People listened to the simple and clear words of Comrade Stalin." In the accounts of Soviet cadres, the words of the constitution and of Stalin's speech traveling over the "invisible waves" of the radio spoke simultaneously to every Soviet citizen at his or her individual level.

According to these cadres, the constitution united leader and people in a mystical and personal communion with one another. In a Moscow City Soviet meeting about the draft constitution, one of the speakers quoted an old Kazakh man's opinion of the draft: "It is as if Stalin himself overheard my thoughts." The constitution thus both reflected and transformed the political consciousness of children, the elderly, and members of the nonRussian nationalities. Cultural and political officials represented ideal reactions to the constitution in a way that downplayed their own roles in the transmission of political consciousness. The sacred words of Stalin acted all by themselves.

The idea that the constitution and Stalin's speech were fascinating and immediately accessible to everyone was a product of socialist realist fantasy rather than reality. Since those who publicly depicted Stalin in any light but the most positive often paid for it with their lives, the portrayal of Stalin as a charismatic statesman and a mesmerizing speaker was inevitable. The representations of the speech as accessible, however, belied the fact that the speech was beyond the understanding of most Soviet elementary schoolchildren or the less-educated segments of the population and had to be explained to be understood. Despite official representations to the contrary, cultural intermediaries such as teachers, librarians, and propagandists were absolutely crucial in the communication of Soviet political ideas from the top leaders in Moscow to the rest of the population. By characterizing the speech as a direct communication between people and leader that did not require explanation, Soviet ideologues complicated the work of these teachers and rank-and-file propagandists, many of whom themselves did not understand the complexities of the constitution.

Teachers of a constitution class for seventh-through tenth-year students were sometimes not skilled enough to make study of the constitution compelling. A March 1937 Central Committee report about constitution teachers complained that "instead of interesting, entertaining explanations of the constitution in a form accessible to the children, in many cases, they give their students boring lectures and reports." The divine words of Stalin lost their luster in the hands of mediocre cadres. In the same month, an education official raised the problem of a class of "mischief-making children" where there existed the "unhealthy and philistine opinion" that it was difficult to read Stalin's speech about the constitution. Teachers could not openly acknowledge the complexity of constitution discourse and this made their task of explaining it all the harder. The reaching for the giant, the mystical, and the fantastic that was an integral part of Soviet life in this period and the use of religious discourse to build the cult of Stalin thus created contradictions that adversely affected the professional credibility of cultural intermediaries and lessened their effectiveness.

The words of the constitution were depicted as having the power to transform not only the consciousness but also the lives of its listeners and readers. At a July 1936 meeting of the Noginskii District Executive Committee in honor of the constitution, a female worker who was a member of her village soviet declared, "When I read the constitution, it was as if I received new strength." In December 1936, a Moscow official reported the remarks of an elderly man: "I am getting younger; who says I am 72 years old?" When collective farmers at the state farm Kudinovo gathered to hear a report about the work of the Eighth Congress of Soviets, one collective farmer stated, "When they read the constitution, then you feel that you want to live and your heart works better." In these instances, the words of the constitution became a healing and life-giving force. To assert the transformative power of the word, however, propagandists defined a "before" and "after" that offered a momentary glimpse at the realities of Soviet life. The collective farmer's statement implied that he did not want to live before he read the constitution. The assertion that the constitution had the power to heal led to the implicit acknowledgment that the population was somehow injured and sick at heart.

Soviet publicists depicted the constitution as ushering in a new era of prosperity. The rhetoric of plenty surrounding the 1936 constitution was one aspect of the government's efforts to convince citizens of the "continuously growing abundance which distinguishes the present moment." At a meeting in honor of the new constitution in Moscow Region, one female collective farmer heralded the new prosperity brought by the constitution, proclaiming that the peasants now "all have cows and pigs and eat meat every day." The poverty of the countryside had been miraculously transformed to abundance by the constitution.

Official propagandists sought to create loyalty to the state by employing a discourse of abundance, miracle, and sudden healing that had much more in common with backward "superstition" and religion than with scientific socialism. The attempt to use such a trope reveals that official Soviet discourse absorbed elements of older "irrational" discourses even as it claimed to eliminate them. This trope offered opportunities to appeal to the emotions of the population, but also complicated the work of propagandists by forcing them to make extravagant, far-fetched, and fantastic claims about the efficacy of the constitution.

Criticism of the Constitution

When the Soviet government published a draft of the new constitution and invited the population to submit suggestions for revision, it opened up a dialogue with the population and created space for comment on and criticism of state policies. While criticism of self and others was an ever present part of Stalinist political culture in the late 1920s and 1930s, public criticism of a document associated with and endorsed by Stalin extended the boundaries of the usual culture of criticism. One puzzled official, for example, announced at a meeting of state farm workers that "suggestions for changes in individual articles or inserting additions into the draft is forbidden." When instructions from the center contradicted this official's experience of how politics in the Soviet Union worked, he ignored directions and behaved according to the dominant political model, entirely excluding the population from decision making. This habitual behavior was now censured by central government officials.

The draft constitution elicited foreign as well as domestic criticism. Stalin admitted in his speech to the Congress of Soviets that the new constitution had been attacked in the foreign "bourgeois" press. By enumerating "bourgeois" criticisms and then responding to them one by one, Stalin disseminated a critique of the constitution to the far corners of the Soviet Union. Stalin used humorous anecdotes and folk sayings to mock his enemies' interpretations, but he nonetheless explained their objections to the constitution in detail. Those Soviet citizens who had enough education and sophistication to understand the implications of Stalin's speech were in formed that the constitution had been criticized both for being "an empty piece of paper" and for being a "rejection of the dictatorship of the proletariat."

Stalin directly addressed the issue of whether the Soviet constitution was actually going to be enforced or whether it was just a propaganda ploy. According to Stalin, Fascist critics believed that the constitution was "an empty promise, calculated to pull off a well-known maneuver and deceive people." Stalin rejected the German charge that the constitution was a deceptive "Potemkin village" by throwing the same charge back at the Germans. He accused them of trying "to hide the truth about the USSR from the people, to delude the people and deceive them." The idea that a government might build up an elaborate facade to deceive its people thus became part of discussions about the constitution. The notion that propaganda could create an alternative reality was an element of public political discourse in the Soviet Union, appearing in the very rhetoric that sought to disguise Soviet reality.

Another charge that Stalin took great pains to rebut was the idea that the constitution was a "shift to the right," rejecting the dictatorship of the proletariat. This criticism from the left in Poland and the United States attacked the Stalin constitution for its resemblance to the constitutions of capitalist countries. Stalin did not reply substantively to this charge, but rather restated his position that the new constitution represented the "transformation of the dictatorship [of the proletariat] into a more flexible... more powerful system of leadership of the State by society." He accused his critics of not understanding what the dictatorship of the proletariat meant and of not being able to tell left from right. Stalin thus publicly defended the transformations in political language that complicated the lives of local cadres. Stalin's speech ensured that broad critiques of Soviet politics became part of a public political vocabulary that could be employed by those who opposed Stalin.

Discussion of the constitution provoked criticisms of the Soviet order and calls for better treatment from various segments of the population. Some Soviet citizens demanded rights based on the constitution's guarantees of freedom of conscience, assembly, speech, and the press and the inviolability of the person. Other criticisms focused on the constitution's definition of the economic and social status of workers, peasants, and employees and on the enumeration of the benefits guaranteed to these groups. National minorities used the constitution's protection of "the equality of rights of citizens of the USSR, irrespective of their nationality or race," to assert their individual rights.

Freedom of Religious Worship

Article 124 of the constitution guaranteed "freedom of religious worship and freedom of anti-religious propaganda." This article of the constitution brought forth a variety of reactions, both against religion and in favor of it, that alarmed Soviet officials. Interest in the religious issues raised by the constitution existed throughout the Russian Republic. Bulletins sent to the Central Executive Committee in the fall of 1936 documented numerous requests to open or repair churches based on Article 124. Interest in religious questions was not limited to the Orthodox Christian population. A propagandist among the Khants and Nenets peoples in Omsk Region reported that in their discussion of the constitution, these peoples "were only interested in the questions of religion. They asked, 'And did the shaman receive rights? We have many shamans.'" In one Muslim area, the population requested the re-opening of twelve mosques and the organization of a system by which mullahs would be paid a salary by the collective farm. Discussions of the constitution brought forth proposals to allow priests, shamans, and mullahs to participate in the social life of their peoples; to support religious leaders financially; and to provide new places of worship. These requests sought to incorporate religious institutions into the Soviet economic and social order.

The declaration of freedom of conscience was interpreted by those who had suffered religious persecution as a sign that religion would now be reintegrated into Soviet life. The clergy of the Viaz'ma diocese wrote a fulsome letter to Stalin, praising "the immortal historical document-the great Stalin Constitution." Other priests offered to propagandize the constitution "from the pulpit." The promulgation of the constitution brought people together for open religious worship as part of both Soviet and religious communities; in the Mordovskii Autonomous Republic, 500 people gathered for prayers to thank God for Article 124. These actions illustrated some citizens' beliefs that there need not be a contradiction between religious worship and loyalty to the Soviet state.

Other Soviet citizens interpreted the separation of church and state guaranteed by the constitution to mean that local control over religious life was at an end. One citizen in Kuibyshev Territory asserted that because of the constitution, "the village soviet does not have the right to manage the church." A bookkeeper in Zel'man Canton told the local population that priests "can freely assemble religious meetings, processions, and so forth, at any time, without the permission of the village soviet and the canton executive committee." According to these interpretations, the constitution created a significant change in local power relations, diminishing the prerogatives of the local soviets as it strengthened the rights of churches....

Soviet citizens read the Stalin Constitution in a variety of idiosyncratic and highly imaginative ways. There were many misinterpretations of Article 124. In the Marinskii Autonomous Region, someone agitated that "the new constitution obliges everyone to pray to God and to sacrifice livestock." Because of this agitation, the peasants on one collective farm tried to slaughter the collectivized bull. In other places, the coming of the new constitution gave the collective farmers incentive to baptize all of the children between the ages of three and six. In the Dagestan Autonomous Republic, a mistranslation turned the "freedom of anti-religious propaganda" clause into "freedom of religious propaganda," leading citizens to believe that an even more sweeping change in the state's attitude toward religion had taken place. There, rumors spread that the constitution encouraged the opening of mosques and learning of the Koran, but that "the village soviets do not want to promulgate this 'document.'"...Rumors accused local officials of distorting legislation from the center and denying the people the freedoms that had been decreed. In 1936, like in 1930, there was an element of truth to the assertion that local officials were unwilling to comply with the dictates of the very document that they were obliged to promote.

The freedom of religious worship guaranteed by the constitution drew criticism from elements of the Soviet population who had embraced the anti-religious doctrine of the Soviet state. These people openly opposed the rights that the constitution had given to priests. One Leningrad propagandist explained that in the course of discussions about the constitution, collective farmers in Leningrad Region proposed a variety of "undesirable corrections" that not only forbade priests to vote and be elected but proposed further limits on their civil rights and demanded that churches be closed. A collective farm Party organizer explained to his audience that priests should not be allowed to vote because they lived off "unearned income." Open hostility to Orthodoxy, which had up until the publication of the draft constitution been a marker of support for Soviet power, suddenly became a statement of protest against the government's policies. By espousing a liberal policy toward religion, even if it was only a policy on paper, the Soviet state placed some of its most vocal supporters at odds with official government doctrine and lessened the enthusiasm and effectiveness of some loyal cadres.

Freedom of Speech

The Stalin Constitution's espousal of freedom of speech also emboldened citizens to challenge local officials. One man in Moscow Region proclaimed, "Now according to the constitution, they cannot arrest me. Freedom of speech means that I can say whatever I want." Because the constitution guaranteed basic civil rights at the same time that NKVD terror was reaching its height, those citizens who dared to claim the civil rights guaranteed in the constitution, were, ironically, in greater peril than ever of suffering arbitrary arrest....

Even if it the guarantee of freedom of speech was not put into practice, the fact that it existed in Soviet public discourse was nonetheless significant. The constitution caused members of the political police to reflect on their activities and their role in the Soviet order. At a meeting of NKVD agents in Western Region to discuss the constitution, a dispute arose. One participant described the controversy: "do we have freedom of criticism or not? Many considered that if we [do] have freedom of criticism, then it is forbidden to prosecute people for anti-Soviet conversations." A Party official was sent to talk to this group and explain their "mistakes" to them. Of course, the agents were not mistaken. Arresting people for anti-Soviet conversations directly contradicted the constitution. The nationwide discussion of the constitution, with its emphasis on political rights, confused even members of the police and made them aware of the contradictions in their own actions. The language of democracy produced new knowledge that made Soviet citizens more aware of the political contradictions surrounding them.

Economic and Social Benefits

In addition to civil rights, the constitution enumerated the economic and social rights of workers and peasants. Articles 119 and 120 ensured "the establishment of annual vacations with pay for workers and employees and the provision of an extensive network of sanataria, rest homes, and clubs for the use of the toilers" and "the extensive development of social insurance for workers and employees at state expense." These provisions promised Soviet toilers that in exchange for productivity, they would receive material benefits and a social safety net.

One propagandist in the Dinamo factory in Moscow admitted that promoting the constitution was a difficult task; in January 1937, he noted that "many of our workers are still in a bad humor and they do not understand the fundamentals of the constitution. Indeed some workers quickly apprehend their rights, but forget about their obligations." This propagandist acknowledged the low morale of Soviet workers and their rejection of the constitution's exhortations to work hard, protect socialist property, and defend the motherland. This propagandist also revealed that workers in the Dinamo factory were particularly receptive to the social welfare provisions of the constitution. The workers took the guarantees of benefits seriously and sought to use them to improve their economic status.

The very popularity of social benefits caused difficulties for Soviet propagandists. Another propagandist at the Dinamo factory in Moscow complained in August 1936 that "as soon as we begin to speak about [the government's] concern for people, then the first thing that pops into our people's heads is a putevka (a place in a sanitarium or on a vacation tour). But everyone knows that it is not possible to provide everyone with a putevka." Soviet workers were quick to comprehend that rhetoric about prosperity, concern for citizens, and the "right to leisure" gave them the opportunity to request attractive social benefits. Since there were not enough resources for everyone, these demands led to friction between workers and factory organizers when organizers used the distribution of benefits to construct social hierarchies. The promises of the constitution raised workers' expectations of economic benefits that were slow in trickling down to rank-and-file workers.

The social benefits in the constitution were guaranteed only to workers and employees, excluding the peasants from even the possibility of receiving these privileges. The constitution thus reaffirmed the hierarchy of urban over rural and defined the peasantry as second-class citizens of the Soviet state. The inequality written into the "most democratic constitution in the world" was not lost on the peasantry. According to J. Arch Getty, in the discussion about the draft constitution, "one-fourth of all suggestions from Smolensk and one-third nationally" demanded equal status for the peasantry in vacation benefits and social insurance. As one female collective farmer in Chernigov Region put it, "Collective farmers who work in the fields do not receive enough for their work compared to those who work in production. We work twenty hours a day, and they work eight hours. We have a common need for clothing and shoes, we walk around in torn dresses and shirts, and they, workers, are provided with everything in full. We don't have free places in resorts, but they do." These provisions of the constitution created much resentment and jealousy, but nothing was done to redress this imbalance in the final draft....

The reactions of younger and older workers to the constitution also revealed a difference in their attitudes towards the Soviet state and their resentment of one another. One young woman complained, "In the constitution it is written that abortions are illegal and they haven't made a lot of nurseries." An older woman responded to this complaint by saying that before "in the factory, pregnant women had to work until the last day [before the baby was born.]" The younger woman answered, "That was before, and now we all speak about [things being] better; that means they should be better." This interchange reveals the older worker's jealousy of the welfare benefits received by younger workers. It also reveals that the younger worker had high expectations of the Soviet welfare state because of official rhetoric about improvements in living conditions. Discussion of the economic and social welfare aspects of the constitution revealed tensions between cadres and citizens, between workers and peasants, between the old and the young. Rather than illuminating the perfection and unity of Soviet society, study of the constitution uncovered unresolved conflicts and inequalities.

The Collective Farm Order

Discussions of the constitution also raised questions about the possibilities of farming outside of the collective farm. Article 9 explicitly permitted the "small-scale private economy of individual peasants and artisans based on their personal labor." While the constitution thus acknowledged that *edinolichniki* (individual peasant-farmers) had a right to exist outside of the collective farm, it also affirmed that the "socialist system of economy...shall be the predominant form of economy in the USSR," upholding the centrality of collective farm agriculture.

Government reports recorded a variety of creative interpretations of this article of the constitution, however. Rumors circulated in Western Region that this article meant that "now individual peasant-farmers will be the preference, and soon Soviet power will return to kulaks the property that had been taken away from them." In Gorkii Region, it was rumored that "individual peasant-farmers will be given a great deal of land and will be freed from all taxes." In Chernigov Region, a peasant proclaimed "there will be no difference between collective farmers, individual peasant-farmers, and kulaks. All will receive full and equal freedom." In the mid-1930s, the peasants circulated the same kind of rumors about land and freedom that they had spread eighty years before. As a result of these kinds of rumors, some people who had been deprived of their property during the collectivization drive asked for it to be returned. Other people decided to leave their collective farms. The arrival of the constitution in villages across the Russian Republic inspired peasants to grasp at freedom by interpreting the constitution as the embodiment of their individual hopes...

The Rights of Nationalities

An important theme of the constitution celebration was that the document reflected the victory of Lenin's nationality policies. The new governmental structure elaborated in the constitution was intended to demonstrate that the eleven Soviet republics were equal members of a voluntary and harmonious federal union. The new Supreme Soviet, for example, had two equal chambers, the Soviet of the Union and the Soviet of Nationalities and Article 17 of the constitution provided for the "right of free secession" from the USSR. In a number of collective farms in the Volga German Autonomous Republic, this "right of free secession" caught the attention of the population. Some peasants proposed that the Volga German Republic be turned into a Union Republic so that it could secede from the Soviet Union. Other peasants advocated a broader interpretation of this article to also include the individual right of "free departure to any country." These proposed revisions to Article 17 articulated the dissatisfaction of the Volga Germans with life in the Soviet Union. These requests both fueled and reflected official paranoia about the loyalty of Volga Germans to the Soviet state, a paranoia that eventually led to the mass deportations of the Volga Germans during World War II.

The constitution could also be used by individuals of one nationality to complain to Moscow authorities about the inappropriate behavior of people of another ethnicity. After the celebration of a festival of Azeri music in Moscow in April 1938, one musician who had not been chosen to travel to Moscow wrote that if he had been excluded from the trip because he was an Italian, this would have violated "Article 123 of the constitution of the Azeri SSR," which like Article 123 of the Union constitution guaranteed equality for all citizens of the USSR "irrespective of their nationality or race." In response to this and other complaints, the Committee on the Arts sent deputies to Azerbaidzhan to investigate charges of nationalism. The central Soviet authorities' vigilance against any sign of "nationalism" made the anti-discrimination article of the constitution a powerful tool for some individuals, while it destroyed the lives and careers of others.

Whatever Stalin's intention was when he decided to draft a new constitution that guaranteed freedom of religion, freedom of speech, and other basic civil rights, this document was interpreted as a signal of change in the status quo at the local level. When peasants took actions based on their understandings or misunderstandings of the constitution, they took advantage of the arrival of an official document to pursue their struggles against local Soviet officials. Those who guarded the status quo in the localities had to promote the constitution and at the same time prevent the peasants from using it as a weapon against them. Local Soviet officials thus had to deal with challenges that were apparently sanctioned from the center. Some officials themselves became conscious that their actions denied Soviet citizens the rights granted by the constitution. The new discourse of democracy made contradictions in Soviet life apparent and revealed a different social and political world to cadres and citizens.

The constitution had a mixed effect on individual rights. In some cases, the rights guaranteed in the constitution caused Soviet citizens to take actions that jeopardized their safety. When citizens exercised their free speech in explicit opposition to the Soviet government, they took a tremendous risk. On the other hand, the constitution might have offered some individuals the opportunity to challenge anti-religious propagandists and justify their right to attend church. The articles of the constitution may also have given minority nationalities in the non-Russian republics a real opportunity to defend themselves against discrimination by the majority in that republic.

New Visions of Government

…The constitution campaign reached many citizens who had never been exposed to Soviet discourse. Since the constitution enumerated benefits to Soviet citizens, this new audience was quite attentive. Official rhetoric about the constitution tapped into pre-revolutionary religious discourse, depicting this document as a holy text invested with the power to transform Soviet life. Some Soviet citizens eagerly accepted the promises that the constitution made to them, becoming frustrated when obtaining the social welfare guaranteed in the constitution proved harder than they had hoped. Other citizens viewed the constitution not as a miraculous document but as a practical one that could possibly be used to achieve concrete social, economic, and political goals.

The celebration of the constitution represented an enormous change in Soviet official rhetoric. It publicized new ideas about elections, local political process, self-government, civil rights, religious freedom, and social benefits to Soviet citizens. Because this rhetoric of democracy served as an alternative to Soviet practices, this document from the center destabilized the status quo between local Soviet officials and Soviet citizens in many parts of the Soviet Union. The document raised expectations of a new social order that never came into being and, by giving rights to priests and kulaks, it stirred up old resentments. Some Soviet citizens embraced the constitution to simultaneously show their loyalty to Soviet power and forward their own battles with local officials, to seek privileges, and to imagine a new kind of local politics.

The constitution campaign, was profoundly affected by the knowledge and experience of the cadres who educated the population. Confusion about the meaning of the constitution was perpetuated by ignorant or bewildered officials who could not themselves understand its basic tenets. Other cadres found themselves challenged by citizens who used the constitution to back up their arguments. Still others were forced to confront the contradictions in Soviet life when readers of the constitution asked them about glaring in consistencies. The introduction of new democratic political rhetoric in the constitution initiated new dialogues about Soviet life. The celebrations surrounding the Stalin Constitution of 1936 show how democratic political concepts were recast in Soviet terms by the central government and mid level officials and then reinterpreted in a wide range of ways by lowerlevel cadres and the Soviet people. Despite the fact that this democracy existed only on paper, the presence of democratic ideals in Soviet political discourse transformed the relationships of Soviet citizens to the Soviet state and its representatives by enabling them to envision alternatives to the Soviet political structure. The actions that Soviet citizens took based on these new visions sometimes led to tragedy for themselves or for the local cadres who they opposed in the name of the Stalin Constitution.

End of Reading 2.4

Further Reading:

Sheila Fitzpatrick, *The Russian Revolution*, 2nd ed. Oxford: Oxford University Press, 1994.

Richard Sakwa, *The Rise and Fall of the Soviet Union, 1917-1991*. London: Routledge, 1999.

Robert Weinberg and Laurie Bernstein, *Revolutionary Russia: A History with Documents*. Oxford: Oxford University Press, 2011.

Ronald Grigor Suny, *The Soviet Experiment: Russia, the USSR, and the Succesor States*. New York: Oxford University Press, 1998.

UNIT THREE

Iran

CHAPTER 10

EARLY IRAN AND ISLAM

If the Russian Revolution gave birth to the world's first communist state, then the revolution in Iran in 1978-79 created a rather different entity: The Islamic Republic of Iran. As one author writes, the Iranian revolution was no less unprecedented: "No modern revolution has been led and supported in the name of ancient religious values claimed to provide a truer and more just foundation for modern society than do Western ideas of progress."[1] And yet as different as the outcome was in these two cases, there are certain similarities between the revolutionary process in Russia and Iran. Moreover, the histories of Russia and Iran have been intertwined at key points, not least of all with reference to constitutional issues. Thus even as we move south from Russia to Iran, what we learned earlier will continue to inform our discussion.

Our focus in this unit will primarily be on the revolution of 1978-79, which ended the rule of **Shah** (or "king") **Mohammed-Reza Pahlavi** (reigned 1941-79) and brought to power the **Ayatollah Ruhollah Khomeini** (1902-89), and furthermore featured the destruction of the Iranian monarchy and its replacement by the Islamic Republic that exists to this day. In order to make full sense of this revolution, however, we need to give some attention to an earlier revolution in 1905-11, which is sometimes called the "**constitutional revolution**." It was then, in 1906, that Iran's first constitution appeared.

In general, the Iranian revolution is less well studied than its Russian counterpart. This is partly because it happened more recently, and the opportunities for western scholars to access Iranian archives has been more limited than was the case in Russia. But it has to do primarily with the central place that the USSR occupied in the Cold War. Especially after World War II, the US government and American universities invested many resources in the study of the USSR, including its history, precisely because that country was the main global adversary of the US. Although relations between the US and Iran have been bad since 1979, Iran never represented the same threat that the USSR constituted in the years 1945-91. The result is that our knowledge of the Russian revolution is more robust, while the continuation of strained relations between the US and Iran makes it harder to evaluate the Iranian revolution objectively.

Our basic goal in this chapter is to provide a very basic outline of Iran's history from antiquity up until the 19th century, with a particular focus on how Iran became a Shia Islamic country—and indeed what it means to make such a statement.

PERSIA TO THE 20TH CENTURY

Known as "Persia" to the western world before 1935,[2] Iran has been familiar to westerners from

---

1   Tim McDaniel, *Autocracy, Modernization, and Revolution in Russia and Iran* (Princeton, 1991), p. 3.

2   The term "Persia" comes from the name of a part of the country known as "Parsa" (now a province in the

antiquity. The Persians were famously the opponents of the ancient Greeks in a series of wars and produced remarkable warrior heroes such as Darius and Xerxes. Iran's rich history and influence have been even more significant for countries to the east. Persians developed an extraordinary high culture, excelling especially in the areas of literature and decorative arts. Their influence is widely felt across a large portion of the Middle East and Central Asia, to such an extent that there was long a common Persian high culture in places as diverse as Azerbaijan, Afghanistan, and Uzbekistan. In this sense, Iranians have made a fundamental contribution to world culture matched by few other civilizations.

While the foundations of the modern Iranian state date from more recent centuries, most Iranians see themselves as the descendants of the **Achaemenid Persian Empire** of antiquity. Primarily the accomplishment of King Cyrus II ("the Great") in the 6th century BCE,[3] by around 500 BCE the empire extended all the way from Libya and Macedon in the west to the Indus River (now in Pakistan) in the east, with a population estimated at 50 million people. Darius the Great, a successor to Cyrus, solidified his predecessor's conquests by creating order and institutions of governance, as well as a royal highway extending some 2600 miles. The country did not really have a capital—the court simply followed the physical presence of the king—but Darius constructed a large palace and ceremonial center at **Persepolis**, whose ruins served in 1971 as the venue for a large commemoration of 2500 years of Iranian monarchy. During this time, the elites of the empire consolidated a new religious tradition, known as **Zoroastrianism**, that posited the existence of both a good and evil god, along with their various supernatural servants. While not monotheism (it is more properly referred to as a "dualist" religion), Zoroastrianism and its sectarian offshoots would have important influences on later monotheist traditions.

The Persian Empire was eventually conquered by Alexander the Great, with the result that by around 330 BCE the empire collapsed and was brought under the rule of Greek successor states. The ancient period of Iranian history is important for our purposes primarily because it nourished the consciousness among Iranians that they had been the creators of a great civilization entitled to respect and a prominent place in world. These sentiments continue to shape Iranian perceptions today.

In fact, the conflict between the "western" Greeks and "eastern" Persians in the ancient world carried on into the early medieval period as well. The Persians threw off Greek rule less than a century after Alexander the Great's conquest, and re-emerged as first the Parthian Empire (247 BCE - 224 CE), and after that, the Sassanid Persian Empire (224-651 CE). These powerful states benefitted from their dominance over the emerging Silk Road trade across Asia, and they effectively blocked the Roman Empire from further expansion into Asia. By the mid—7th century a new force appeared that would reshape the geography of the Middle East within a few decades. That force was the first generation of Arab Muslims from the tribal groups inhabiting the Arabian peninsula. By 650 CE, they became masters of the entire region of the former imperial space governed by the Persian Empires. The coming of Islam was to be so important to Persian history that we should turn to an expert in the field to provide a clear and accurate overview. The author of the text below is **John Curry**, a professor at UNLV who has published extensively on an Islamic form of mysticism known as Sufism.[4] His overview provides a brief history of the appearance and early spread of Islam, including its move into Persia in the 7th century, and accounts for the split of Muslims into two major sects—**Sunni and Shia**. Iran is notable for being one of a relatively small number of countries where the **Shiites** outnumber Sunnis, and this particular sectarian outlook is critical for understanding Iran's politics and culture even in the late 20th century.

---

southwest). In antiquity the rulers of Parsa established an empire that became know to the Greeks and thus to the West as "the Persian Empire." The name "Iran" is a contraction of the longer "Airyana Vaeja", meaning "land of the Aryans." In 1935 the Iranian ruler insisted that foreign governments use "Iran" rather than "Persia." In this book, we will use the two terms more or less interchangeably, though most often "Iran" when referring to the later 20th century.

3   This text will use the abbreviations "BCE" to signify "before the Christian era" and "CE" to designate "the Christian era."

4   Curry's most noteworthy publications are *The Transformation of Muslim Mystical Thought in the Ottoman Empire: The Rise of the Halveti Order* (Edinburgh, 2010); and *The Nexus of Sufism and Society: Arrangements of the Mystical in the Muslim World, 1200-1800*, co-edited with Erik S. Ohlander (London, 2012).

READING 3.1

JOHN CURRY, "EMERGENCE OF ISLAM AND ITS SHI'A SECTARIAN BRANCHES"

The word "Islam" itself means the act of submitting to an all-powerful, single God, and such is the name of the religion itself. The followers of Islam are referred to as "Muslims," meaning those who submit to God. While the term "God" is rendered as "Allah" in the Arabic language, the word itself literally means "the [one] God," and therefore represents the same general concept as in the monotheisms of Judaism and Christianity.

Where Islam diverges from those religions is in terms of theology and sacred texts. The religion of Islam, according to most accounts, emerged between 610 to 632 CE as a series of revelations from God to the **Prophet Muhammad**. These revelations, at first transmitted orally among the Arabic-speaking peoples of the western Arabian peninsula, were eventually codified into a written text known as the **Qur'an** (or "Recitation") by the mid-7th century CE.[5] Composed of 114 chapters of lengths varying from hundreds of verses to just a few, and arranged largely from longest verse to shortest, the Qur'an is the basic religious touchstone for all Muslims regardless of the specific sect to which they adhere. The verses clearly reflect the period of Muhammad's life in which they were revealed. The Meccan verses, which were revealed between 610 and 622, represent the earliest verses in the Qur'an, and they show the Prophet Muhammad trying to convince a skeptical, largely polytheistic Meccan Arab community of the truth of the new revelation.

Indeed, the text of the Qur'an teaches us a good deal about Muhammad's audience in early 7th-century Arabia. Stories of various prophets from the Judaic and Christian biblical tradition, such as Abraham, Moses, Jesus and Mary, make frequent appearances throughout the text, while various figures from the local Arabian tradition appear in the narrative as well. The Qur'an narrates stories about these figures with the assumption that the audience already knew them, and seeks primarily to reorient that existing knowledge about them to fit them into an Islamic framework.

Because the Meccan community's political, economic, and social life was bound up with its location as a pilgrimage site for various tribal gods, and because the Meccan elites of Muhammad's tribe drew their power from control over this system, they began to persecute Muhammad and his followers in an attempt to eliminate the threat that his monotheistic teaching represented. Over time, the persecutions escalated into acts of violence as younger members of prominent tribal elites defected to Muhammad's group and began to divide local families. By 622, hostilities had reached the point where Muhammad and his followers could no longer live safely among the Meccans; they therefore fled several hundred miles northward to the oasis of Yathrib (subsequently renamed "Medina") in search of refuge. This *hijra* (meaning "emigration") marks the start of Muslim history, and the Muslim community dates events in its history from this date (thus, the year 2015 by the western calendar is 1436 for Muslims).

At this point, the Prophet Muhammad became not just the conduit for the revelations of the Qur'an, but a political leader of a community as well. Muhammad and his followers made an agreement with the people of Medina to mediate between conflicting sides in a series of bloody tribal disputes there in return for his community's protection. As a result, the focus of the Qur'anic verses in the final ten years of the Prophet's life (622 to 632) changes somewhat. Chapters on subjects such as family law, divorce, inheritance, relations with other religious communities, and the proper conduct of warfare now became more prominent. In addition, the pre-existing conflict with the Meccans escalated into open warfare fairly rapidly after the arrival of Muhammad and his community, as the latter began to raid the caravans of their enemies. The escalation of the conflict quickly involved not only the Meccan and Medinan tribes, but other tribes resident in the Arabian peninsula, as they were drawn into supporting one side or the other. After nearly a decade of alternating conflict and negotiation with the Meccans, Muhammad emerged victorious and managed to unify much of the Arabian peninsula under his rule by 630.

However, the Prophet died less than two years later, leaving a number of questions about how the nascent Muslim community should proceed thereafter. The most obvious question involved designating Muhammad's successor, and determining whether this person could continue the Prophet's role as a conduit for divine revelation. Since the Prophet did not have a son, there was no obvious candidate

---

5   An older way of writing "Qu'ran" is "Koran."

waiting in the wings, and many of the Arabian tribes viewed their adherence to Islam strictly as a matter of allegiance to Muhammad; when he died, some simply ended their alliance and went their own way. According to most Muslim sources, the leaders of the Muslim community, after a short debate, acclaimed the Prophet's father-in-law and trusted adviser Abu Bakr (d. 634) as the best person to lead the community. The community gave him the title of *khalifa* or "caliph," a term that basically meant "successor" or "deputy." However, some narratives suggest that the Prophet's son-in-law, a much younger man named Ali ibn Abu Talib (d. 661), contested this decision. By this narrative, he and his supporters had to be forced to give their grudging consent to Abu Bakr's succession. Whatever the truth of these conflicting accounts, by the end of Abu Bakr's short two-year reign as caliph, all of the rebelling tribes had been brought back into the fold, and he nominated the powerful Arab warrior Umar (d. 644) as his own successor before his death. Still, there are reasons to suppose that Ali and his supporters remained disgruntled.

Even before Umar's accession, the campaigns to re-unify the Muslim community had begun to spill over into the Arab tribal groups along the frontiers of the Sassanid Persian Empire. For a variety of reasons, the weakened Sassanid state was dissolving into multiple competing factions at the time, and while some of those managed to resist the Arab advance for a time, others made agreements with the Muslim leaders and thus retained some semblance of local power under an emerging Arab empire. The last of the Sassanid territories fell under Muslim control when the last Sassanid king fell in battle while fleeing eastward into Central Asia. It is in this way that the lands of modern-day Iran came under Muslim rule for the first time, although this does not mean that the peoples of the region promptly became Muslim. Probably only the Arab tribal groups that invaded and settled in the region even knew anything about Islam. It was moreover physically impossible to convert everyone in one fell swoop, and the Qur'an itself states that "there can be no compulsion in religion" (2:256). Given the rapid nature of the conquest of the Near East, which was completed in less than 20 years, a series of *ad hoc* arrangements emerged in various places so that the Muslims could govern them. Most of the time, the non-Arab and non-Muslim populations such as Christians, Jews and Zoroastrians were granted status as *dhimmi* or "protected peoples," although the fact that the dhimmi paid a higher rate of tax than the Muslims created the possibility for economic incentives in exchange for conversion in subsequent eras. Such incentives do indeed seem to have played a role in attracting non-Arab groups to Islam.

As the Arab conquests extended over thousands of miles, the early Muslim community began to fragment, as groups that had formerly been in close geographic proximity now found themselves at opposite ends of the known world. The rapid transformation of the Muslim community from a tight-knit group into a global imperial power created serious tensions among its members and their leaders. In 644, the caliph Umar was mortally wounded by an assassination attempt, and before he died, he called together a council of six leading Muslims and asked them to choose one of their number as his successor. One of the six was the aforementioned Ali ibn Abu Talib, and another was Uthman ibn Affan (d. 656), who was eventually chosen by a deeply divided vote to become the third caliph. Uthman proved to be a controversial choice, in that he often relied heavily upon his experienced Meccan kinsmen to govern the expanding empire— that is, some of the same people who had fought the Prophet Muhammad at an earlier stage and who had converted to Islam only grudgingly after the Meccan defeat. Furthermore, the massive wealth and plunder that came out of the initial conquests was often distributed in an unequal way, and some tribal groups began to chafe at the emerging inequalities. It was out of these tensions that the first signs of the sectarian split into the Sunni and Shi`a sects of Islam began to emerge.

By 656, tensions had reached a point where some tribal groups openly rebelled against the caliph Uthman, and the community was thrown into turmoil when one group murdered him. In order to regain control over an increasingly chaotic situation, the community leaders quickly elevated Ali ibn Abu Talib as the fourth caliph, based partially on the proposition that he had been the alternate candidate in the council vote twelve years earlier. The gambit did not work, however, and Ali's caliphate quickly devolved into a five-year civil war between different factions that ended in Ali's defeat. Although Ali himself was killed in the civil war, his supporters, who increasingly came to be known as the "shi`at `Ali," or "partisans of Ali"—the basis for the words "Shiite" and "Shia"—refused to accept the rule of Uthman's powerful extended family, known as the Umayyads. When the first Umayyad ruler who had defeated Ali died in 680, the Prophet's grandson and Ali's son, Husayn, launched an abortive rebellion in which both he and the members of his small force were massacred. Most Muslims, even those who supported the Umayyads, were horrified that a direct descendant of the Prophet had met such a fate, and attitudes hardened across the political spectrum. Another civil war between 683 and 692 further reinforced the growing divisions, and increasingly heavy-handed responses from the Umayyad leadership gave them a reputation for brutality and impiety among the broader Muslim community. By the mid-eighth century, internal family struggles undermined the power of the Umayyads, while a coalition of forces against them grew. The "partisans of Ali," other descendants of the Prophet's extended family lineage, and various non-Arab communities of converts to Islam all directed their ire against the Umayyads.

By 750, the Umayyad government had been overthrown, though even then there was disagreement about what to do next. Whereas the "partisans of Ali" presumed that one of Ali's descendants would be placed on the throne, a different faction supporting the descendants of the Prophet's uncle Abbas proved better-organized and more powerful, in part because they demonstrated a willingness to accept non-Arab converts on equal terms. For their part, the "partisans of Ali" would be increasingly radicalized by having their dreams dashed when victory had seemed so close.

Yet despite the disappointments of "partisans of Ali," by the end of the eighth century alternative sources of power and legitimacy in Muslim societies were emerging. As the political and religious legitimacy of the caliphates weakened as a result of the aforementioned conflicts, religious authority began to devolve to local pious figures with extensive knowledge of the Qur'an and the actions of the Prophet and other early Muslim leaders. As believers sought answers to various questions pertaining to proper belief and practice in the new faith—and this included a growing number of converts who were unfamiliar with Arab culture and history—they gravitated to these immediately accessible local figures who could provide answers. The result was the emergence of a group of religious specialists known as the _ulama_ (literally, "those who know"). By the ninth century, even the political rulers of the Abbasid caliphate found that they could not undertake policy that touched on religious matters without consulting the most renowned and prestigious _ulama_. Eventually, the most educated and well-traveled members of this Muslim intellectual elite compiled books of _hadith_—oral traditions that could be verified through a chain of authority as reaching back to the generation of the Prophet Muhammad himself. With the growing acceptance of these works, Muslim scholars of succeeding generations elaborated various schools of Islamic law to answer the numerous questions that were not addressed directly by either the Qur'an or the oral tradition literature.

For the "partisans of Ali"—who were eventually known as Shiites—this process took a very specific form, which lies at the foundation of the primary sectarian split within Islam right up to the present. The "partisans" recognized only one legitimate source of religious authority: the Prophet's direct descendants via his son-in-law, Ali, who had seen his authority wrongfully usurped from the time of the Prophet's death. For the Shi`ites, therefore, the _hadith_ reports are almost always sourced to this carefully bounded lineage of descendants, who are called _Imams_. The majority of Sunnis, by contrast, take their traditions from a much wider range of pious or educated figures in Islamic history—including the Shiite Imams. What sets the two sects apart, then, is the range and types of traditions that they accept as authoritative and the manner in which they elaborate legal arguments from that base. They otherwise draw upon the exact same text of the Qur'an as the foundation for their religion.

Up until the latter half of the 9th century, the emerging Shia sect was able to look to a series of descendants from Ali ibn Abu Talib's line. But what would happen if one of the Imams did not have a surviving son to continue the line? Shiites eventually had to confront this very scenario. In 874, during yet another civil war, the eleventh Imam, Hasan al-Askari, died and left behind only a young child as his successor, Muhammad al-Mahdi. In light of the disturbed state of affairs, Muhammad was never seen in public due and did not emerge to lead the community thereafter. Instead, he communicated with his followers via four prominent deputies for the next seven decades in a period called the "Minor Occultation" (with the term "occultation" meaning something that is hidden from view or concealed). Shortly before the last of these deputies died in 941, the Imam supposedly issued a letter stating that no future communication would take place until God commanded it, and that the community of believers should be led by the transmitters of Shia traditions until this twelfth Imam could re-emerge. This signaled the beginning of the "Major Occultation" of the twelfth Imam, and his followers accordingly refer to themselves as "Twelver Shiites" in reference to their expectation that one day the Twelfth Imam will return. This expectation gives the theology of **Twelver Shiism** a distinctly messianic overtone, as the return of the Imam is presumed to include the return of justice and order to a fallen world.

Shortly after these developments, some Shi`ite groups were able to seize power in various parts of the Muslim world and thereby to establish a set of public holidays, such as Ashura, where public reenactments of the martyrdom of Ali's son Husayn at Karbala took place, and where the Shia faithful may engage in acts of penance for the failure of the community to come to Husayn's aid. However, the Shia always remained a distinct minority in most parts of the Muslim world even if they controlled the levers of power locally. It is quite telling that after decades of rule by various Shia leaders in centers such as Egypt and Mesopotamia, the majority of the population remained Sunnis. Only geographically-remote regions, such as the area around the Persian Gulf island of Bahrain and the mountains of Lebanon and northern Iran, saw the emergence of permanent Shia majorities.

Such would be the situation, more or less, all the way until the 16th century, when a new situation developed in Iran. By the mid-15th century, Iran and its surrounding regions had become highly decentralized, featuring groups of nomadic warriors who made their living preying on others. Once such group, the **Safavids**, claimed descent from a medieval religious leader named Safi al-Din (d. 1334). While Safi al-Din himself was most likely not a follower of the Shia, by the late 15th century his descendants and their followers appear to have adopted some elements from Twelver Shiism. Although the details are murky, in 1500 a twelve-year old leader named Ismail emerged from the mountainous northern regions of Iran with an army of followers and began to subjugate the region of the Caucasus (further north) and Iranian plateau (to the south). Contact with Shiite scholars resident in the province of Gilan may have further strengthened the Safavids' affiliation with Shiite beliefs. By 1510, Ismail had carved out a large empire roughly encompassing present-day Iran and its surrounding regions. As his power grew, he began to persecute various Sunni leaders and groups that had previously been dominant, and his successors invited various Shiite scholars and leaders from other parts of the Muslim world to join them. By the early 17th century, a combination of this in-migration, conversion, and the flight of Sunnis to other parts of the Middle East made the region of modern-day Iran into a Shia-majority population for the first time. In fact, the Safavid state became strong enough to seize much of Mesopotamia (which today would constitute most of Iraq) from the Ottomans for several decades, and invested heavily in developing the Shiite pilgrimage centers, such as the tombs of Ali ibn Abu Talib in Najaf and his son Husayn in Karbala. As a result, around half of the modern-day population of Iraq remains Twelver Shiite right up to the present. In short, as a result of the Safavids, most of Iran and a portion of what is now Iraq became Shia.

By the early 18th century, the Safavid Dynasty weakened to the point where it was overthrown by invading forces from Afghanistan. The country thereafter fractured into a host of highly decentralized and unstable regions that were often at the mercy of powerful nomadic tribes in the area. The lack of a strong central government had a critical impact on the doctrines of Twelver Shiism. The previous generations of Shiite leadership had closely followed the Qur'an and the textual traditions handed down from the time of the Twelve Imams in a highly literal fashion; they had accordingly declined to recognize the independent reasoning of any scholar as a legitimate source of law. But in the unstable world of the 18th and early 19th centuries, local religious authorities often became *de facto* sources of political authority as well. As a result, over the course of a generation, many of the most prominent Shiite scholars began to introduce a more activist practice of independent reasoning (or *ijtihad*) as a necessary component of Twelver Shiism's ability to confront new problems. As a result, a doctrine developed whereby the most prominent Shiite scholars were acclaimed as "sources of emulation" (called *marja` al-taqlid*). In theory, all Twelver Shia were compelled to choose one of these living "sources" and to follow their ruling and judgments without question. If their "source" were to die, they would be required to choose another, in contrast to previous practice where continuing to follow the teachings of long-deceased scholars was perfectly acceptable. The highest-ranking of these members of the Shiite clerical hierarchy in turn came to be referred to as *ayatollah* ("Sign of God"). This gave the Shia clerical hierarchy unprecedented power and influence over their followers and distinguishes this branch of Islam from its Sunni counterpart.

Let us make a few broad points in summarizing the complex story presented above. First, Islam, meaning "submission to God," appeared as a distinct religion in the 7th century based on the revelations from God to the Prophet Muhammad. While these were initially transmitted orally, they were eventually compiled into the written text of the Qu'ran, whereas other oral traditions recounting the activities and sayings of the Prophet and his Companions were recorded as the *hadith*. Islam had roots in both Judaism and Christianity—it claimed to represent a more perfect and final revelation of those earlier faiths—and it embraced an uncompromising monotheism. Islam eventually spread into what is now Iran as part of a rapid conquest that only slowly converted the Persian-speaking population to Islam. Second, questions of both political and religious succession occupied a critical place in the lives of Muslims after the death of the Prophet, and the resulting conflicts played a critical role in determining the character of the Muslim community and the degree of its unity. Indeed, struggles over succession did much to define the first several centuries of Islamic history after the Prophet's death in 632. Third, one of the most important disagreements produced the division of Muslims into two major sects, Sunnis and Shiites, although it took several centuries for that division to solidify. With a few minor exceptions, the Shiites, or "partisans of Ali," remained a minority throughout the Muslim world until the Safavids asserted control over Iran in the 16th century and established Shiism as the predominant form of Islam there. Finally, Shi'ites recognized only a strict line of succession from the Prophet through Ali and referred to that succession as Imams. Most Shi'ites held that the Twelfth Imam had disappeared into occultation and would appear only subsequently to restore justice and order. Whereas Shi'ites had initially shunned religious interpretation in favor of strict adherence to inherited textual traditions, in the context of political decentralization in the 18th and 19th century, they gradually embraced the principle of independent reasoning, which allowed for a more hierarchical organization than was characteristic for Sunnis.

End of Reading 3.1

By the early 16th century, then, Shia Islam had become the official religion of Iran, which had distinct repercussions for the rest of Iran's history. By embracing Twelver Shiism, Iran now distinguished itself clearly from the major Sunni powers, and the country's attachment to Twelver Shiism continued even after the Safavid dynasty had dissipated. Indeed, this religious distinction shapes its rivalry with Saudi Arabia for prominence in the Middle East even today.

By the late 18th century a new dynasty, the **Qajars**, secured power over Iran. Despite their success, the Qajars faced a series of significant challenges over the course of their reign (1796-1925). They were a Turkic-speaking tribe and did not actually have an integral connection to Shiism. The Qajars did try to justify themselves as defenders of Shiism and as supporters of religious projects such as mosques and charitable endowments. They eagerly publicized their pilgrimages to various Islamic shrines. They really had little choice but to defer to the wishes and the interests of religious leaders, and the authority of Shia ulama accordingly grew. The state and the religious establishment thus coexisted in a condition of tension. The Qajars did not really have a proper state or a bureaucracy, with the result that their real jurisdiction over the country was sharply restricted to the vicinity of the capital. The result was that the country was not well integrated. Geography made it hard to unify the country, and the population was thus fragmented into small self-contained tribes, villages and towns. Despite a few attempts, for the most part the Qajars could take only very limited steps to modernize the country.

In other circumstances this might not have mattered so much, but in the 19th century Iran found itself increasingly pressured by European powers — most importantly Britain and Russia. Both of those countries were becoming global empires extending across large portions of the world, and Iran was one of the places where their paths intersected. Russia exploited the existence of Christian kingdoms in the south Caucasus as the justification for extending its power towards Iran. The Persians were forced to fight two unsuccessful wars against Russia in 1804-13 and 1826-28, as a result of which Russia annexed what is now Georgia, Armenia, and Azerbaijan — previously Persian territory — and made the Aras river the border between itself and Iran. Russia also extracted economic concessions and privileges of extraterritoriality for Russian subjects and property in Iran,[6] as well as a large sum in war reparations. As the century progressed the British became more involved as well. They were eager, first of all, to protect their colony in India, and Iran was central to their strategy in this regard. The British also sought special economic concessions in Iran — that is, the exclusive right to develop areas of the economy such as banking, mines, and public works. Trade treaties limited custom duties to a low percent, thus effectively creating a free trade area for western imports, which then often undersold domestic Iranian handicrafts and created economic hardships for the local population. Writes one historian, "Vital aspects of national life passed into foreign hands": the military, transportation, banking, etc. "Even the borders of the country — with Russia, Afghanistan, and British India — were being determined by outside powers, with Iran being reduced to little more than a spectator."[7] In short,

---

6   "Extraterritoriality" means that foreigners — in this case Russians in Iran — were subject to their own laws rather than those of the country in which they resided.

7   Elton L. Daniel, *The History of Iran* (Westport, Conn., 2001), 114.

western encroachments intensified over the course of the 19th century, and the Qajars had only limited possibilities to resist. Such encroachments were to be an important factor in Iranian revolutionary upheaval at several stages, as we shall see in the next chapter.

Further Reading:

Elton L. Daniel, *The History of Iran*. Westport, Conn.: Greenwood Publishers, 2001.

John L. Esposito. *Islam: The Straight Path*. Oxford: Oxford University Press, 2011.

Malise Ruthven, *Islam: A Very Short Introduction*. Oxford: Oxford University Press, 1997.

CHAPTER 11

REVOLUTIONARY UPHEAVAL & AUTOCRATIC MODERNIZATION TO THE 1970S

We saw in the previous chapters that the Qajars faced significant obstacles in their efforts to modernize Iran and thus to resist encroachments from imperial powers like Britain and Russia. Those encroachments proved to be an important factor in the first revolutionary stirrings in Iran, which began in the late 19th century. Our goal in this chapter is accordingly to take the story up until the crisis years of the 1970s and thus to identify the most important sources of the revolution in 1978-79. We first briefly recount prominent cases of revolutionary upheaval in Iran before the 1970s, focusing on two major events that occurred within a twenty-year period between 1890 and 1911: the so-called **Tobacco Rebellion of 1890-92** and the constitutional revolution of 1905-1911. Subsequently, we explore the Iran's experience under the **Pahalvi dynasty**, beginning in 1921 when **Colonel Reza Shah** seized power from the ailing Qajars, creating his own dynasty in 1925. A major feature of the reigns of both Pahlavi shahs was **autocratic modernization**, a process whereby the ruler actively encouraged economic and social change while preserving the main elements of political autocracy.

REVOLUTIONARY UPHEAVAL BEFORE THE 1970S

The first revolutionary tremble in Iran began in 1890, though there was not a full-blown revolution at the time. The immediate cause for the so-called Tobacco

Rebellion was the granting of a tobacco concession to a British subject, Major General Talbot. This meant that Talbot could form an Imperial Tobacco Corporation that would have an exclusive right for fifty years to the production, sale, and export of all tobacco in Iran, with the shah receiving an immediate payment and a portion of the profits. Several groups were upset by this concession. The most directly affected were indigenous Iranian producers of tobacco, but they were merely one example of a much larger group—all of those in Iran who were engaged in largely traditional, urban, small-scale production and trade. Collectively, this group was known as the bazaar, or bazaaris. As early as the 1830s the bazaaris were complaining to the government about how the large-scale importation of foreign manufactures was undermining their own production and trade. Coming after many other economic concessions that undermined the bazaar's economy, the tobacco concession caused particular irritation. Joining the bazaar in protest were religious clerics. Recall that the Shiite religious authorities had a good deal of independence from the state in Iran, and this gave them the opportunity to articulate the grievances of the bazaar and other traditional elements of Iranian society. Clerics were also angry about the possibilities given to western missionaries to teach Christianity in Iran. There was, finally, a small group of secularized intellectuals who had at least some familiarity with Western ways and sought to emulate those at home in Iran. They especially appreciated western economic development, comparative justice, and the lack of arbitrary rule. Although their visions for the future were quite different, these groups—the bazaar and religious clerics, on the one hand, secularized liberals and radicals, on the other—revolted against the tobacco concession and engaged in a boycott of tobacco dealing and smoking. In early 1892, the shah was compelled to cancel the tobacco monopoly.[1]

Two things especially are noteworthy in the Tobacco Rebellion of 1890-92. The first is the alliance formed among clerics, the bazaar, and some secular intellectuals. This is a pattern that would be partially replicated later. The other is the strong anti-imperialist and anti-foreign component of the protest. This, too, would figure prominently in later revolutionary upheaval. Still, the Tobacco Rebellion was itself not a revolution, since it altered neither the political or social order in Iran. Its principal accomplishment was to end the tobacco concession.

The events of 1905-11, in contrast, warrant the label of "revolution"—indeed, they are usually referred to as Iran's "constitutional revolution." The events began essentially as a continuation and intensification of the Tobacco Rebellion. Aside from the end of the tobacco concession, the issues that produced dissatisfaction persisted, and Iran continued to endure pressure from foreign powers. Moreover, the Iranian government had been compelled to borrow money in order compensate the British tobacco company for the loss of the concession. So opposition and discontent continued. Events in Russia helped to precipitate a new crisis. As we know, Russia experienced its own revolution in 1905-07, which blocked the tsar's regime from intervening in Iranian affairs to prevent revolution there. The revolution in Russia extended all the way down to the South Caucasus, and many of the oil workers in Baku were migrants from Iran who could easily communicate revolutionary ideas to their families and friends back in Iran. In fact, the city of Tabriz in the northwest, near the Russian border, stood at the vanguard of the revolution. Moreover, the fact that Japan, an Asian power, had defeated a European one inspired Iranians, who had been facing foreign intervention for almost a century. The revolution itself is usually seen to have started in December of 1905, when the governor of Tehran subjected several sugar merchants to corporal punishment for not lowering their sugar prices as ordered (the merchants insisted that this was beyond their control due to high import prices). Demonstrations followed, in which religious clerics occupied a prominent place. The shah felt compelled to make certain concessions to the crowd, including the dismissal of the unpopular governor. The unrest nonetheless continued.

Though there was some talk initially of a constitution, for the most part the intellectual foundations for constitutionalism in Iran were relatively weak. In fact the revolution acquired its support from an eclectic mix of tradesmen, clerics, religious dissidents, intellectuals, journalists, and some government officials. They had a range of motivations, extending from patriotism to pure self-interest, and positions shifted frequently as the revolution unfolded. Nonetheless constitutional ideology and principles eventually emerged from the revolutionary process. One consideration was the fact that Japan, in contrast to Russia, actually had a constitution already, having produced one in 1889. Thus, writes Nikki Keddie, "Many [in Iran] considered it significant that the only Asian power with a constitution had defeated the only Western power without one, and constitutions came to be looked upon as the 'secret of strength' of Western governments."[2] By the summer a group of merchants, bazaaris, and clerics were calling for a representative assembly—they used the term *Majles*—and there was increasing talk of a constitution. The first Majles opened in October of 1906, and a new Fundamental Law, based largely on the constitution of Belgium, was drafted in late 1906. This formed the core of the Iranian constitution that existed until the revolution of 1979. "The intent of the constitution was to set up a true constitutional monarchy in which Majles approval was required on all important matters, including foreign loans and treaties, and in which ministers would be responsible to the Majles. Equality before the law and personal rights and freedoms, subject to a few limits, were also guaranteed."[3] Ultimately, the revolution was chiefly political in nature: its goal, to

1   Nikki Keddie, "Iranian Revolution in Comparative Perspective," in Albert Hourani, Philip S. Khoury, and Mary C. Wilson, eds., *The Modern Middle East: A Reader* (Berkeley, 1983), 604-06.

2   Keddie, "Iranian Revolution," 608.

3   Nikki R. Keddie, *Modern Iran: Roots and Results of Revolution* (New Haven, 2003), 68. Observant readers will immediately recognize certain parallels with tsarist Russia and its Duma and Fundamental law.

the extent that its participants could agree, was to reduce monarchical and foreign power through the introduction of a constitution and parliament. There is of course a certain irony in that the revolutionaries sought to resist western influence by introducing western institutions, but after all Japan had already showed how effective this approach could be.

But while the framers of the constitution had intended real power to reside in the parliament and its ministers, rather than in the crown, the Majles proved largely unsuccessful in wresting power from the shah. The shah who signed the constitution—literally on his deathbed—was replaced in early 1907 by a successor who was adamantly opposed to radical reform, the Majles, and constitutionalism. Once he felt secure on the throne, the new shah moved against all three of them, and indeed managed to close the Majles in a coup in 1908. There also began to appear divisions among the constitutionalists between secular nationalists and conservative Islamists. Whereas the former desired an order akin to European constitutional systems, the religious conservatives became alarmed by this drift towards secularism and by the un-Islamic character of the constitution. They accordingly managed to insert an article requiring that any law passed by the Majles had to be approved by a council of religious clerics— although for reasons that are unclear this council was never formed.

Further undermining the revolution were the actions of Russia and Britain. As we know, the tsarist autocracy had regained its footing by 1907, once Peter Stolypin's "coup" had secured an acceptable Duma and the countryside had been "pacified." Russia was now in a position to reassert its influence over Iranian affairs, and indeed the Russian-led Cossack brigade in Iran played a role in the shah's closing of the Majles in 1908. Thus the basic dynamic in Russia was replicated in Iran, not least of all because of Russian involvement in the latter case. Still more important, Britain and Russia, long imperial rivals that had come close to fighting wars in Asia over colonial claims, came to a diplomatic settlement at the expense of Iran in 1907. The two imperial powers divided Iran into clearly defined spheres of influence—Russia in the north and Britain in the southeast—with a neutral zone between them. The division was designed to insure that the two countries would not accidentally start a war because of a misunderstanding or skirmish. Iranians were

neither consulted nor properly informed of the terms of the agreement. The Iranian effort to end foreign influence had obviously proved unsuccessful, and now the Iranians could not even play the Russians and the British off against each other as they had before. When in 1911 Iran was compelled by Britain and Russia to dismiss an American advisor enlisted to help with the country's financial affairs, the revolution was effectively over.

Iran's constitutional revolution had not been a complete failure. The country now had a constitution, even if the shah frequently ignored it. The Majles met at least some of the time, even though it was marginalized. Women also became politically active in a way that they had not been before. And the alliance of religious clerics, the bazaaris, and secular intellectuals had shown a remarkable capacity for political action. But the country still remained under foreign domination— all the more significant when oil was discovered in Iran in 1908—and the shah still was not effectively limited by constitutional restraints.

THE PAHLAVIS AND AUTOCRATIC MODERNIZATION

The First World War created fundamentally new conditions for Iran. As we know, Russia entered the war in 1914, experienced two revolutions in 1917, and signed the treaty of Brest-Litovsk with the Central Powers in 1918. This effectively spelled the withdrawal of Russia from Iran, as well as the (temporary) loss of Armenian, Georgia, and Azerbaijan, which for a few years became independent states. Indeed, in 1919 the Bolsheviks formally terminated the special concessions that the tsarist government had extracted from Iran. For a time, then, Russia was effectively out of Iran. The influence of the British, by contrast, increased. The British had established the Anglo-Persian Oil Company (a predecessor to today's BP, or British Petroleum) and were determined to protect the vitally important operations of the company. They were also determined to block any intrusion from Germany and the Ottoman Empire, both of which were fighting Britain in the war. Shortly after the war ended, the British imposed a new agreement on Iran. While ostensibly designed to provide technical expertise and protection to Iran, the agreement was more likely intended to secure and extend

British domination in Iran—in essence to create a protectorate.

Opposition to the agreement of 1919 led the British to the conclusion that it was better to have a stable if independent Iran than to have a protectorate. It was unclear who could lead such an Iran, but Colonel Reza Khan soon answered the question by taking power in a coup in 1921. Historians disagree about what exactly happened in this coup and who, precisely, was behind it, but for us it is enough to note that Reza Khan proved willing to defy the British and, in 1925, had himself declared shah, thereby ending the Qajar dynasty. Reza's surname, Pahlavi, gave its name to the new dynasty, which featured two shahs, father and son: Reza Shah (1925-1941) and Mohammed-Reza Shah (1941-1979). It was this dynasty that was overthrown by the Islamic Revolution of 1978-79.

Both Pahlavi shahs were notable as modernizers: they made extensive efforts to make Iran into a modern nation-state and eventually into a leading regional power in the Middle East. Thus Reza Shah sought to build up a modern professional army with mechanized transport and aircraft; he began construction of a Trans-Iranian Railroad; he built new highways; he sought to establish greater centralization of power, by breaking the power of Iran's tribes; he promoted a strong sense of Iranian nationality at the expense ethnic, regional, and religious identities, for example by discouraging the use of non-Iranian languages like Kurdish and Turkish; and he took steps toward the emancipation of women, for example by outlawing full-length covering for women in certain contexts. Some of these measures generated opposition among more traditional elements of Iranian society, and especially among some religious clerics. Reza Shah was not hostile to Islam, but he was determined to ensure that it not prevent needed reforms. In general, Reza Shah was an autocratic modernizer: he sought to change the country in fundamental ways, but he did so in an autocratic fashion, without taking much stock of those who had different views. He especially disliked communists and socialists, who were effectively outlawed in the early 1930s. In essence, Reza Shah wanted controlled change imposed from above, not revolutionary upheaval from below.

Despite Reza Shah's efforts, the country was still susceptible to foreign intervention. In the 1920s and 30s, even the British had been prepared to allow the shah to rule the country with minimal interference. The situation changed fundamentally when Nazi Germany invaded the USSR in June of 1941. Suddenly Britain and the USSR, separated by ideological opposition in the 1920s and 30s, found themselves allied to one another against Germany. Meanwhile, Reza Shah had cultivated political and economic ties with Nazi Germany, partly to avoid dependence on Britain and Russia and partly because Nazi race theories of Aryan superiority sounded attractive (the very name of the country, "Iran," meant "land of the Aryans"). The Soviets and British were determined to block German access to Iranian oil. And the allies also needed Iran as a corridor for bringing war matériel from the Persian Gulf to the USSR.[4] The allies accordingly issued various ultimatums to Reza, and when the shah rejected those, they invaded the country. They removed Reza Shah from power and, after considering the resurrection of the Qajar dynasty but lacking an appropriate Qajar candidate, transferred the crown to Reza's son, Mohammed Reza. Deposed, Reza went into exile, eventually dying in South Africa in 1944. Iran was once again divided into spheres of influence: the Soviets in the north and the British in the south. Once the United States entered the war in December of 1941, American influence in Iran became significant as well.

The new shah, Mohammed Reza, was relatively young (22 years old) and inexperienced when he took the throne. In the initial stages of the postwar period another figure, **Mohammed Mossadeq**, emerged as the central figure. Mossadeq headed a group of liberal, anti-royalist and nationalist factions that had banded together in 1949. He was notable for his integrity and charisma, and he opposed foreign economic concessions, while also striving to subordinate the shah to the constitution. His most striking act, in 1951, was to propose the nationalization of the Anglo-Iranian Oil Company (AIOC), which meant claiming the country's oil wealth for Iranians and terminating the concession to the British company. This became the basis for Mossadeq's appointment as prime minister, though the shah made the appointment only reluctantly. The bill on the nationalization of oil was signed later

---

4   It is worth emphasizing that the vast majority of German forces after 1941 were deployed against the USSR, which gave all of the allies a strong incentive to get trucks, airplanes, and other goods into Soviet hands.

in 1951, and Mossadeq then produced legislation to dismantle the AIOC and to replace it with a purely Iranian company. Britain was of course angered by this unilateral nationalization, which represented a challenge to both their strategic interests—their access to oil—and their imperial pride. Britain organized a boycott and blockade of Iranian oil, while British employees, whose technical expertise was indispensible, refused to work for the new Iranian company. Britain also encouraged the US to help in pressuring Iran, and the Americans indeed joined an unofficial worldwide boycott featuring the major oil companies. Faced with this mounting crisis, Mossadeq found it impossible to back down, and in response adopted a more authoritarian and leftist approach, which included not only various populist measures but also efforts to oppose and even humiliate the shah. He became increasingly dependent on the support of radical parties to back his policies through street demonstrations. In the end, Mossadeq's actions on the nationalization issue had been based on the propositions that he would be able to sell Iranian oil despite British opposition and that he would receive support from the US. Both turned out to be false. The Americans were actually not entirely unsympathetic—they felt that the British should have negotiated a new deal that was more favorable to the Iranian side—but in the context of the Cold War US leaders were deeply concerned that the crisis in Iran would give the USSR a pretext to intervene and foment revolution. Thus in both Britain and the US Mossadeq was pictured increasingly "as a dangerous fanatic, likely to deliver Iran to the Soviets," even though it would be more accurate to characterize Mossadeq as "an anti-imperialist nationalist who intended to keep Iran from being controlled by any foreign country or company."[5] In 1953 the CIA and its British counterpart, MI-6, organized a coup to oust Mossadeq from power. The exact course of events remains unclear, as does precise responsibility for it. But the end result was that, with the shah's reluctant agreement, Mossadeq was removed from power, convicted of treason, and then placed under house arrest until his death in 1967.

Although Iranians themselves probably played a bigger role in Mossadeq's removal than many are prepared to recognize, the events of 1953 had tremendous resonance over the longer term.

Many in Iran saw Mossadeq as a patriot and a martyr and were disturbed by what they regarded as the harmful meddling of the US and Britain (although some, clearly, were bothered less by this meddling as such and more by the fact that foreign powers had intervened against Mossadeq rather than in his favor). In any event, the removal of Mossadeq not only reversed the nationalization of oil, but also opened up space for Mohammed Reza Shah, by then in his mid-30s, to take a more active role in ruling the country. Indeed, in the years after 1953 the shah would create a new autocracy or a royal dictatorship—but one that also aggressively promoted modernization.

This combination of political conservatism (autocracy) and the promotion of socio-economic change (modernization) is critical for understanding the revolution of 1978-79, and we must therefore focus carefully on each of those strands.[6] Let us begin with autocracy. For the remainder of the 1950s the shah focused his efforts heavily on consolidating his control over Iranian political life. In 1957, he created a domestic security apparatus, known as SAVAK, for keeping opposition groups and parties under control. SAVAK moved aggressively against the regime's opponents, putting them in prison, subjecting many to torture, and exiling some from the country entirely. For example, in 1963 the religious cleric Ruhollah Khomeini was arrested and exiled to neighboring Iraq for opposing an agreement with the US that gave diplomatic immunity to American military personnel. By the mid-1960s, writes Elton Daniel, "politics in Iran revolved completely around the will of the shah."[7] The Majles continued to function, but its actions were largely symbolic, and it was dominated by just two government-sponsored parties. In 1975, the shah eliminated all parties save one—the Rastakhiz, or Revival party—thus making Iran into a monolithic, one-party state. For a full twelve years, from 1965 to 1977, there was only one prime minister, and he was utterly loyal to the shah. Mohammed Reza also engaged in elaborate ceremony to bolster his image and power. In 1967 he staged a dramatic coronation ceremony for himself and the empress (he had postponed coronation until

6   The idea of "autocratic modernization" as a source of the Iranian Revolution is central to Tim McDaniel, *Autocracy, Modernization, and Revolution in Russia and Iran* (Princeton, 1991).

5   Keddie, *Modern Iran*, 125.

7   Daniel, *History of Iran*, 158

he felt fully secure in power). The coronation was part of larger effort of the shah to portray himself as a natural successor to the great imperial Persian monarchs of the past. Along the same lines, in 1971 the shah organized a lavish celebration at Persepolis to commemorate the accession to the throne of Cyrus the Great and thus 2500 years of monarchy in Iran. The shah likewise introduced a new calendar that used the creation of the Persian Empire rather than the Islamic era as its starting point.

Yet modernization and change also occupied a central place in the shah's vision for the country's future. In other words, the shah constructed and perpetuated an autocracy in the country not simply in order to hold on to power for its own sake, but in order to transform Iran into a modern country that would become the principal regional power in the Middle East. At the center of the shah's efforts was a reform program that he called "the White Revolution," or the "Revolution of the Shah and the People." Initiated in 1963 on the basis of a referendum which provided almost unanimous support, the White Revolution consisted of a series of reform measures such as land reform, the nationalization of forests, privatization of state industries, a profit-sharing program for workers, the promotion of literacy, and the extension of voting rights to women. Other reform projects were added later. The shah used the term "White Revolution" to distinguish the reform from more radical plans, such as those promoted by the communists and other leftists (the "red"). The emphasis was on controlled reform that would advance the country and break the resistance of the conservative and reactionary forces that he saw as a brake on the country's progress ("the black"),[8] which often involved reducing power at the local level in favor of the central government. The larger goal of the reform, for the shah, was the creation of what he called the "Great Civilization," which as one historian has written entailed "a program that would lift Iran into the ranks of the most important countries in the world, on a par with a Japan or Germany."[9] Another historian characterizes the White Revolution as "a bloodless revolution from above, led by a dynamic, populist, 'revolutionary monarch,' which would anticipate and prevent the possibility of a red

revolution, and ensure the stability and durability of the regime."[10] As we shall see later, the White Revolution generated much more dissatisfaction than the shah was prepared to recognize.

Contributing to the shah's modernization program were the aspirations of the United States. As the British Empire gradually crumbled after World War II, the US came to occupy a more prominent place as the main global power (though always in competition with the USSR). Thus the removal of Mossadeq had involved the CIA as well as the MI-6, and the Americans had soon replaced the British as the principal supporters of the shah's regime. The US was eager to have a major and dependable ally in the region, and Iran emerged as an excellent candidate. The shah was hostile to communism—for example, he outlawed the major leftist party in Iran, the Tudeh party—and this opposition ensured that the Soviet Union would have only limited influence in Iran and would thus help to "contain" the USSR—one of the principal goals of the American foreign policy. Iran could also help to regulate affairs in the Middle East in a manner advantageous to the US. For example, the US, already preoccupied in Vietnam, would have less of a need to have a massive presence in the region if it could work through its Iranian ally and proxy. And of course Iran continued to be a major source of oil, which was of great significance given the industrialized character of the American economy and its reliance on cars. Iran also represented a significant market for the sale of US arms. At the same time, the Americans wanted to see liberalization and reform in the countries that it supported and even put a certain emphasis on respect for human rights. The shah thus sensed that successive American administrations favored "progressive" leaders, which to a significant degree coincided with his own desire for modernization and progress. In short, there was a good foundation for an alliance between the two countries. The US wanted a regional ally that would help to rule the Middle East in a way favorable to American interests; that would resist communism and the USSR; that would sell its oil and purchase arms; and that would engage in careful reform in order to attain some socio-economic progress and prevent radicals from fomenting disorder. The shah wanted to have a dependable market for Iran's oil; to

---

8   We shall return to this color scheme later, but it is worthwhile to note it for now.

9   Daniel, *History of Iran*, 158.

10   Ali M. Ansari, *Modern Iran since 1921: The Pahlavis and After* (London, 2003), 148.

have a major world power as its backer and as a source of advanced military technology; to become the Middle East's main regional power; and to modernize the country in a careful and controlled fashion. To be sure, the interests of the two sides did not overlap completely. The US refused to sell Iran nuclear weapons, for example, and the shah was less concerned with human rights than some of the American administrations would have liked. But to a substantial degree the interests of the two sides converged.

CONCLUSION

Thus as Iran approached the late 1970s, we see the following picture. Iran had a long but complicated history extending back over two millennia, and yet only at certain points was the country unified more or less in its present form. Even at later stages, under the Qajars and the Pahlavis, rulers had attained only partial success in unifying the country, and initiatives like the White Revolution were designed at least partly to address that deficit. Gradually over the course of a few centuries, Islam, which originated among Arab tribes, became the main religion of Persian speakers, who added their own contributions to Islamic civilization. After the Safavids had established power in the early 16th century, the country gradually became predominantly Shia—indeed the state before the 20th century where Shiites represented a majority of the population. Most Shites embraced the "Twelver" version of the sect's teaching, which proposed that the 12th Imam had gone into occultation and would appear only later. Even in the 1970s by most reckonings the "hidden Imam" had not yet reappeared. Especially in the 19th and 20th century—the "age of imperialism"—Iran had found itself increasingly under foreign pressure. The Russians and the British were prominent in earlier stages, while the Americans became more important after World War II. Many Iranians resented this foreign intervention, and this dissatisfaction played a key role in the Tobacco Rebellion of 1890-92 and in the actions of Mossadeq when he sought to nationalize Iranian oil in the early 1950s. As we shall see, a desire to be free from it was certainly one of the sources of the revolution of 1978-79. Finally, the Pahlavis were autocratic modernizers, which is to say that they constructed a largely dictatorial political system that was nonetheless energetic in pursuit of social, economic, and technical change. Reza Shah began this process, though he was then ousted from power by the British and the Soviets in 1941. Once Mossadeq had been deposed in the coup of 1953 and Mohammed Reza Shah was able to consolidate power, the younger Pahlavi shah could embark on his White Revolution. That project transformed Iran in significant ways, but it also generated a great deal of opposition, as we shall see in the next chapter.

Further Reading:

Ali M. Ansari, *Modern Iran since 1921: The Pahlavis and After*. London: Longman, 2003.

Elton L. Daniel, *The History of Iran*. Westport, Conn.: Greenwood Publishers, 2001.

Nikki R. Keddie, *Modern Iran: Roots and Results of Revolution*. New Haven: Yale University Press, 2003.

Tim McDaniel, *Autocracy, Modernization, and Revolution in Russia and Iran*. Princeton: Princeton University Press, 1991.

CHAPTER 12

OPPOSITION TO THE SHAH

In the previous chapter we saw that Mohammed-Reza Shah, after consolidating power in the 1950s following the coup against Mossadeq, began to promote a significant program of modernization—the White Revolution—even as he strengthened his own personal autocracy. The 1970s saw the high point of the shah's personal power as well as significant successes for his program. Yet the shah also became a prisoner of his own rhetoric and grew increasingly convinced not only that his reform efforts were fundamentally correct, but also that they enjoyed broad support among the Iranian people. In fact, both his autocratic methods and the reform program itself—or at least the manner in which it was implemented—generated a significant degree of opposition. But the constraints imposed by his political system offered few legal outlets for the expression of this dissent. Moreover, Mohammed-Reza increasingly became convinced that those who opposed his programs were simply traitors who had no place in Iran. As a result, the shah, for all of his talk of enjoying an intimate connection to his people, was dangerously isolated and therefore unaware of the dissatisfaction that was brewing in the country. This disconnect was undoubtedly one of the major sources of the revolution that broke out in 1978-79.

The principal goal of this chapter is to account for this opposition to the shah. We will do so in greater detail below, but a useful way to think about the opposition is in terms of colors—something that the shah himself did, in fact. In the previous chapter we noted that the White Revolution set itself in opposition to two other forces: the "red," or socialists and similar leftists, most of whom were drawing on Marxism in one form or another; and the "black," or religious clerics and other forces in society that were generally understood to be conservative or even reactionary. The striking feature of the Iranian Revolution was the alliance of these two major strands of opposition, which created a powerful force that succeeded in toppling the shah's regime in 1979. The alliance is so remarkable because it seemed to unite two forces, one radical and the other conservative, that were presumably at odds with one another. So one of the major tasks of this chapter is to show how this union could occur—how the opposition was able to combine elements of Marxism and socialism, on the one hand, with clericalism and Islam, on the other. To be sure, we cannot understand the entire opposition to the shah with reference to "the red and the black," but it certainly helps us to grasp a very complex phenomenon.

Before turning to the opposition, however, let us briefly recount the apogee of the shah's autocracy in the 1970s. We have already alluded to some of the key elements, but those are worth recounting briefly so that we may extend the analysis down to the late 1970s.

THE APOGEE OF THE SHAH'S AUTOCRACY

There are indications that Mohammed-Reza initially had reservations about the idea of the White Revolution, as he sensed the contradiction between the principles of monarchy and revolution. Perhaps it was for this reason that he put the main provisions of the White Revolution to a referendum in 1963. Incredibly, the program was supported by 99% of the voters in the referendum. However that result was secured—and any such result immediately raises suspicions—the shah seems to have convinced himself that there was strong popular support for the White Revolution and for him personally. Accordingly, he spoke less and less over time about democracy. At earlier stages of his reign, Mohammed-Reza had implied that he would be only a transitional autocrat who would develop the country and then oversee an eventual transition to democracy. As time went by, he abandoned this idea, arguing instead that each country needed to find its own system of government by and for the people. Rather than a "democratic sovereign," the shah increasingly presented himself as a "revolutionary monarch," who was both egalitarian and autocratic.[1] He accordingly emphasized the role of monarchy for the history of Iran. This was the principal message of the commemoration at Persepolis in 1971, and the shah also declared the upcoming year to be Cyrus the Great Year, in acknowledgement of the ancient king. All the while, the shah cast ever greater doubt on western conceptions of democracy, positing that this was not appropriate for Iran. In response to a British interviewer in 1974, he asked, "Who says the people of Iran want to have the type of democracy that you have in Britain?" Better than democracy for Iranians, the shah declared, was a paternalistic monarch who knew what was best for his people: "The people and the Shah of Iran are so close to each other that they consider themselves to be the members of one family. I think that the people of Iran respect their Shah in the same way that children of Iranian families respect their fathers."[2] The decision to establish a single governing party, the Rastakhiz party, reflected this idea that democracy was not appropriate to Iran. The intended function of party itself was not political representation but rather political education—not to listen to the people and their concerns, but to instruct them in how to engage in politics "correctly."

Gradually, a cult of personality developed around the shah as well. The cult began with the coronation in 1967, in which the shah crowned himself (though he claimed that his hand represented the people of Iran). Statues of Mohammed-Reza proliferated, while the shah was also described more and more in messianic terms—i.e., as a savior. The commemoration at Persepolis in 1971 identified him with Cyrus the Great and as a worthy successor to that ancient king. Not long after that, the shah initiated construction of a massive monument near the Tehran airport, Shahyad Aryamehr, which was designed to incorporate Achaemenid, Safavid, and modern Iranian influences so as to link the ancient and the modern. It was presented as the gift of a grateful nation to the shah. Mohammed-Reza's toleration of dissent accordingly disappeared, and he was inclined to see domestic traitors behind any expressions of opposition. At a press conference in 1971, he declared, "I can tell you that the number of political prisoners in this country is exactly amounting to the number of traitors in this country."[3] The creation of the Rastakhiz party in 1975 merely reinforced this cult of personality, and at a Rastakhiz commemoration of the 15th anniversary of the start of the White Revolution, in 1977, a huge portrait of the shah was unveiled, with the ruler standing among the clouds with his hands raised. On the 50th anniversary of the Pahlavi dynasty, in 1976, the shah imposed an entirely new calendar on the country, dating back to Cyrus the Great, instead of the Islamic calendar. In all of this the shah became more confident and assertive.

In fact, Mohammed-Reza did have achievements to celebrate. He introduced significant reforms in the White Revolution, including critical changes to the old order on the issue land. The country was also taking steps to eliminate illiteracy and to involve women in politics and other aspects of modern life. The shah could point to major developments in the construction of roads, factories, dams, and other attributes of a modern society. In the decade between 1963 and 1973 the economy grew at an average of 10% per year—an enviable rate—and many began to comment that Iran was the new Japan. The shah

---

1   Ali M. Ansari, *Modern Iran Since 1921: The Pahlavis and After* (London, 2003), 158.

2   Ansari, *Modern Iran*, 184-85.

3   Cited in Ansari, *Modern Iran*, 180.

talked with greater frequency of an impending "Great Civilization," which would include, by the shah's own account, "the kind of welfare state where everybody born, until he is dead, will enjoy every kind of social insurances to permit him to go into industry, to other jobs, to work and to die in peace and tranquility."[4] Many foreign observers were impressed by Iran's achievements and accepted the idea that his White Revolution reflected the aspirations of Iranians. The American press, for example, portrayed the shah as a progressive, modernizing ruler faced with a backward population and some resistant fanatics. Iran also began to play a more important role in the international arena, especially in the Middle East. As a weakened British Empire found itself withdrawing from the region east of the Suez Canal in 1971, new space opened up for the shah to become "Policeman of the [Persian] Gulf." American President Richard Nixon was prepared to sell the shah advanced weaponry—essentially everything short of nuclear weapons—with the idea that Iran would become regional hegemon after the British withdrawal. The shah talked of making Iran an Asian financial center, and he expressed the expectation that soon Iran would be among the five most prosperous countries in the world with the third largest military. To be sure, the shah was becoming arrogant, but there was some foundation to his claims and to his predictions for the near future.

Yet the shah's confidence clearly got the better of him. Inclined to regard critics as traitors, he felt that he could safely ignore their critique, and in any event SAVAK ensured that he actually heard comparatively little criticism. Even underground and exile groups were decimated, and Iranians became increasingly hesitant to discuss politics at all. Elections to the Majles had become largely a farce, while the outlawing of all parties save the Rastakhiz ensured that there was little by way of political competition. At one point Mohammed-Reza stated directly that those who rejected the Rastakhiz party warranted either prison or exile. The constitution of 1906 was effectively ignored. The shah, in short, seems to have believed his own propaganda, and he was insulated from anything that might have disrupted this belief. The historian Ali Ansari concludes forcefully, "Surrounded by sycophants, there was a palpable sense that by the end of 1975 the Shah was becoming cocooned

within a semiological chain of his own construction, and was increasingly alienated from the social reality beyond the boundaries of the court."[5] This isolation made it impossible to respond to the crisis effectively.

THE CAUSES OF OPPOSITION

The discussion so far already hints at some of the reasons for opposition to the shah. The absence of democracy—indeed, the absence even of any steps in that direction—clearly represented one major source. Critics on the left wrote in one article that even constitutional monarchy was simply undemocratic and at worst "profoundly reactionary." Moreover, "The idea of omniscient, omnipotent leaders can only appeal to the imbecile. It cannot deceive the wise."[6] Iranians with any political aspirations were either subjected to repression by SAVAK—including arrest, imprisonment, and torture—or were co-opted by the shah's political machine. There were few opportunities for independent political activity. This situation was to have important consequences. As Nikki Keddie writes, the suppression and co-optation of the opposition over the years "made it increasingly likely that eventual effective opposition would come from those who could appeal to the traditional disaffected masses more than from Westernized liberals or leftists."[7] Here already we see how religious clerics became politically important.

But the problem was not only a dearth of democracy. At issue was also the problematic attitude of Mohammed-Reza Shah to Islam. The shah was by no means hostile to Islam, and at points he deployed Islamic imagery and concepts in the service of monarchy. He claimed to believe in God, regarded himself as a religious man, and declared that he had God's sanction for his modernization projects. But in large measure he was a secular monarch who proved inattentive to the Islamic sensibilities of his subjects, especially the traditional classes. Mohammed-Reza after all received his education in Switzerland and was thus largely cut off from the religious culture of

---

4   Cited in Ansari, *Modern Iran*, 173.

5   Ansari, *Modern Iran*, 187.

6   Cited in Ansari, *Modern Iran*, 171. This was an article of the Tudeh Party.

7   Nikki R. Keddie, *Modern Iran: Roots and Results of Revolution* (New Haven, 2003), 135.

his country. Moreover, both Mohammed-Reza and his father, Reza Shah, had invested much energy in the task of promoting a single Iranian identity that could overcome various regional, religious, and tribal affiliations.[8] This included, for example, trying to purge the Persian language of some of its Arabic vocabulary and grammar (Arabic being the language of the Qu'ran, the hadith, and a good deal of Islamic scholarship). Both Pahlavi Shahs—and Mohammed-Reza in particular—glorified the *pre-Islamic* Iranian past by focusing on ancient Persian history (the Achaemenid Empire, Cyrus the Great, etc.). They sponsored numerous archeological expeditions to uncover the greatness of the ancient Persian past, and the celebration of 2500 years of Persian monarchy at Persepolis in 1971 hearkened back to a history hundreds of years before the Prophet Muhammad had even been born. The Pahlavis' efforts on behalf of women were also understood by many to entail an attack on Islamic values and strictures. Thus in 1934, when Reza Shah prohibited female students and teachers from wearing the chador (the full-length covering), some Shia clerics condemned this as an un-Islamic innovation. Other efforts to promote women's rights likewise ran afoul of traditionalist Islamic views. In short, although the two Pahlavi Shahs were by no means as resolutely secularist as Mustafa Kemal (Atatürk) in neighboring Turkey, and neither was openly hostile to religion as such, their aspirations to modernize Iran meant that they confronted a traditionalism that was strongly associated with Islamic clerics, the *ulama*. They accordingly became intolerant of clerical criticism, and their plans for modernization made them more anti-clerical than they might have been otherwise.

The shah's land reform—the centerpiece of the first stage of the White Revolution—also had contradictory effects. The reform was designed to break up large estates and transfer land to impoverished peasants, and to a degree that result was secured. But there was also much resistance from large landlords, some of whom were, or had connections with, religious clerics. Moreover, private property was considered inviolable by Islamic Law. Some of the leading *ulama* thus came out against reform, and the shah was compelled to grant numerous exceptions to the law. In general,

the situation in the countryside was complicated, and the drafters of the law may not have been aware of all the complexities (there were for example no cadastral surveys for many villages).[9] The result was that the land reform proved quite uneven, with some peasants getting more land, some less, and still others none at all. In other cases landlords proved adept at evading the law, for example by making fictitious sales or gifts to relatives or friends in order to reduce their holdings on paper. The shah and his advisors were also seduced by the idea of introducing western agricultural technology to Iranian farms, with the result that western equipment was given preferential treatment over Iranian equipment—thus creating another source of dissatisfaction. It should be emphasized that some peasants did indeed receive land as a result of the reform, which can therefore not be regarded as an outright failure. But too little was done to provide even those more fortunate peasants with the appropriate means to increase their productivity and thus make them prosperous. As for those who did not receive land, many of them made their way to the cities, where they swelled the urban slums. Indeed, there was a rapid stream of rural migrants to Tehran in particular, where there was insufficient housing and jobs to accommodate the influx. In short, the shah's government adopted a reform policy that was economically rational for a different kind of country, but not really for Iran at the time. The irony was that this important measure of reform, designed to improve the lot of peasants, did so only for some and created dislocation, confusion, and eventually anger among the others.[10]

Mohammed Reza's ties to the Americans likewise proved problematic, especially against the background of extensive foreign interference since the early 19th century. Here again the picture is complex. It would certainly be wrong to regard the last shah as just a lackey of the West. We have seen, for example, that he questioned western conceptions of democracy and their relevance for Iran, and that he looked to ancient Persia as inspiration for his ideas of a Great Civilization. The shah's rhetoric also had an anti-colonial dimension. In 1972 he remarked

---

8   It is a striking fact that only about half of the population spoke Persian at the start of the 20th century.

9   A cadastre is a register of property showing the extent and value of land for the purposes of taxtion. Without cadastres, one cannot really know who owns how much land and what the land is actually worth.

10   The account based largely on Keddie, *Modern Iran*, 148-56.

on Tehran radio that "colonial powers" had become "accustomed to sucking the blood of nations," and that the Iranian nation "has already seen the ugliness of colonialism." He became increasingly dismissive of the West and predicted the imminent collapse of Western civilization, with his own Great Civilization overtaking it.[11] Yet at the same time, his ties with the United States were close. It was after all the CIA, along with the British MI-6, that had perpetrated the coup against Mossadeq in 1953, thereby opening the way to the shah's royal dictatorship in subsequent decades. The shah decided to undertake land reform and other aspects of the White Revolution partly under the influence of the administration of John F. Kennedy, who signaled that it would be easier to support leaders abroad who exhibited some degree of enthusiasm for progress and modernization. Mohammed-Reza also found himself agreeing to extraterritoriality for American advisors in 1963—a development that some in Iran regarded as an imposition on the country's sovereignty. Similarly, Iran's pretensions to regional leadership were in no small measure dependent on the willingness of the US to sell arms, which of course implied some element of dependence on American wishes. When the shah agreed to become "Policeman of the Gulf"—the principal power upholding order in the region—some Iranians saw not an emerging regional power worthy of respect and marvel, but instead a servile "gendarme" that was merely doing the West's dirty work. In short, just as foreign intervention had remained a consistent problem over the course of the 19th and 20th centuries, the situation developing in Iran in the 1960s-70s appeared to entail not the liberation of the country from western influence, but rather its continued dependence and subservience. Poorly informed about the true sentiments of his subjects, the shah remained largely unaware of this problem as well.

THE FORMS OF OPPOSITION

What specific forms did opposition to the shah's regime actually take, then? We may point to three basic organized forms. One was the Tudeh Party ("the party of the masses"), consisting primarily of secular Iranian leftists generally with communist sympathies. The party was originally formed in 1941, as the British and Soviets intervened to send Reza Shah into exile. It received some support, not surprisingly, from the USSR. After an assassination attempt on Mohammed-Reza Shah in 1949, the party was formally banned, though it continued to exist in an illegal form. The party retained significant clout, registered in its ability to generate strikes and street demonstrations. In the 1960s-70s, the effectiveness of the Tudeh Party was reduced, on the one hand, by growing disagreements among various strands of leftist thought (Marxism, Maoism, terrorism, etc.); and, on the other by, SAVAK's infiltration and repression. To adopt the color scheme that we raised earlier, the Tudeh Party and its adherents represented "the red"—that is, the proponents of radical secular revolution.

A bit more difficult to place is the National Front (and we have no color to deploy in this case). The National Front was initially associated with Mossadeq and the kind of liberal, anti-royalist and nationalist sentiments that he expressed (for example in the context of nationalizing Iran's oil in the early 1950s). Adherents to the National Front also opposed foreign economic concessions and called for the constitution of 1906 to be respected (although Mossadeq's own commitment to constitutionalism was rather conditional). Like the Tudeh Party, the National Front faced repression from SAVAK and had difficulty mounting an effective challenge to the shah. But people in that camp became gradually more and more convinced that the Pahlavi autocracy needed to be destroyed rather than merely reformed.

Finally, there was a religious faction—"the black"—that started out on the right. This faction opposed what it regarded as the secular and un-Islamic tendencies of shah's modernization project, as well as the foreign influences that they saw standing behind it. And the faction was also concerned about the position and prerogatives of the *ulama*. They accordingly became more and more critical of what they saw as Iran's subservience to the West and deviations from Islamic norms. Earlier in the 20th century, clerics had generally supported the idea of a constitution; indeed, they were prominent in the coalition that produced both the Tobacco Rebellion and the constitutional evolution of 1905-11. But by the 1960s they were drawing the conclusion that the constitution was too feeble a defense against the Pahlavi autocracy. "The black" was not coordinated as a political party, like the Tudeh or the National Front, but the *ulama*

---

11   Ansari, *Modern Iran*, 177-85 (citation at 180).

had some organization as a hierarchy.[12] This in fact gave it a certain degree of protection, since the shah could not legitimately shut down the mosques or religious schools where the clerical faction was actually located. As Keddie concludes, "The effective suppression of secular oppositionists, whether from the National Front or Tudeh, left room for the religious opposition, whose sermons, processions, and plays with themes like the martyrdom of Imam Hosain [in the year 680] by tyrants were understood to refer to contemporary tyranny, but could not be suppressed."[13]

Here already we can detect part of the reason why opposition to Mohammed-Reza Shah eventually coalesced around the *ayatollah* Ruhollah Khomeini. Secularists like those of the National Front and Tudeh were blocked from opposing the regime by the repression of SAVAK (and to a degree by their own internal disagreements); the religious clerics, for their part, proved willing to adopt some of the concerns and the rhetoric of the left and also to emphasize some aspects of the Shia religious tradition over others. But the critical role of Khomeini was also a function of his charismatic personality, his political skill, and his uncompromising opposition to the shah's regime. His biography warrants closer attention.

Khomeini was born in 1902 into a family of religious clerics and landowners. In 1921 he went to Qom, the center of Islamic scholarship in Iran, to study. In 1936, after the death of his teacher, he became a mujtahid, which is to say that he had been recognized as an Islamic religious scholar with the competence to practice independent judgment on religious matters (ijtihad). In 1944, Khomeini published his first critique of the Pahlavi regime, which was a fairly modest call to unite against immorality in public life. Khomeini emerged as a much more prominent figure in reaction to the initiation of the White Revolution in 1963, and indeed it was from that time that he really took up political activism and became an uncompromising critic of Shah and his reforms. Not without some foundation, Khomeini began to criticize the reforms of the White Revolution as being imposed on Iran indirectly by the US, and as being concerned primarily with increasing the Shah's power and wealth.

Of critical significance was a request of the US for immunity from prosecution for all American personnel, diplomats and others, living in Iran. This request, in 1964, hit a raw nerve and reminded Iranians of all the indignities to which the country had been subjected in the age of imperialism.[14] Because the US had just extended a large loan to Iran for the purchase of arms, many concluded that the US was brazenly trying to purchase extraterritoriality for its citizens in Iran. Khomeini was among the most indignant: "I cannot express the sorrow I feel in my heart.... They have sold us, they have sold our independence.... Our dignity has been trampled underfoot; the dignity of Iran has been destroyed! ... [A]ll American military advisors, together with their families, technical and administrative officials, and servants—in short, anyone in any way connected with them—are to enjoy legal immunity with respect to any crime that they may commit in Iran. If some American's servant, some American's cook, assassinates your *marja*[15] in the middle of the bazaar, or runs over him, the Iranian police do not have the right to apprehend him! Iranian courts do not have the right to judge him! The dossier must be sent to America, so that our masters there can decide what is to be done!"[16] Khomeini's furious denunciation of this violation of Iranian sovereignty earned him a reputation for fearlessness and incorruptibility. He accordingly acquired a dedicated, intensely loyal, and well-organized group of followers.

Khomeini's denunciation also earned him exile. His diatribe revealed him to be precisely the kind of critic that the shah regarded as a traitor. Khomeini was accordingly expelled from the country later in 1964. He went initially to Turkey and then, in 1965, settled more permanently in the city of Najaf in Iraq, south of Baghdad.[17] Yet Khomeini's exile failed to marginalize him. On the contrary, he remained politically active in Iraq and continued to criticize

---

12   See the discussion by John Curry in chapter 10.

13   Keddie, *Modern Iran*, 169. On the martyrdom of Hosain, see the text by Curry in an earlier chapter.

14   The Americans had wanted to handle the matter quietly through an exchange of diplomatic letters, but the matter was brought to the Majles, which expressed deep dissatisfaction even though that body was filled mostly with the shah's supporters.

15   Recall that a *marja al-taqlid* was one of a small number of the most prominent Shiite scholars who were acclaimed as "sources of emulation." See chapter 10.

16   Cited in Ansari, *Modern Iran*, 162.

17   Najaf was the location of the tomb of Ali for whom the Shiites (the "partisans of Ali") were named, so this was a major Shiite shrine.

the shah's regime. Students and others interested in his ideas came to see him in Najaf, recorded his speeches and lectures, and then smuggled them back into Iran. In some ways, Khomeini managed to be better connected with his followers from Iraq than might have been possible within Iran itself.

Among Khomeini's more remarkable compositions was the set of lectures in Najaf that were recorded and transcribed by students in early 1970 and then published as *Islamic Government*. Its principal audience consisted of students of the religious sciences, who were likely to occupy important positions in Muslim society later. It does show the kinds of issues with which Khomeini was engaged during his time in Najaf, and it also provides a basic blueprint for what he would

do following the revolution. Among the more interesting propositions of Khomeini is the doctrine of "the governance of the faqih" (*velayat-i faqih*), the idea that legitimate political authority may be held by a meritorious Shiite religious scholar. As we shall see later, this doctrine was incorporated directly in the new constitution of the Islamic republic in 1979, after the revolution.

As you read the selection, think about the role that Khomeini ascribes to Islam in government. In his view, to what extent does Islam regulate human affairs and the affairs of society? What is the attitude of Islam toward the principle of monarchy and hereditary succession? For Khomeini, what is the principal function of government? What is his attitude toward the constitution of 1906?

DOCUMENT 3.1

RUHOLLAH KHOMEINI, ISLAMIC GOVERNMENT (1970)[18]

In the name of God, the Beneficent, the Merciful

All Praise be to God, the Lord of the worlds

And may His blessings be upon the best of His creation,

Muhammad and His Descendants.

The subject of the governance of the jurist (velayet-i faqih)[19] provides us with the opportunity to discuss certain related matters and questions. The governance of the faqih is a subject that in itself elicits immediate assent and has little need of demonstration, for anyone who has some general awareness of the beliefs and ordinances of Islam will unhesitatingly give his assent to the principle of the governance of the faqih as soon as he encounters it; he will recognize it as necessary and self-evident. If little attention is paid to this principle today, so that it has come to require demonstration, it is because of the social circumstances prevailing among the Muslims in general, and the teaching institution in particular. These circumstances, in turn, have certain historical roots to which I will now briefly refer.

From the very beginning, the historical movement of Islam has had to contend with the Jews, for it was they who first established anti-Islamic propaganda and engaged in various stratagems, and as you can see, this activity continues down to the present. Later they were joined by other groups, who were in certain respects, more satanic than they. These new groups began their imperialist penetration of the Muslim countries about three hundred years ago, and they regarded it as necessary to work for the extirpation of Islam in order to attain their ultimate goals. It was not their aim to alienate the people from Islam in order to promote Christianity among them, for the imperialists really have no religious belief, Christian or Islamic. Rather, throughout this long historical period, and going back to the Crusades,[20] they felt that the major obstacle in the path of their materialistic ambitions and the chief threat to their political power was nothing but Islam and its ordinances, and the belief of the people in Islam. They therefore plotted and campaigned against Islam by various means.

---

18   Translated by Hamid Algar. Text from: http://www.al-islam.org/islamicgovernment/

19   Faqih: one learned in the principles and ordinances of Islamic law.

20   Crusades is the name of a series of war campaigns waged by the European Christians against the Muslims (11th-13th centuries) for the control of the Holy Land, particularly Jerusalem.

The preachers they planted in the religious teaching institution, the agents they employed in the universities, government educational institutions, and publishing houses, and the orientalists who work in the service of the imperialistic states—all these people have pooled their energies in an effort to distort the principles of Islam. As a result, many persons, particularly the educated, have formed misguided and incorrect notions of Islam.

Islam is the religion of militant individuals who are committed to truth and justice. It is the religion of those who desire freedom and independence. It is the school of those who struggle against imperialism. But the servants of imperialism have presented Islam in a totally different light. They have created in men's minds a false notion of Islam. The defective version of Islam, which they have presented in the religious teaching institution, is intended to deprive Islam of its vital, revolutionary aspect and to prevent Muslims from arousing themselves in order to gain their freedom, fulfill the ordinances of Islam, and create a government that will assure their happiness and allow them to live, lives worthy of human beings.

For example, the servants of imperialism declared that Islam is not a comprehensive religion providing for every aspect of human life and has no laws or ordinances pertaining to society. It has no particular form of government. Islam concerns itself only with rules of ritual purity after menstruation and parturition. It may have a few ethical principles, but it certainly has nothing to say about human life in general and the ordering of society.

This kind of evil propaganda has unfortunately had an effect. Quite apart from the masses, the educated class—university students and also many students at the religious teaching institutions—have failed to understand Islam correctly and have erroneous notions. Just as people may, in general, be unacquainted with a stranger, so too they are unacquainted with Islam. Islam lives among the people of this world as if it were a stranger.[21] If somebody were to present Islam as it truly is, he would find it difficult to make people believe him. In fact, the agents of imperialism in the religious teaching institutions would raise a hue and cry against him.

In order to demonstrate to some extent, the difference between Islam and what is presented as Islam, I would like to draw your attention to the difference between the Holy Qur'an and the books of hadith,[22] on the one hand, and the practical treatises of jurisprudence, on the other. The Holy Qur'an and the books of hadith, which represent the sources for the commands and ordinances of Islam, are completely different from the treatises written by the mujtahids of the present age both in breadth of scope and in the effects they are capable of exerting on the life of society. The ratio of Qur'anic verses concerned with the affairs of society to those concerned with ritual worship is greater than a hundred to one. Of the approximately fifty sections of the corpus of hadith containing all the ordinances of Islam, not more than three or four sections relate to matters of ritual worship and the duties of man toward his Creator and Sustainer. A few more are concerned with questions of ethics, and all the rest are concerned with social, economic, legal, and political questions—in short, the gestation of society.

You who represent the younger generation and who, God willing, will be of service to Islam in the future must strive diligently all your lives to pursue the aims I will now set forth and to impart the laws and ordinances of Islam. In whatever way you deem most beneficial, in writing or in speech, instruct the people about the problems Islam has had to contend with since its inception and about the enemies and afflictions that now threaten it. Do not allow the true nature of Islam to remain hidden, or people will imagine that Islam is like Christianity (nominal, not true Christianity), a collection of injunctions pertaining to man's relation to God, and the mosques will be equated with the church.

At a time when the West was a realm of darkness and obscurity—with its inhabitants living in a state of barbarism, and America still peopled by half-savaged redskins—and the two vast empires of Iran and Byzantium were under the rule of tyranny, class privilege, and discrimination, and the powerful dominated all without any trace of law or popular government, God, Exalted and Almighty, by means of the Most Noble Messenger(s), sent laws that astound people with their magnitude. He instituted laws and practices for all human affairs and laid injunctions for man extending from even before the embryo is formed until after he is placed in the tomb. In just the same way that there are laws setting forth the duties of worship for man, so too there are laws, practices, and norms for the affairs of society and government. Islamic law

---

21   This is an allusion to the saying of the Prophet: "Islam will again become a stranger among men, as it was in the beginning, but blessed is the state of the stranger."

22   On the hadith, see reading 3.1.

is a progressive, evolving, and comprehensive system. All the voluminous books that have been compiled from the earliest times on different areas of law, such as judicial procedure, social transactions, penal law, retribution, international relations, regulations pertaining to peace and war, private and public law—taken together, these contain a mere sample of the laws and injunctions of Islam. There is not a single topic in human life for which Islam has not provided instructions and established a norm.

In order to make the Muslims, especially the intellectuals, and the younger generation, deviate from the path of Islam, foreign agents have constantly insinuated that Islam has nothing to offer, that Islam consists of a few ordinances concerning menstruation and parturition, and that this is the proper field of study for the akhunds.[23]

There is something of truth here, for it is fitting that those akhunds who have no intention of expounding the theories, injunctions and worldview of Islam and who spend most of their time on precisely such matters, forgetting all the other topics of Islamic law, be attacked and accused in this manner. They too are at fault; foreigners are not the only ones to be blamed. For several centuries, as might be expected, the foreigners laid certain plans to realize their political and economic ambitions, and the neglect that has overtaken the religious teaching institution has made it possible for them to succeed. There have been individuals among us, the *ulama*, who have unwittingly contributed to the fulfillment of those aims, with the result that you now see.

It is sometimes insinuated that the injunctions of Islam are defective, and said that the laws of judicial procedure, for example, are not all that they should be. In keeping with this insinuation and propaganda, agents of Britain were instructed by their masters to take advantage of the idea of constitutionalism in order to deceive the people and conceal the true nature of their political crimes (the pertinent proofs and documents are now available). At the beginning of the constitutional movement, when people wanted to write laws and draw up a constitution, a copy of the Belgian legal code was borrowed from the Belgian embassy and a handful of individuals (whose names I do not wish to mention here) used it as the basis for the constitution they then wrote, supplementing its deficiencies with borrowings from the French and British legal codes. True, they added some of the ordinances of Islam in order to deceive the people, but the basis of the laws that were now thrust upon the people was alien and borrowed.

What connections do all the various articles of the Constitution as well as the body of Supplementary Law concerning the monarchy,[24] the succession, and so forth, have with Islam? They are all opposed to Islam; they violate the system of government and the laws of Islam.

Islam proclaims monarchy and hereditary succession wrong and invalid. When Islam first appeared in Iran, the Byzantine Empire, Egypt, and the Yemen, the entire institution of monarchy was abolished. In the blessed letters that the Most Noble Messenger (s) wrote to the Byzantine Emperor Heraclius and the Shahanshah of Iran, he called upon them to abandon the monarchical and imperial form of government, to cease compelling the servants of God to worship them with absolute obedience, and to permit men to worship God, Who has no partner and is the True Monarch. Monarchy and hereditary succession represent the same sinister, evil system of government that prompted the Doyen of the Martyrs [the Imam Hosain], to rise up in revolt and seek martyrdom in an effort to prevent its establishment. He revolted in repudiation of the hereditary succession of Yazīd,[25] to refuse it his recognition.

Islam, then, does not recognize monarchy and hereditary succession; they have no place in Islam. If that is what is meant by the so-called deficiency of Islam, then Islam is indeed deficient. Islam has laid down no laws for the practice of usury, for banking on the basis of usury, for the consumption of alcohol, or for the cultivation of sexual vice, having radically prohibited all of these. The ruling cliques, therefore, who are the puppets of imperialism and wish to promote these vices in the Islamic world, will naturally

---

23 Ākhūnd: a word of uncertain etymology that originally denoted a scholar of unusual attainment, but was later applied to lesser-ranking scholars, and then acquired a pejorative connotation, particularly in secularist usage.

24 Articles 35 through 57 of the Supplementary Constitutional Laws approved on October 7, 1906 relate to "the rights of the throne."

25 In 60/680, Imām Husayn refused to swear allegiance to Yazīd, son of Mu'āwiyah and second caliph of the Umayyad dynasty, since Yazīd did not possess legitimate authority and had succeeded to the caliphate by hereditary succession. The ensuing death of the Imām in battle at Karbala has always been commemorated by Shī'ah Muslims as the supreme example of martyrdom in the face of tyranny. It served as an important point of both ideological and emotive reference throughout the Islamic Revolution in Iran.

regard Islam as defective. They must import the appropriate laws from Britain, France, Belgium, and most recently, America. The fact that Islam makes no provision for the orderly pursuit of these illicit activities, far from being a deficiency, is a sign of perfection and a source of pride.

The conspiracy worked out by the imperialist government of Britain at the beginning of the constitutional movement had two purposes. The first, which was already known at that time, was to eliminate the influence of Tsarist Russia in Iran, and the second was to take the laws of Islam out of force and operation by introducing Western laws.

The imposition of foreign laws on our Islamic society has been the source of numerous problems and difficulties. Knowledgeable people working in our judicial system have many complaints concerning the existing laws and their mode of operation. If a person becomes caught up in the judicial system of Iran or that of analogous countries, he may have to spend a whole lifetime trying to prove his case. In my youth I once encountered a learned lawyer who said, "I can spend my whole life following a litigation back and forth through the judicial machinery, and then bequeath it to my son for him to do the same thing!" That is the situation that now prevails, except, of course, when one of the parties has influence, in which case the matter is examined and settled swiftly, albeit unjustly.

Our present judicial laws have brought our people nothing but trouble, causing them to neglect their daily task and providing the occasion for all kinds of misuse. Very few people are able to obtain their legitimate rights. In the adjudication of cases, it is necessary not only that everyone should obtain his rights, but also that correct procedure be followed. People's time must be considered, as well as the way of life and profession of both parties, so that matters are resolved as swiftly and simply as possible.

A case that a shariah[26] judge in earlier times settled in one or two days cannot be settled now in twenty years. The needy, young, and old alike, must spend the entire day at the Ministry of Justice, from morning to evening, wasting their time in corridors or standing in front of some official's desk, and in the end they will still not know what has transpired. Anyone who is more cunning, and more willing and able to give bribes, has his case settled expeditiously, but at the cost of justice. Otherwise, they must wait in frustration and perplexity until their entire lives are gone.

The agents of imperialism sometimes write in their books and their newspapers that the legal provisions of Islam are too harsh. One person was even so impudent as to write that the laws of Islam are harsh because they have originated with the Arabs, so that the "harshness" of the Arabs is reflected in the harshness of Islamic law!

I am amazed at the way these people think. They kill people for possessing ten grams of heroin and say, "That is the law" (I have been informed that ten people were put to death some time ago, and another person more recently, for possession of ten grams of heroin).[27] Inhuman laws like this are concocted in the name of a campaign against corruption, and they are not to be regarded as harsh. (I am not saying it is permissible to sell heroin, but this is not the appropriate punishment. The sale of heroin must indeed be prohibited but the punishment must be in proportion to the crime). When Islam, however, stipulates that the drinker of alcohol should receive eighty lashes, they consider it "too harsh." They can execute someone for possessing ten grams of heroin and the question of harshness does not even arise!

Many forms of corruption that have appeared in society derive from alcohol. The collisions that take place on our roads, and the murders and suicides are very often caused by the consumption of alcohol. Indeed, even the use of heroin is said to derive from addiction to alcohol. But still, some say, it is quiet unobjectionable for someone to drink alcohol (after all, they do it in the West); so let alcohol be bought and sold freely.

But when Islam wishes to prevent the consumption of alcohol—one of the major evils—stipulating that the drinker should receive eighty lashes, or sexual vice, decreeing that the fornicator be given one hundred lashes (and the married man or woman be stoned), then they start wailing and lamenting: "What a harsh law that is, reflecting the harshness of the Arabs!" They are not aware that these penal provisions of Islam are intended to keep great nations from being destroyed by corruption. Sexual vice has now reached such proportions that it is destroying entire generations, corrupting our youth, and causing them to neglect all

---

26   Shariah: the all-embracing law of Islam derived from the Qur'an, the normative practice and authoritative pronouncements of the Prophet, and a number of secondary sources.

27   A law promulgated in July 1969 provided the death penalty for anyone in possession of more than two kilograms of opium or ten grams of heroin, morphine, or cocaine. The first ten executions were carried out in December, 1969.

forms of work. They are all rushing to enjoy the various forms of vice that have become so freely available and so enthusiastically promoted. Why should it be regarded as harsh if Islam stipulates that an offender must be publicly flogged in order to protect the younger generation from corruption?

At the same time, we see the masters of this ruling class of ours enacting slaughters in Vietnam over fifteen years, devoting enormous budgets to this business of bloodshed, and no one has the right to object! But if Islam commands its followers to engage in warfare or defense in order to make men submit to laws that are beneficial for them, and kill a few corrupt people or instigators of corruption, then they ask: "What's the purpose for that war?"

All of the foregoing represent plans drawn up several centuries ago that are now being implemented and bearing fruit.

First, they opened a school in a certain place and we overlooked the matter and said nothing. Our colleagues also were negligent in the matter and failed to prevent it from being established so that now, as you can observe, these schools have multiplied, and their missionaries have gone out into the provinces and villages, turning our children into Christians or unbelievers.

Their plan is to keep us backward, to keep us in our present miserable state so they can exploit our riches, our underground wealth, our lands, and our human resources. They want us to remain afflicted and wretched, and our poor to be trapped in their misery. Instead of surrendering to the injunctions of Islam, which provide a solution for the problem of poverty, they and their agents wish to go on living in huge places and enjoy lives of abominable luxury.

These plans of theirs are so broad in scope that they have even touched the institutions of religious learning. If someone wishes to speak about an Islamic government and the establishment of Islamic government, he must observe the principle of *taqiyyah*[28] and count upon the opposition of those who have sold themselves to imperialism. When this book was first printed, the agents of the embassy undertook certain desperate measures to prevent its dissemination, which succeeded only in disgracing themselves more than before.

Matters have now come to the point where some people consider the apparel of a soldier incompatible with true manliness and justice, even though the leaders of our religion were all soldiers, commanders, and warriors. They put on military dress and went into battle in the wars that are described for us in our history; they killed and they were killed. The Commander of the Faithful[29] himself would place a helmet on his blessed head, don his coat of chain mail, and gird on a sword. Imam Hasan[30] and the Doyen of the Martyrs, acted likewise. The later Imams did not have the opportunity to go into battle, even though Imam Baqir[31] was also a warrior by nature. But now the wearing of military apparel is thought to detract from a man's quality of justice, and it is said that one should not wear military dress. If we want to form an Islamic government, then we must do it in our cloaks and turbans; otherwise, we commit an offense against decency and justice!

This is all the result of the wave of propaganda that has now reached the religious institution and imposed on us the duty of proving that Islam also possesses rules of government.

That is our situation then—created for us by the foreigners through their propaganda and their agents. They have removed from operation all the judicial processes and political laws of Islam and replaced them with European importations, thus diminishing the scope of Islam and ousting it from Islamic society. For the sake of exploitation they have installed their agents in power.

So far, we have sketched the subversive and corrupting plan of imperialism. We must now take into consideration as well certain internal factors notably the dazzling effect that the material progress of the imperialist countries has had on some members of our society. As the imperialist countries attained a high degree of wealth and affluence—the result both of scientific and technical progress and of their plunder of the nations of Asia and Africa—these individuals lost all their self-confidence and imagined that the only way to

---

28   Taqiyyah: prudential dissimulation of one's true beliefs under conditions of acute danger, a practice based on Qur'an, 3:28.

29   The reference is to Ali ibn Abi Tālib, as in the "partisans of Ali."

30   Imām Hasan: son of Imām 'Ali and second of the Imāms. He was poisoned in 50/670 after spending most of his life in seclusion in Medina.

31   Imām Bāqir: the fifth Imām. He was born in 57/675 and spent most of his life in Medina, until his martydom there in 114/732.

achieve technical progress was to abandon their own laws and beliefs. When the moon landings took place, for instance, they concluded that Muslims should jettison their laws! But what is the connection between going to the moon and the laws of Islam? Do they not see that countries having opposing laws and social systems compete with each other in technical and scientific progress and the conquest of space? Let them go all the way to Mars or beyond the Milky Way; they will still be deprived of true happiness, moral virtues and spiritual advancement and be unable to solve their own social problems. For the solution of social problems and the relief of human misery require foundations in faith and moral; merely acquiring material power and wealth, conquering nature and space, have no effect in this regard. They must be supplemented by, and balanced with, the faith, the conviction, and the morality of Islam in order truly to serve humanity instead of endangering it. This conviction, this morality, and these laws that are needed, we already possess. So, as soon as someone goes somewhere or invents something, we should not hurry to abandon our religion and its laws, which regulate the life of man and provide for his well being in this world and hereafter.

The same applies to the propaganda of the imperialists. Unfortunately some members of our society have been influenced by their hostile propaganda, although they should not have been. The imperialists have propagated among us the view that Islam does not have a specific form of government or governmental institutions. They say further that even if Islam does have certain laws, it has no method for enforcing them, so that its function is purely legislative. This kind of propaganda forms part of the overall plan of the imperialists to prevent the Muslims from becoming involved in political activity and establishing an Islamic government. It is in total contradiction with our fundamental beliefs.

We believe in government and believe that the Prophet(s) was bound to appoint a successor, as he indeed did. Was a successor designated purely for the sake of expounding law? The expounding of law did not require a successor to the Prophet. He himself, after all, had expounded the laws; it would have been enough for the laws to be written down in a book and put into people's hands to guide them in their actions. It was logically necessary for a successor to be appointed for the sake of exercising government. Law requires a person to execute it. The same holds true in all countries of the world, for the establishment of a law is of little benefit in itself and cannot secure the happiness of man. After a law is established, it is necessary also to create an executive power. If a system of law or government lacks an executive power, it is clearly deficient. Thus Islam, just as it established laws, also brought into being an executive power.

There was still a further question: who was to hold the executive power? If the Prophet (s) had not appointed a successor to assume the executive power, he would have failed to complete his mission, as the Qur'an testifies. The necessity for the implementation of divine law, the need for an executive power, and the importance of that power in fulfilling the goals of the prophetic mission and establishing a just order that would result in the happiness of mankind—all of this made the appointment of a successor synonymous with the completion of the prophetic mission. In the time of the Prophet(s), laws were not merely expounded and promulgated; they were also implemented. The Messenger of God was an executor of the law. For example, he implemented the penal provisions of Islam: he cut off the hand of the thief and administered lashings and stonings. The successor to the Prophet(s) must do the same; his task is not legislation, but the implementation of the divine laws that the Prophet(s) has promulgated. It is for this reason that the formation of a government and the establishment of executive organs are necessary. Belief in the necessity for these is part of the general belief in the Imamate, as are, too, exertion and struggle for the sake of establishing them.

Pay close attention. Whereas hostility toward you has led them to misrepresent Islam, it is necessary for you to present Islam and the doctrine of the Imamate correctly. You must tell people: "We believe in the Imamate; we believe that the Prophet(s), appointed a successor to assume responsibility for the affairs of the Muslims, and that he did so in conformity with the divine will. Therefore, we must also believe in the necessity for the establishment of government, and we must strive to establish organs for the execution of law and the administration of affairs." Write and publish books concerning the laws of Islam and their beneficial effects on society. Improve your style and method of preaching and related activity. Know that it is your duty to establish an Islamic government. Have confidence in yourselves and know that you are capable of fulfilling this task. The imperialists began laying their plans three or four centuries ago; they started out with nothing, but see where they are now! We too will begin with nothing, and we will pay no attention to the uproar created by a few "xenomaniacs"[32] and devoted servants of imperialism.

Present Islam to the people in its true form, so that our youth do not picture the akhunds as sitting

---

32   Xenomaniacs: those infatuated with foreign and especially Western models of culture. This is a translation of a Persian term, gharbzādeh-ha, popularized by Jalal Al-i Ahmad (see below).

in some corner in Najaf or Qum, studying the questions of menstruation and parturition instead of concerning themselves with politics, and draw the conclusion that religion must be separate from politics. This slogan of the separation of religion from politics and the demand that Islamic scholars should not intervene in social and political affairs have been formulated and propagated by the imperialists; it is only the irreligious who repeat them. Were religion and politics separate in the time of the Prophet (s)? Did there exist, on one side, a group of clerics, and opposite it, a group of politicians and leaders? Were religion and politics separate in the time of the caliphs—even if they were not legitimate—or in the time of the Commander of the Faithful ('a)? Did two separate authorities exist? These slogans and claims have been advanced by the imperialists and their political agents in order to prevent religion from ordering the affairs of this world and shaping Muslim society, and at the same time to create a rift between the scholars of Islam, on the one hand, and the masses and those struggling for freedom and independence, on the other. They will thus been able to gain dominance over our people and plunder our resources, for such has always been their ultimate goal.

If we Muslims do nothing but engage in the canonical prayer, petition God, and invoke His name, the imperialists and the oppressive governments allied with them will leave us alone. If we were to say "Let us concentrate on calling the *azan* [call to prayer] and saying our prayers. Let them come and rob us of everything we own—God will take care of them! There is no power or recourse except in Him, and God willing, we will be rewarded in the hereafter!"—if this were our logic, they would not disturb us.

Once during the occupation of Iraq, a certain British officer asked, " Is the azan I hear being called now on the minaret harmful to British policy?" When he was told that it was harmless, he said: "Then let him call for prayers as much as he wants!"

If you pay no attention to the policies of the imperialists, and consider Islam to be simply the few topics you are always studying and never go beyond them, then the imperialists will leave you alone. Pray as much as you like; it is your oil they are after—why should they worry about your prayers? They are after our minerals, and want to turn our country into a market for their goods. That is the reason the puppet governments they have installed prevent us from industrializing, and instead, establish only assembly plants and industry that is dependent on the outside world.

They do not want us to be true human beings, for they are afraid of true human beings. Even if only one true human being appears, they fear him, because others will follow him and he will have an impact that can destroy the whole foundation of tyranny, imperialism, and government by puppets. So, whenever some true human being has appeared they have either killed or imprisoned and exiled him, and tried to defame him by saying: "This is a political akhund!" Now the Prophet (s) was also a political person. This evil propaganda is undertaken by the political agents of imperialism only to make you shun politics, to prevent you from intervening in the affairs of society and struggling against treacherous governments and their anti-national and anti-Islamic politics. They want to work their will as they please, with no one to bar their way.

End of reading 3.1

Annoyed by the continuing criticism from Najaf, the shah eventually requested the ruler of Iraq, Saddam Hussein, to expel Khomeini, with the hope of thereby depriving him of his base of operations. In 1978 the Iraqi dictator fulfilled this request, and Khomeini found himself in exile again. He considered moving to another Muslim country, for example Syria or Algeria, but no Muslim country was willing to grant him the assurance that he could continue his political activity freely. Khomeini therefore made his way to France, settling in a suburb outside of Paris. There was some irony in the fact that Khomeini's communications with Iran were actually better from France than from Iraq, given modern technology and travel. Many Iranians from the US, from Europe, and of course from Iran itself came to France to see him and to hear his lectures and sermons. By that time the revolution itself was arguably already beginning, and so Khomeini spent comparatively little time in France, returning to Iran on 1 February 1979 to lead the revolution. We shall return to those developments in the next chapter.

Although Khomeini attracted strongly devoted followers, there were other important figures who also contributed to the intellectual opposition to the shah. It is noteworthy that because censorship and SAVAK proved quite effective at blocking direct attacks on the shah and his regime, opposition took the form of critiques of western culture and defenses of indigenous Iranian and Islamic values. Let us consider two such critiques that were to prove particularly influential.

The first is Jalal Al-i Ahmad (1923-69), who in the 1960s condemned what he called "Westoxication" in a pamphlet by the same name.[33] Although Al-i Ahmad was born into a clerical family, he himself remained a largely secular figure and even became a communist for a time. After a pilgrimage to Mecca in 1964 he began to search for cultural roots and ties of the Iranian people to Islam. He presented "Westoxication" as "an illness, a disease imported from abroad, and developed in an environment receptive to it." He construed the distinction between "East" and "West" largely in terms of a confrontation between rich and poor, and criticized the fact that "we of the developing nations… must be polite and servile consumers of the products of Western industry, or at best we must be satisfied, subservient, and low-paid repairmen for whatever comes form the West." He went on to identify the "basic point" of his book to be "that we have not been able to preserve our 'cultural-historical' personality in the face of the machine [modernity] and its unavoidable onslaught. Rather we have been crushed by events. The point is that we have not been able to maintain a well-thought-out and considered position vis-à-vis this monster of the modern age. The fact is that until we have actually grasped the essence, basis, and philosophy of Western civilization and no longer superficially mimic the West in our consumption of Western products, we shall be just like the ass who wore a lion skin."[34] Al-i Ahmad represents a key development in Iranian political thought in the 60s-70s: the shift of many important intellectuals from socialism and other secular ideologies towards political Islam. Al-i Ahmad was effectively proposing that Islam, which was already becoming the symbol of a national struggle against the Pahlavi monarchy, occupy its rightful position in politics and become what it had been in distant past: a source of liberation.

This idea was taken further by Ali Shariati (1933-77), who became a figure of extraordinary influence on the eve of the revolution in Iran. In Keddie's estimation, he did "the most to prepare Iranian youth for revolutionary upheaval."[35] Also born into a clerical family, Shariati became involved with the pro-Mossadeq opposition in his youth. After finishing university in Iran, he won the chance to study further in Paris. This was in the early 1960s, a critical phase in the Algerian struggle for independence from France,[36] and Shariati actively sympathized with the Algerian liberation movement. Back in Iran, he devoted more thought to the problem of colonialism, especially its capacity to alienate people from their own cultural roots. Shariati sought refuge from this colonialism, for Iranians at least, in Shia Islam. He referred frequently to the early Shia heroes, such as Ali and Hosain, while also condemning what he called "Safavid Shiism"—that is, the form that had developed in Iran since the Safavids in the 16th century. This Safavid Shiism, he thought, had degraded Islam into a mere institution, making it a means of political enslavement rather than a basis for the search for justice. Instead, Shariati emphasized the revolutionary and liberationist element of Shiism. Indeed, for him the true essence of Shiism was revolution against all forms of repression: feudalism, capitalism, and imperialism. Genuine Shiism, in his telling, was a militant and revolutionary force that would lead to a populist and egalitarian utopia.

Shariati thus radicalized Shiism and converted Islam from a religion into a political ideology. His nativist call to preserve Iranian identity—especially its Shiite Islamic dimensions—from foreign influences enjoyed tremendous resonance among Iranians. Here was a thinker who was familiar with modern ideologies but had not ceased to be a believer. In fact one of Shariati's more striking achievements was his synthesis of Marxism and Shiism. He sought "to translate Marxist ideas into cultural symbols that the Shia masses could relate to."[37] He was therefore able to speak a language accessible to Iranians seeking a way to refute the ideologies of the western imperialists.

---

33   The Persian *gharbzadegi* can be translated variously as "westoxicatopn," "westitis," "occidentosis," and other variants. It essentially transmits the idea of having been stricken by the West, as if by disease. Publication of the pamphlet was long blocked by censorship in Iran.

34   Jalal Al-i Ahmad, "Westoxication," in Mansoor Moaddel and Kamran Talatoff, eds., *Contemporary Debates in Islam: An Anthology of Modernist and Fundamentalist Thought* (New York, 2000), citations at 343 and 346.

35   Keddie, *Modern Iran*, 200.

36   France fought a nasty and brutal war in an unsuccessful attempt to hold on to Algeria in the years 1954-62.

37   Vali Nasr, *The Shia Revival* (New York, 2007), 128.

To be sure, Shariati's ideas were obscure in a number of key points, and his grasp of Iranian history was actually rather limited. Nevertheless, as Elton Daniel concludes, "his work was of fundamental importance in paving the way for an Islamic revolution in Iran."[38] Whereas previously Iran's intellectuals had seen Islam as something disconnected from the modern world's needs, Shariati equipped young Iranians with a revolutionary Iranian Shia response. For many, Islam now appeared as the natural ideological base from which to fight both the West and the Pahlavi autocracy. Iran's salvation was to lie not in westernization pushed by the shah, but in a return to an idealized indigenous Iranian Islam. From Shariati's death in the summer of 1977, his books sold hundreds of thousands of copies, just as the political crisis leading to the revolution was beginning.

CONCLUSION

By the late 1970s, then, a dangerous situation was developing. On the one hand, the shah, protected by censorship and SAVAK, had become isolated from his people (despite his claims to the contrary) and ever more confident of the wisdom of the White Revolution. He accordingly ceased even making gestures towards democracy, asking rhetorically whether Iranians actually desired such a political system. Instead, he glorified monarchy, created a one-party dictatorship, promoted a cult of personality, proved insensitive to Iranians' religious sensibilities, and dismissed his critics as traitors. Meanwhile, ordinary Iranians, especially those migrating from the countryside to the cities, faced socio-economic hardships, even as Iran as a whole could claim certain successes. Traditional classes, such as peasants and bazaaris, faced dislocation and competition from western goods, while also perceiving that Iran had become a servant of the United States, much like the country had endured foreign intervention in the past. One hesitates to posit a single cause to an event as complex as a revolution, but the cluster of factors that can be subsumed under the idea of "autocratic modernization" do much to explain the crisis that had developed.[39]

On the other hand, the opposition to the shah experienced a key shift beginning in the early 1960s that in due course created new possibilities for revolution in an Islamic key. Up until that point, modern secular ideologies such as nationalism and socialism had been prominent among those resisting the shah and foreign powers. Recall that even the *ulama*, beginning as early as the Tobacco Rebellion in the early 1890s, had been proponents of constitutionalism. The great majority of Iranian writing, until about 1960, saw the evils plaguing Iran, either explicitly or implicitly, as a result of Iranian customs and traditions that needed to be modified or discarded, not as a result of western imperialism as such. The critiques of people like Khomeini, Al-i Ahmad, and Shariati, by contrast, emphasized the destructive effects of western culture and shifted the focus back to the native traditions of Iran, and to Shia Islam in particular, as the most promising basis for Iran's successful future. To quote Keddie, "Once dependence on the West was associated with Western culture, and Western culture with moral decay, it was natural to seek Iran's salvation not in the Westernization pushed by the shah's regime but in a return to an idealized indigenous Islam."[40] This indigenous Islam, it bears repeating, was presented by Shariati and his allies as a revolutionary force for justice and liberation; it could therefore serve as an ideological foundation for revolution.

This shift created space for religious clerics to play a prominent role in the revolution. Partly the issue was that the shah's repression of secular critics, such as the Tudeh Party and the National Front, left the *ulama* as the main oppositional force still standing. Of course clerics had to be careful and could not criticize the shah too directly. But as we noted, their sermons and processions were understood as a critique of the contemporary tyranny, yet could not be suppressed so easily. At the same time, Khomeini was noteworthy for his consistent, direct, and uncompromising opposition to the shah. In contrast to many clerics who were calling merely for constitutional reforms, Khomeini emerged in 1963 as the most vocal and incorruptible opponent of Mohammed-Reza, monarchy, and foreign intervention—and he continued that opposition in exile for some fifteen years (1965-79). Moreover, with his concept of *velayet-e faqih*, Khomeini also presented Islam

---

38   Daniel, *History of Iran*, 164.

39   Tim McDaniel provides an argument along these lines in *Autocracy, Modernization, and Revolution in Russia and Iran* (Princeton, 1991).

40   Keddie, *Modern Iran*, 188.

as a legitimately political force and indicated a clear role for religious clerics, such as himself, in politics. The growing crisis of the Pahlavi regime would soon give Khomeini the opportunity to exercise political power in a new revolutionary regime.

Further Reading:

Ali M. Ansari, *Modern Iran since 1921: The Pahlavis and After*. London: Longman, 2003.

Elton L. Daniel, *The History of Iran*. Westport, Conn.: Greenwood Publishers, 2001.

Nikki R. Keddie, *Modern Iran: Roots and Results of Revolution*. New Haven: Yale University Press, 2003.

Tim McDaniel, *Autocracy, Modernization, and Revolution in Russia and Iran*. Princeton: Princeton University Press, 1991.

Ehsan Naraghi, *From Palace to Prison: Inside the Iranian Revolution*, trans. Nilou Mobasser. Chicago: Ivan R. Dee, 1994.

Vali Nasr, *The Shia Revival*. New York: W. W. Norton, 2007.

CHAPTER 13

FROM REVOLUTION TO CONSTITUTION IN IRAN

Even at the beginning of 1978 it would have been hard to imagine that the shah's regime would collapse by the first month of the next year. To be sure, the regime faced many problems and a growing opposition, but even the ayatollah Khomeini himself gave little indication that he expected to be in power a short time later. Likewise, US President **Jimmy Carter**, visiting Tehran on New Year's of 1977, famously declared Iran to be "an island of stability in one of the more troubled areas of the world," chalking this up to the shah's leadership and "the respect, admiration and love" of the Iranian people for their ruler.[1] Yet by mid-January of 1979 the shah was forced to abandon Iran, and on 1 February of the same year Khomeini returned in triumph to his native country. In March Iran held a referendum to declare the country now to be an "Islamic Republic," and by the end of the year a new constitution had been produced. At the same time, crucial issues concerning the future of the country were yet to be resolved, and the two years between 1979 and 1981 saw something of low-level civil war within Iran to define the character of the revolution. To return to the color scheme adopted earlier, this struggle represented a contest between "the red" and "the black"—between a secular leftist orientation and a more distinctly Islamist one. Sorting out these distinctions is difficult, however, since, as we saw in our discussion of Ali Shariati in the previous chapter, leftism and Islamism had become so thoroughly intertwined in the years leading up the revolution. The argument in this chapter is that whereas the designation of Iran as an "Islamic Republic" served to paper over those distinctions for the time being, the constitution itself represented a crucial step in asserting the Islamic character of the revolution.

In order to demonstrate this thesis, there are several issues on which we need to focus. We will first consider the basic course of events from early 1978 to the fall of the shah's regime a year later. We next focus on the behavior and ideology of Khomeini, about which we know a little bit already. Although Khomeini had remarkable charisma, it would be a mistake to ascribe his success entirely to this factor, as if the Iranian population simply became a bunch of mesmerized dupes. Probably more important were, on the one hand, Khomeini's inflexible and uncompromising opposition to the shah, which made him attractive to everyone who has hostile to the monarchy; and, on the other hand, his ability simultaneously to reflect the aspirations of diverse groups of the population. In effect, this discussion allows us to identify the ideology of the revolution. Finally, we turn to constitutional issues—the designation of Iran as an "Islamic Republic" and, more importantly, the process leading to the new constitution and the content and character of the constitution itself. That process permits us to engage briefly with the main episode of the revolution as far as Americans were concerned: the taking of the US embassy staff hostage in November of 1979.

---

1   Cited in Ali M. Ansari, *Modern Iran since 1921: The Pahlavis and After* (London, 2003), 196.

THE COURSE OF THE REVOLUTION

There were several precursors to the crisis that struck Iran in 1978-79. From 1975 or so there was an economic downturn that was partly a function of oil prices. The Arab-Israeli War of 1973 produced a dramatic increase in oil prices, when Arab members of OPEC (Organization of Petroleum Exporting Countries) imposed an embargo on the United States and thus caused a significant spike in the worldwide price for oil. This of course benefited Iran, as an oil-producing country, but it also caused serious inflation, which led to a considerable drop in real incomes in Iran (i.e., the wages of most workers did not keep pace with the increase in prices). When oil prices fell again a few years later, many large construction projects in Iran stalled, and unemployment became a problem. Generally speaking wage earners and bazaar merchants were the ones hardest hit by this combination of inflation and unemployment. All of this occurred against a general backdrop of growing inequality within Iranian society, which demonstrates that the shah's modernization project was affecting the country's population in an uneven fashion. Some wealthy Iranians showed their lack of faith in the economy by transferring large qualities of wealth abroad, into Swiss bank accounts. In short, the years 1975-78 saw the Iranian economy endure significant difficulties, which served to exacerbate the dissatisfaction that had already appeared with the shah and his policies.

Moreover, disappointment with the US grew when President Carter, who had given considerable attention to the issue of human rights in his 1976 election campaign, did not push the shah harder on this issue. Carter's campaign raised the hopes of many in Iran that the United States would confront the shah and encourage both political liberalization and the imposition of new limits on SAVAK. Yet the capacity of the United States actually to compel the shah to do one thing or another was quite limited. Nor could Carter afford to ignore American geopolitical interests, which included access to oil and thus required a good relationship with Iran. The shah's opponents saw hypocrisy in the disconnect between Carter's words and actions, and their frustration on this score seems merely to have increased their anger.

By most accounts the revolution can be said to have begun with the publication of a newspaper article highly critical of Khomeini on 7 January 1978.

How exactly the article appeared and what it was intended to achieve remain unclear. Presumably it was designed to respond to the intense criticism of the shah that continued to emanate from Khomeini, then still in Iraq. In any event the semi-official character of the newspaper, *Ettela'at*, led many to presume that the article reflected the shah's views, which it likely did. Entitled "Iran and the Colonization of the Red and the Black," the article attacked the supposedly unholy alliance between religious reactionaries and communist subversives, and condemned Khomeini as a British agent and even a homosexual. It is a sign of Khomeini's stature that the reaction to the article was swift and dramatic. The newspaper's offices were quickly attacked, and demonstrations occurred in the bazaars and in Qom, the center of religious learning in Iran. A massive demonstration also occurred in the city of Tabriz, focusing on visible emblems of state power and foreign influence— liquor stores, theatres, hotels, and the office of the Rastakhiz party. When the shah's police forces shot into crowds in Qom, killing several, a new dynamic appeared, drawing the country further into revolutionary chaos. Shia custom requires the commemoration of the dead after 40 days, and then those commemorative demonstrations precipitated new confrontations with the police, thus causing new deaths, which in turn had to be commemorated 40 days later. And so on. This pattern signaled an important shift, whereby the initiative in the protest movement swing from secular forces to a religiously led opposition. Whereas the regime had been fairly effective at dealing with the secular opposition, it proved much more complicated to combat the religious one.

Still, even in the summer of 1978 it seemed that the shah might be able to weather the storm. Outside analysts were still not inclined to see the shah's regime as being in any fundamental danger, and few envisioned that it would collapse within months. But three key events pushed matters in a considerably more radical direction in the second half of 1978. The first was a major fire at a movie theater in a poor district of Tehran in August. Because escape doors had been locked and the fire department was late to arrive, some 400 people perished. What in other circumstances might have been treated as a simple tragedy quickly acquired political significance in Iran. Rumors quickly spread that SAVAK had set the fire, with diverse conspiracy theories providing varying degrees of elaboration. What SAVAK would have gained by perpetrating such an act is completely unclear, and the accusations were almost certainly without any foundation. But they reveal the general climate in Iran at the time, the fear and hatred of SAVAK that pervaded the country, and the tendency among Iranians towards conspiratorial thinking. Demonstrations and protest reached the level that the shah felt compelled to declare martial law, while also granting certain concessions.

The second event was "Black Friday" (8 September 1978), when a massive demonstration in Tehran began despite martial law. Matters turned violent when protestors began to call for the ouster of the shah and the return of Khomeini. The shah's troops fired indiscriminately on protestors, thereby creating a kind of Iranian Bloody Sunday. This indeed was the bloodiest incident so far, and it probably made the gulf between the shah and the public unbridgeable. The incident also showed that armed insurrection was a real possibility.

Finally, the expulsion of Khomeini from Iraq also contributed significantly to the crisis. Saddam Hussein was already worried about the effects of Khomeini on Iraq's Shiites (recall that Shiites made up around 60% of Iraq's population), and he therefore agreed to the shah's request to expel the ayatollah. But as we noted earlier, Khomeini was actually able to influence events more effectively from France than from Iraq, given modern communications. In important ways he became even more accessible to Iranians now, while his message of uncompromising opposition to the shah became ever more attractive to the mass of discontented Iranians.

These three events made the opposition to the shah harsher and more militant. Strikes and demonstrations spread to various sectors of the economy—for example the bazaaris, who closed their shops in protest against the shah, and oil workers, who refused to pump and process oil for his regime. Soon virtually the entire country was on strike. Meanwhile Khomeini—the figure who had criticized the shah over some fifteen years and had paid for it with exile—gained support. Indeed, the opposition began to coalesce around the ayatollah. It is worth highlighting that Khomeini was neither the only major oppositional figure nor the highest in the Iranian Shia religious hierarchy; but his opposition had been the most consistent and uncompromising. Thus as the opposition became more militant, Khomeini became the obvious figure around whom to rally. And the ayatollah proved adept at

shaping his message in such a way as to appeal to an extraordinarily wide range of the political spectrum.

The shah's response to all of this was confused and inconsistent. He combined elements of concession and repression, but without any apparent logic or system. He also arrested some of his longtime supporters while releasing prominent clerical opponents. How to explain this incoherent response? The answer probably has partly to do with illness: the shah was diagnosed with cancer, and he indeed died of the disease within the next year (this occurred in Egypt in July of 1980). It is also unclear what kind of information the shah was actually receiving about the crisis. SAVAK seems to have been quite effective as an instrument of repression, but not as an intelligence unit. Subordinates, whether in SAVAK or elsewhere in the shah's governmental apparatus, were apparently reluctant to provide information that he had not requested. In general, the shah was quite isolated from the society that he ruled, despite his claims to enjoy a unique and close bond with the people. He probably did not understand the full magnitude of the disorders, and perhaps nothing could have been done in 1978 to save the regime. Finally, the shah was also receiving mixed signals from the United States. To be sure, the shah was by no means fully dependent on the US, but he remained sensitive to American opinion. He was reluctant to take forceful action against the protestors without clear signs of support from the US. At one point he thought it best "to let Tehran burn" so as to impress upon Washington the need for repression. But the Carter administration was itself conflicted about what kind of advice to give. There was after all a great deal at stake in all of this: the US had major investments in the shah, in terms of economic and security ties. Some in the administration were inclined to support the shah strongly, while others thought that the fall of the shah would vindicate a principled stance on human rights.

The culmination started at the very end of 1978. In December, some army troops began to defect. The government meanwhile banned all demonstrations, citing the upcoming and emotionally charged Islamic holy days. Some two million people in Tehran alone simply ignored the ban. Many treated this as a referendum on the shah's regime—and as an unequivocal rejection of it. The shah was finally convinced to leave the country "on vacation" in January of 1979. He was never to return. The shah's departure opened the way for Khomeini's return to Iran, which occurred on 1 February 1979. Within two weeks, the shah's regime had been terminated. On 11 February 1979, Radio Tehran made the historic statement: "This is the voice of Iran, the voice of true Iran, the voice of the Islamic Revolution."[2]

KHOMEINI AND THE REVOLUTION'S IDEOLOGY

The fall of the shah's regime and the return of Khomeini, both in early 1979, were dramatic and decisive. But what exactly had triumphed in February of that year? What kind of state and social order would replace the shah's system? Was it actually Khomeini's intention to rule the country—that is, to have a religious cleric wield political power? And what exactly did Khomeini stand for? These were all critical questions for which there were no immediate answers.

In the previous chapter we saw the curious fusion of religious sensibilities and socialist ideas that informed the work of people like Ali Shariati and commanded striking popularity in the late 1970s. Indeed, this fusion of Marxism and Islam, combined with nationalism and hostility to foreign imperialism, effectively *was* the ideology of the revolution. And it was precisely this combination that explains the strength of this ideology, which was able to encompass a wide range of grievances against the regime. And yet there were important tensions here as well. The goals of secular leftists were distinct from the goals of Iranians who were focused primarily on Islam. Shariati's conception of a revolutionary Islam could paper these differences over to a degree, but not entirely. In 1978, the fact that this fusion of Marxism and Islam was still incomplete, awkward, and very fluid was actually a source of strength. To quote Ansari, "Ambiguity allowed a disparate plurality of groups to unite against the Shah. A lack of definition allowed differences to be buried in the interests of the immediate focus of discontent."[3] Yet once the shah had departed and the revolution had triumphed, a

struggle began for defining its essence and its future. To simplify a bit, the question was this: Was the revolution to be primarily "red" or "black"?

If we look even at just Shariati and Khomeini—and demonstrations in Tehran featured crowds carrying portraits of both of them simultaneously—we can detect divergences between the two. Shariati was, after all, a secular intellectual for whom Marxist ideas were important. For him the challenge was "how to translate Marxist ideas into cultural symbols that the Shia masses could relate to—how to make Marx go down easier by giving him a Shia coating, so to speak."[4] Shariati criticized "Safavid Shiism" as a repressive invention of the ruling class, and the traditional clergy as its reactionary accomplices. In other words, he criticized the existing Shia establishment of which Khomeini was a part. It should not surprise us, then, that Khomeini criticized some of Shariati's followers on the grounds that there could not really be Islam without the ulama, and one could not really be a Muslim if one did not recognize their authority.[5] Other clerics were even more critical of Shariati, whom they accused of being a Sunni in disguise. Yet these clerical critiques did little to diminish Shariati's appeal, and in any event many of the younger ulama accepted his ideas. Others, including Khomeini, concluded that the only way to curb Shariati's influence was to appropriate some of his ideas as their own. As a result, writes Vali Nasr, "Shariati's Marxist reading of Shiism came to define Khomeini's movement. Khomeini's arguments against the monarchy and in favor of clerical rule were thus married to Shariati's Shia Marxism to forge a revolutionary movement."[6]

Indeed, Khomeini possessed a flexibility and a political acumen that allowed him to position himself as the embodiment of the hopes and aspirations of wide circles in Iranian society. He had already distinguished himself by his uncompromising stance with respect to the regime. As others were imprisoned or co-opted by the shah's regime, he—albeit from afar—continued to criticize mercilessly. For this reason alone, he emerged as a compelling figure to anyone who opposed the regime. But this was not all. Despite his traditional appearance (turban, beard, gown, etc.), Khomeini was "an

---

2   Cited in Ervand Abrahamian, *Khomeinism* (Berkeley, 1993), 162. My account of the revolution itself is based primarily on Elton L. Daniel, *The History of Iran* (Greenwood, 2001), 175-95.

3   Ansari, *Modern Iran*, 202.

4   Vali Nasr, *The Shia Revival* (New York, 2007), 128.

5   Daniel, *History of Iran*, 163-64; Nikki R. Keddie, *Modern Iran: Roots and Results of Revolution* (New Haven, 2003), 206-97.

6   Nasr, *Shia Revival*, 130.

unusually unorthodox mullah, in many ways thoroughly modern in outlook." His interpretation of *velayet-e faqih* was actually highly unorthodox, and not all major Shia clerics were prepared to accept it. Khomeini was also familiar with western philosophy and even taught that subject, while also being well aware of figures like Shariati. In effect, Khomeini was able simultaneously to project different things to different constituencies. If some saw in him an image of turbaned austerity, others saw a figure who transcended both the modern and the traditional. Khomeini effectively became the embodiment of the complex synthesis of ideas that was Islamic Marxism. This synthesis, to quote Ansari, "while rough around the edges, possessed the immediate attraction of reconciling two traditions into an authentic whole regarded as both national and legitimate. Khomeini became the personalization of this synthesis, symbolizing and in some ways possessing both its potency and its inherent contradictions. For the traditional masses of religious Iranians, he represented all that was traditional and authentic about Shi'a Iranian culture. For the young idealistic students who were to become the ideological vanguard of the movement, he represented unorthodoxy and rebelliousness."[7] In a word, various groups with different visions for the future could all convince themselves that their vision had triumphed early in 1979 and that Khomeini was their champion. To be sure, the Marxists and the Islamists shared certain views beyond just opposition to the shah. Both groups were essentially nationalist and anti-imperialist, for example. But on some basic level, the two orientations—Islamic or Marxist—were different and perhaps even irreconcilable. Which would predominate going forward?

In this context Khomeini proved to be remarkably astute. He apparently recognized that both major strands of opposition had given the revolution the force necessary to overthrow the shah. He was careful, therefore, not to emphasize the Islamic dimensions of the revolution at the expense of the Marxist ones. The early language of the revolution—including Khomeini's—was as much (or even more) populist (even Marxist) than it was Islamic. There was much talk about a "classless" society, about the redistribution of wealth and about the elimination of "unwarranted privileges."

Shortly after returning to Iran, Khomeini declared, "World capitalism and its affiliate, the Shah's regime, were bent on finishing Iran's oil resources within the next twenty years in order to make possible their own survival."[8] Especially in the run-up to the revolution Khomeini increasingly used terms and slogans with a strongly socio-economic flavor (even as they referred also to Islam). Consider the following examples:

- ❖ Islam belongs to the oppressed, not to the oppressors

- ❖ Islam will eliminate class differences

- ❖ Islam originates from the masses, not from the rich

- ❖ Islam represents the slum-dwellers, not the palace dwellers

- ❖ We are for Islam, not for capitalism and feudalism

- ❖ In a truly Islamic society, there will be no shantytowns

- ❖ The duty of the clergy is to liberate the hungry from the clutches of the rich.[9]

Meanwhile, Khomeini played down the ideas that he had articulated in *Islamic Government*. He thus made almost no public references to *velayet-e faqih* and associated ideas. Khomeini and other clerics gave numerous indications that they themselves did not seek to rule directly. Many Iranians thus assumed that he might act as an important moral force after the revolution, but would not actually seek to rule.

Khomeini's distinctly Muslim appearance made many in the West, and in the United States in particular, regard him as a "fundamentalist." Likewise, his supporters were often portrayed as religious fanatics or as dupes mesmerized by Khomeini's charisma. The best research on these questions shows that such interpretations are deeply misleading if not simply false. "Fundamentalism" generally presumes religious inflexibility and intellectual purity, political traditionalism and social conservatism, the rejection of the modern world, and a hankering for an earlier age. Very little of this can be applied to Khomeini's thought. It is probably

---

7   Ansari, *Modern Iran*, 200-201.

8   Ansari, *Modern Iran*, 216.

9   These slogans and others like them are provided in Abrahamian, *Khomeinism*, 31-32.

better to regard Khomeinism as a particular kind of leftist populism that was designed to mobilize the lower classes and above all the urban poor against the regime on the basis of class grievances. Khomeini actively used the language of class in his post-1970 writings (though without directly using the Marxist categories of "bourgeoisie" and "proletariat"). Thus he spoke of the oppressed vs. the oppressors, of poor vs. rich, of slum dwellers vs. palace dwellers, of the lower class vs. the upper class, of the needy class vs. the aristocratic class, and so on. Khomeini likewise criticized the shah's regime precisely on a series of socio-economic issues: its failure to alleviate rural and urban poverty; its failure to provide basic services and low-income housing; its failure to address crime, alcoholism, prostitution and drug addiction; its submission to what Khomeini called *kravatis* (literally, "wearers of ties"—by which he meant westerners and westernized Iranians).[10] Khomeini rarely invoked religious doctrine. He did not give much attention to discussions of religious interpretation, and he said comparatively little after 1970 about *velayet-e faqih*. He even reinterpreted early Islamic history to reinforce populist notions. By the late 1970s Khomeini was using terms like "revolution" and "republic" that he previously avoided. In short, Khomeini's thought was hardly "fundamentalism," but was instead flexible, forward-looking, and even materialistic in its focus on socio-economic issues. To a very significant degree, over the course of the 1970s and especially as the revolution approached, Khomeini subordinated the religious element to socio-economic questions and class antagonisms. In light of these pronouncements, it is not hard to see how and why secular leftists in Iran supported him.[11]

TOWARD A NEW CONSTITUTION

Early constitutional developments likewise reflected efforts to accommodate both major strands of the revolutionary movement while even implying a preference for the secular leftist dimensions. By insisting that the new country explicitly be a "republic," Khomeini seemed to be signaling his recognition of ascendant leftists. According to one account, even before the revolution, when presented with a draft

constitution for an "Islamic state," Khomeini crossed out the word "state" and replaced it with "republic." And of course by retaining the designation "Islamic," he sought to bind the two strands of opposition together. The formulation "Islamic Republic," writes Ansari, "was sufficiently ambiguous to be open to interpretation, and hence inclusive. It reassured traditional constituents by the emphasis on Islam, while at the same time appealing to 'modernists' by being republican and hence progressive."[12] Perhaps more worrisome to secular leftists might have been Khomeini's negative remarks on the inclusion of the word "democratic" in the republic's name: "What the nation needs is an Islamic Republic—not a Democratic Republic nor a Democratic Islamic Republic. Don't use the Western term 'democratic.' Those who call for such a thing don't know anything about Islam."[13] When a referendum was held on the new name for the country in March of 1979, some 98% supported "Islamic Republic." It appears that some groupings on the left boycotted the referendum because there was only this one option, but the result was so decisive in part, one supposes, because that formulation offered something for different groupings in the revolutionary coalition that had brought down the shah. As Ansari writes, "For authoritarian Islamists, the implication of the referendum was simply the popular affirmation of a political reality dictated from the top. For the 'republicans,' many Muslim activists included, the referendum was symbolic of the popular roots of the revolution and the reconnection of the state with society."[14] Once again, both sides of the revolutionary coalition—leftists and Islamists—could convince themselves that the new name of the country reflection the triumph of "their" version of the revolution.

The first draft of the constitution, produced around the same time, also played down the Islamic dimension of the new state. It was also far more democratic than the final version. There was no mention of *velayet-e faqih*, and the constitution granted no powers to religious clerics beyond those granted by the original constitution of 1906 to a so-called **Guardian Council**.[15] By no means did this

---

10   Note that to this day virtually no one representing the present Iranian regime wears a tie.

11   On these issues, see *Abrahamian, Khomeinism*, esp. 13-38.

12   Ansari, *Modern Iran*, 221.

13   Abrahamian, *Khomeinism*, 163.

14   Ansari, *Modern Iran*, 221.

15   Recall that the constitution of 1906 had called for the creation of such a council of clerics to vet every proposed law to ensure its compatibility with Islam.

signify that Sharia (Islamic law) was to become the basis for law in the new republic, but rather (and merely) that all laws had to be compatible with it. The draft constitution moreover drew heavily on that of the French Fifth Republic and included an elected president and prime minister, as well as the separation of powers into executive, legislative, and judicial branches. And whatever Khomeini might have said earlier about female suffrage being un-Islamic, women received the right to vote by the new constitution. In general, the first year of the revolution saw no imposition of Islamic strictures on Iranian society. Thus, for example, the veil (*hejab*) for women remained voluntary throughout the year.

All of this is to say that the revolution was not strictly Islamic at first. Rather, because diverse oppositional forces had brought down the Shah's regime, their interests were reflected in the institutions and practices of the revolution's early stages. To be sure, Khomeini—an Islamic cleric with beard and turban—was clearly the most prominent figure of the revolution. But he was not advancing the idea of *velayet-e faqih* openly and explicitly—some of Khomeini's secular supporters were not even aware of this concept, since the ayatollah had not emphasized it in the years leading up to 1979. He was giving indications that neither he nor other clerics were planning actually to rule. Shortly after the fall of the shah's regime, Khomeini authorized the establishment of a provisional government under Mehdi Bazargan, a secular figure. Many presumed that Khomeini would be a moral force dispensing advice from Qom, rather than a political figure directly running the show. Others assumed that if Khomeini actually chose to exercise power, the incompetence of clerical rule would soon reveal itself and give way to secular rulers. Thus many allied with and supported Khomeini not because they wanted or expected him to come to power, but *tactically*—in order to exploit his ability to mobilize the population against shah.

It is difficult to tell precisely what Khomeini was thinking in the early stages of the revolution. One possibility is that he had a plan, based on the idea of *velayet-e faqih*, and was merely waiting for the right moment to implement it more fully. Another possibility is that Khomeini had no plan as such and instead began to move towards greater Islamism when he saw the initiative of some of the Islamic radicals at the grassroots level. Perhaps it was a combination of the two.

For much of 1979 an arrangement of "dual power" characterized the political situation in Iran, although this arrangement was rather different from what we encountered in the case of Russia. As noted above, Khomeini authorized the creation of a provisional government under **Mehdi Bazargan**, a secular intellectual who nonetheless argued that religion should control and inspire politics rather than vice versa. As an engineer and professor, he tried to show that Islam was in accord with scientific and technical progress.[16] With such views, the new country's first prime minister was broadly aligned with Khomeini, while not necessarily agreeing with him on all points. But the government of Bazargan was neither the only nor the most important center of power in Iran; it was designed explicitly as a transitional entity, until Khomeini and his circle could figure what to do next. Khomeini thereafter created a kind of parallel government in the form of an **Islamic Revolutionary Council** (IRC), which was under the direction of his close clerical followers. Revolutionary activists spontaneously created hundreds of **komitehs** (revolutionary committees) and tribunals that quickly took de facto control of various administrative and judicial functions. With Khomeini's apparent blessing, these revolutionary committees embarked on the task of purging the bureaucracy, the military, and educational institutions of the shah's supporters or simply anyone with whom they disagreed. Bazargan accordingly had little control over anything of significance, even his own ministries. In fact by accepting appointment from Khomeini and IRC, Bazargan had essentially acknowledged that his legitimacy was dependent on them. At one point he himself remarked, "They put a knife in my hands, but it's a knife with only a handle. Others are holding the blade."[17] As Bazargan proved ineffective, Khomeini intervened more and more, advocating a tougher approach to various problems. Other institutions where Khomeini's supporters rose to prominence were the **Islamic Republic Party** (IRP), armed paralegal forces like the **Revolutionary Guard** (created in May of 1979 to deal with threats to the revolution), and violent groups called *hezbollah* (consisting primarily of men from the lower classes who were intensely loyal to Khomeini).

Two major conclusions flow from all of this. The first is that Bazargan's provisional government

---

16   Keddie, *Modern Iran*, 198-200.

17   Abrahamian, *Khomeinism*, 163.

was only one of many power centers in post-revolution Iran, and it was partly for this reason that it became so marginalized. The other is that because of this complex political arrangement, over which Khomeini never asserted complete control, Iran after 1979 "never became a dictatorship but always had a complex variety of power centers."[18] Even the term "dual power" probably simplifies things too much. At key moments it even makes it hard to determine exactly what was happening and who was calling the shots. Was Khomeini directing the revolution or largely reacting to the initiatives of others?

In any event, the institutions most closely connected with Khomeini—or more accurately, perhaps, the institutions with a strongly Islamist orientation—were on the ascent over the course of 1979. Their rise proved critical for the next stage of the constitution. Only a draft constitution had been produced at the time of the referendum on whether Iran should be an "Islamic Republic," but subsequently an **Assembly of Experts** was elected to produce a final version to the text. The rise of the Islamists secured their strong representation on the 73-person Assembly, and the final version of the constitution differed quite significantly from the earlier draft. True, the constitution retained a good deal of populist rhetoric and made a series of promises on issues of pensions, social security, medical services, education, etc. In this sense the class issues that were prominent in the revolution's success by no means disappeared. But in important ways the constitution was now drastically revised in a more conservative and Islamic direction. Ideas from *Islamic Government* were now incorporated, which included the establishment of an all-powerful office of **Faqih** (translated as "**Religious Leader**" in document 3.2). In this way Khomeini received constitutional powers unimagined by the shahs, and he was furthermore made Faqih for life. The new draft also delineated a more decisive and direct role for clergy in politics, which served to marginalize the Majles considerably. Women also received less than equal status under the final constitution, and part of the document's preamble associated them explicitly with the institutions of family and motherhood.[19]

It should come as no surprise that there was resistance to this new version of the constitution, which still needed to be approved by referendum.

Leftists were concerned about the drift towards clericalism and Islamism, but they were not especially unified, and they had a harder time communicating with Iranian masses. After all, their vocabulary was relatively abstract, often based on western concepts, and was therefore not readily intelligible to the masses. The language of the Islamists, by contract, was much more accessible to the traditional classes—peasants, urban laborers, bazaaris, etc.—because they were rooted in Islam and the actual life of those people. So when it came to mobilizing supporters—and at a certain stage, revolutions are almost always about this more than anything else—the Islamists simply proved superior to their leftist counterparts. Thus when it came to electing the Assembly of Experts that produced the final draft of the constitution, the Revolutionary Guard, *hezbollah*, and similar organizations managed to organize and intimidate the electorate.

Yet crucial to the final passage of the constitution was also a major crisis involving the United States, which served to divert attention from the constitutional question. The crisis had above all to do with the ultimate fate of the shah, now effectively deposed and in exile. He had been diagnosed with cancer and had made his way to Mexico and now sought entry to the US in order to receive medical treatment from leading specialists. For its part, the United States was unsure how to proceed given the volatile situation in Iran itself. Eventually, however, Carter's administration acquiesced, and on 22 October 1979 the shah received permission to enter the country. The decision produced a storm of indignation in Iran, where many citizens, having chanted "death to the shah!" during the demonstrations and protest in 1978, demanded that the former ruler be returned to Iran for trial, where he would presumably be found guilty and executed. The US government refused to return the shah to Iran. In retaliation, and also because they feared a 1953-style coup that would end the revolution, radical Iranian students attacked the American embassy in Tehran and took the staff there hostage on 4 November 1979. For most Americans, the Iranian revolution is associated principally with the image of American embassy staff in blindfolds, arrested by radical Iranian students. Indeed, from this point forward the revolution would be defined to a significant degree by its antagonistic relationship with the United States. But for our purposes here, the **hostage crisis** is important

---

18   Keddie, *Modern Iran*, 242.

19   Keddie, *Modern Iran*, 246-48.

primarily as a diversion. It is hard to tell whether the students acted spontaneously, or whether they were somehow directed by Khomeini and his circle. But in any event, Khomeini congratulated the students with their act, while Bazargan resigned, since he could not negotiate with the US without looking like a lackey of the imperialists. It was precisely in this context that Khomeini submitted the final draft of the constitution for popular approval, adding that a "no" vote would only benefit the Americans and thus associating those opposed to the constitution with "Satan" and "imperialism." He furthermore warned that any sign of disunity within Iran would impel the Americans to attack Iran. Thus by picking a fight with "the Great Satan" (the US), Khomeini created the impression that the Islamic Republic was under siege and thereby limited dissent on consti-tutional issues. Those bold enough to oppose the constitution boycotted the referendum in December of 1979, thus allowing the revised draft to be passed by 99.5% of the vote.

A portion of the resulting constitution of 1979 is provided here. It includes an extensive preamble, which, unlike the very brief preamble of the US Constitution, provides a history of the revolution and specifies some of the ideological issues at stake. As you read through the selection, consider the place that the constitution affords to Islam, the Qu'ran, and clerics. How does the constitution define the power of the "religious leader" (Faqih)? Where does it seem that the constitution locates sovereignty? To what degree have elements of populism been retained in the constitution?

DOCUMENT 3.2

CONSTITUTION OF THE ISLAMIC REPUBLIC OF IRAN (1979)[20]

Preamble

The Constitution of the Islamic Republic of Iran advances the cultural, social, political, and economic institutions of Iranian society based on Islamic principles and norms, which represent an honest aspiration of the Islamic *Ummah* [community]. This aspiration was exemplified by the nature of the great Islamic Revolution of Iran, and by the course of the Muslim people's struggle, from its beginning until victory, as reflected in the decisive and forceful calls raised by all segments of the populations. Now, at the threshold of this great victory, our nation, with all its beings, seeks its fulfillment.

The basic characteristic of this revolution, which distinguishes it from other movements that have taken place in Iran during the past hundred years, is its ideological and Islamic nature. After experiencing the anti-despotic constitutional movement and the anti-colonialist movement centered on the nationalization of the oil industry, the Muslim people of Iran learned from this costly experience that the obvious and fundamental reason for the failure of those movements was their lack of an ideological basis. Although the Islamic line of thought and the direction provided by militant religious leaders played an essential role in the recent movements, nonetheless, the struggles waged in the course of those movements quickly fell into stagnation due to departure from genuine Islamic positions. Thus it was that the awakened conscience of the nation, under the leadership of Imam Khomeini, came to perceive the necessity of pursuing a genuinely Islamic and ideological line in its struggles. And this time, the militant "ulama" of the country, who had always been in the forefront of popular movements, together with the committed writers and intellectuals, found new impetus by following his leadership.

The Dawn of the Movement

The devastating protest of Imam Khomeini against the American conspiracy known as the *"White Revolution,"* which was a step intended to stabilize the foundations of despotic rule and to reinforce the political, cultural, and economic dependence of Iran on world imperialism, brought into being a united movement of the people and, immediately afterwards, a momentous revolution of the Muslim nation in June 1963. Although this revolution was drowned in blood, in reality it heralded the beginning of the blossoming of a glorious and massive uprising, which confirmed the central role of Imam Khomeini as an Islamic leader. Despite his exile from Iran after his protest against the humiliating law of capitulation

---

20 Source: http://www.oefre.unibe.ch/law/icl/ir00000_.html.

(which provided legal immunity for American advisers), the firm bond between the Imam and the people endured, and the Muslim nation, particularly committed intellectuals and militant 'ulama', continued their struggle in the face of banishment and imprisonment, torture and execution.

Throughout this time, the conscious and responsible segment of society was bringing enlightenment to the people from the strongholds of the mosques, centers of religious teaching, and universities. Drawing inspiration from the revolutionary and fertile teachings of Islam, they began the unrelenting yet fruitful struggle of raising the level of ideological awareness and revolutionary consciousness of the Muslim people. The despotic regime which had begun the suppression of the Islamic movement with barbaric attacks on the Faydiyyah Madrasah, Tehran University, and all other active centers of revolution, in an effort to evade the revolutionary anger of the people, resorted to the most savage and brutal measures. And in these circumstances, execution by firing squads, endurance of medieval tortures, and long terms of imprisonment were the price our Muslim nation had to pay to prove its firm resolve to continue the struggle. The Islamic Revolution of Iran was nurtured by the blood of hundreds of young men and women, infused with faith, who raised their cries of *"Allahu Akbar"* [God is Great] at daybreak in execution yards, or were gunned down by the enemy in streets and marketplaces. Meanwhile, the continuing declarations and messages of the Imam that were issued on various occasions, extended and deepened the consciousness and determination of the Muslim nation to the utmost.

Islamic Government

The plan of the Islamic government as proposed by Imam Khomeini at the height of the period of repression and strangulation practiced by the despotic regime, produced a new specific, and streamline motive for the Muslim people, opening up before them the true path of Islamic ideological struggle, and giving greater intensity to the struggle of militant and committed Muslims both within the country and abroad.

The movement continued on this course until finally popular dissatisfaction and intense rage of the public caused by the constantly increasing repression at home, and the projection of the struggle at the international level after exposure of the regime by the "ulama" and militant students, shook the foundations of the regime violently. The regime and its sponsors were compelled to decrease the intensity of repression and to *"liberalize"* the political atmosphere of the country. This, they imagined, would serve as a safety valve, which would prevent their eventual downfall. But the people, aroused, conscious, and resolute under the decisive and unfaltering leadership of the Imam, embarked on a triumphant, unified, comprehensive, and countrywide uprising.

The Wrath of the People

The publication of an outrageous article meant to malign the revered "ulama" and in particular Imam Khomeini on 7 January 1978 by the ruling regime accelerated the revolutionary movement and caused an outburst of popular outrage across the country. The regime attempted to quiet the heat of the people's anger by drowning the protest and uprising in blood, but the bloodshed only quickened the pulse rate of the Revolution. The seventh-day and fortieth-day commemorations of the martyrs of the Revolution, like a series of steady heartbeats, gave greater vitality, intensity, vigor, and solidarity to this movement all over the country. In the course of this popular movement, the employees of all government establishments took an active part in the effort to overthrow the tyrannical regime by calling a general strike and participating in street demonstrations. The widespread solidarity of men and women of all segments of society and of all political and religious factions, played a clearly determining role in the struggle. Especially the women were actively and massively present in a most conspicuous manner at all stages of this great struggle. The common sight of mothers with infants in their arms rushing towards the scene of battle and in front of the barrels of machine-guns indicated the essential and decisive role played by this major segment of society in the struggle.

The Price the Nation Paid

After slightly more than a year of continuous and unrelenting struggle, the sapling of the revolution, watered by the blood of more than 60,000 martyrs and 100,000 wounded and disabled, not to mention property damage, came to bear fruit amidst the cries of *"Independence! Freedom! Islamic government!"* This great movement, which attained victory through reliance upon faith, unity, and the decisiveness of its leadership at every critical and sensitive juncture, as well as the self-sacrificing spirit of the people, succeeded in upsetting all the calculations of imperialism and destroying all its connections and institutions, thereby opening a new chapter in the history of all-embracing popular revolutions of the world.

On 12 and 13 February 1979, the world witnessed the collapse of the monarchical regime. Domestic tyranny and foreign domination, both of which were based upon it, were shattered. This great success proved to be the vanguard of Islamic government – a long-cherished desire of the Muslim people – and brought with it the glad tidings of final victory.

Unanimously, the Iranian people declared their final and firm decision, in the referendum on the Islamic Republic, to bring about a new political system, that of the Islamic Republic. A majority of 98.2% of the people voted for this system. The Constitution of the Islamic Republic of Iran, setting forth as it does the political, social, cultural, and economic institutions and their relations that are to exist in society, must now provide for the consolidation of the foundations of Islamic government, and propose the plan of a new system of government to be erected on the ruins of the previous order.

The Form of Government in Islam

In the view of Islam, government does not derive from the interests of a class, nor does it serve the domination of an individual or a group. Rather, it represents the fulfillment of the political ideal of a people who bear a common faith and common outlook, taking an organized form in order to initiate the process of intellectual and ideological evolution towards the final goal, i.e., movement towards Allah. Our nation, in the course of its revolutionary developments, has cleansed itself of the dust and impurities that accumulated during the past and purged itself of foreign ideological influences, returning to authentic intellectual standpoints and world-view of Islam. It now intends to establish an ideal and model society on the basis of Islamic norms. The mission of the Constitution is to realize the ideological objectives of the movement and to create conditions conducive to the development of man in accordance with the noble and universal values of Islam.

With due attention to the Islamic content of the Iranian Revolution, the Constitution provides the necessary basis for ensuring the continuation of the Revolution at home and abroad. In particular, in the development of international relations, the Constitution will strive with other Islamic and popular movements to prepare the way for the formation of a single world community (in accordance with the Koranic verse *"This your community is a single community, and I am your Lord, so worship Me"* [21:92]), and to assure the continuation of the struggle for the liberation of all deprived and oppressed peoples in the world....

Woman in the Constitution

Through the creation of Islamic social infrastructures, all the elements of humanity that served the multifaceted foreign exploitation shall regain their true identity and human rights. As a part of this process, it is only natural that women should benefit from a particularly large augmentation of their rights, because of the greater oppression that they suffered under the old regime.

The family is the fundamental unit of society and the main center for the growth and edification of human being. Compatibility with respect to belief and ideal, which provides the primary basis for man's development and growth, is the main consideration in the establishment of a family. It is the duty of the Islamic government to provide the necessary facilities for the attainment of this goal. This view of the family unit delivers woman from being regarded as an object or instrument in the service of promoting consumerism and exploitation. Not only does woman recover thereby her momentous and precious function of motherhood, rearing of ideologically committed human beings, she also assumes a pioneering social role and becomes the fellow struggler of man in all vital areas of life. Given the weighty responsibilities that woman thus assumes, she is accorded in Islam great value and nobility.

An Ideological Army

In the formation and equipping of the country's defence forces, due attention must be paid to faith and ideology as the basic criteria. Accordingly, the Army of the Islamic Republic of Iran and the Islamic Revolutionary Guards Corps are to be organized in conformity with this goal, and they will be responsible not only for guarding and preserving the frontiers of the country, but also for fulfilling the ideological mission of jihad in God's way; that is, extending the sovereignty of God's law throughout the world (this is in accordance with the Koranic verse *"Prepare against them whatever force you are able to muster, and strings of horses, striking fear into the enemy of God and your enemy, and others besides them"* [8:60]).

The Judiciary in the Constitution

The judiciary is of vital importance in the context of safeguarding the rights of the people in accordance with the line followed by the Islamic movement, and the prevention of deviations within the Islamic nation. Provision has therefore been made for the creation of a judicial system based on Islamic justice and operated by just judges with meticulous knowledge of the Islamic laws. This system, because of its essentially sensitive nature and the need for full ideological conformity, must be free from every kind of unhealthy relation and connection (this is in accordance with the Koranic verse *"When you judge among the people, judge with justice"* [4:58]).

Executive Power

Considering the particular importance of the executive power in implementing the laws and ordinances of Islam for the sake of establishing the rule of just relations over society, and considering, too, its vital role in paving the way for the attainment of the ultimate goal of life, the executive power must work toward the creation of an Islamic society. Consequently, the confinement of the executive power within any kind of complex and inhibiting system that delays or impedes the attainment of this goal is rejected by Islam. Therefore, the system of bureaucracy, the result and product of old forms of government, will be firmly cast away, so that an executive system that functions efficiently and swiftly in the fulfillment of its administrative commitments comes into existence.

Mass-Communication Media

The mass-communication media, radio and television, must serve the diffusion of Islamic culture in pursuit of the evolutionary course of the Islamic Revolution. To this end, the media should be used as a forum for healthy encounter of different ideas, but they must strictly refrain from diffusion and propagation of destructive and anti-Islamic practices....

Representatives

The Assembly of Experts, composed of representatives of the people, completed its task of framing the Constitution, on the basis of the draft proposed by the government as well as all the proposals received from different groups of the people, in one hundred and seventy-five articles arranged in twelve chapters, in 1979, and in accordance with the aims and aspirations set out above, with the hope that this century will witness the establishment of a universal holy government and the downfall of all others.

CHAPTER I: GENERAL PRINCIPLES

Article 1 [Form of Government]

The form of government of Iran is that of an Islamic Republic, endorsed by the people of Iran on the basis of their longstanding belief in the sovereignty of truth and Koranic justice, in the referendum of 29 and 30 March 1979, through the affirmative vote of a majority of 98.2% of eligible voters, held after the victorious Islamic Revolution led by Imam Khumayni.

Article 2 [Foundational Principles]

The Islamic Republic is a system based on belief in:

1. the One God (as stated in the phrase *"There is no god except Allah"*), His exclusive sovereignty and right to legislate, and the necessity of submission to His commands;

2. Divine revelation and its fundamental role in setting forth the laws;

3. the return to God in the Hereafter, and the constructive role of this belief in the course of man's ascent towards God;

4. the justice of God in creation and legislation;

5. continuous leadership and perpetual guidance, and its fundamental role in ensuring the uninterrupted process of the revolution of Islam;

6. the exalted dignity and value of man, and his freedom coupled with responsibility before God...

Article 3 [State Goals]

In order to attain the objectives specified in Article 2, the government of the Islamic Republic of Iran has the duty of directing all its resources to the following goals:

1. the creation of a favorable environment for the growth of moral virtues based on faith and piety and the struggle against all forms of vice and corruption;

2. raising the level of public awareness in all areas, through the proper use of the press, mass media, and other means;

3. free education and physical training for everyone at all levels, and the facilitation and expansion of higher education;

4. strengthening the spirit of inquiry, investigation, and innovation in all areas of science, technology, and culture, as well as Islamic studies, by establishing research centers and encouraging researchers;

5. the complete elimination of imperialism and the prevention of foreign influence;

6. the elimination of all forms of despotism and autocracy and all attempts to monopolize power;

7. ensuring political and social freedoms within the framework of the law;

8. the participation of the entire people in determining their political, economic, social, and cultural destiny;

9. the abolition of all forms of undesirable discrimination and the provision of equitable opportunities for all, in both the material and the intellectual spheres;

10. the creation of a correct administrative system and elimination of superfluous government organizations;

11. all round strengthening of the foundations of national defence to the utmost degree by means of universal military training for the sake of safeguarding the independence, territorial integrity, and the Islamic order of the country;

12. the planning of a correct and just economic system, in accordance with Islamic criteria, in order to create welfare, eliminate poverty, and abolish all forms of deprivation with respect to food, housing, work, health care, and the provision of social insurance for all;

13. the attainment of self-sufficiency in scientific, technological, industrial, agricultural, and military domains, and other similar spheres;

14. securing the multifarious rights of all citizens, both women and men, and providing legal protection for all, as well as the equality of all before the law;

15. the expansion and strengthening of Islamic brotherhood and public cooperation among all the people;

16. framing the foreign policy of the country on the basis of Islamic criteria, fraternal commitment to all Muslims, and unsparing support to the freedom fighters of the world.

Article 4 [Islamic Principle]

All civil, penal, financial, economic, administrative, cultural, military, political, and other laws and regulations must be based on Islamic criteria. This principle applies absolutely and generally to all articles of the Constitution as well as to all other laws and regulations, and the wise persons of the Guardian Council are judges in this matter.

Article 5 [Office of Religious Leader]

During the occultation of the Wali al-'Asr (may God hasten his reappearance), the leadership of the Ummah [Muslim community] devolves upon the just and pious person, who is fully aware of the circumstances of his age, courageous, resourceful, and possessed of administrative ability, will assume the responsibilities of this office in accordance with Article 107.

Article 6 [Administration of Affairs]

In the Islamic Republic of Iran, the affairs of the country must be administered on the basis of public opinion expressed by the means of elections, including the election of the President, the representatives of the Islamic Consultative Assembly, and the members of councils, or by means of referenda in matters specified in other articles of this Constitution.

Article 11 [Unity of Islam Principle]

In accordance with the sacred verse of the Koran *"This your community is a single community, and I am your Lord, so worship Me"* [21:92], all Muslims form a single nation, and the government of the Islamic Republic of Iran have the duty of formulating its general policies with a view to cultivating the friendship and unity of all Muslim peoples, and it must constantly strive to bring about the political, economic, and cultural unity of the Islamic world.

Article 12 [Official Religion]

The official religion of Iran is Islam and the Twelver Ja'fari school, and this principle will remain eternally immutable. Other Islamic schools are to be accorded full respect, and their followers are free to act in accordance with their own jurisprudence in performing their religious rites....

Article 13 [Recognized Religious Minorities]

Zoroastrian, Jewish, and Christian Iranians are the only recognized religious minorities, who, within the limits of the law, are free to perform their religious rites and ceremonies, and to act according to their own canon in matters of personal affairs and religious education.

CHAPTER II: THE OFFICIAL LANGUAGE, SCRIPT, CALENDAR, AND FLAG OF THE COUNTRY

Article 15 [Official Language]

The Official Language and script of Iran, the lingua franca of its people, is Persian. Official documents, correspondence, and texts, as well as textbooks, must be in this language and script. However, the use of regional and tribal languages in the press and mass media, as well as for teaching of their literature in schools, is allowed in addition to Persian.

Article 16 [Arabic Language]

Since the language of the Koran and Islamic texts and teachings is Arabic, and since Persian literature is thoroughly permeated by this language, it must be taught after elementary level, in all classes of secondary school and in all areas of study.

Article 17 [Official Calendar]

The Official Calendar of the country takes as its point of departure the migration of the Prophet of Islam – God's peace and blessings upon him and his Family.... The official weekly holiday is Friday.

Article 18 [Official Flag]

The Official Flag of Iran is composed of green, white, and red colors, with the special emblem of the Islamic Republic, together with the State Motto.

CHAPTER V: THE RIGHT OF NATIONAL SOVEREIGNTY

Article 56 [Divine Right of Sovereignty]

Absolute sovereignty over the world and man belongs to God, and it is He Who has made man master of his own social destiny. No one can deprive man of this divine right, nor subordinate it to the vested interests of a particular individual or group. The people are to exercise this divine right in the manner specified in the following articles.

Article 57 [Separation of Powers]

The powers of government in the Islamic Republic are vested in the legislature, the judiciary, and the executive powers, functioning under the supervision of the absolute religious Leader and the Leadership of the Ummah, in accordance with the forthcoming articles of this Constitution. These powers are independent of each other.

CHAPTER VI: THE LEGISLATIVE POWERS

Article 62 [Election of the Islamic Consultative Assembly]

1. The Islamic Consultative Assembly is constituted by the representatives of the people elected directly and by secret ballot.

2. The qualifications of voters and candidates, as well as the nature of election, will be specified by law.

Article 72 [Limits]

The Islamic Consultative Assembly cannot enact laws contrary to the official religion of the country or to the Constitution. It is the duty of the Guardian Council to determine whether a violation has occurred, in accordance with Article 96.

Article 91 [Guardian Council]

With a view to safeguard the Islamic ordinances and the Constitution, in order to examine the compatibility of the legislation passed by the Islamic Consultative Assembly with Islam, a council to be known as the Guardian Council is to be constituted with the following composition:

1. six religious men, conscious of the present needs and the issues of the day, to be selected by the Leader, and

2. six jurists, specializing in different areas of law, to be elected by the Islamic Consultative Assembly from among the Muslim jurists nominated by the Head of the Judicial Power.

Article 94 [Review of Legislation]

All legislation passed by the Islamic Consultative Assembly must be sent to the Guardian Council. The Guardian Council must review it within a maximum of ten days from its receipt with a view to ensuring its compatibility with the criteria of Islam and the Constitution. If it finds the legislation incompatible, it will return it to the Assembly for review. Otherwise the legislation will be deemed enforceable.

Article 98 [Authoritative Interpretation]

The authority of the interpretation of the Constitution is vested with the Guardian Council, which is to be done with the consent of three-fourths of its members.

CHAPTER VIII: THE LEADER OR LEADERSHIP COUNCIL

Article 107 [Religious Leader]

1. After the demise of Imam Khomeini, the task of appointing the Leader shall be vested with the experts elected by the people. The experts will review and consult among themselves concerning all the religious men possessing the qualifications specified in Articles 5 and 109....

2. The Leader is equal with the rest of the people of the country in the eyes of law.

Article 109 [Leadership Qualifications]

1. Following are the essential qualifications and conditions for the Leader:

    a. Scholarship, as required for performing the functions of religious leader in different fields.

    b. Justice and piety, as required for the leadership of the Islamic Ummah.

    c. Right political and social perspicacity, prudence, courage, administrative facilities, and adequate capability for leadership.

2. In case of multiplicity of persons fulfilling the above qualifications and conditions, the person possessing the better jurisprudential and political perspicacity will be given preference.

CHAPTER IX: THE EXECUTIVE POWER

Article 113 [President]

After the office of Leadership, the President is the highest official in the country. His is the responsibility for implementing the Constitution and acting as the head of the executive, except in matters directly concerned with the office of the Leadership.

Article 122 [Responsibility]

The President, within the limits of his powers and duties, which he has by virtue of this Constitution or other laws, is responsible to the people, the Leader and the Islamic Consultative Assembly.

Article 150 [Islamic Revolution Guards Corps]

The Islamic Revolution Guards Corps, organized in the early days of the triumph of the Revolution, is to be maintained so that it may continue in its role of guarding the Revolution and its achievements. The scope of the duties of this Corps, and its areas of responsibility, in relation to the duties and areas of responsibility of the other Armed Forces, are to be determined by law with emphasis on brotherly cooperation and harmony among them.

End of document 3.2

The approval of the constitution by referendum at the end of 1979 was a crucial step in asserting the Islamic character of the revolution at the expense of more leftist and secularist visions of the revolution's future. But the battle was by no means over. The first figure to be elected president by the new constitution and with Khomeini's approval, Abol-Hassan Bani-Sadr, tried to bind together the two wings of the revolutionary movement, the leftist and the Islamist, but his experience largely replicated that of Bazargan. The Islamists continued to push strongly for the Islamization of society, and though they were a fairly amorphous group, they had deeper roots among the disaffected in both the cities and villages. The leftists, for their part, watched the rise of the Islamic wing of the movement with apprehension. They were not especially unified—internal disputes continued to divide them—and unlike the religious clerics, who were heavily supported economically by the bazaaris and other traditional groups—they had little economic support. For the first half of 1980 the future the still looked unclear.

Yet in September of 1980 the situation changed fundamentally, when the dictator of Iraq, Saddam Hussein, decided to attack Iran. There were several reasons for Hussein to have done so. For one, the two countries had long been rivals, and Hussein saw a unique opportunity to exploit the revolutionary chaos within Iran for his own benefit. Indeed, his assumption was that such an attack would meet relatively weak resistance, and that he would thereby be in a position to dictate the peace terms to a defeated Iran. This might allow him not only to assert more control over the waterway at the very end of the Persian Gulf (the Shatt al-Arab waterway, which made up the border between Iran and Iraq in the southwest, at the very end of the Persian Gulf), but possibly also to annex the Iranian border

region of Khuzestan, which was both rich in oil and populated primarily by Arabs. His assumption was also that the Americans, previously the backers of the shah, were much more hostile to the new revolutionary regime in Iran, especially after the beginning of the hostage crisis. Equally important in Hussein's calculations was the ideology of the revolution itself. Khomeini made clear that the revolution was not only an affair for Shiites but for all Muslims. It was bad enough for Hussein that a majority of Iraq was Shiite (if only a majority of around 60%), whereas he himself was a Sunni. More important still was that his Baathist regime was strictly secularist, and an "Islamic Revolution"— especially one that sought its own export—looked dangerous. In short, Hussein's Iraq attacked Iran both to block the export of "Islamic Revolution" and to gain geopolitical advantage over his Persian rival.

The Iraqi invasion actually proved to be a valuable gift to the Islamists and similar supporters of Khomeini. Combined with the Soviet invasion of Persian-speaking Afghanistan in December of 1979, the Iraqi invasion created the impression that the entire Persian world was under assault. This provided a powerful cause to mobilize the Iranian people against the invasion. More generally, it created the impression that the revolution was in danger and needed to be defended, not least since the operative assumption was that the Americans almost surely stood behind Hussein. For one, this meant that many who were resisting Khomeini's consolidation of power and the growing strength of the Islamists abandoned their opposition and supported the new regime in its struggle against Iraq. For the opponents that remained, Khomeini's regime now found it easier to marginalize them, since, the ayatollah could claim, they were undermining the "holy war" against Iraq. The religious establishment used the context of the war to push harder for Islamization. In other words, the war with Iraq both mobilized Iranians, especially young men, to fight for the new revolutionary state while also creating the basis for repressing the leftist wing of the revolutionary movement.

The nail in the coffin of the leftists came in June of 1981, when a bomb exploded at the headquarters of the Islamic Republican Party, the main party supporting Khomeini. Over 70 people died in the blast, and the revolutionary regime "launched a reign of terror against leftist opponents, which resulted in their decimation as a distinct political force in Iran." Probably several thousand opponents of the regime were executed, oftentimes in public and with great enthusiasm. "The destruction of the Left was merciless."[21] By the end of 1981, the Left had essentially been neutralized, and more elements of Islamization could be introduced. To take a few prominent examples, in 1981 the Majles passed a law requiring all women in Iran to wear "Islamic dress" and later reintroduced flogging, amputation, and stoning to death, as well as capital punishment for sodomy.

Nor was Saddam Hussein's attack ultimately successful. Iran after all inherited a good deal of advanced military technology from the shah, and there were many pilots and mechanics who, if otherwise uncertain about whether to support Khomeini's revolutionary regime, had no doubts about whether to defend the country. Iran also proved able to mobilize even young boys and older men to engage in human wave assaults or to clear minefields by walking through them. Many young men accepted the prospect of their own martyrdom with enthusiasm.

By 1982 Iran was able to reverse the course of the war and initiate a counteroffensive. The recapture of the city of Khorramshahr in May of 1982 was a crucial moment that had a catalytic effect on Iranian society: It demonstrated what the country could do when unified, and it confirmed the righteousness of the revolution—for many there was really no better proof. Especially striking is Ehsan Naraghi's description of the reaction to the taking of the city even among the regime's prisoners in Evin prison. The capture of the port city, he writes, "was received with great joy by prisoners and jailors alike. From the beginning of the Iran-Iraq War a great many Iranians who were otherwise hostile to the Islamic Republic had fallen in line behind Khomeini with the aim of pushing Saddam's troops out of southwestern Iran. It is not surprising then, that at the time of the liberation of Khorramshahr virtually everyone allowed himself to be carried along by the spirit of patriotism, with a large majority of the people supporting the policies of the regime."[22] The war dragged on for another six years, ending only in 1988. But for us, the main significance was already clear by 1981: the war allowed the clerical regime to solidify its control over Iranian society. It produced a wave of patriotism and nationalism and thus support for the regime. It allowed Khomeini to dispense with the moderate secular president Bani-Sadr, and to replace him with Hojjatoleslam Ali Khamenei, a cleric, who later went on to become *Faqih* after Khomeini's death in 1989 and holds that position to this day. And it allowed the regime to suppress the leftist wing of the revolutionary movement. By around 1982, then, the revolution had not only triumphed but had become, for all intents and purposes, Islamic.

Further Reading

Ervand Abrahamian, *Khomeinism*. Berkeley: University of California Press, 1993.

Ali M. Ansari, *Modern Iran since 1921: The Pahlavis and After*. London: Longman, 2003.

Elton L. Daniel, *The History of Iran*. Westport, Conn.: Greenwood Publishers, 2001.

Nikki R. Keddie, *Modern Iran: Roots and Results of Revolution*. New Haven: Yale University Press, 2003.

Tim McDaniel, *Autocracy, Modernization, and Revolution in Russia and Iran*. Princeton: Princeton University Press, 1991.

Ehsan Naraghi, *From Palace to Prison: Inside the Iranian Revolution*, trans. Nilou Mobasser. Chicago: Ivan R. Dee, 1994.

Vali Nasr, *The Shia Revival*. New York: W. W. Norton, 2007.

Asghar Schirazi, *The Constitution of Iran: Politics and the State in the Islamic Republic*. London: I. B. Tauris, 1998.

---

21   Ansari, *Modern Iran*, 233.

22   Ehsan Naraghi, From Palace to Prison: *Inside the Iranian Revolution* (Chicago, 1994), 252.

INDEX

A

Abbasid caliphate, 149
Abkhaz minorities, 115
Abraham, Richard, 90
Abrahamian, 181, 182, 183
absolutism, 4, 5
Abu Bakr, 148
Accomac, 38
Achaemenids, 146, 162, 164
Affirmative action, 113, 118, 119
Afghanistan, 146, 150, 151
Africa, 35, 171
African Americans, 39, 45
African-American emigration, 34
Age of Modernization and Revolution, 81
Agitation and Propaganda Department, 134
Ahmad, 174
All-Russian Congress of Soviets, 93
AIOC (Anglo-Iranian Oil Company), 156, 157
Airyana Vaeja, 146
Akhil Reed Amar, 22, 29, 30, 31, 49
Ākhūnd, 169
Alabama, 38
Alexander I, 60
Alexander II, 58, 61, 62, 70, 80
Alexander III, 57, 62, 63, 70, 73
Alexander, 55, 59, 60, 73, 146
Algar, Hamid, 167
Algeria, 173, 174
Al-i Ahmad, 174, 175
Allah, 147, 187
Alleghanies, 35
All-Russia Central Executive Committee, 100
All-Russia Soviet Government, 100
All-Russian Central Executive Committee, 93, 99
All-Russian Communist party, 115
All-Russian Congress of Soviets and VTsIK, 93, 95
All-Russian Congress of Soviets, 88, 93, 94, 95, 97, 98, 100, 108
All-Russian Emperor, 76
All-Russian Extraordinary Commission, 90
All-Russian Workers Commune, 94
American colonies, 3, 8, 11, 15, 53, 54
American conspiracy, 185
American economy, 158
American embassy, 184
American federalism, 47
American geopolitical interests, 44, 158, 178
American history, 46

American influence in Iran, 156
American military personnel, 157
American political community, 21, 33
American political thinking, 8, 47, 158, 159
American President Richard Nixon, 163
American press, 163
American Republic, 22, 30
American Revolution, 11, 22, 30, 53, 105
American Slavery, 39, 57, 66
American universities, 145
Ancient Greeks, 146
Ancient Persia, 164
Anglo-Iranian Oil Company (AIOC), 156, 157
Anglo-Persian Oil Company, 155
Ansari, 158, 159, 162, 163, 165, 166, 176, 177, 180, 181, 182, 193
Anti-Bolshevik, 108, 121
Anti-Catholic hysteria, 5
Anti-Islamic practices, 167, 173, 188
April Theses, 86
Arab culture, 146, 147, 148, 149, 159, 164, 170, 190, 192
Arab warrior Umar, 148
Arabian peninsula, 146, 147
Arab-Israeli War, 178
Aras river, 151
Arch Getty, 140
Archangel Gabriel, 114
Arkansas, 38
Armenia, 56, 100, 105, 107, 110, 111, 117, 151, 155
Articles of Confederation, 16, 18, 23, 28, 29
Ascher, Abraham, 81
Ashura, 149
Asia, 35, 100, 146, 155, 171
Assent to Laws for establishing Judiciary Powers, 12
Atatürk, 164
Rosa Luxembourg's denial, 115
Attorney General Edward Bates, 45
Austria, 60, 105, 107
Austria-Hungary, 84, 85, 86, 106, 114
Authoritarian Islamists, 182
Avdienko, 124
ayatollah, 150, 177, 179, 183, 192
Azerbaijan, 105, 110, 111, 141, 146, 151, 155
Azeri music in Moscow in April, 141

B

Baathist regime, 192
Baghdad, 166
Bahrain, 150

Baku, 108, 154
Balkans, 60, 84
Baltic Provinces and Finland, 59, 66
Baltic region, 56, 84, 109, 110
Baltimore, 33
Bani-Sadr, Abol-Hassan, 192, 193
Barron decision, 33
Barron, 33
Bashkir leadership, 109
Bashkirs, 105, 109, 115
Bazaaris, 153, 154, 155, 175, 179, 184, 192
Bazargan, Mehdi, 183, 185, 192
Belarus, 55, 105, 106, 110, 115, 116
Belgian embassy, 169
Belgian, 169
Belgium, 154, 170
beliefs, 94, 114, 115, 138, 163, 167, 171, 172, 187, 188
Berkeley, 38, 154, 180, 193
Bernstein, 87, 124, 125, 126, 127
Bernstein, Laurie, 87, 102, 124, 142
Biography, 22, 29, 30, 31, 49, 166
Black Friday, 179
Black Hundred Great Russians, 115
Blackwell Encyclopedia, 90
Blessings of Liberty, 23
Bloody Sunday, 74, 75
Bloomington, 133
Bolshevik chauvinism in Ukraine, 115
Bolsheviks, 59, 83, 85, 88-90, 93, 94, 96, 103-104, 106-108, 110, 113, 115-116, 121-125, 132
Bolshevik Revolution, 67, 89, 92, 102, 105, 106, 119, 121, 123
Bonaparte, Napoleon, 54
Bone, Jon, 75
Boston, 40
bourgeois constitutions, 96, 131
bourgeois counter-revolution, 90
Bourgeois Criticism, 132
bourgeois democracy, 94, 97, 115, 136
bourgeois specialists, 125, 128
bourgeois state, 91, 96, 97, 110
bourgeois, 71, 86, 87, 91, 94, 96, 114, 115, 137
Brest-Litovsk, 90, 93, 106, 107
Brethren, 13
Breunig, Charles, 54, 55, 66
Britain, 3, 4, 5, 15, 55, 58, 70, 151, 153, 155-159, 162, 165, 169-170
British law, 5, 169
British and French capitalists, 127
British history, 3, 4, 5, 13, 15, 35, 151, 156, 158,
British MI-6, 165
British Tobacco Company, 154
Brussels, 81
Brutus, 18, 20, 23, 29
Buddhism, 56
Bukharin, 113, 114, 115, 118, 125
Bulgaria, 60, 65

Bushkovitch, Paul, 76, 81, 125
Byzantine Empire, 168, 169

C
California Press, 193
California, 44
Caliph Umar, 148
Caliph Uthman, 148
Caliph, 148, 173
Calvinist, 3
Cambridge University Press, 81
Cambridge, 57, 66, 76, 81, 125
Canada acceding, 17
Capital, 30, 57, 70-72, 88, 92- 93, 99-101, 107, 112, 124-125, 130, 132,146, 151
Capitalism, 70-73, 80, 86, 107, 114-115, 118, 123, 125, 129-130, 132, 137, 174
Capitation, 26
Carr, Edward H., 92–93, 98, 102, 104, 106, 107, 119
Carter, President Jimmy, 177-179,
Catholicism, 3-6, 8, 56
Caucasian, 49
Caucasus, 150
Central Asia, 146, 148
Central Executive Committee, 111, 112, 133, 134, 138
Central government, 47, 95, 96, 134, 141, 158
Central Powers, 107, 155
Century Rulers and Writers in Political Dialogue, 57
Charles II, 4, 5, 7
Charles, 5
Charters, 12
Chauvinism
Chechens Germans, 105
Cheka, 90
Chernigov Region, 140
Chicago, 176, 193
Chisholm, 31
Christianity, 3, 8, 56, 147-148, 150, 151, 167-168, 171
Church of Rome, 7
Church, 4, 5, 54, 58, 93, 96, 100, 138, 139, 141, 168
Chuvash, 109
CIA, 157, 158, 165
City, Elizabeth, 38
Civil rights, 41, 60, 63, 73, 74, 77, 79, 86, 133, 135, 139, 141
Civil War Amendments, 34, 47
Civil war, 32, 33, 34, 38, 44, 45, 46, 98, 103, 104, 109, 113, 121, 122, 149
Clark County, 48, 49
Clark, 48
Classes, 24, 69, 70, 71, 92, 94, 99, 100, 106, 113, 114, 122, 130, 131, 132
Clemens, 45
Clerics, 153, 154, 165, 173, 175, 180, 181, 182, 183, 185, 193
Codifying Russian, 59
Cold War US leaders, 157
Cold War, 145, 157
Collectivization, 121, 122, 125, 126, 127, 134, 136, 138, 140

Colonies, 12, 13, 15, 17, 23, 32, 44, 46, 100, 131, 151
Colorado, 35
Commissar of Nationalities, 114
Commissioners, 6, 7
Commissions, granting, 27
Communism, 92, 94, 128, 130, 131, 158
Communist League Marx, 107
Communist Manifesto, 70–72, 91
Communist Party, 104, 110, 118, 119, 121, 122, 123, 132, 134
Comstock Lode, 45, 46
Confederacies, 16, 21, 37
Confederate States, 45, 46
Confederation Congress, 18
Confederation, 15, 16, 17, 19, 21, 26, 29, 117, 119
Conference, special TsK,
Connecticut, 16, 24
Constantine, 55
Constituent Assembly, 75, 85, 86, 87, 89, 90, 98, 108
Contemporary Debates in Islam, 174
Cossacks, 101, 155
Council of Baltimore, 33
Council of Ministers, 77, 78, 79
Council of People's Commissars, 89, 100
Council of Peoples' Commissars, 93
counterrevolution, 113, 114
Court of Commissioners for Ecclesiastical, 6, 7
Court of King's Bench, 6
Courts of Law, 27
Crimea, 58, 118
Cromwell, Oliver, 4
Crusades, 167
Curry, John, 146, 147, 166
Cyrus, 146, 158, 162, 164
Czech legions, 108

D
Dagestan Autonomous Republic, 138
Dakota, 35
Daniel, 157, 158, 175, 180
Daniel, Elton L., 151–52, 157, 159, 175-176, 180, 193
Darius, 146
Decembrists, 55, 60, 65, 67
Declaration, influenced Nevada's, 47
Dee, Ivan R., 176, 193
DeKalb, 57, 66
Delaware, 16, 24
Democracy in capitalist countries, 132
Democracy, 48, 59, 63, 64, 65, 71, 92, 132, 133, 139, 141, 142, 162, 163, 164
Democratic Islamic Republic, 182
district congresses of, 93, 95
Dnevnik imperatora Nikolaia II, 75
Douglass, Frederick, 39–40
Doyen, 169, 171
Dred Scott decision, 33
Duma, 67, 74, 75, 76, 78, 79–80, 85, 86, 154, 155
Dungan, 48

Dunn, Richard S., 5, 13
Dzerzhinskii, denounced, 115

E
Early 7th-century Arabia, 147
Early constitutional developments, 182
Early Iran and Islam, 145, 147, 149, 151
East Slavs, 55
Eastern Europe, 54, 117
Egypt, 150, 169, 179
Ehsan Naraghi, 176, 193
Eighteen-Century Rulers and Writers in Political Dialogue, 66
Eighth Communist Party Congress, 113
Eighth Congress of Soviets, 136
Eighth Extraordinary Congress of Soviets, 133, 134, 135
Electoral College, 34, 46, 96
Emancipation of Labor Group, 72
Emancipation Proclamation, 34, 37, 38
Emerging Silk Road, 146
Emperor Alexander I, 55
Emperor Nicholas II, 61, 70, 74, 80
Emperor Nicholas, 79
Engels, Friedrich, 70-71, 91, 93, 107, 108
England, 3, 4, 5, 7, 47, 56, 108
English Catholics, 4
English Civil War, 4, 55
English Declaration of Rights, 5, 6, 23
English political traditions, 3, 5, 12
English Protestantism, 4, 5
Enlightenment, 8, 55, 66, 136, 186
Erfurt programme, 108
Ervand Abrahamian, 180, 193
Esposito, John L., 152
Essay Concerning Human Understanding, 8
Estonia, 105, 107, 109
Ettela'at, 178
European continent, 54, 55, 57, 74, 90
European geopolitical stage, 59
European importations, 171
European liberals, 54
Evin prison, 193
Exile System, 69
Expansion, State government's, 49
Expropriated kulaks, 126

F
faqih, 167, 175, 181, 182, 183, 184, 185, 193
Fatherland, 77
Faydiyyah Madrasah, 186
February Revolution, 83, 84, 86
Federal government, 23, 33, 44, 46, 96, 100, 108
Federalism, 47, 93, 106, 107, 108, 109
Federalists, 20, 34
Fifth All-Russia Congress of Soviets, 102
Fifth Congress, 99

Finland, 59, 60, 65-66, 75, 87, 88, 91, 100, 105-106, 107, 113-114, 109, 113, 116
First US Congress, 29
First World War, 83, 155
Fitzpatrick, Sheila, 89, 102, 104, 119, 122, 125, 128, 129,133, 142
Five-Year Plan, 127
Florida, 38
Florinsky, Michael T., 60, 66, 102
Foner, Eric, 49
Fort Sumter, 45
Founding Fathers, 30, 31, 46, 47
France, 3, 4, 5, 54, 55, 56, 58, 64, 65, 67, 68, 105, 106, 173, 174
Francisco, San, 35, 45
Franco-Prussian War, 58Roosevelt's New Deal, 48
Franklin, Benjamin, 15
Freeman, 71
French capitalists, 127
French Estates-General, 62
French Fifth Republic, 183
French parliament, 62
French Revolution, 53–54, 56, 64, 68, 70, 105, 107
French revolutionary tradition, 107
Fundamentalist Thought, 174

G
Geifman, Anna, 73, 81
Gellner, Ernest, 114
General Congress, 13
General Secretary, 123
Georgia, 16, 24, 31, 38, 110, 111, 115, 117, 151
Georgian Republic, 105,110, 115
German bourgeois democrats, 107
German cities, 114
German military, 84-85, 90, 106-107, 108, 156
German revolution, 90
German territory, 86
Germany, 3, 55, 58, 84-87, 90, 106–7, 109, 114, 121, 122, 132–33, 155-156, 158
Gettysburg Address, 32
Gilan, 150
Glorious Revolution, 3, 5, 7
Gorkii Region, 140
Gotha Program, 91
Grand Duke of Finland, 75
Grand Jury, 30
Great Britain and Germany, 41
Great Britain and Russia, 55
Great Britain, 11, 12, 13, 20, 21, 47, 48, 53, 55, 84
Great Britain's North American, 3
Great Depression, 121
Great Reforms, 53, 58, 62, 65, 68
Great Russians, 113, 115, 118
Great War, 102
Great Year, 162
Greece, 54, 146

Green, Michael, 44, 49
Greenwood, 180
Gregorians, 56
Grundgesetz, 59
Guadalupe Hidalgo, 44
Guam, 44
Guardian Council, 182, 189, 191

H
Habeas Corpus, 26, 60
Hadiths, 149, 150, 164, 168
Haiti, 34
Hallett, Edward, 92
Halveti Order, 146
Hamilton, Alexander, 20
Hasan al-Askari, 149
Hay, John, 37
Henry VIII, 3
Hitler, Adolph, 121
Hojjatoleslam, 193
Holy Qur'an, 168
Holy Synod, 62
Hosain, 166, 174
Hourani, Albert, 154
House of Commons, 21
House of Representatives, 23, 24, 25, 27, 32, 34, 42, 43, 48
Hroch, 117–119
Hungary, 3, 114, 115, 121, 122
Husayn, 148, 150
Hussein, 192

I
ibn Abu Talib, 148-150, 171
ibn Abu Talib's line, 149
Illinois, 35
Imam Baqir, 31, 171
Imām Hasan, 171
Imam Hosain, 166, 169
Imām Husayn, 169
Imam Khomeini, 185, 186, 191
Imam Khumayni, 188
Imām, 169, 171
Imamate, 172
Imams, 149, 150, 151, 159, 171, 186
Imperial Tobacco Corporation, 153
Imperialism, 99, 119, 167-168, 169, 171-174, 185, 187, 189
India, 151
Indian Tribes, 25
Indiana, 35
Indians, 16, 17, 24, 39
Industrialization, 41, 55, 58, 65, 68, 72, 74, 105, 125, 127, 128
Interior Minister Loris-Melikov, 63
interior minister Michael Loris-Melikov, 61
International Women's Day, observing, 84
Iowa, 35
Iran, 143, 145–46, 148, 150, 151, 153-159, 161, 162–70, 173-193

Iranian Revolution in Comparative Perspective, 154
Iranian Revolution, 145, 152, 154, 157, 161, 176, 184, 187, 193
Iranian Shia, 179
Iranian society, 153, 156, 162, 164, 178, 180, 183, 185, 193
Iranian youth for revolutionary upheaval, 174
Iranians, 146, 155-157, 161-163, 173-175, 179-181, 192-193
Iranians, Christian, 190
Iran-Iraq War, 193
Iraq, 150, 166, 167, 173, 178, 179, 192–93
IRC (Islamic Revolutionary Council), 183
Ireland, 7
IRP (Islamic Republic Party), 183
Islam commands, 171
Islam Principle, 190
Islam, 147-149, 150–52, 167-168-172, 174, 175, 180, 181, 187
Islamic brotherhood and public cooperation, 189
Islamic calendar, 162
Islamic Consultative Assembly, 190, 191, 192
Islamic form of mysticism, 146
Islamic Government, 167, 171, 172, 181, 184, 186, 187
Islamic history, 149, 151
Islamic khanate, 56
Islamic law, 149, 164, 167, 168, 169, 170, 183, 188
Islamic leader, 185
Islamic line of thought, 185
Islamic Marxism, 181
Islamic radicals, 183
Islamic Republic Of Iran, 145, 185, 187, 189, 190
Islamic Republic, 145, 167, 177, 182-185, 187, 188, 190, 192-193
Islamic Revolution of Iran, 169, 175, 186
Islamic Revolution, 156, 180, 188, 192
Islamic Revolutionary Council (IRC), 183
Islamic scholars, 173
Islamic scholarship in Iran, 166
Islamic scholarship, 164
Islamic schools, 190
Islamic shrines, 151
Islamic society, 170, 171, 181, 188
Islamic Ummah, 185, 191
Islamic values, 164, 174
Islamism, 177, 183, 184
Islamists, 177, 181, 182, 184, 192
Islamization of society, 192, 193
Ismail, 150
Italian states, 55
Italy, 3, 54, 121
Ithaca, 68, 81, 119
Izvestiya, 98

J
Jacksonian Democracy, 47
Jalal Al-i Ahmad, 172, 174
James II, 5, 8
Japan, 74, 75, 154, 155, 158

Jay, John, 20
Jefferson, Thomas, 11, 38
Jelavich, Charles, 60
Jerusalem, 167
Jesus, 147
Jewish Bund, 107
Jews, 56,
John Locke, 3, 5
Judaism, 56, 63, 73, 105, 147-148, 150, 167, 190
Jupiter, 10

K
Kadets, 73, 89, 90
Kamran Talatoff, 174
Kansas, 35
Karaites, 56
Karakozov, 68, 81
Karbala, 150, 169
Kazakhstan, 105, 110,127, 136
Kazan, 56, 90
Keddie, Nikki R., 154, 157, 159, 163, 164, 175-176, 180, 183-184, 193
Kemal, Mustafa, 164
Kennan, George, 69
Kennedy, 165
Kentucky, 35
Kerensky, Alexander, 87
Khamenei, 193
Khants, 138
Khomeini, 166, 167, 173, 175–85, 192, 193
Khorramshahr, 193
Khoury, Philip S., 154
Khristian Rakovskii, 117
Khuzestan, 192
Kiev Region, 55, 58, 74, 115, 134
king and parliament, 4
King Charles I, 4
King Cyrus II, 146
King George III, 47
King James II, 5
King Louis XIV, 4
King's brother James II, 5
Kingdom of Poland, 60, 105
Kolchin, Peter, 57
Konstantin Pobedonostsev, 62, 63
Kopelev, 127
Koran and Islamic texts and teachings, 190
Koran, 138, 147, 187-188, 190
Korea, 74
korenizatsiia, 116, 117
Kronstadt naval base, 122
Kuibyshev Territory, 138
kulaks, 63, 113, 125, 126, 128, 130, 132, 133, 140, 141
Kurdish, 156
Kursk Region, 134
Kyrgyz, 110

L

Labor Group, 72
Lafourche, 38
Lake City Mormons, 45
Las Vegas, 44, 46, 48
late King James, 6
Latin America, 53
Latvia, 106, 107, 109
Latvians, 105
Law of Nations, 25
Laws for Naturalization of Foreigners, 12
    laws of, 169, 170, 172
Leadership Council, 191
Leadership Qualifications, 191
Lebanon and northern Iran, 150
Lebed, Dmitri, 118
Left SRs, 73, 89, 94, 98
Lenin and Stalin, 109, 113, 114, 116, 117
Lenin and Stalin's terminology, 115
Lenin, 73, 86, 88, 91, 94, 96-98, 104, 107, 108, 110, 113-115,
    118, 122-123, 136, 140
Leningrad propagandist, 138
Leningrad Region, 134, 138
Leszek Kolakowski, 68, 81
Lev Kopelev, 126
Levinger, 55
Levinger, Matthew, 54, 66
Liberia, 34
Librarie Encyclopédique, 81
Libya, 146
Lincoln, Abraham, 32, 34, 37, 38, 45-46
Lithuania, 105, 106, 107, 109
Locke, John, 7-10, 18
Locke's discussion, 10
London, 88, 102, 122, 142, 146, 158, 159, 162, 176, 177, 193
    long, 87
Longman, 66, 81, 159, 176, 193
Loris-Melikov, 61, 65, 67, 70
Louis XIV, 5, 56
Louisiana, 38
Lutheran churches, 3
Lutheranism, 3, 56
Luxembourg, Rosa, 115

M

Macedon, 146
Macmillan, 66, 81, 102, 119
Madison, James, 18, 20, 29, 34
Maier, Pauline, 18, 22
Main Currents of Marxism, 68, 81
Majles approval, 154
Majles, 154, 155, 157, 163, 166, 184, 193
majorities, permanent Shia, 150
Malise Ruthven, 152
Manchuria, 74
Manner chuse, 27

Mansoor Moaddel, 174
Maoism, 165
March Nicholas, 85
Marinskii Autonomous Region, 138
Maris, 105
Martin, Terry, 112, 113, 119Martyrdom, 150, 166, 169, 193
Marx, Karl, 70, 71, 91
Marxism, 55, 65-68, 70-72, 75, 80, 81, 89-94, 96, 106, 113,
    161, 165, 174, 180, 182
Maryland, 16, 24,
Massachusetts Bay Colony, 16, 46
Massachusetts, 24, 35
McDaniel, Tim, 145, 157, 159, 175, 176, 193
Mecca, 147, 148,174
Medina, 147, 171
Melikov, 68
member Republics, 111–12
Mensheviks, 73, 85, 87, 88, 89
Mexican-American War, 44, 46
Mexico, 3, 44, 184
MI-6, 157, 158
Michigan, 35
Mid-1930s, 122, 127, 128, 129, 140
Middle East and Central Asia, 146
Middle East, 54, 146, 150, 151, 156, 158, 159, 163
Minnesota, 35
Minor Occultation, 149
Mirbach, 98
Miroslav Hroch, 117
Mississippi, 33, 49, 38
Missouri, 35
Modern Iran, 157-159, 162-166, 174, 175–77, 180-182, 184,
    193
Modern Middle East, 154
Mohammed, 114
Mohammed-Reza Shah, 145, 156, 157, 159,161, 163, 165,
    166
Mohammed-Reza, 161, 162, 163–65, 175
Moldavia, 134
Mongols, 6, 127
Monks and ministers of religion, 101
Mordovskii Autonomous Republic, 138
Mordvins, 105
Mormon Church, 47
Mormons, 45
Moscow, 55-58, 74, 75, 88, 93, 104, 107, 110, 112, 129, 134,
    136, 137, 139, 141
Moses, 147
Moskvaly, 113
Mossadeq, Mohammed, 156, 157, 159, 161, 165
Mu'āwiyah, 169
Muhammad al-Mahdi, 149
Muhammad, 113, 147, 148, 149, 167
Munck, Thomas, 13
Murav'ev, Nikita, 60, 61
Muslims, 146, 147, 148, 149, 150–51, 167, 168, 169, 172,
    173,185, 186, 187, 189, 192

N

Najaf, 150, 166–67, 173
Napoleon III, 54
Napoleon, 54, 55, 57, 58, 59, 60
Nasr, 180
National Front and Tudeh, 166
National Front, 165–66, 175
Native Americans, 33, 44, 60
Naturalization, 12, 25
Nays, 25
Nazi Germany, 121, 132, 133, 156
Nebraska, 35
Neighboring Belgium, 54
Nenets peoples, 138
NEP (New Economic Policy), 122, 123, 124, 125, 126, 128, 129
Netherlands, 3, 5, 7
Neva, 63
Nevada Constitution, 44, 46, 47, 48, 49
Nevada Constitution's Declaration of Rights, 46, 47
Nevada Press, 44, 49
Nevada Revised Statutes, 49
Nevada Territory, 44, 45
Nevada, 31, 33, 35, 37, 39, 41, 43, 44–49
New Communist State, 83, 85, 87, 89, 91, 93, 95, 97, 99, 101
new country, 3, 15, 83, 103, 107, 182, 183
New Hampshire, 16, 23, 24
New Jersey, 16, 24
New Mexico, 45
New Orleans, 35
New York Supreme Court, 18
Nicholas I, Emperor, 55
Nicholas II, 57, 75, 76, 84
Nicholas, 75, 80, 85
Nicholas's military advisors, 85
Nicolay, John G., 37
Nilou Mobasser, 176, 193
Nineteenth Amendment, 48
NKVD, 139
Noginskii District Executive Committee, 136
North America, 15, 59
North Carolina, 16, 24, 29, 38
North Caucasus, 127
Northampton, 38
Northwest Ordinance, 44
Norton, 5, 13, 22, 30, 66, 81, 176, 193
Notorious Georgian Affair, 115
Nye of New York, 45, 46
Nye, James W., 45

O

October coup, 104
October Manifesto, 75, 76, 79, 80
October Revolution, 83, 88, 90, 108, 134
Office of Trust, 27
Official Flag of Iran, 190

Official Flag, 190
Official Language and script of Iran, 190
Ohio, 35
Ohlander, Erik S., 146
Omsk Region, 138
OPEC, 178
Ordzhonikidze, 115
Orion Clemens, 45
Orleans, 38
Orthodox Christian population, 138
Orthodox Christians, 56, 139
Orthodox Church, 57
Ossetine, 115
Ottoman Empire, 56, 58, 84, 146, 155
Ottomans, 60, 150
Oxford English Dictionary, 15, 104
Oxford University Press, 56, 87, 102, 119, 142, 152
Oxford University, 102
Oxford, 56, 89, 102, 104, 113, 119, 122, 124, 142, 152

P

Pacific Ocean, 56, 58, 59
Pahlavis, 153,155-156, 158-159, 162, 164-166, 174-177, 193
Pakistan, 146
Palace, Winter, 63, 74, 88
Paris commune, 97, 107
Parliament, 4–7, 54, 56, 58, 64, 65, 67, 79, 85, 97, 155
Parsa, 145, 146
Parthian Empire, 146
Paul cathedral, 63
Paul fortress, 63
Pavel Pestel, 60
Peasants' Deputies, 95, 99, 100
Peasants' Republic, 99
Pennsylvania, 15, 16, 24
People Debate, 18, 22
People's Commissariat, 95, 96, 97, 99
People's Commissars, 89, 100
People's time, 170
Peoples' Commissars, 93
Persepolis, 146, 158, 162, 164
Persia, 100, 145, 146, 151, 158, 159, 163-164, 190, 192,
Persian gharbzadegi, 174
Persian Gulf, 150, 156, 192
Pestel, 61
Peter, 53, 56, 57, 63
Peterhof, 76
Petersburg, 74, 89
Petrograd Soviet, 85–86, 88, 89
Petrograd, 85, 86, 88, 89, 93, 106, 123
Petroleum Exporting Countries, 178
Petrone, Historian Karen, 133
Philadelphia, 18, 23, 31
Philippines, 44
Piatakov, 113, 114, 115, 118
Piatakov's policy, 113

Piatikov, 114
Pobedonostsev, 62, 63, 67, 76
Poland, 3, 56, 59-61, 65, 73, 75, 87, 105, 106-107, 109-110, 113, 115, 127, 137
Policeman of the Gulf, 165
Polnoe sobranie zakonov Rossiiskoi Imperii, 75
Pope's authority, 4
Portsmouth, 38
Portugal, 3, 53
Potemkin village, 137
Pravda, 108
Prentice Hall, 66
Presbyterian, 3
Present Islam, 168, 172
President Abraham Lincoln, 32
President and Vice President, 27, 39, 42, 43
President, 24, 25, 26, 27, 28, 31, 32, 36, 37, 38, 42, 43, 112, 189, 191–92
Princeton, 59, 66, 73, 81, 145, 157, 159, 175, 176, 193
prison chaplain Father Grigorii Gapon, former, 74
Progressive Era, 41, 48
Propaganda, anti-Islamic, 167
Propagandists, 135, 136, 137, 138, 139
Prophet Muhammad, 147, 148, 149, 150, 151, 164, 168, 170, 172, 173 190,
Protestantism, 3-7, 56
Proudhon, 107
Providence Plantations, 16, 24
Provinces, former Baltic, 108
Prussia, 60, 105
Public Education, 99
Public Records, 12
Publius, 20, 22, 23
Puerto Rico, 44
Pushkin, 134

Q
Qajar dynasty, 156
Qajars, 151, 152, 153, 159
Qom, 166, 173, 178, 183
Qu'ran, 147, 150, 164, 185
Queen Elizabeth I, 3
Qur'an, 147, 148, 149, 150, 168, 170, 171

R
Raeff, Marc, 61, 62, 66
Rastakhiz commemoration, 162
Rastakhiz party, 162, 163, 178
Rastakhiz, 157, 163
Red Army, 97, 103, 104, 126
Red Square, 123
Reds, 90, 103, 104
Reed, 31
Reformation, 3
REFSR, 93
Reisner, 97
Religious cleric Ruhollah, 157

Religious Wars, 3, 5, 13
Reno, 44, 46, 48, 49
Republican Party, 45
Revolution in Russia and Iran, 145, 157, 159, 175, 176, 193
Revolution to Constitution in Iran, 179, 181, 183, 185, 187, 189, 191,
Revolutionary Era, 53, 54, 55, 66
Revolutionary Guard, 183, 184
Revolutionary Russia, 87, 102, 104, 124, 125, 126, 127, 142
Revolutionary Terrorism in Russia, 73, 81
Reynolds, 48
Reza Khan, 156
Reza Shah, Colonel, 153, 156, 159, 164, 165
Reza, Mohammed, 156, 157, 164
Rhode Island, 23, 24, 29
Riga, 116
Right SRs, 73, 87, 123
Rights and Obligations of Russian Subjects, 77
River, Neva, 63
Rocky mountains, 35
Rogger, 74, 75, 81
Roland Grigor Suny, 113
Roman Catholicism, 5
Roman Catholics, 3, 56
Roman Empire, 3, 146
Romanovs, 83
Rome and Catholic countries, 4
Rome, 3–4, 7
Rome's teaching of Christianity, 3
Ronald Grigor Suny, 119, 142
Routledge, 102, 142
RSFSR, 18, 72-73, 91-99, 102, 107-109, 110
Rumanians, 116
Russia, 55, 56–63, 67-68, 72-74, 83, 84, 85, 86–90, 103, 105-106, 151, 155
Russia's ruling elite, 59
Russian history, 53, 55, 60, 65, 78, 83, 87, 102, 105, 106
Russian Orthodox Church, 62
Russian Republic, 99, 100, 101, 108, 110, 134, 138, 140
Russian Revolution, 53, 73, 83, 89, 90, 92, 102, 104, 119, 122, 125, 128, 129, 142, 145
Russian Serfdom, 57, 66
Russian Socialist Federative Soviet Republic, 92, 99, 100, 101, 102
Russian tsars, 57, 58, 62,
Russians, 55, 56, 58, 59, 63, 69, 73, 74, 84, 86, 87, 104–5, 117, 118, 119
Russification, 59, 66, 74, 105
Russkii Arkhiv, 62

S
Sabotage, 90
Saddam Hussein, 173, 179, 192, 193
Safavids, 150, 151, 159, 162, 174, 180
Safi al-Din, 150
Sagebrush Rebellion, 46

Sakwa, 88, 89, 122, 123
Sakwa, Richard, 88, 102, 122, 142
Samuel, 45
Sanborn, Josh, 102
Sanford, 33
Sassanid Persian Empire, 146, 148
Saudi Arabia, 151
Saunders, David, 60, 66
SAVAK, 157, 163, 165, 166, 173, 175, 178–79
Sawyer, 48
Scandinavia, 3
Shirazi, Asghar, 193
scholars, prominent Shiite, 150, 166
Scholarship, 191
Scotland, 3, 4
Seattle, 60
Senate and House of Representatives, 23, 25, 27, 32
Senate, 23, 24, 25, 27, 29, 32, 41, 42, 43, 47, 48
Seneca, 47
Seventeenth Century Europe, 13
seventeenth century, 3, 4, 55
Seward, William Henry, 45
Shah of Iran, 154-158,162-167, 175-183
Shahyad Aryamehr, 162
Shakhty region of Ukraine for deliberate sabotage, 128
Sharia, 183
Shariati, 174, 175, 177, 180, 181
Shatt al-Arab, 192
Shi'a sects, 148
Shī'ah Muslims, 169
Shi'ite groups, 149
Shi'ites, 146-151, 153, 159, 161, 164, 166, 169, 174-175,
    178-179, 181, 192
Shukman, Harold, 90
Siberia, 55, 58, 61, 69, 83, 86, 104, 108, 125
Sierra Nevada, 45
Silver State, 44, 49
Sims, 48
Slavery, 10, 32-40, 45, 46, 55, 57, 71
Slavic peoples, 105
Smolensk, 140
Socialism, 68, 69, 70, 72, 80, 85–87, 90, 92, 94, 114-115, 128,
    130–31, 174, 175
Socialist revolution, 80, 86, 91, 97, 101, 128
Socialist Revolutionaries, 73
Socialist Soviet Republic of Armenia, 111
Socialist Soviet Republic of Azerbaijan, 111
Socialist Soviet Republic of Transcaucasia, 111
Socialist Soviet Republic of Ukraine, 111
Socialist Soviet Republic of White Russia, 111
South Africa, 156
South America, 35
South Carolina, 16, 24, 33, 38
South Caucasus, 151, 154
South Caucuses, 110
South's rebellion, 46

Soviet holidays, 134
Soviet ideologues, 136
Soviet institutions, 99, 108, 135
Soviet intelligentsia, 130
Soviet invasion of Persian-speaking Afghanistan, 192
Soviet nationalities policy agenda, 117
Soviet nationalities policy, 113, 115, 116, 117, 118, 119
Soviet of Nationalities and Article, 140
Soviet of Nationalities,
Soviet Republics, 99, 100, 102, 110, 111, 140
Soviet society, 128, 129, 130, 131, 132, 140
Soviet state, 94, 109, 114, 116, 117, 119, 133, 134, 135,
    138-142
Soviet Union, 51, 113, 114, 115, 116, 117, 119, 122, 133-135,
    137, 140-142
Soviets, 85, 86, 88, 93, 94–100, 108–12, 118, 119, 133-137,
    142, 156
Sovnarkom, 89, 93, 97
Spain, 3, 53, 54
St Petersburg, 75, 76
St. Bernard, 38
St. Charles, 38
St. James, 38
St. John, 38
St. Louis, 45
St. Martin, 38
St. Martin's Press, 13
St. Mary, 38
St. Petersburg, 55, 57, 58, 61, 63, 74
Stalin Constitution, 121, 133, 134, 135, 137, 138, 139, 141,
    142
Stalin Revolution, 121, 122, 123, 125, 127, 129, 131, 133,
    135, 137, 139, 141
Stalin, 106, 113, 114, 115–18, 121, 124-129, 132–33, 135-137
Stalin, Joseph, 106, 121, 123, 129
Stanford, 55, 66, 81
State Council and State Duma, 77, 79
State Council, 62, 76, 77, 78–79
State Duma and representatives, 76
State Duma, 77, 78–79
state farm Kudinovo, 136
State of Great Britain, 13
Statues of Mohammed-Reza, 162
Steam, 35
Steinberg, 84, 85, 86, 90, 102
Steklov, 98
Stewart, 46
Stile, 16
Stolypin, Peter, 80, 83, 84, 155
Stuart dynasty, 4
Suez Canal, 163
Suffrage, equal, 29, 86, 135
Sufism, 146
Sunnis, 146, 148, 149, 150, 151, 180, 192
Sutter's Mill, 44
Svod Zakonov Rossiiskoi Imperii, 76

Sweden, 56, 59, 86, 105
Swiss bank accounts, 178
Swiss, 108
Switzerland, 3, 67, 86, 107, 163
Syndey, 129
Syria, 173
Szeftel, Marc, 81

T
Tabriz, 154, 178
Tadzhikistan, 134
Tajiks, 110
Talbot, Major General, 153
Tatars, 105, 109, 136
Tatarstan, 118
Tauris, 193
Tehran, 154, 162, 164, 165, 177, 178, 179, 180, 184, 186
Tennessee, 35
Tenth Amendment, 49
Terre Bonne, 38
Texas, 38
text, standard Bolshevik proof, 116
Thaden, Edward C., 59, 66
Third All-Russia Congress of Soviets, 99, 100
Third Congress of Soviets, 99, 100
Thirteenth Amendment, 46
Tobacco Rebellion, 153, 154, 159, 165, 175
Trade, emerging Silk Road, 146
Transcaucasia, 108, 111
Transformation of Muslim Mystical Thought, 146
Trans-Iranian Railroad, 156
Treaties, 16, 17, 19, 26, 27, 28, 29, 35, 46, 77, 107, 110, 111, 154, 155
Treaty of Guadalupe Hidalgo, 44
Treaty of Riga, 116
Trotsky, Leon, 104, 123-125
Tsar Nicholas, 74, 75
Tsar of Poland, 75
Tsar's Foreign Faiths, 56
Tsarist chauvinism, 113
Tsarist regime, 53, 65, 67, 68, 72, 73, 74, 76, 79, 80, 83, 115
Tsarist Russia in Iran, 170
Tsarist Russia, 53, 55, 56, 57, 59, 61, 63, 65, 95, 154
Tsars, 56, 57, 58, 59, 60, 62, 63, 65, 67, 68, 69, 74, 75, 96, 110
Tudeh Party, 158, 163, 165-166, 175
Turkey & Turkic people, 56, 105, 110, 151, 166
Twain, Mark, 45
Twelfth Imam, 149, 151
Twelfth Party Congress, 114, 116
Twelver Shiism, 149, 150, 151, 159, 190
Twentieth Anniversary, 134

U
Udmurts, 105
Ukraine, 55, 87, 89, 105-111, 113, 115-118, 127-128
ulama, 149, 164, 165, 169, 175, 180, 185, 186
Umar's accession, 148

Umayyads, 148, 149, 169
Ummah, 189, 190
Unified Political Administration of State, 112
Unified State Political Administration, 112
Union Army, 34
Union of America, 21
Union of Liberation, 75
Union of Socialist Soviet Republics, 111
Union of Unions, 75
Union Republics, 132, 140
United States in Congress, 16, 17, 22
United States in politics and civil rights, 41
United States, 11, 13, 16, 17, 19-29, 32, 33, 36, 38, 39, 43
Unity of Islam Principle, 190
Universal male suffrage, 54
University of Nevada, 44
Urals, 125
US Constitution, 18, 20, 23, 25, 27, 29, 32, 39, 41, 60, 98, 185
US embassy staff hostage, 177
US South, 40
US territories, 44
US West, 44
Utah territory, 45
Utah, 45
Uthman ibn Affan, 148
Uthman, 148
Uzbekistan, 105, 110, 146

V
Vali Nasr, 174, 176, 180, 193
Valuev, 61
Valuev's project, 61
Verhoeven, Claudia, 68, 81
Vermont, 23
Viaz'ma diocese, 138
Vice President, 24, 26, 27, 28, 31, 32, 39, 42, 43
Victors, 128
Vietnam, 158, 171
Virginia, 16, 24, 35, 38
Vladimir Il'ich Ulianov, 73
Volga German Autonomous Republic, 140-141
Volga region, 90
Volga River, 56, 108

W
Wade, Rex A., 110
Wali al-'Asr, 189
Walicki, Andzrej, 55, 66
Warren, Chief Justice Earl, 48
Warsaw, 58, 74
Washington, 38, 45–47, 179
Washoe, 48
Weinberg, 87, 124, 125, 126, 127
Weinberg, Robert, 87, 102, 124, 142
Werth, Paul W., 56, 62
West Virginia, 38, 44
Western civilization, 165, 174

Western constitutional forms, 61
Western Europe, 3, 62, 133
Western Frontier, 47
Western governments, 154
Western ideas, 145
Western industry, 174
Western laws, 170
Western models of culture, 172
Western power, 133, 154
Western products, 174
Western Region, 139, 140
Westminster, 6
Westoxication, 174
Westport, 151–52, 159, 176, 193
White armies, 104
White Revolution, 108-109, 111, 158-159, 16-166, 175, 185
Whittaker, Cynthia Hyhla, 57, 66
William, 5, 6, 8
Wilson, Mary C., 154
Wilson, Woodrow, 113
Wisconsin, 35
Witte, 75

Wood, Gordon S., 22, 30
Wood, Gordon, 11, 126, 135
World Cup, 5
World War II, 83, 141, 145, 158, 159

X
Xerxes, 146

Y
Yolinsky. Avraham, 81
Yates, Robert, 18
Yathrib, 147
Yazīd, 169
Yemen, 169
York, 38

Z
Zasulich, Vera, 61
Zel'man Canton, 138
Zinoviev, 118
Zoroastrianism, 146, 148, 190
Zoroastrians, 148, 190